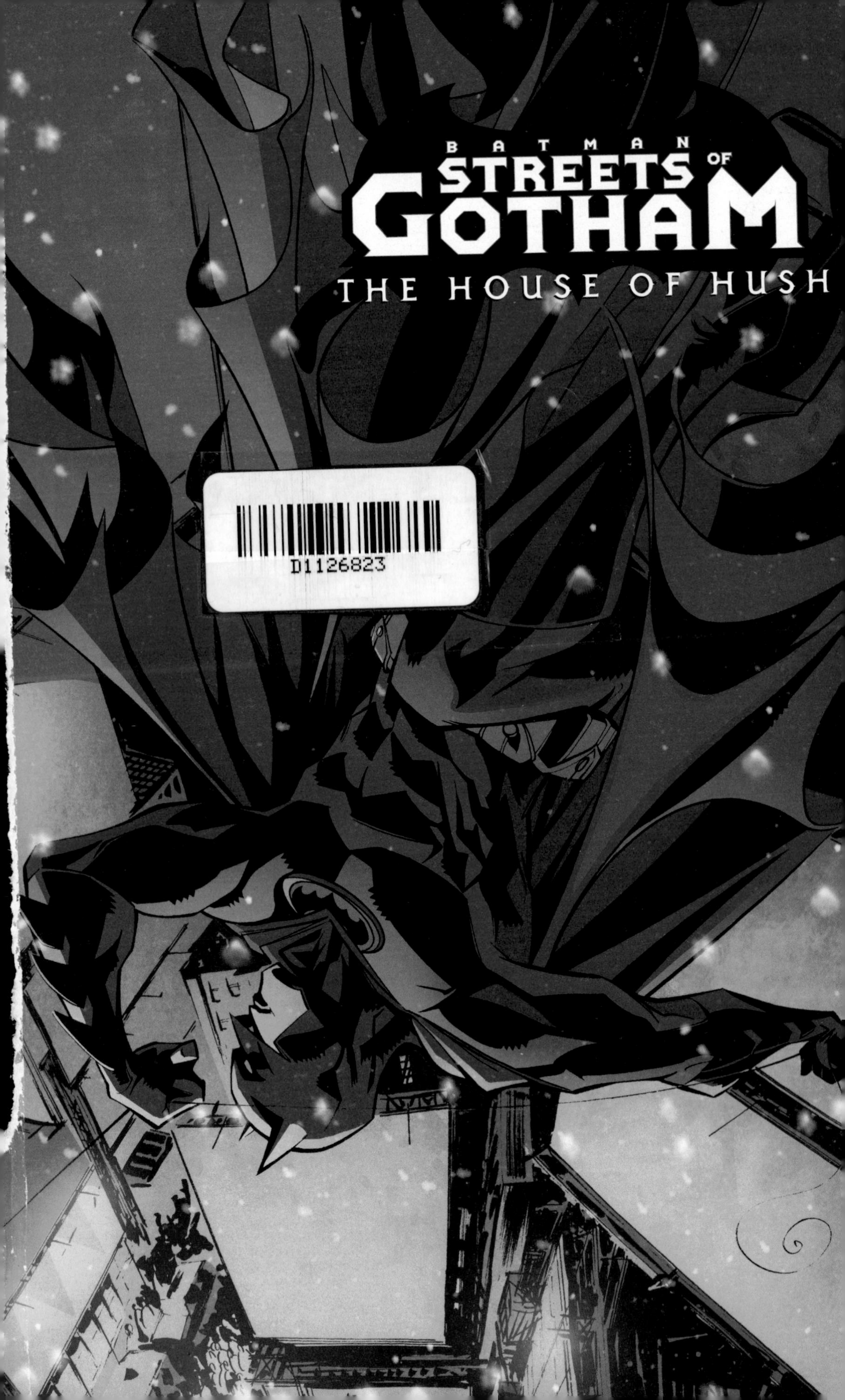
BATMAN
STREETS OF
GOTHAM
THE HOUSE OF HUSH

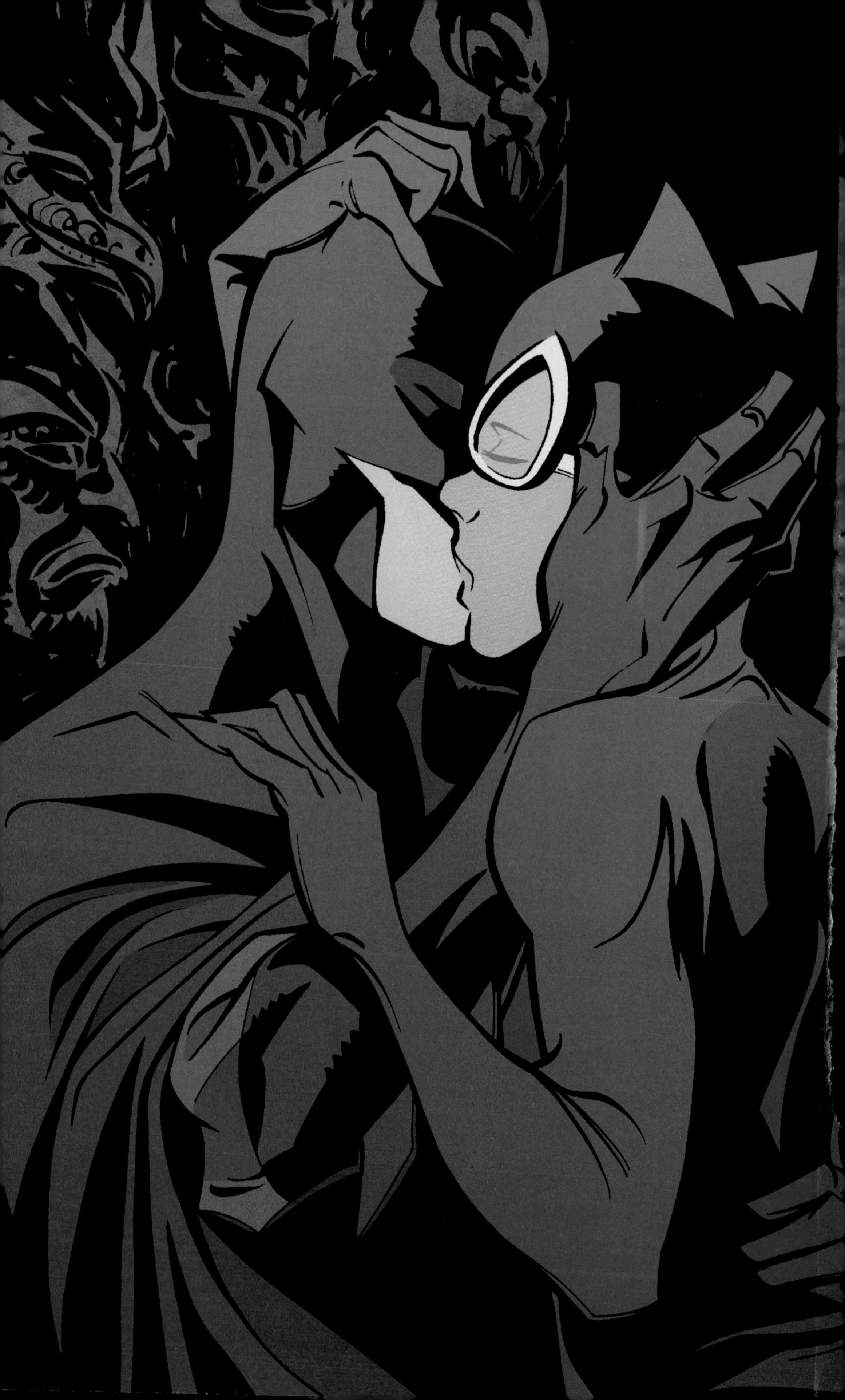

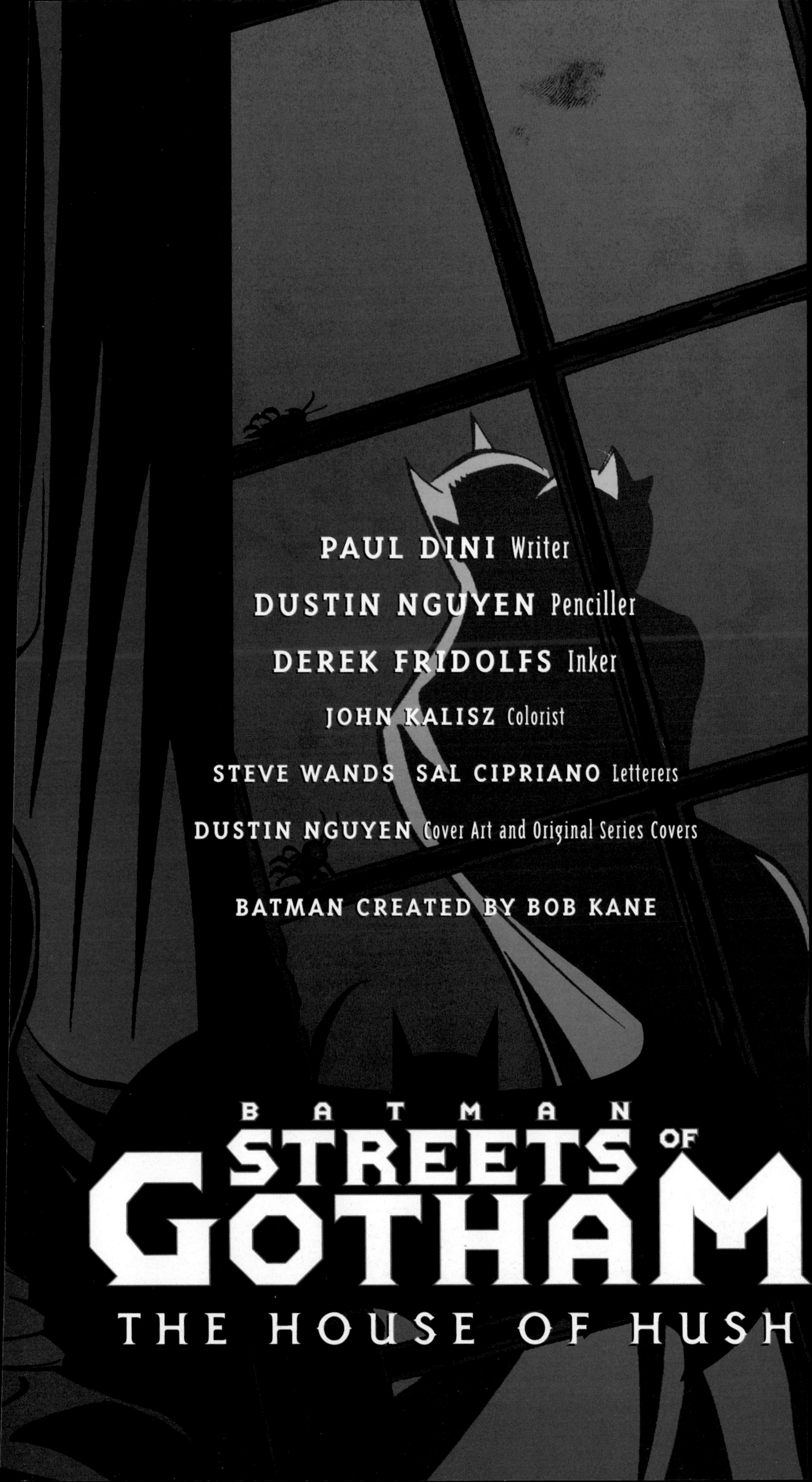

PAUL DINI Writer

DUSTIN NGUYEN Penciller

DEREK FRIDOLFS Inker

JOHN KALISZ Colorist

STEVE WANDS SAL CIPRIANO Letterers

DUSTIN NGUYEN Cover Art and Original Series Covers

BATMAN CREATED BY BOB KANE

BATMAN STREETS OF GOTHAM

THE HOUSE OF HUSH

Mike Marts
Editor – Original Series

Harvey Richards
Janelle Asselin
Associate Editors – Original Series

Katie Kubert
Assistant Editor – Original Series

Ian Sattler
Director Editorial, Special Projects and Archival Editions

Scott Nybakken
Editor

Robbin Brosterman
Design Director – Books

Eddie Berganza
Executive Editor

Bob Harras
VP – Editor in Chief

Diane Nelson
President

Dan DiDio and Jim Lee
Co-Publishers

Geoff Johns
Chief Creative Officer

John Rood
Executive VP – Sales, Marketing and
Business Development

Amy Genkins
Senior VP – Business and Legal Affairs

Nairi Gardiner
Senior VP – Finance

Jeff Boison
VP – Publishing Operations

Mark Chiarello
VP – Art Direction and Design

John Cunningham
VP – Marketing

Terri Cunningham
VP – Talent Relations and Services

Alison Gill
Senior VP – Manufacturing and Operations

David Hyde
VP – Publicity

Hank Kanalz
Senior VP – Digital

Jay Kogan
VP – Business and Legal Affairs, Publishing

Jack Mahan
VP – Business Affairs, Talent

Nick Napolitano
VP – Manufacturing Administration

Ron Perazza
VP – Online

Sue Pohja
VP – Book Sales

Courtney Simmons
Senior VP – Publicity

Bob Wayne
Senior VP – Sales

TABLE OF CONTENTS

BATMAN

STREETS OF GOTHAM

THE HOUSE OF HUSH

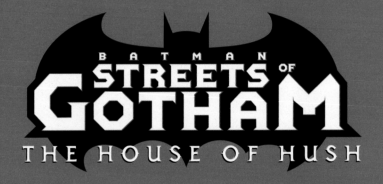

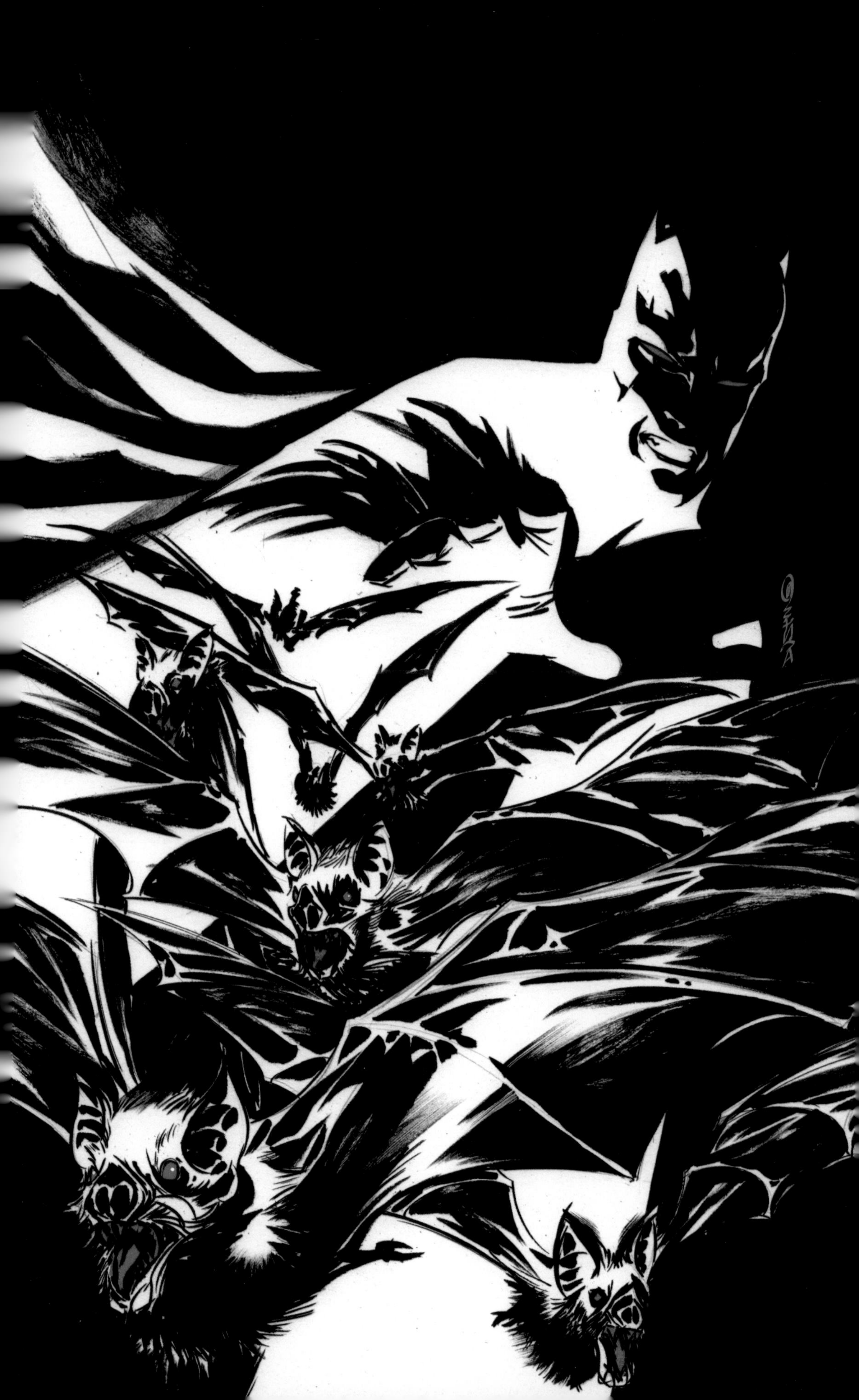

"Of course it's alligators. The wackos **always** want alligators."

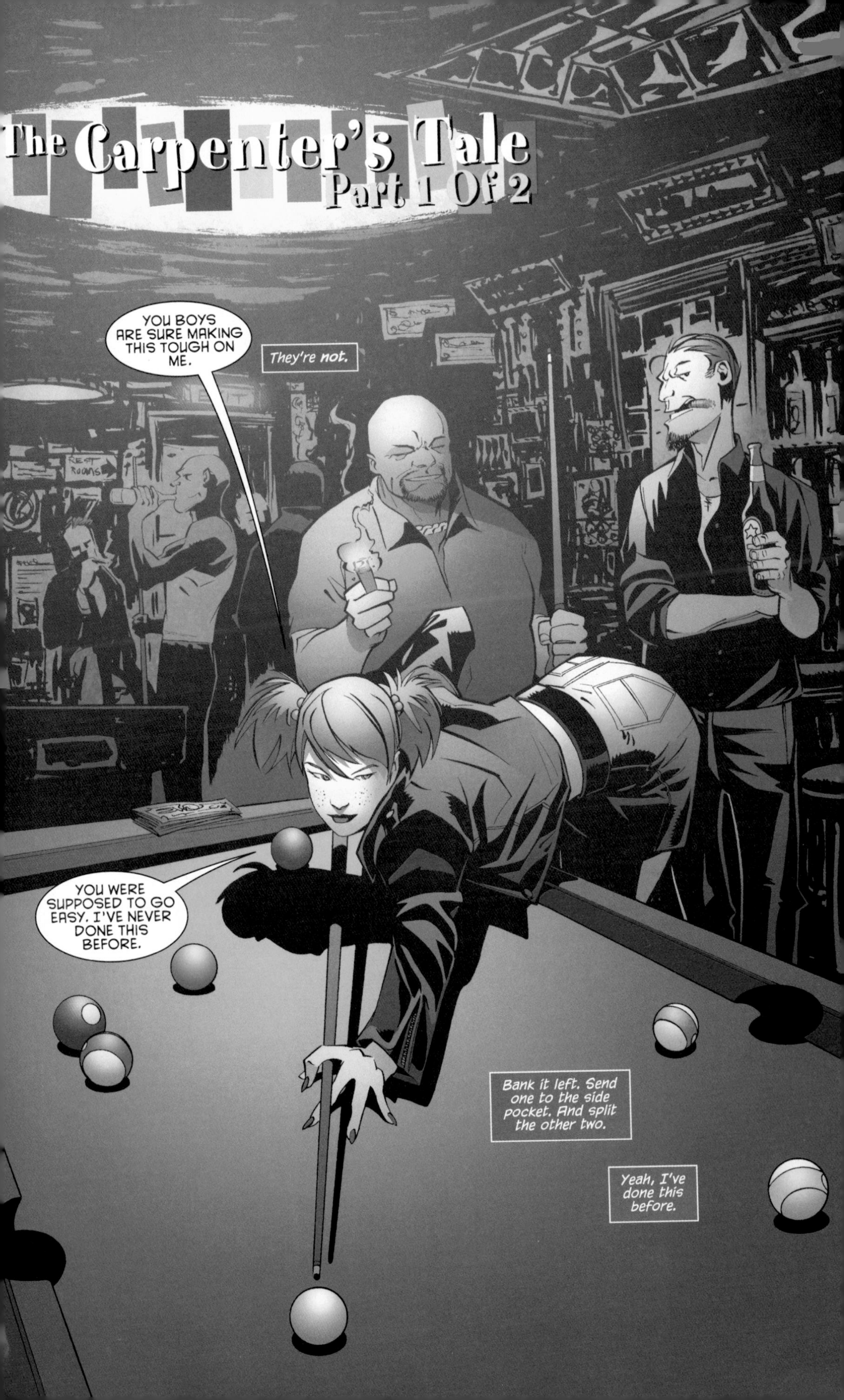
The Carpenter's Tale
Part 1 Of 2
YOU BOYS ARE SURE MAKING THIS TOUGH ON ME.
They're not.
YOU WERE SUPPOSED TO GO EASY. I'VE NEVER DONE THIS BEFORE.
Bank it left. Send one to the side pocket. And split the other two.
Yeah, I've done this before.

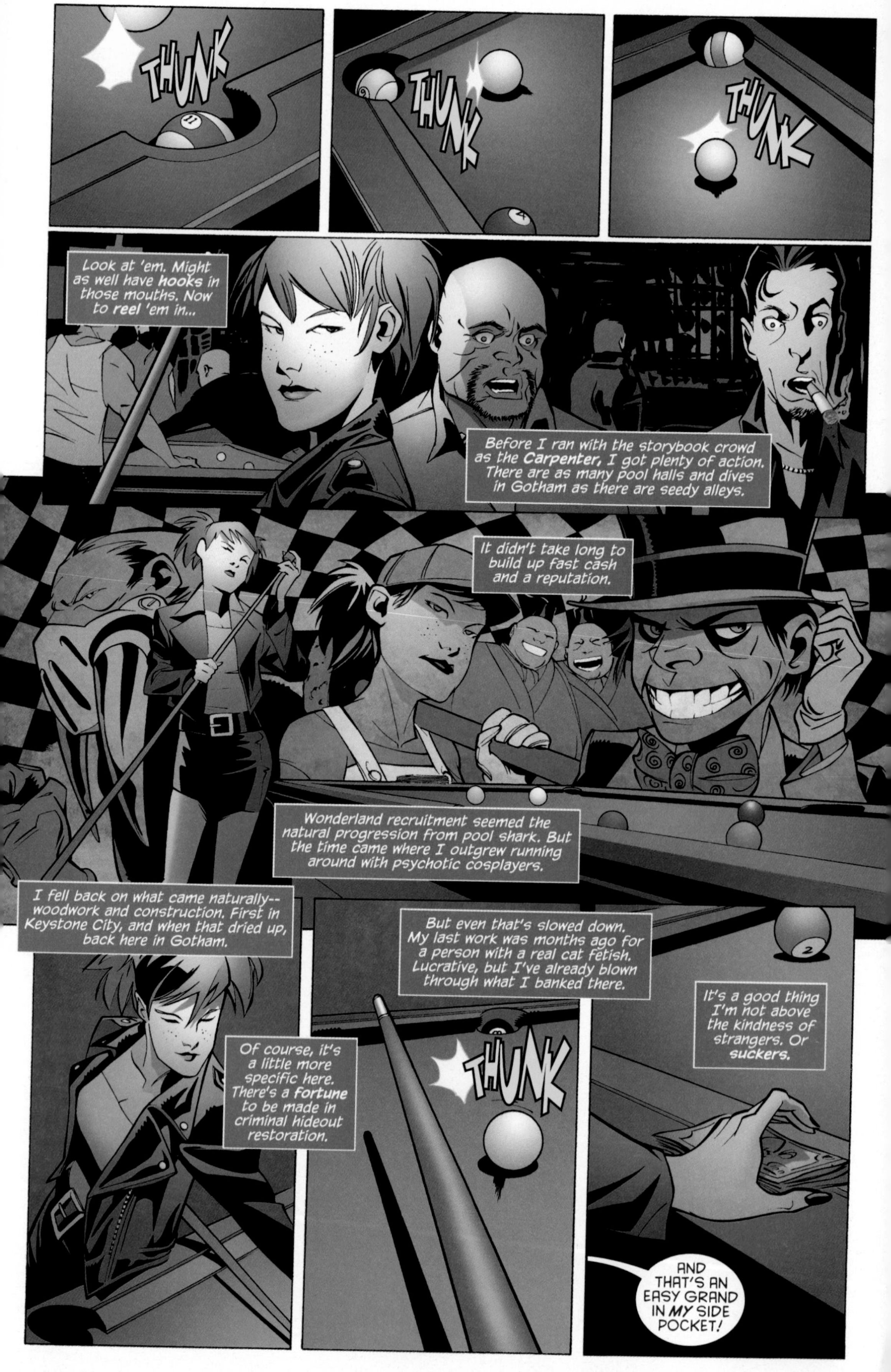

THUNK
THUNK
THUNK
Look at 'em. Might as well have hooks in those mouths. Now to reel 'em in...
Before I ran with the storybook crowd as the Carpenter, I got plenty of action. There are as many pool halls and dives in Gotham as there are seedy alleys.
It didn't take long to build up fast cash and a reputation.
Wonderland recruitment seemed the natural progression from pool shark. But the time came where I outgrew running around with psychotic cosplayers.
I fell back on what came naturally--woodwork and construction. First in Keystone City, and when that dried up, back here in Gotham.
Of course, it's a little more specific here. There's a fortune to be made in criminal hideout restoration.
But even that's slowed down. My last work was months ago for a person with a real cat fetish. Lucrative, but I've already blown through what I banked there.
THUNK
It's a good thing I'm not above the kindness of strangers. Or suckers.
AND THAT'S AN EASY GRAND IN MY SIDE POCKET!

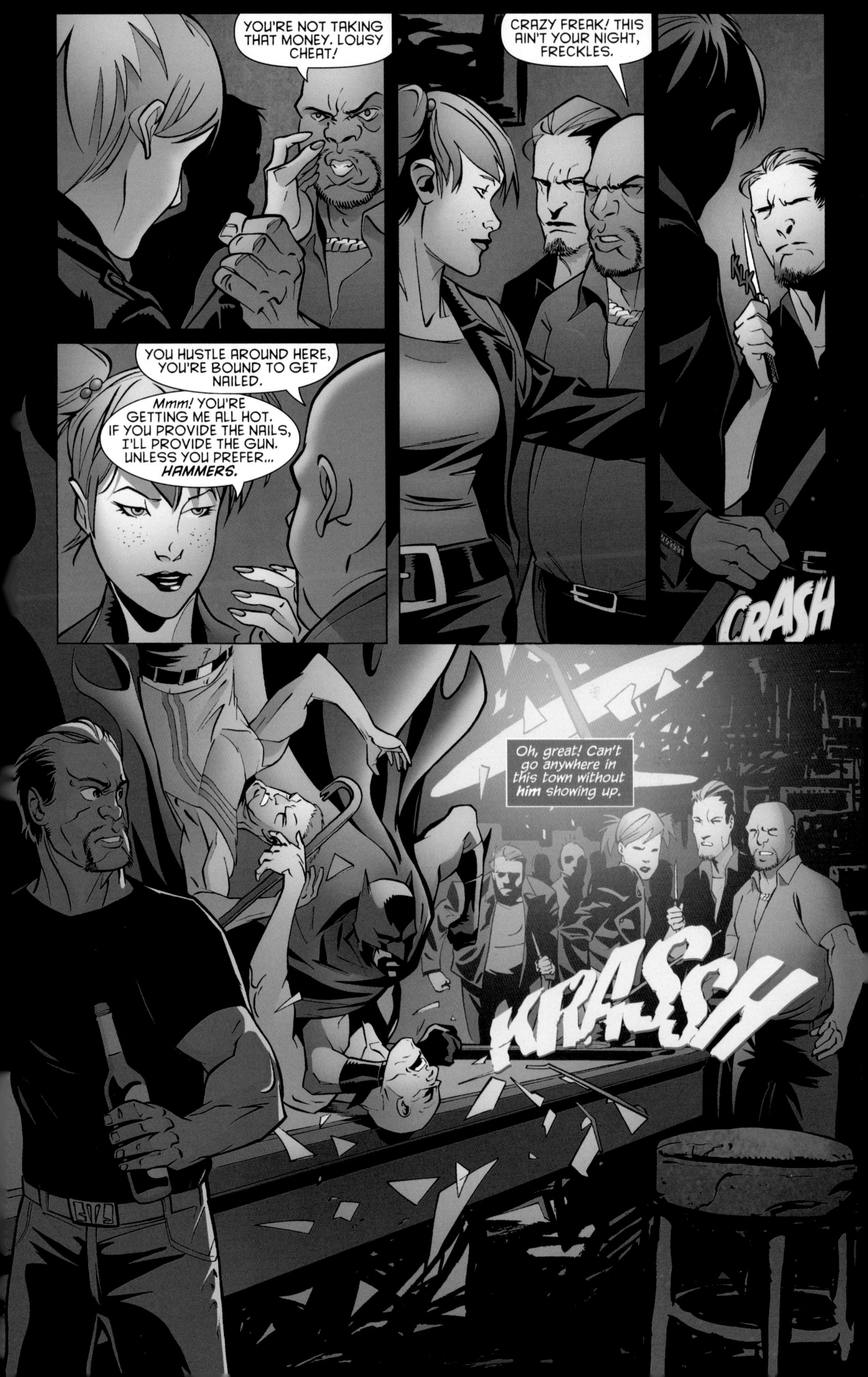
YOU'RE NOT TAKING THAT MONEY. LOUSY CHEAT!
CRAZY FREAK! THIS AIN'T YOUR NIGHT, FRECKLES.
KLK
YOU HUSTLE AROUND HERE, YOU'RE BOUND TO GET NAILED.
Mmm! YOU'RE GETTING ME ALL HOT. IF YOU PROVIDE THE NAILS, I'LL PROVIDE THE GUN. UNLESS YOU PREFER... HAMMERS.
CRASH
Oh, great! Can't go anywhere in this town without him showing up.
KRASSH

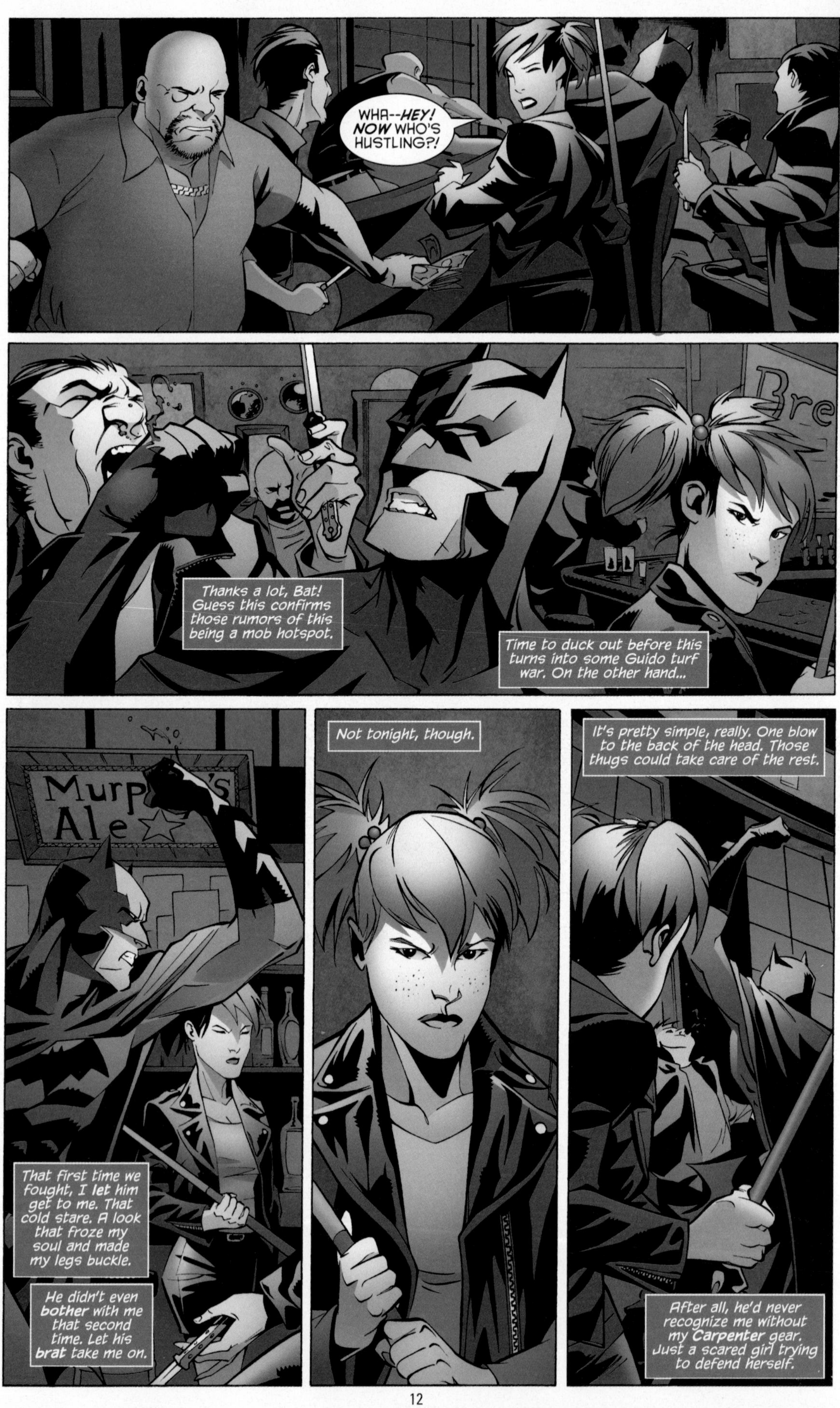
WHA--HEY! NOW WHO'S HUSTLING?!
Bre
Thanks a lot, Bat! Guess this confirms those rumors of this being a mob hotspot.
Time to duck out before this turns into some Guido turf war. On the other hand...
Murp 's Ale
That first time we fought, I let him get to me. That cold stare. A look that froze my soul and made my legs buckle.
He didn't even bother with me that second time. Let his brat take me on.
Not tonight, though.
It's pretty simple, really. One blow to the back of the head. Those thugs could take care of the rest.
After all, he'd never recognize me without my Carpenter gear. Just a scared girl trying to defend herself.

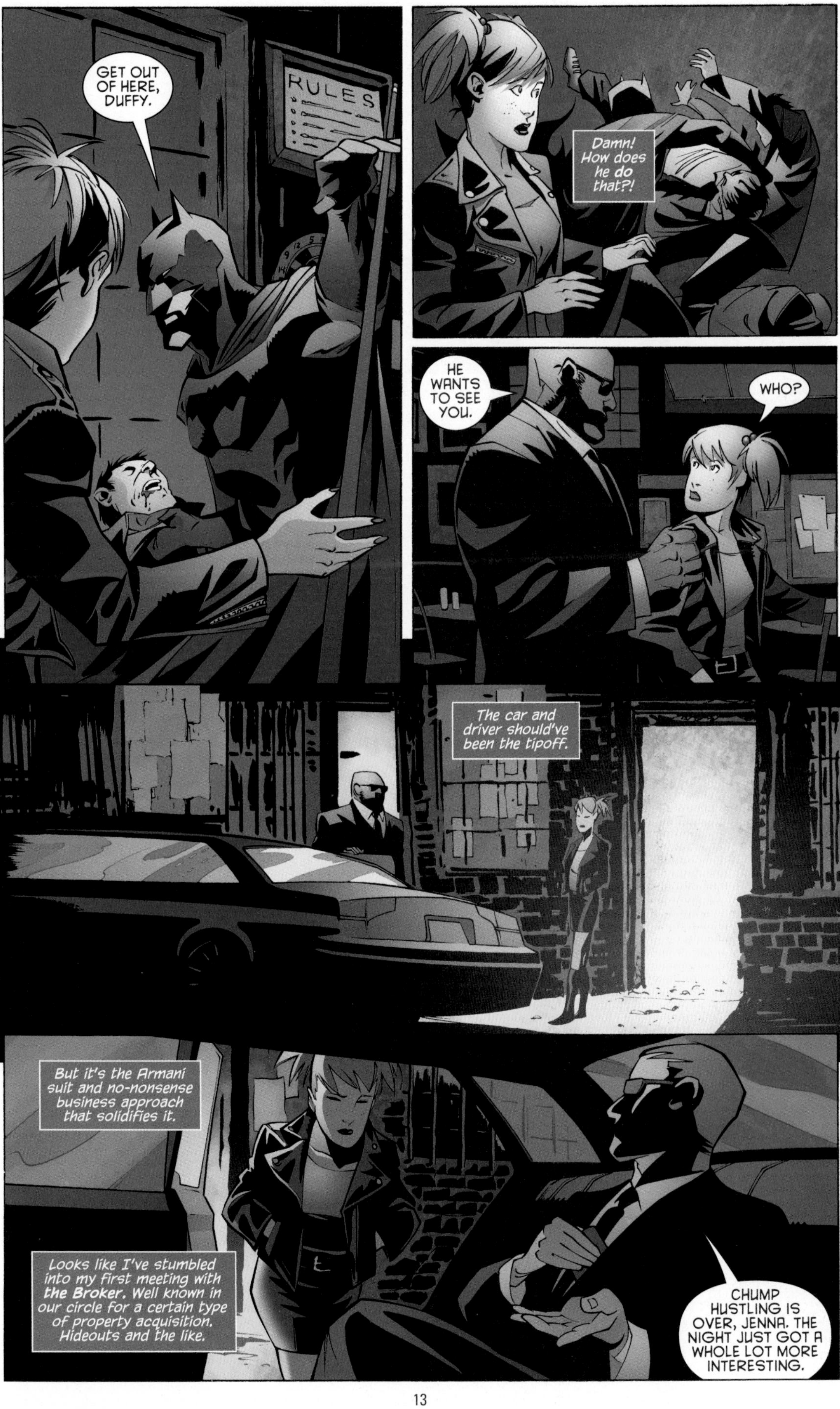
GET OUT OF HERE, DUFFY.
RULES
Damn! How does he do that?!
HE WANTS TO SEE YOU.
WHO?
The car and driver should've been the tipoff.
But it's the Armani suit and no-nonsense business approach that solidifies it.
Looks like I've stumbled into my first meeting with the Broker. Well known in our circle for a certain type of property acquisition. Hideouts and the like.
CHUMP HUSTLING IS OVER, JENNA. THE NIGHT JUST GOT A WHOLE LOT MORE INTERESTING.

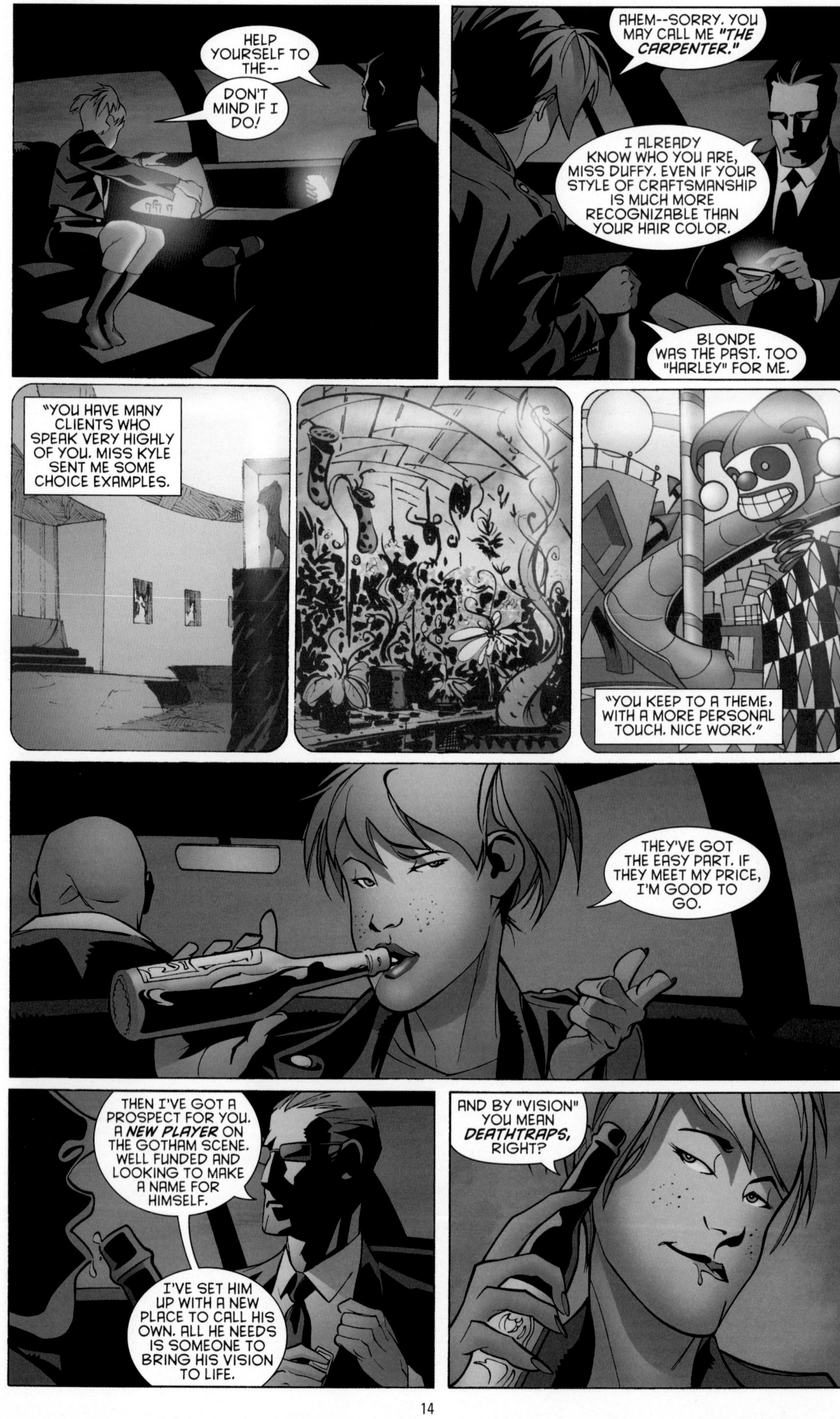

HELP YOURSELF TO THE--
DON'T MIND IF I DO!
AHEM--SORRY. YOU MAY CALL ME *"THE CARPENTER."*
I ALREADY KNOW WHO YOU ARE, MISS DUFFY. EVEN IF YOUR STYLE OF CRAFTSMANSHIP IS MUCH MORE RECOGNIZABLE THAN YOUR HAIR COLOR.
BLONDE WAS THE PAST. TOO "HARLEY" FOR ME.
"YOU HAVE MANY CLIENTS WHO SPEAK VERY HIGHLY OF YOU. MISS KYLE SENT ME SOME CHOICE EXAMPLES.
"YOU KEEP TO A THEME, WITH A MORE PERSONAL TOUCH. NICE WORK."
THEY'VE GOT THE EASY PART. IF THEY MEET MY PRICE, I'M GOOD TO GO.
THEN I'VE GOT A PROSPECT FOR YOU. A *NEW PLAYER* ON THE GOTHAM SCENE. WELL FUNDED AND LOOKING TO MAKE A NAME FOR HIMSELF.
I'VE SET HIM UP WITH A NEW PLACE TO CALL HIS OWN. ALL HE NEEDS IS SOMEONE TO BRING HIS VISION TO LIFE.
AND BY "VISION" YOU MEAN *DEATHTRAPS,* RIGHT?

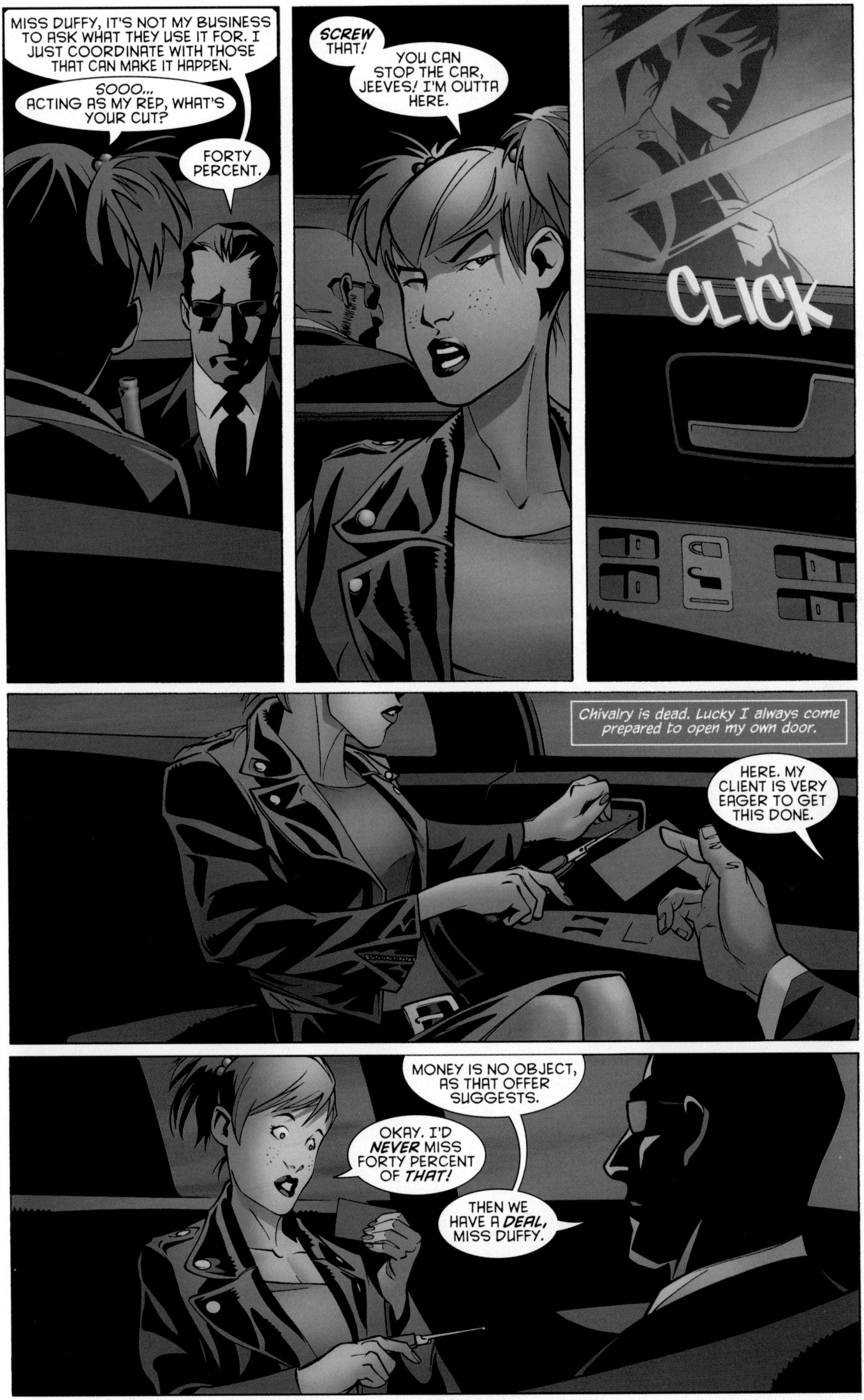
MISS DUFFY, IT'S NOT MY BUSINESS TO ASK WHAT THEY USE IT FOR. I JUST COORDINATE WITH THOSE THAT CAN MAKE IT HAPPEN.
SOOO... ACTING AS MY REP, WHAT'S YOUR CUT?
FORTY PERCENT.
SCREW THAT!
YOU CAN STOP THE CAR, JEEVES! I'M OUTTA HERE.
CLICK
Chivalry is dead. Lucky I always come prepared to open my own door.
HERE. MY CLIENT IS VERY EAGER TO GET THIS DONE.
MONEY IS NO OBJECT, AS THAT OFFER SUGGESTS.
OKAY. I'D NEVER MISS FORTY PERCENT OF THAT!
THEN WE HAVE A DEAL, MISS DUFFY.

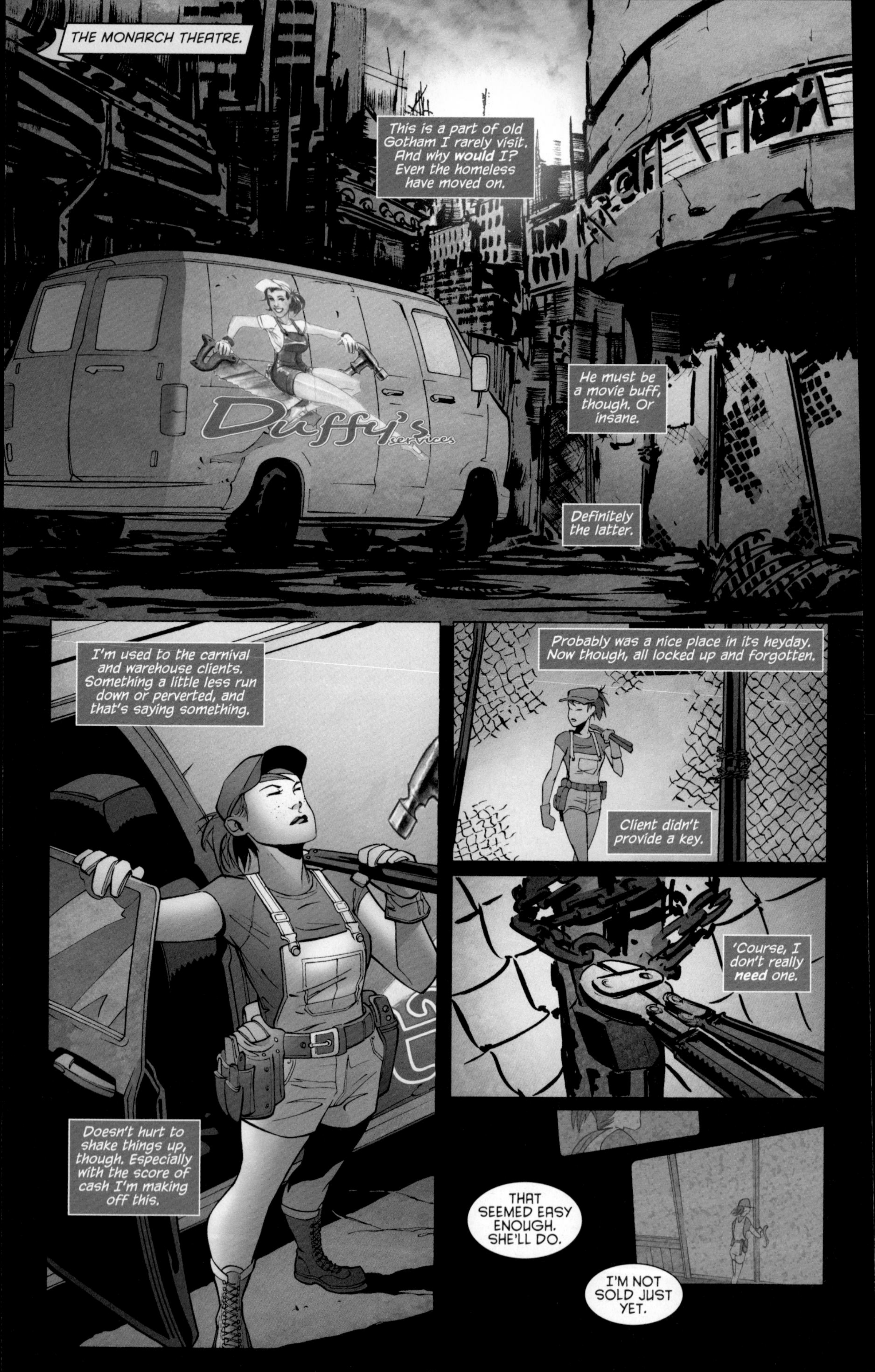
THE MONARCH THEATRE.
This is a part of old Gotham I rarely visit. And why **would** I? Even the homeless have moved on.
Duffy's services
He must be a movie buff, though. Or insane.
Definitely the latter.
I'm used to the carnival and warehouse clients. Something a little less run down or perverted, and that's saying something.
Doesn't hurt to shake things up, though. Especially with the score of cash I'm making off this.
Probably was a nice place in its heyday. Now though, all locked up and forgotten.
Client didn't provide a key.
'Course, I don't really **need** one.
THAT SEEMED EASY ENOUGH. SHE'LL DO.
I'M NOT SOLD JUST YET.

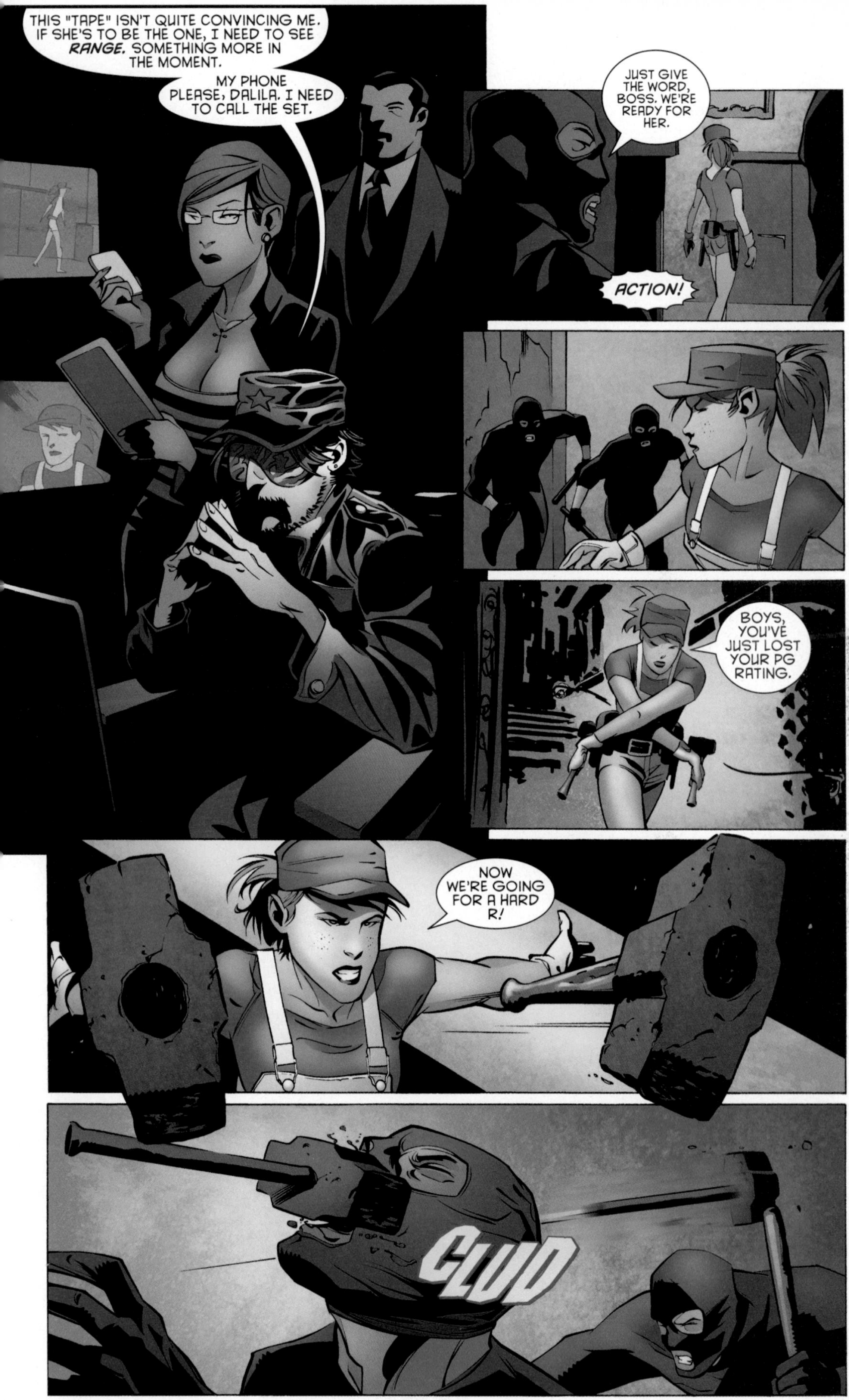
THIS "TAPE" ISN'T QUITE CONVINCING ME. IF SHE'S TO BE THE ONE, I NEED TO SEE *RANGE.* SOMETHING MORE IN THE MOMENT.
MY PHONE PLEASE, DALILA. I NEED TO CALL THE SET.
JUST GIVE THE WORD, BOSS. WE'RE READY FOR HER.
ACTION!
BOYS, YOU'VE JUST LOST YOUR PG RATING.
NOW WE'RE GOING FOR A HARD R!
CLUD

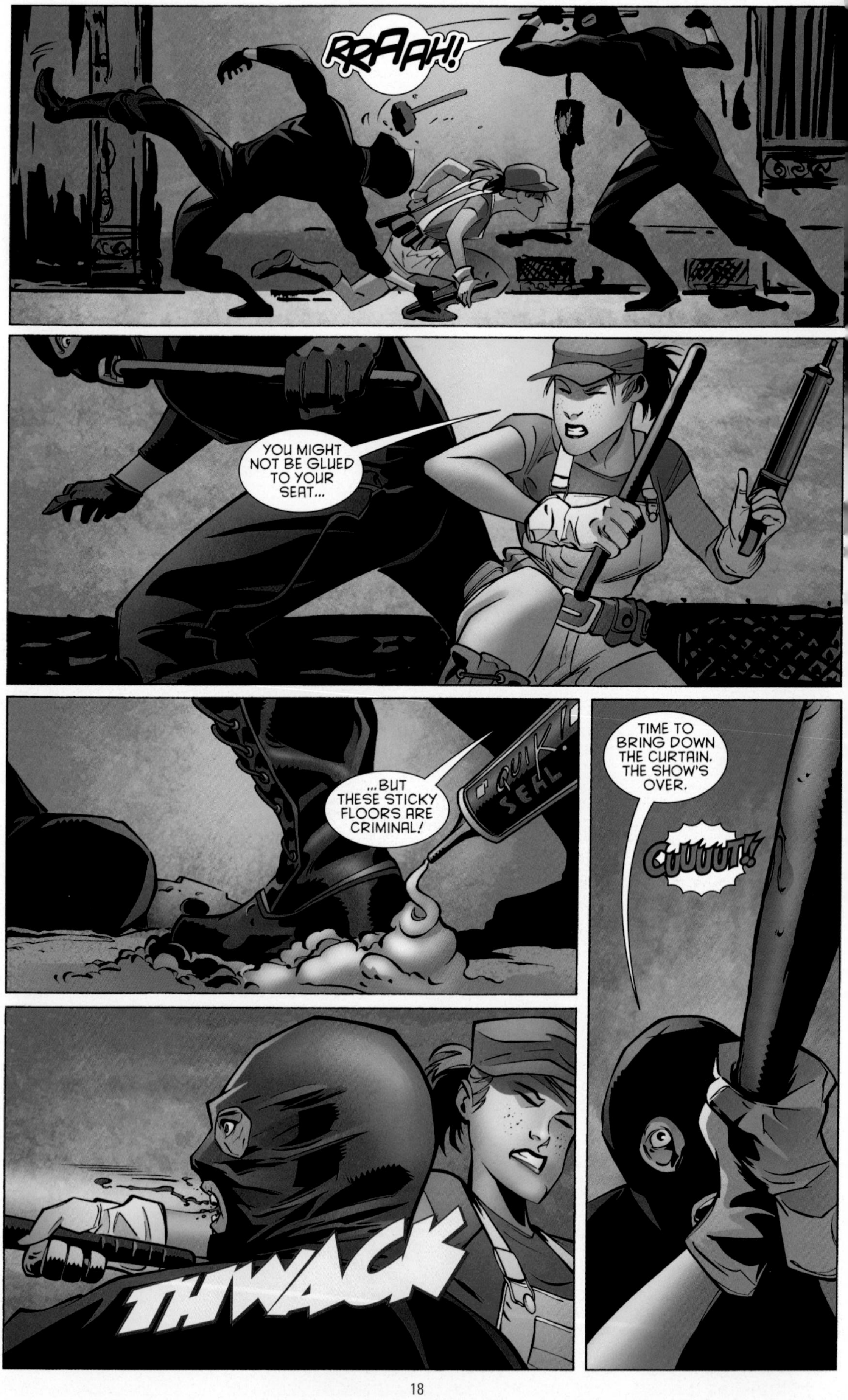
RRAAAH!
YOU MIGHT NOT BE GLUED TO YOUR SEAT...
...BUT THESE STICKY FLOORS ARE CRIMINAL!
QUIK SEAL
TIME TO BRING DOWN THE CURTAIN. THE SHOW'S OVER.
CUUUUT!!
THWACK

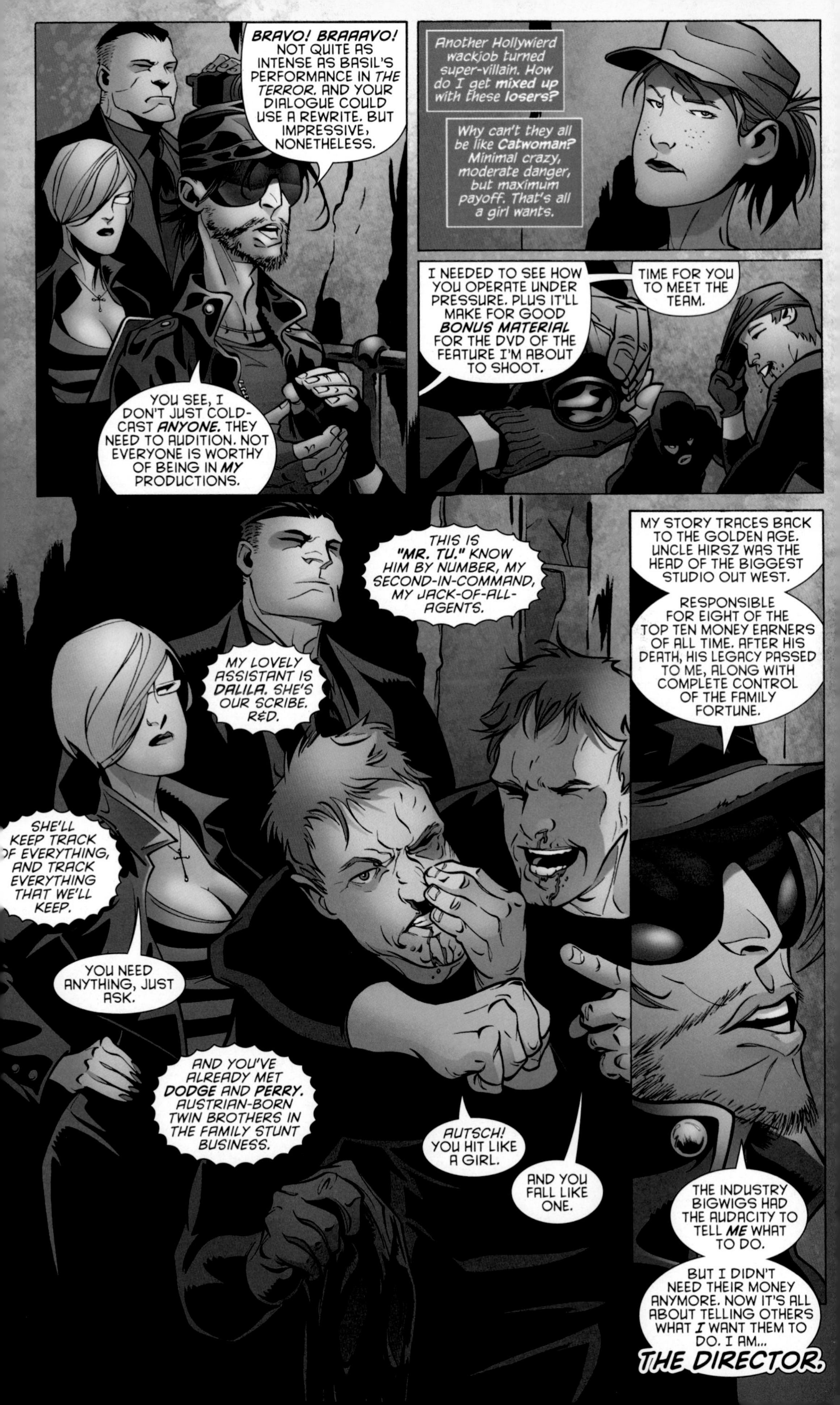

BRAVO! BRAAAVO! NOT QUITE AS INTENSE AS BASIL'S PERFORMANCE IN THE TERROR. AND YOUR DIALOGUE COULD USE A REWRITE. BUT IMPRESSIVE, NONETHELESS.
YOU SEE, I DON'T JUST COLD-CAST ANYONE. THEY NEED TO AUDITION. NOT EVERYONE IS WORTHY OF BEING IN MY PRODUCTIONS.
Another Hollywierd wackjob turned super-villain. How do I get mixed up with these losers?
Why can't they all be like Catwoman? Minimal crazy, moderate danger, but maximum payoff. That's all a girl wants.
I NEEDED TO SEE HOW YOU OPERATE UNDER PRESSURE. PLUS IT'LL MAKE FOR GOOD BONUS MATERIAL FOR THE DVD OF THE FEATURE I'M ABOUT TO SHOOT.
TIME FOR YOU TO MEET THE TEAM.
THIS IS "MR. TU." KNOW HIM BY NUMBER, MY SECOND-IN-COMMAND, MY JACK-OF-ALL-AGENTS.
MY LOVELY ASSISTANT IS DALILA. SHE'S OUR SCRIBE. R&D.
SHE'LL KEEP TRACK OF EVERYTHING, AND TRACK EVERYTHING THAT WE'LL KEEP.
YOU NEED ANYTHING, JUST ASK.
AND YOU'VE ALREADY MET DODGE AND PERRY. AUSTRIAN-BORN TWIN BROTHERS IN THE FAMILY STUNT BUSINESS.
AUTSCH! YOU HIT LIKE A GIRL.
AND YOU FALL LIKE ONE.
MY STORY TRACES BACK TO THE GOLDEN AGE. UNCLE HIRSZ WAS THE HEAD OF THE BIGGEST STUDIO OUT WEST.
RESPONSIBLE FOR EIGHT OF THE TOP TEN MONEY EARNERS OF ALL TIME. AFTER HIS DEATH, HIS LEGACY PASSED TO ME, ALONG WITH COMPLETE CONTROL OF THE FAMILY FORTUNE.
THE INDUSTRY BIGWIGS HAD THE AUDACITY TO TELL ME WHAT TO DO.
BUT I DIDN'T NEED THEIR MONEY ANYMORE. NOW IT'S ALL ABOUT TELLING OTHERS WHAT I WANT THEM TO DO. I AM...
THE DIRECTOR.

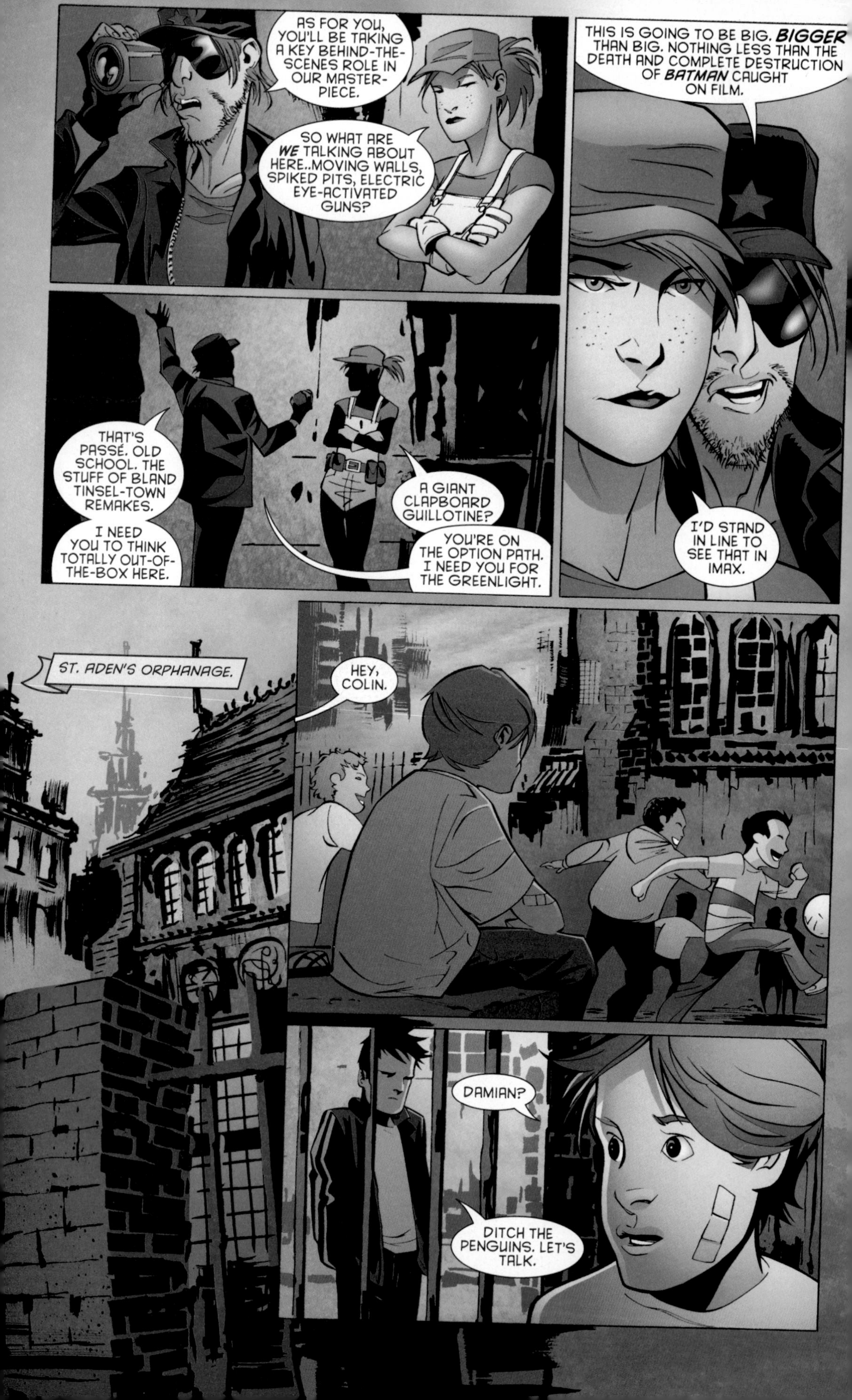
AS FOR YOU, YOU'LL BE TAKING A KEY BEHIND-THE-SCENES ROLE IN OUR MASTER-PIECE.
SO WHAT ARE WE TALKING ABOUT HERE..MOVING WALLS, SPIKED PITS, ELECTRIC EYE-ACTIVATED GUNS?
THAT'S PASSÉ. OLD SCHOOL. THE STUFF OF BLAND TINSEL-TOWN REMAKES.
I NEED YOU TO THINK TOTALLY OUT-OF-THE-BOX HERE.
A GIANT CLAPBOARD GUILLOTINE?
YOU'RE ON THE OPTION PATH. I NEED YOU FOR THE GREENLIGHT.
THIS IS GOING TO BE BIG. BIGGER THAN BIG. NOTHING LESS THAN THE DEATH AND COMPLETE DESTRUCTION OF BATMAN CAUGHT ON FILM.
I'D STAND IN LINE TO SEE THAT IN IMAX.
ST. ADEN'S ORPHANAGE.
HEY, COLIN.
DAMIAN?
DITCH THE PENGUINS. LET'S TALK.

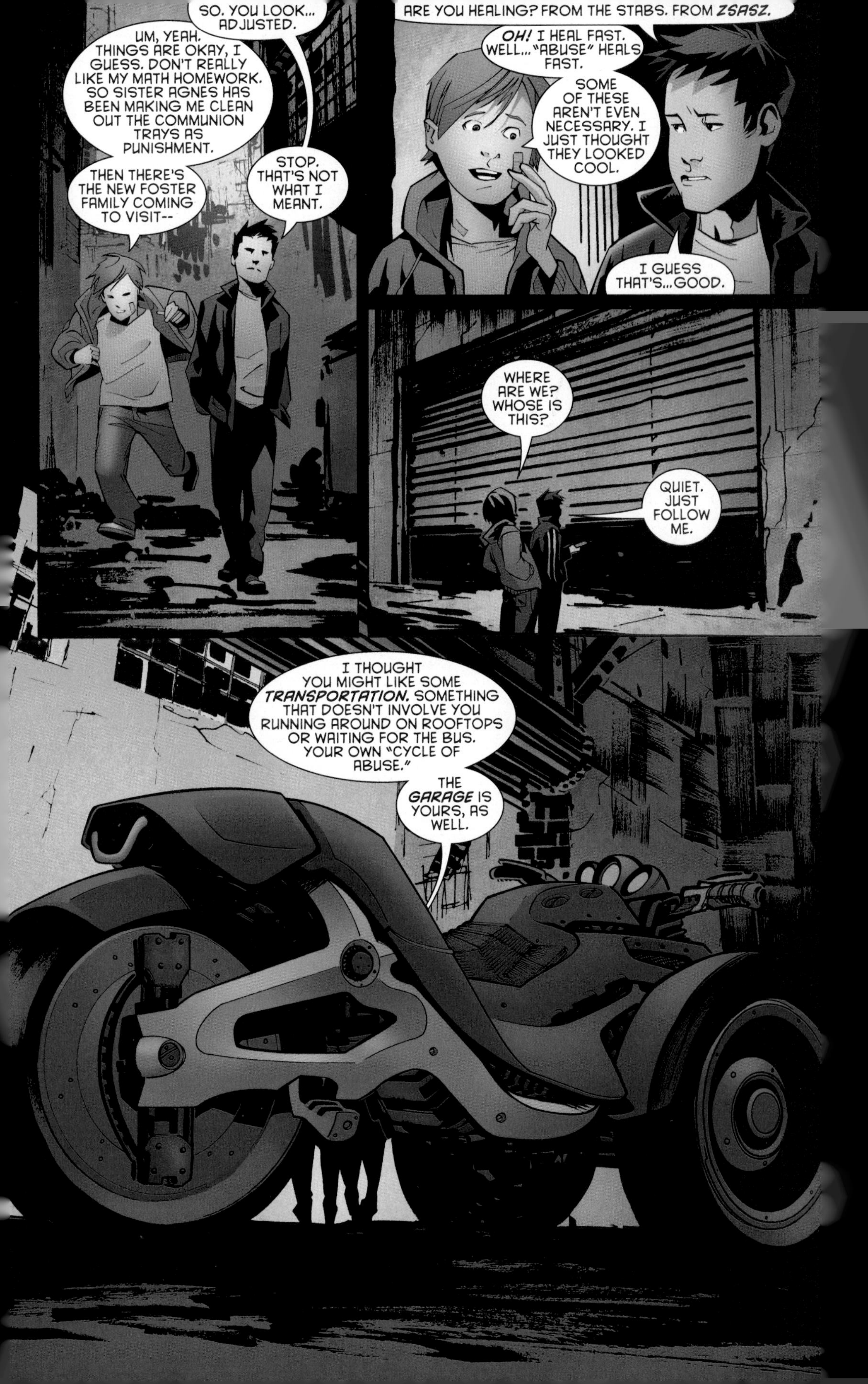
SO. YOU LOOK... ADJUSTED.
UM, YEAH. THINGS ARE OKAY, I GUESS. DON'T REALLY LIKE MY MATH HOMEWORK. SO SISTER AGNES HAS BEEN MAKING ME CLEAN OUT THE COMMUNION TRAYS AS PUNISHMENT.
THEN THERE'S THE NEW FOSTER FAMILY COMING TO VISIT--
STOP. THAT'S NOT WHAT I MEANT.
ARE YOU HEALING? FROM THE STABS. FROM ZSASZ.
OH! I HEAL FAST. WELL... "ABUSE" HEALS FAST.
SOME OF THESE AREN'T EVEN NECESSARY. I JUST THOUGHT THEY LOOKED COOL.
I GUESS THAT'S...GOOD.
WHERE ARE WE? WHOSE IS THIS?
QUIET. JUST FOLLOW ME.
I THOUGHT YOU MIGHT LIKE SOME TRANSPORTATION. SOMETHING THAT DOESN'T INVOLVE YOU RUNNING AROUND ON ROOFTOPS OR WAITING FOR THE BUS. YOUR OWN "CYCLE OF ABUSE."
THE GARAGE IS YOURS, AS WELL.

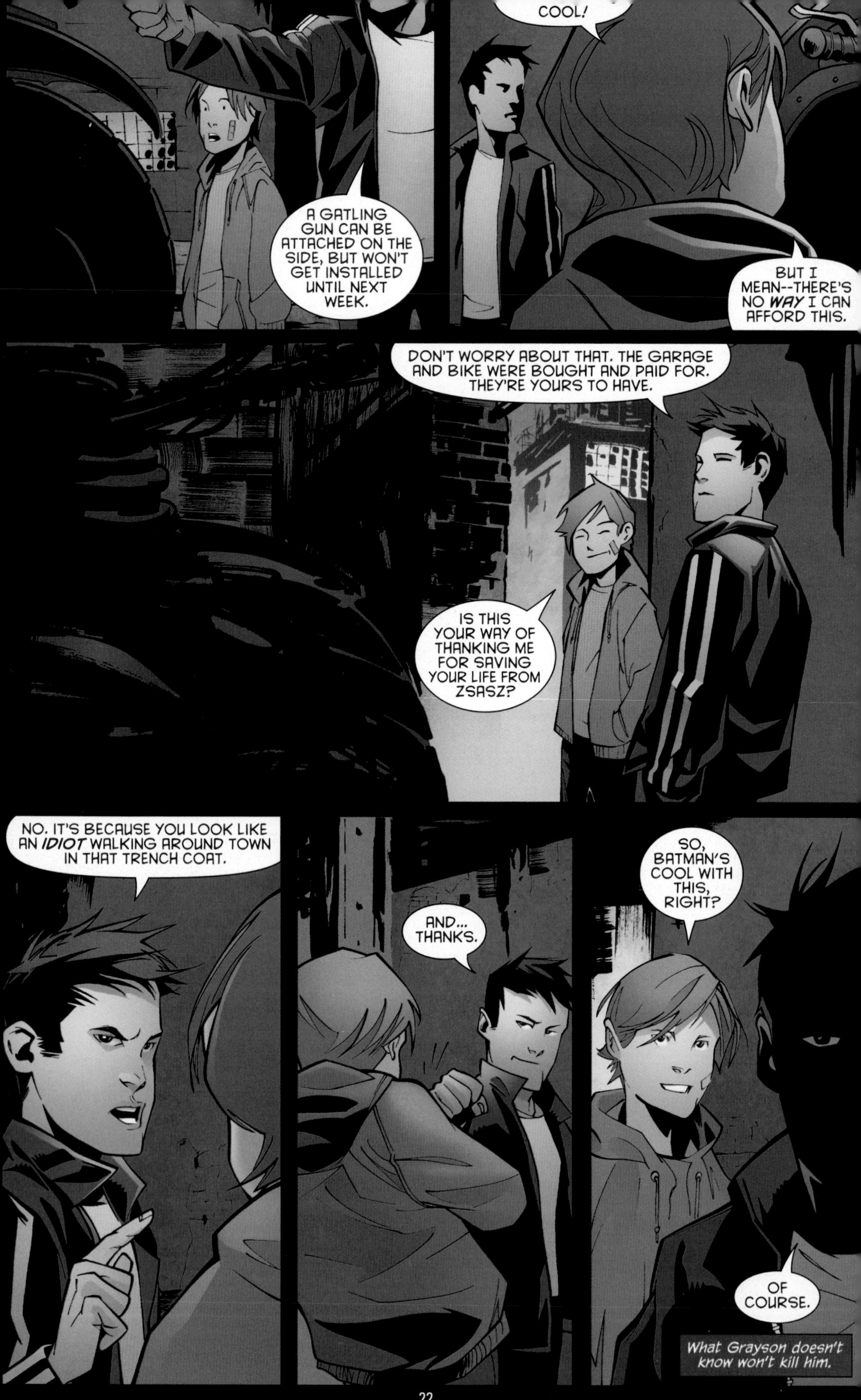
COOL!
A GATLING GUN CAN BE ATTACHED ON THE SIDE, BUT WON'T GET INSTALLED UNTIL NEXT WEEK.
BUT I MEAN--THERE'S NO *WAY* I CAN AFFORD THIS.
DON'T WORRY ABOUT THAT. THE GARAGE AND BIKE WERE BOUGHT AND PAID FOR. THEY'RE YOURS TO HAVE.
IS THIS YOUR WAY OF THANKING ME FOR SAVING YOUR LIFE FROM ZSASZ?
NO. IT'S BECAUSE YOU LOOK LIKE AN *IDIOT* WALKING AROUND TOWN IN THAT TRENCH COAT.
AND... THANKS.
SO, BATMAN'S COOL WITH THIS, RIGHT?
OF COURSE.
What Grayson doesn't know won't kill him.

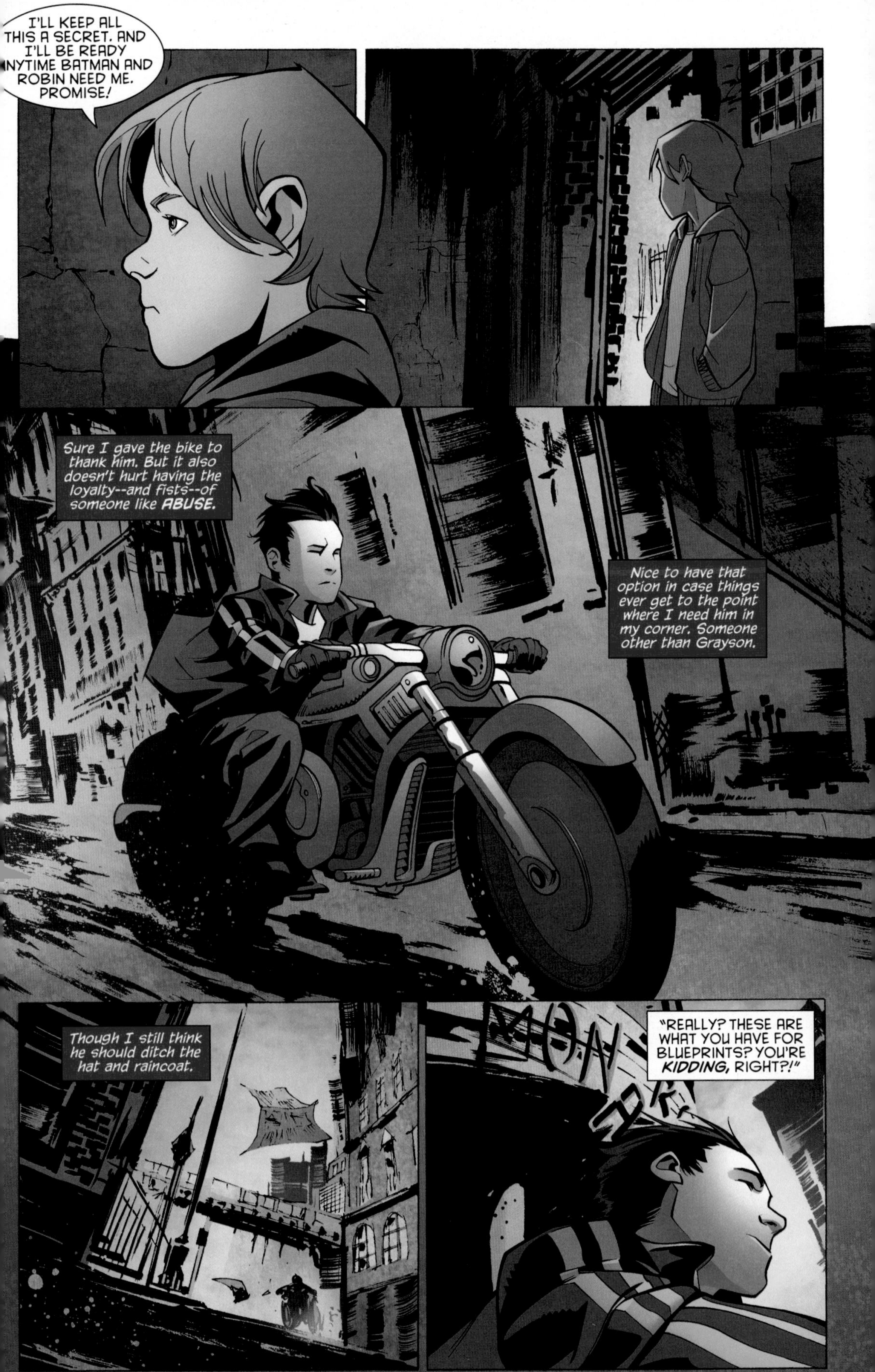
I'LL KEEP ALL THIS A SECRET. AND I'LL BE READY NYTIME BATMAN AND ROBIN NEED ME. PROMISE!
Sure I gave the bike to thank him. But it also doesn't hurt having the loyalty--and fists--of someone like ABUSE.
Nice to have that option in case things ever get to the point where I need him in my corner. Someone other than Grayson.
Though I still think he should ditch the hat and raincoat.
"REALLY? THESE ARE WHAT YOU HAVE FOR BLUEPRINTS? YOU'RE KIDDING, RIGHT?!"

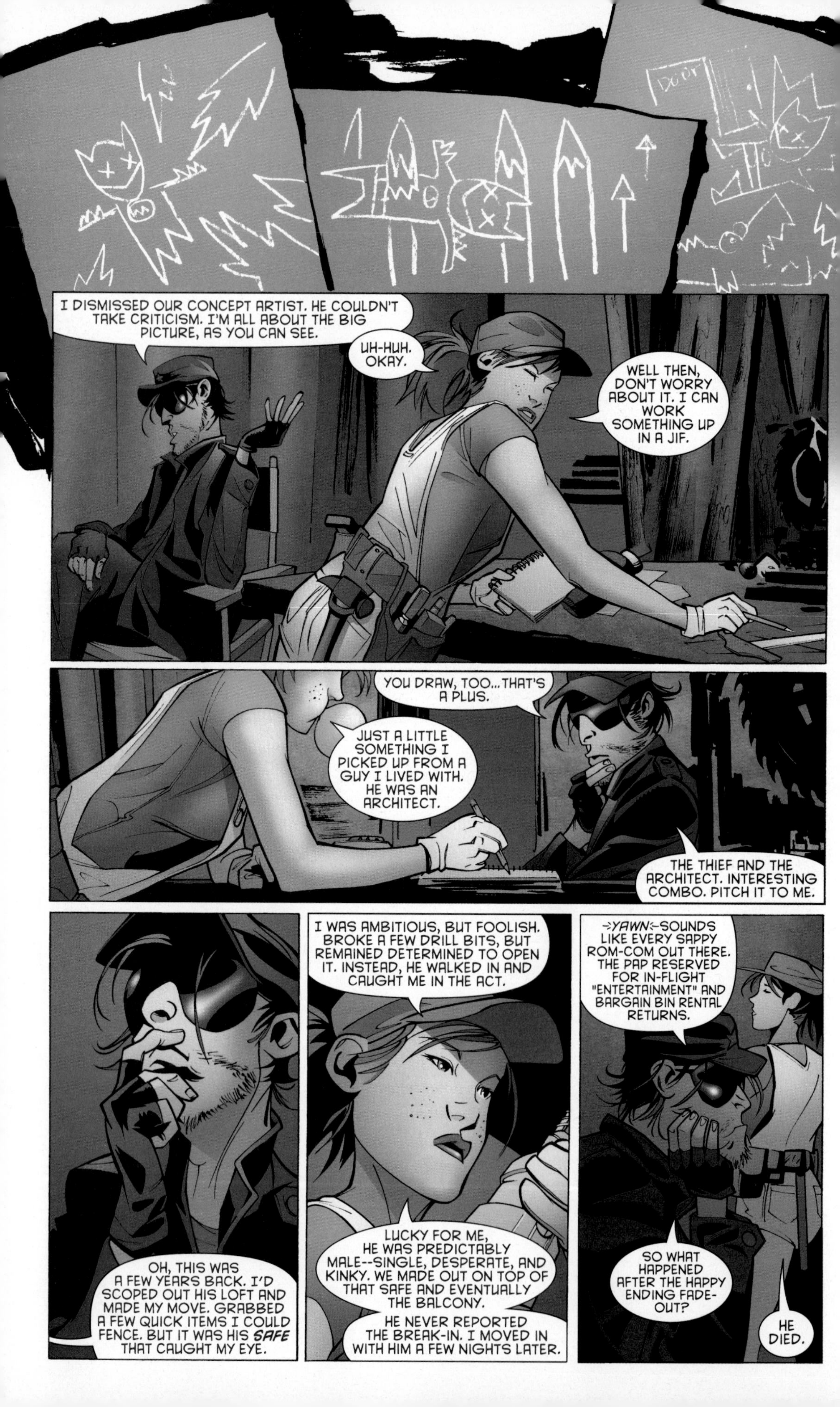
DOOR
I DISMISSED OUR CONCEPT ARTIST. HE COULDN'T TAKE CRITICISM. I'M ALL ABOUT THE BIG PICTURE, AS YOU CAN SEE.
UH-HUH. OKAY.
WELL THEN, DON'T WORRY ABOUT IT. I CAN WORK SOMETHING UP IN A JIF.
YOU DRAW, TOO...THAT'S A PLUS.
JUST A LITTLE SOMETHING I PICKED UP FROM A GUY I LIVED WITH. HE WAS AN ARCHITECT.
THE THIEF AND THE ARCHITECT. INTERESTING COMBO. PITCH IT TO ME.
OH, THIS WAS A FEW YEARS BACK. I'D SCOPED OUT HIS LOFT AND MADE MY MOVE. GRABBED A FEW QUICK ITEMS I COULD FENCE. BUT IT WAS HIS *SAFE* THAT CAUGHT MY EYE.
I WAS AMBITIOUS, BUT FOOLISH. BROKE A FEW DRILL BITS, BUT REMAINED DETERMINED TO OPEN IT. INSTEAD, HE WALKED IN AND CAUGHT ME IN THE ACT.
LUCKY FOR ME, HE WAS PREDICTABLY MALE--SINGLE, DESPERATE, AND KINKY. WE MADE OUT ON TOP OF THAT SAFE AND EVENTUALLY THE BALCONY.
HE NEVER REPORTED THE BREAK-IN. I MOVED IN WITH HIM A FEW NIGHTS LATER.
=>*YAWN*<=SOUNDS LIKE EVERY SAPPY ROM-COM OUT THERE. THE PAP RESERVED FOR IN-FLIGHT "ENTERTAINMENT" AND BARGAIN BIN RENTAL RETURNS.
SO WHAT HAPPENED AFTER THE HAPPY ENDING FADE-OUT?
HE DIED.

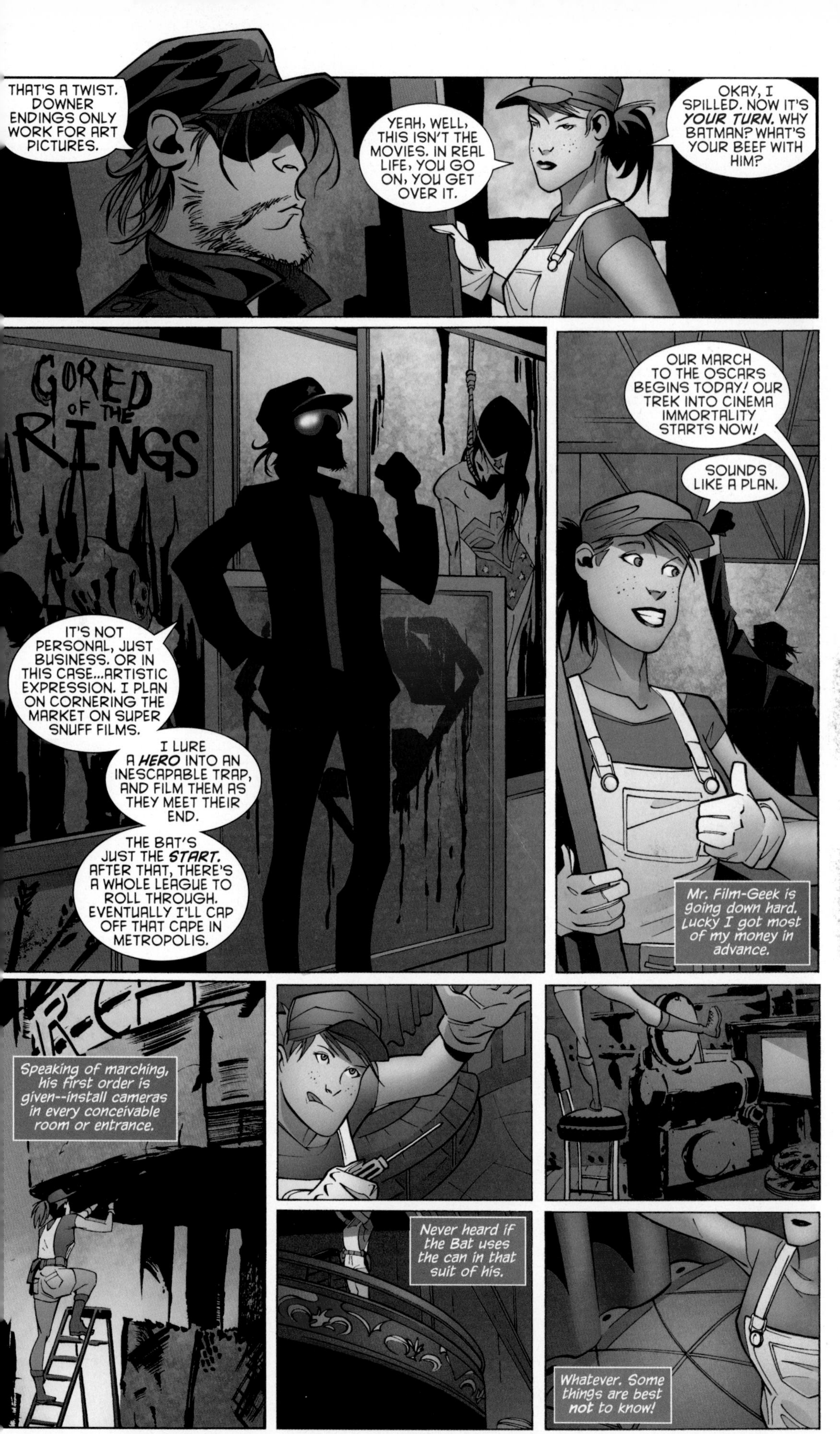
THAT'S A TWIST. DOWNER ENDINGS ONLY WORK FOR ART PICTURES.
YEAH, WELL, THIS ISN'T THE MOVIES. IN REAL LIFE, YOU GO ON, YOU GET OVER IT.
OKAY, I SPILLED. NOW IT'S YOUR TURN. WHY BATMAN? WHAT'S YOUR BEEF WITH HIM?
GORED OF THE RINGS
IT'S NOT PERSONAL, JUST BUSINESS. OR IN THIS CASE...ARTISTIC EXPRESSION. I PLAN ON CORNERING THE MARKET ON SUPER SNUFF FILMS.
I LURE A HERO INTO AN INESCAPABLE TRAP, AND FILM THEM AS THEY MEET THEIR END.
THE BAT'S JUST THE START. AFTER THAT, THERE'S A WHOLE LEAGUE TO ROLL THROUGH. EVENTUALLY I'LL CAP OFF THAT CAPE IN METROPOLIS.
OUR MARCH TO THE OSCARS BEGINS TODAY! OUR TREK INTO CINEMA IMMORTALITY STARTS NOW!
SOUNDS LIKE A PLAN.
Mr. Film-Geek is going down hard. Lucky I got most of my money in advance.
Speaking of marching, his first order is given--install cameras in every conceivable room or entrance.
Never heard if the Bat uses the can in that suit of his.
Whatever. Some things are best not to know!

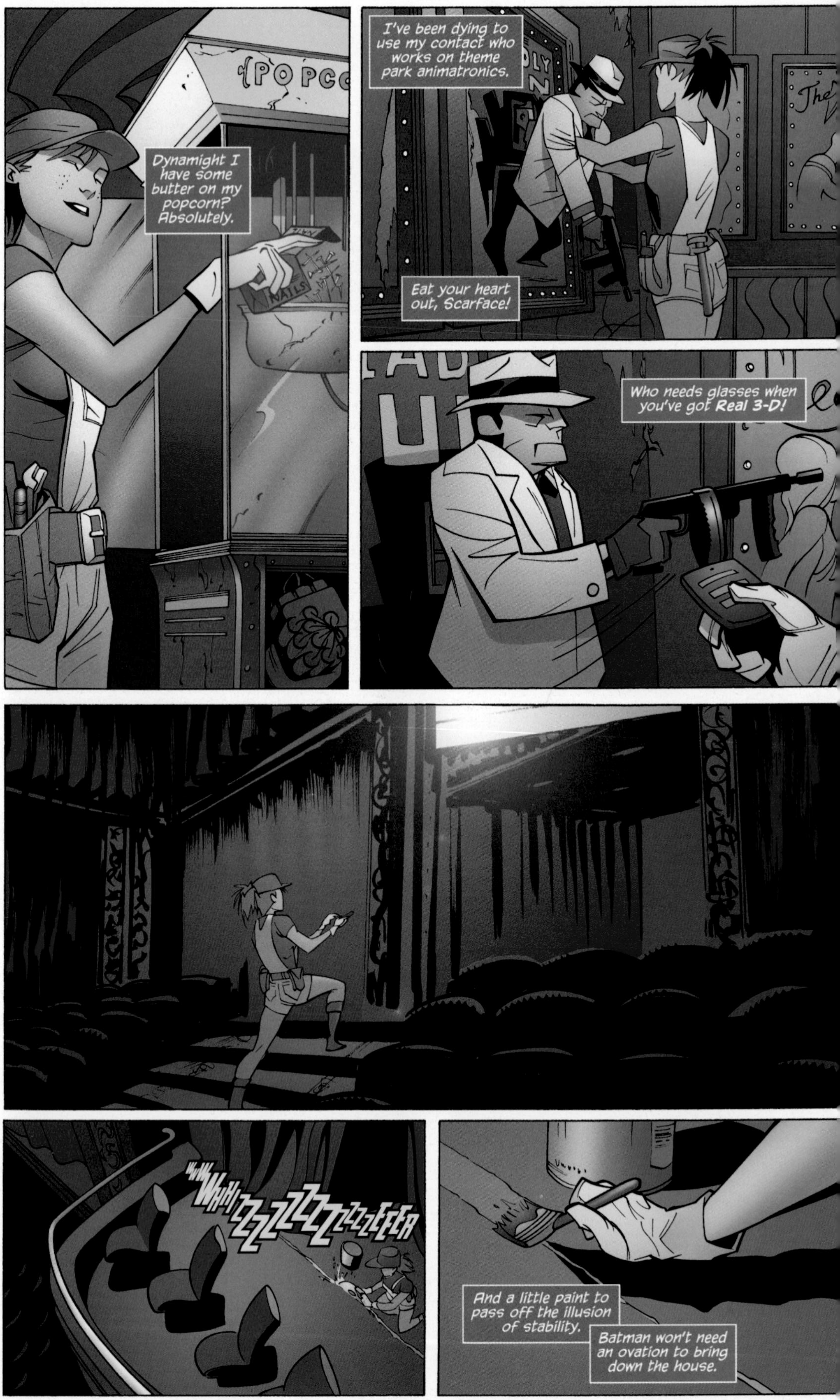
POPCO
Dynamight I have some butter on my popcorn? Absolutely.
NAILS
I've been dying to use my contact who works on theme park animatronics.
Eat your heart out, Scarface!
Who needs glasses when you've got **Real 3-D!**
WHHIZZZZZZZZZZZZEEER
And a little paint to pass off the illusion of stability.
Batman won't need an ovation to bring down the house.

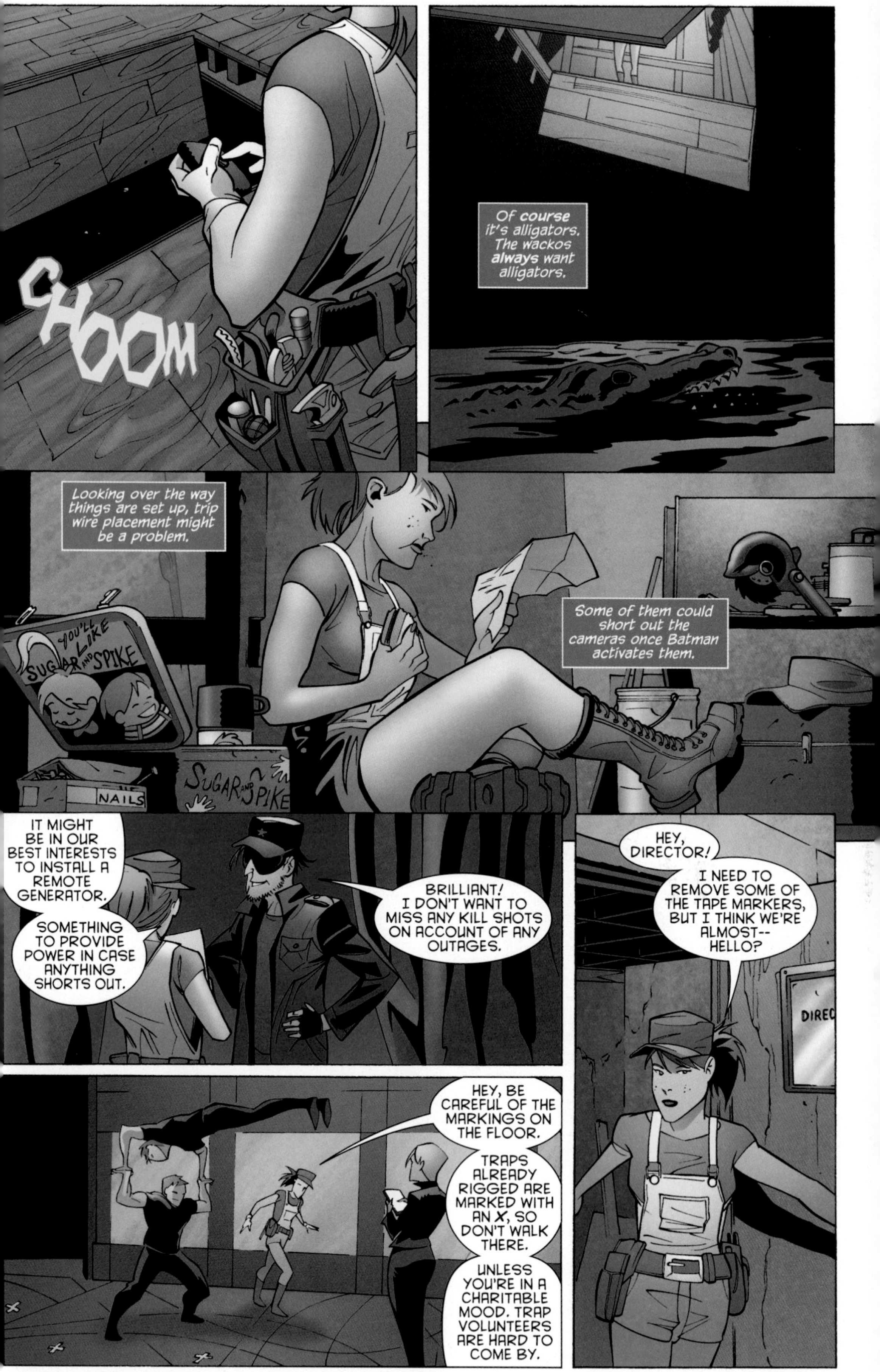

CHOOM
Of course it's alligators. The wackos always want alligators.
Looking over the way things are set up, trip wire placement might be a problem.
YOU'LL LIKE SUGAR AND SPIKE
SUGAR AND SPIKE
NAILS
Some of them could short out the cameras once Batman activates them.
IT MIGHT BE IN OUR BEST INTERESTS TO INSTALL A REMOTE GENERATOR.
SOMETHING TO PROVIDE POWER IN CASE ANYTHING SHORTS OUT.
BRILLIANT! I DON'T WANT TO MISS ANY KILL SHOTS ON ACCOUNT OF ANY OUTAGES.
HEY, DIRECTOR!
I NEED TO REMOVE SOME OF THE TAPE MARKERS, BUT I THINK WE'RE ALMOST-- HELLO?
DIREC
HEY, BE CAREFUL OF THE MARKINGS ON THE FLOOR.
TRAPS ALREADY RIGGED ARE MARKED WITH AN X, SO DON'T WALK THERE.
UNLESS YOU'RE IN A CHARITABLE MOOD. TRAP VOLUNTEERS ARE HARD TO COME BY.

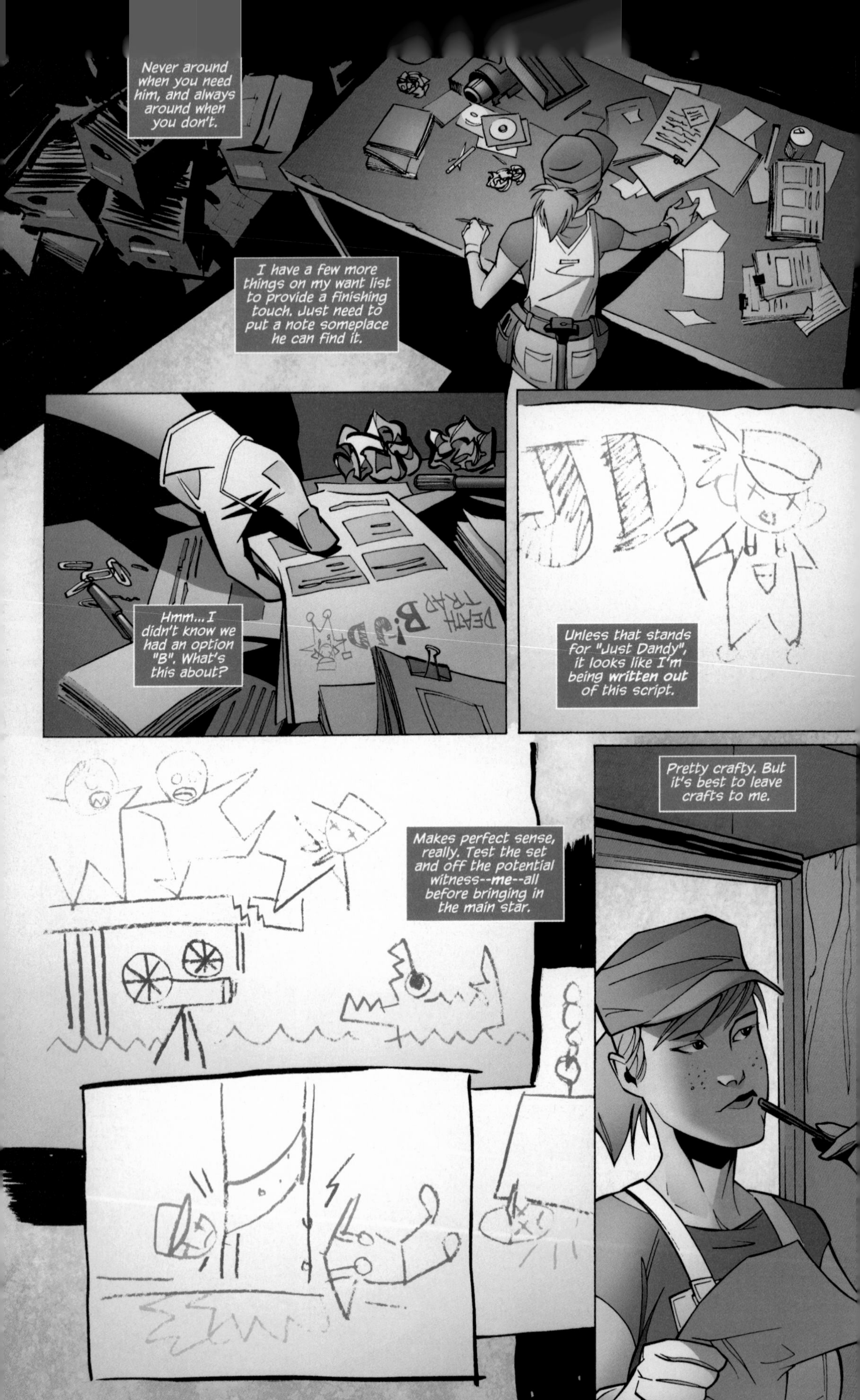

Never around when you need him, and always around when you don't.
I have a few more things on my want list to provide a finishing touch. Just need to put a note someplace he can find it.
Hmm...I didn't know we had an option "B". What's this about?
Unless that stands for "Just Dandy", it looks like I'm being **written out** of this script.
Makes perfect sense, really. Test the set and off the potential witness--**me**--all before bringing in the main star.
Pretty crafty. But it's best to leave crafts to me.

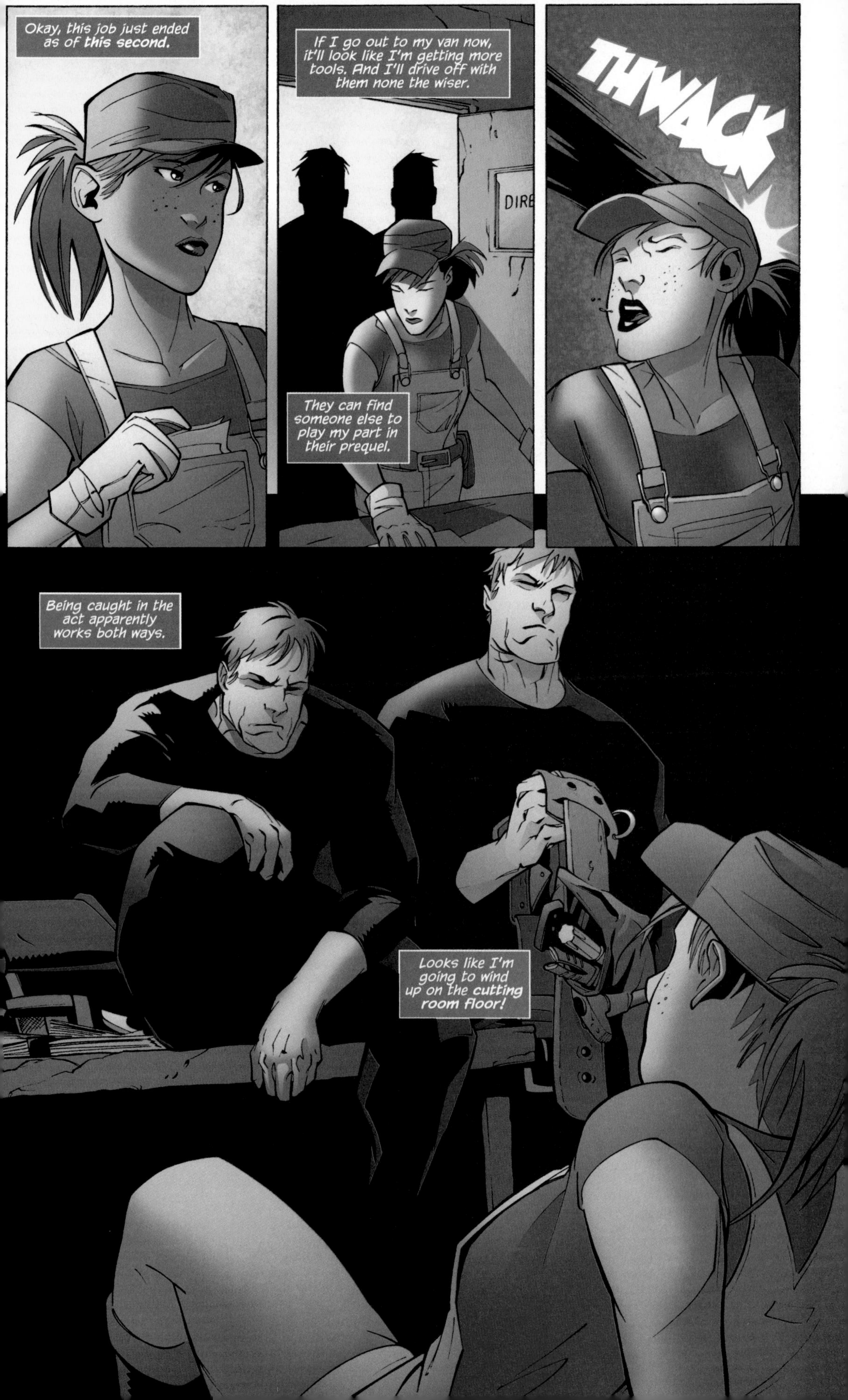
Okay, this job just ended as of this second.
If I go out to my van now, it'll look like I'm getting more tools. And I'll drive off with them none the wiser.
DIRE
They can find someone else to play my part in their prequel.
THWACK
Being caught in the act apparently works both ways.
Looks like I'm going to wind up on the cutting room floor!

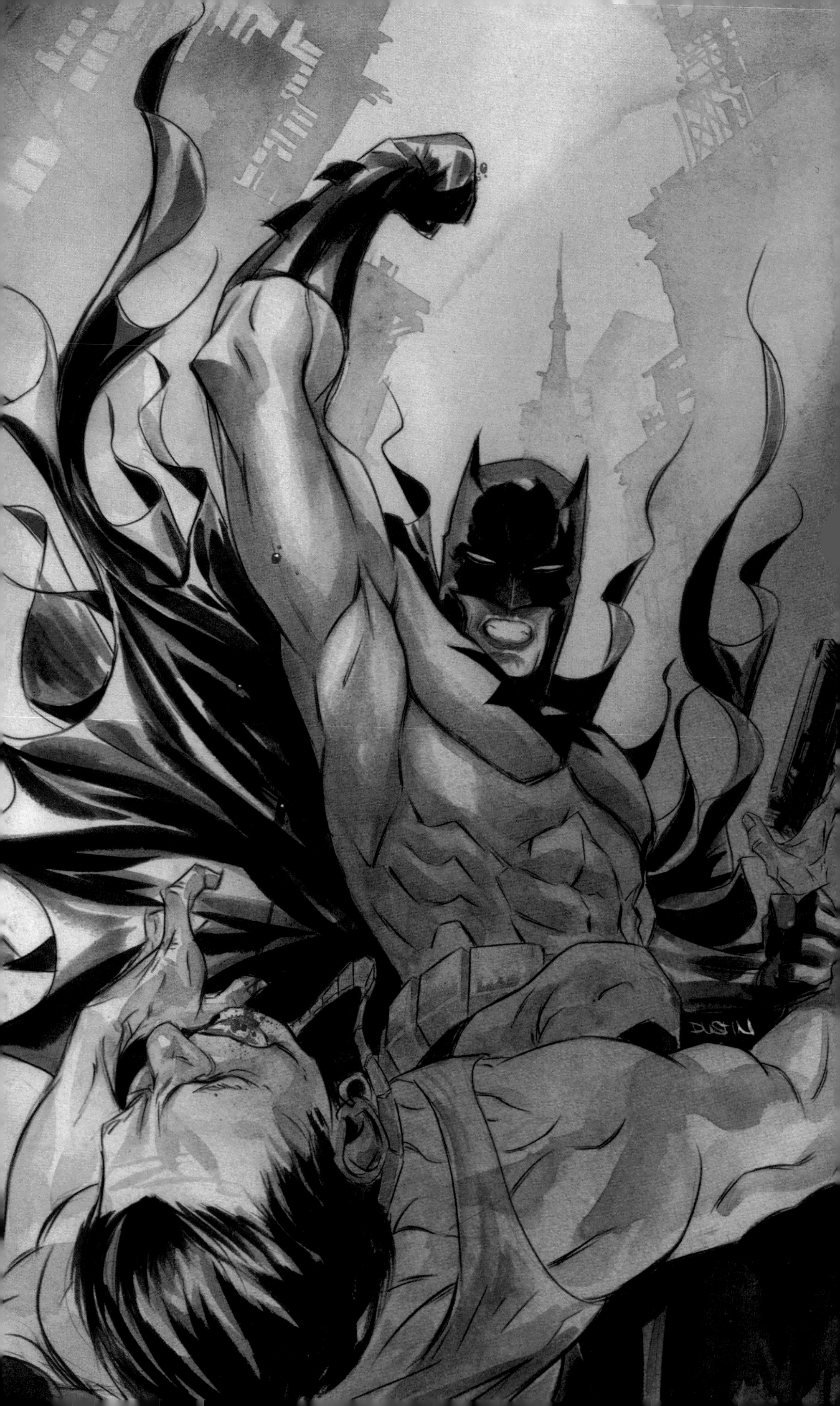
DUSTIN

"I wanted a closed set! **No spoilers allowed!**"

Way to go, Jenna. Captured by the very people that hired me.
I was entrusted to create the ultimate deathtrap scenario for my boss, The Director, to capture Batman's demise on film.
Too bad there wasn't enough trust to go around, as the hidden notes I just found in his office plan for my own death.
How do I get myself into these situations?
WHUMP
Better yet, how do I get out of them?

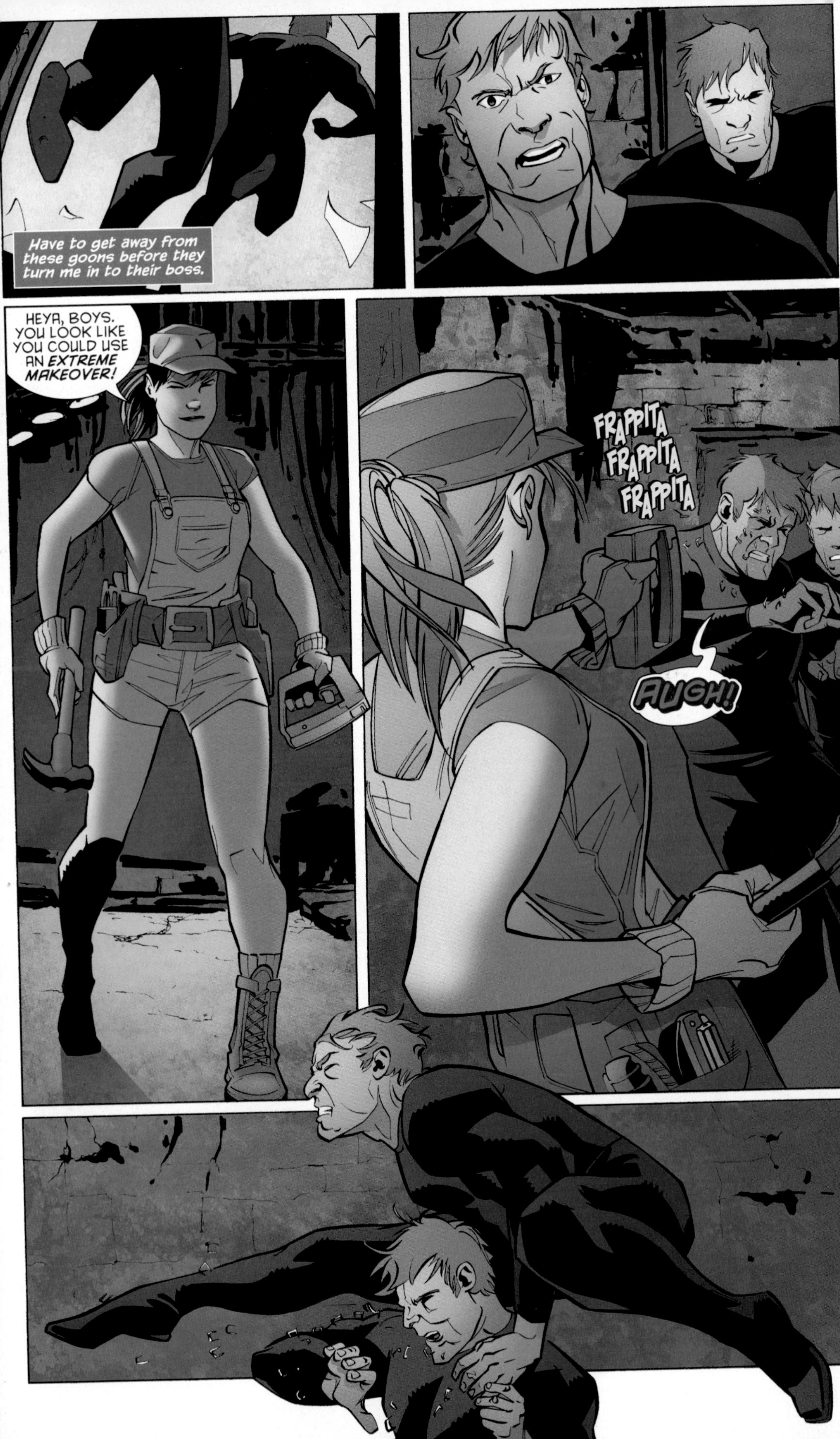
Have to get away from these goons before they turn me in to their boss.
HEYA, BOYS. YOU LOOK LIKE YOU COULD USE AN EXTREME MAKEOVER!
FRAPPITA FRAPPITA FRAPPITA
AUGH!

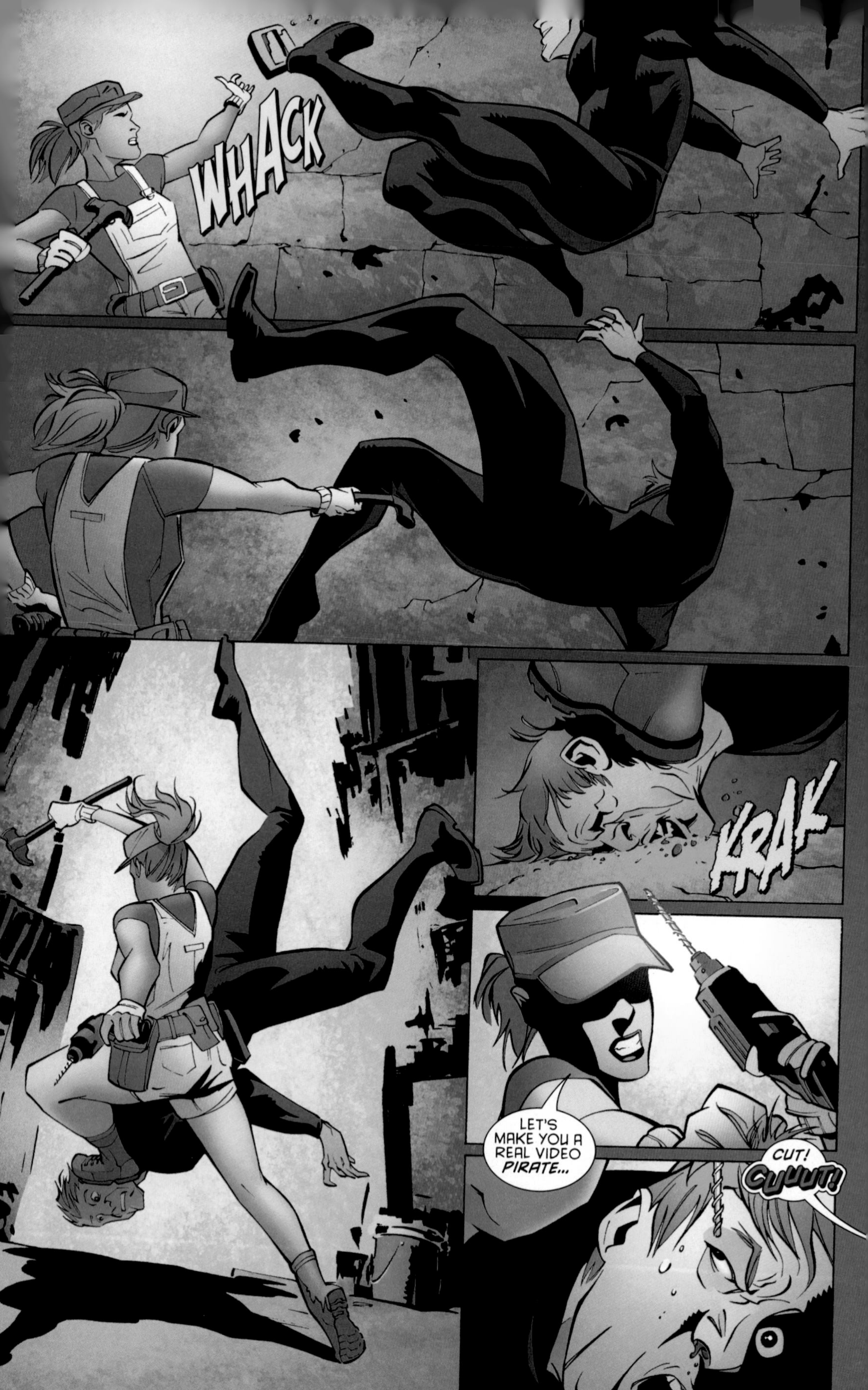
WHACK
KRAK
LET'S MAKE YOU A REAL VIDEO *PIRATE...*
CUT!
CUUUT!

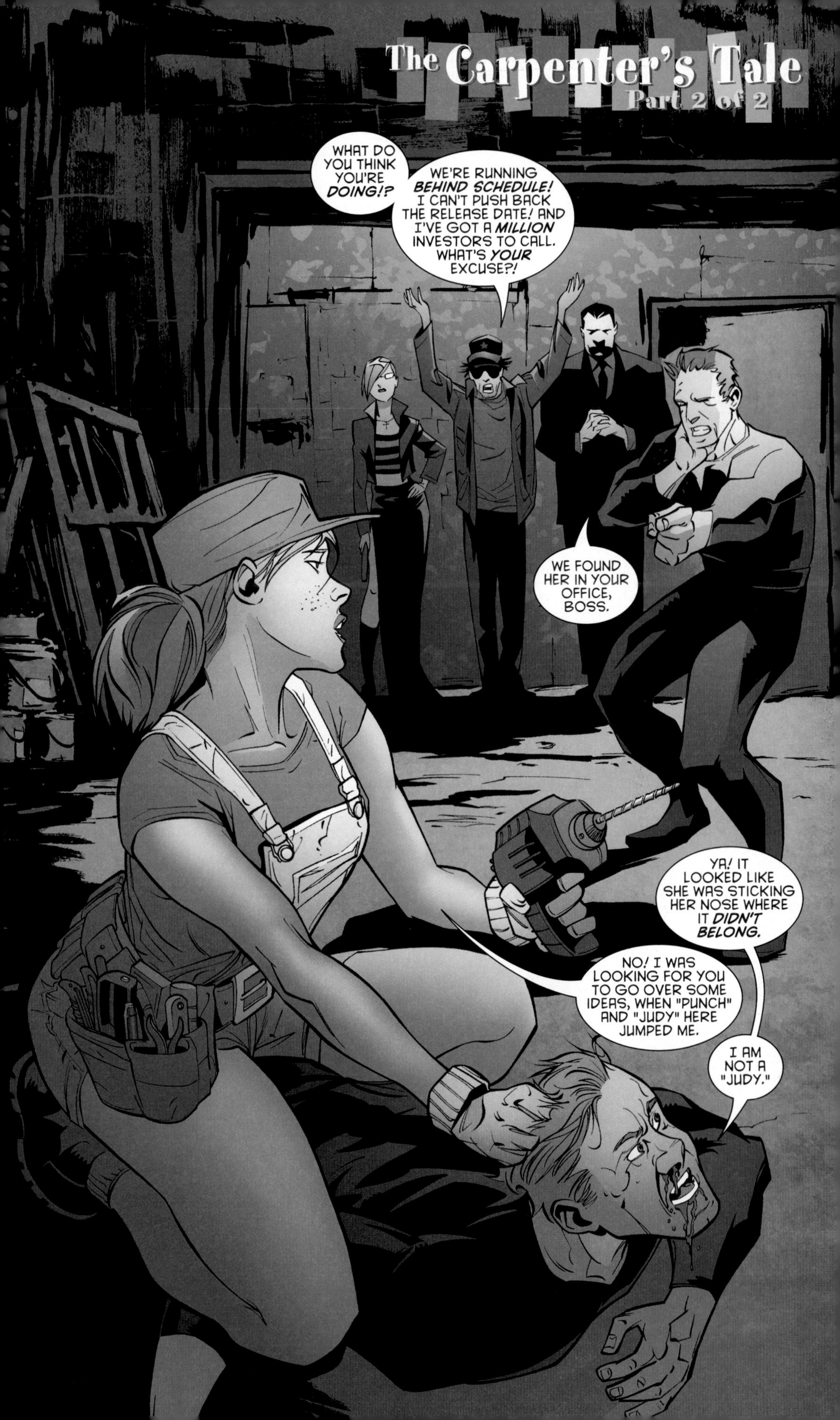
The Carpenter's Tale
Part 2 of 2
WHAT DO YOU THINK YOU'RE DOING!?
WE'RE RUNNING BEHIND SCHEDULE! I CAN'T PUSH BACK THE RELEASE DATE! AND I'VE GOT A MILLION INVESTORS TO CALL. WHAT'S YOUR EXCUSE?!
WE FOUND HER IN YOUR OFFICE, BOSS.
YA! IT LOOKED LIKE SHE WAS STICKING HER NOSE WHERE IT DIDN'T BELONG.
NO! I WAS LOOKING FOR YOU TO GO OVER SOME IDEAS, WHEN "PUNCH" AND "JUDY" HERE JUMPED ME.
I AM NOT A "JUDY."

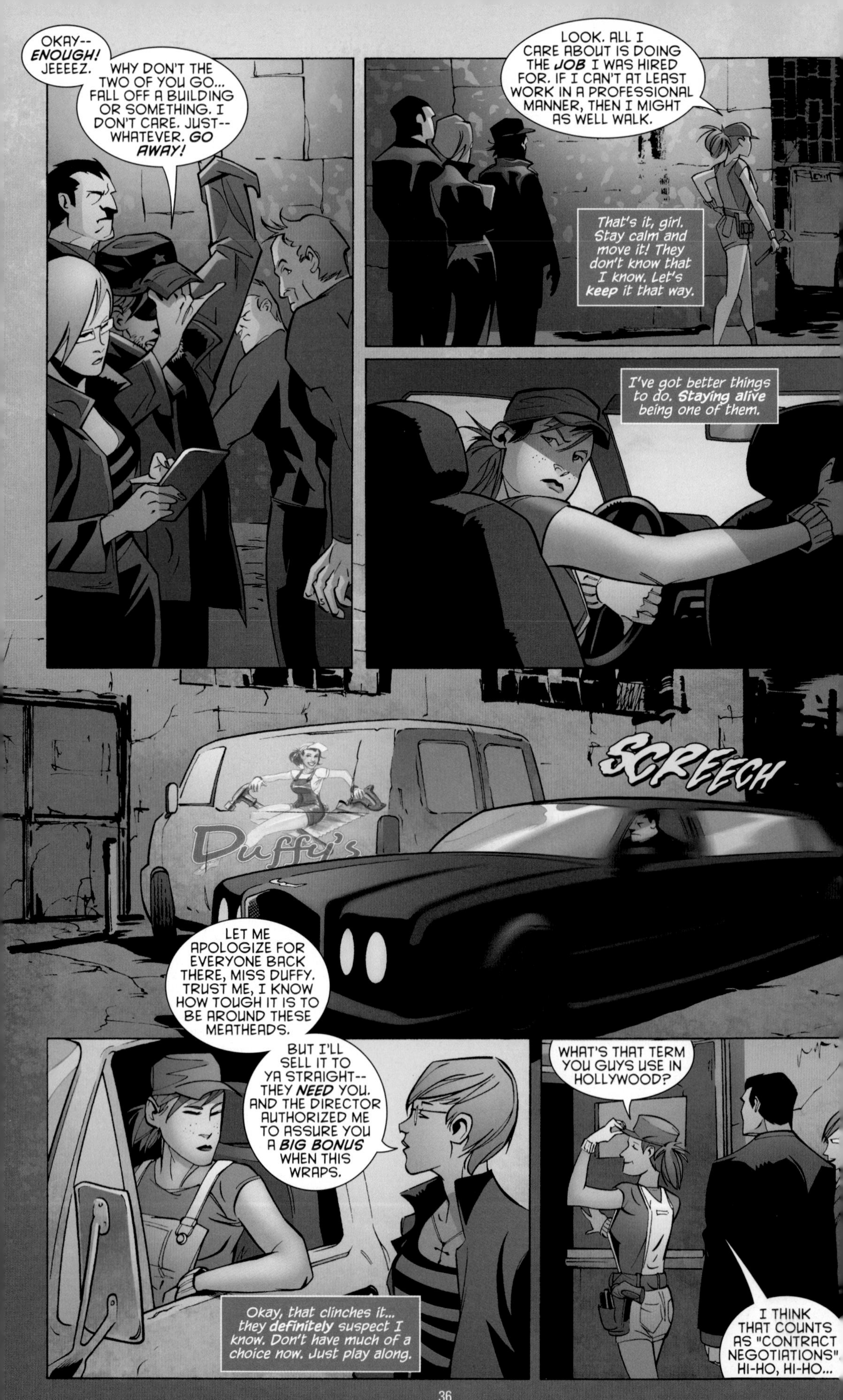
OKAY-- ENOUGH! JEEEEZ.
WHY DON'T THE TWO OF YOU GO... FALL OFF A BUILDING OR SOMETHING. I DON'T CARE. JUST-- WHATEVER. GO AWAY!
LOOK. ALL I CARE ABOUT IS DOING THE JOB I WAS HIRED FOR. IF I CAN'T AT LEAST WORK IN A PROFESSIONAL MANNER, THEN I MIGHT AS WELL WALK.
That's it, girl. Stay calm and move it! They don't know that I know. Let's keep it that way.
I've got better things to do. Staying alive being one of them.
SCREECH
Duffy's
LET ME APOLOGIZE FOR EVERYONE BACK THERE, MISS DUFFY. TRUST ME, I KNOW HOW TOUGH IT IS TO BE AROUND THESE MEATHEADS.
BUT I'LL SELL IT TO YA STRAIGHT-- THEY NEED YOU. AND THE DIRECTOR AUTHORIZED ME TO ASSURE YOU A BIG BONUS WHEN THIS WRAPS.
Okay, that clinches it... they definitely suspect I know. Don't have much of a choice now. Just play along.
WHAT'S THAT TERM YOU GUYS USE IN HOLLYWOOD?
I THINK THAT COUNTS AS "CONTRACT NEGOTIATIONS". HI-HO, HI-HO...

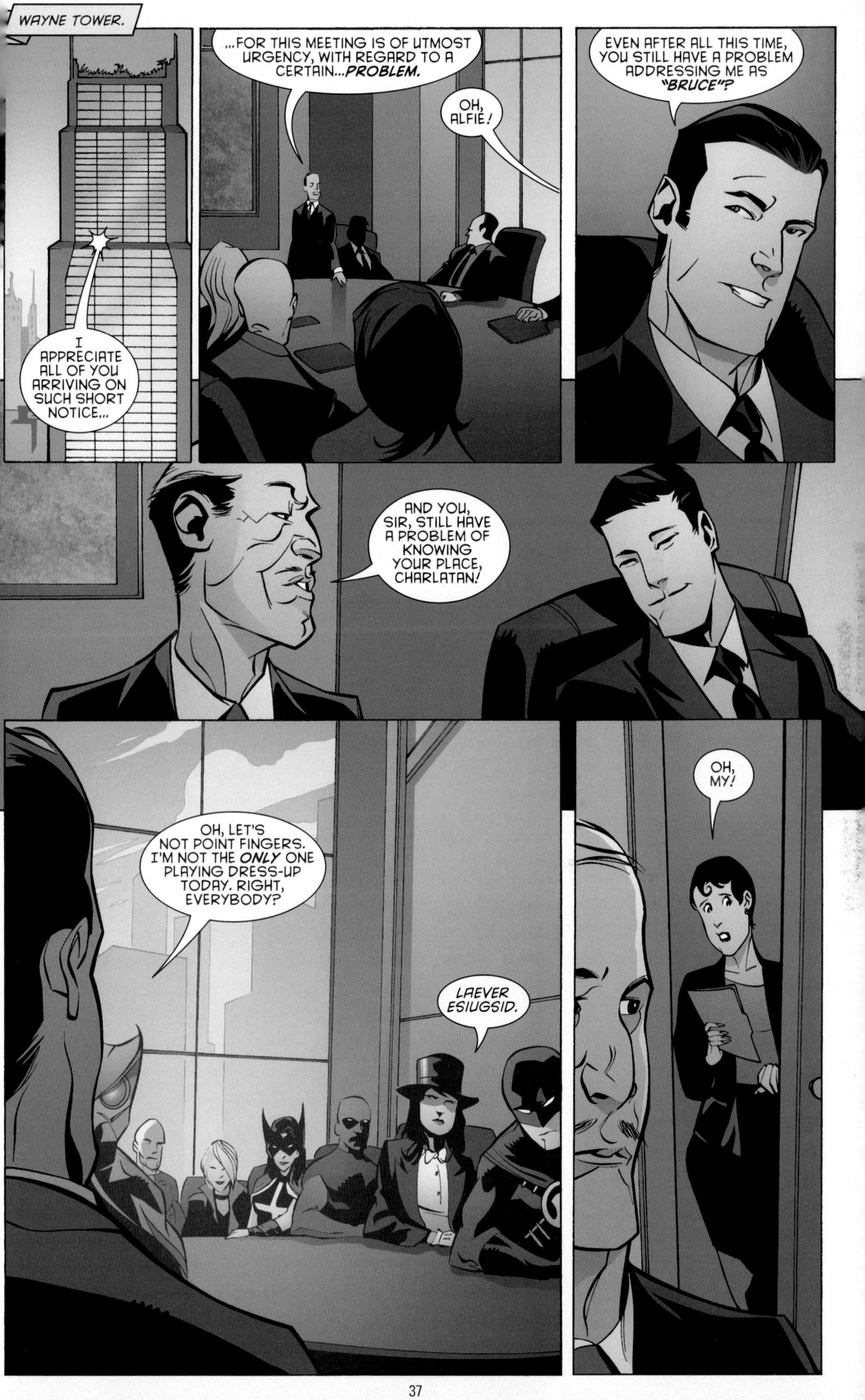
WAYNE TOWER.
I APPRECIATE ALL OF YOU ARRIVING ON SUCH SHORT NOTICE...
...FOR THIS MEETING IS OF UTMOST URGENCY, WITH REGARD TO A CERTAIN...PROBLEM.
OH, ALFIE!
EVEN AFTER ALL THIS TIME, YOU STILL HAVE A PROBLEM ADDRESSING ME AS "BRUCE"?
AND YOU, SIR, STILL HAVE A PROBLEM OF KNOWING YOUR PLACE, CHARLATAN!
OH, LET'S NOT POINT FINGERS. I'M NOT THE ONLY ONE PLAYING DRESS-UP TODAY. RIGHT, EVERYBODY?
LAEVER ESIUGSID.
OH, MY!

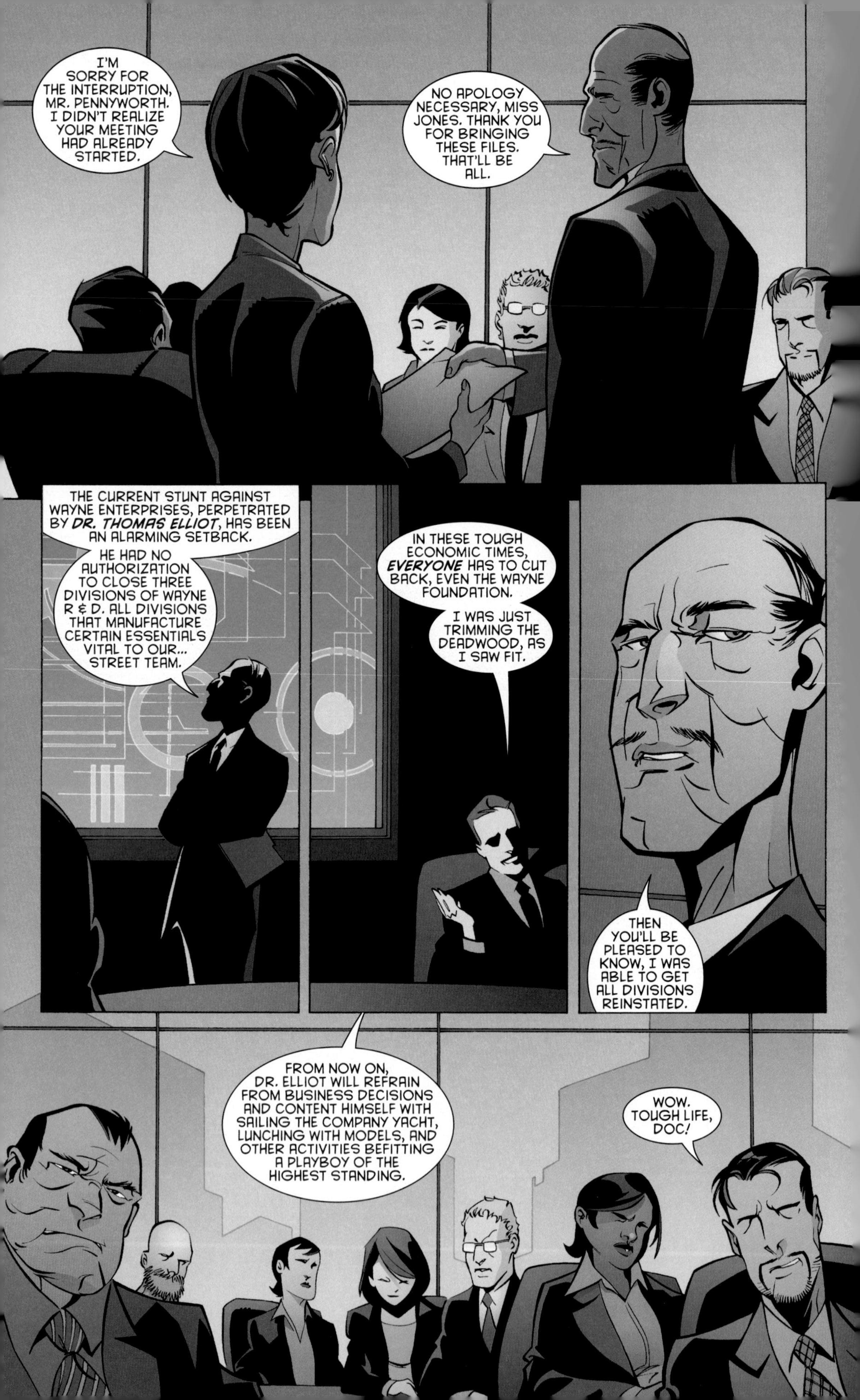
I'M SORRY FOR THE INTERRUPTION, MR. PENNYWORTH. I DIDN'T REALIZE YOUR MEETING HAD ALREADY STARTED.
NO APOLOGY NECESSARY, MISS JONES. THANK YOU FOR BRINGING THESE FILES. THAT'LL BE ALL.
THE CURRENT STUNT AGAINST WAYNE ENTERPRISES, PERPETRATED BY *DR. THOMAS ELLIOT*, HAS BEEN AN ALARMING SETBACK.
HE HAD NO AUTHORIZATION TO CLOSE THREE DIVISIONS OF WAYNE R & D. ALL DIVISIONS THAT MANUFACTURE CERTAIN ESSENTIALS VITAL TO OUR... STREET TEAM.
IN THESE TOUGH ECONOMIC TIMES, ***EVERYONE*** HAS TO CUT BACK, EVEN THE WAYNE FOUNDATION.
I WAS JUST TRIMMING THE DEADWOOD, AS I SAW FIT.
THEN YOU'LL BE PLEASED TO KNOW, I WAS ABLE TO GET ALL DIVISIONS REINSTATED.
FROM NOW ON, DR. ELLIOT WILL REFRAIN FROM BUSINESS DECISIONS AND CONTENT HIMSELF WITH SAILING THE COMPANY YACHT, LUNCHING WITH MODELS, AND OTHER ACTIVITIES BEFITTING A PLAYBOY OF THE HIGHEST STANDING.
WOW. TOUGH LIFE, DOC!

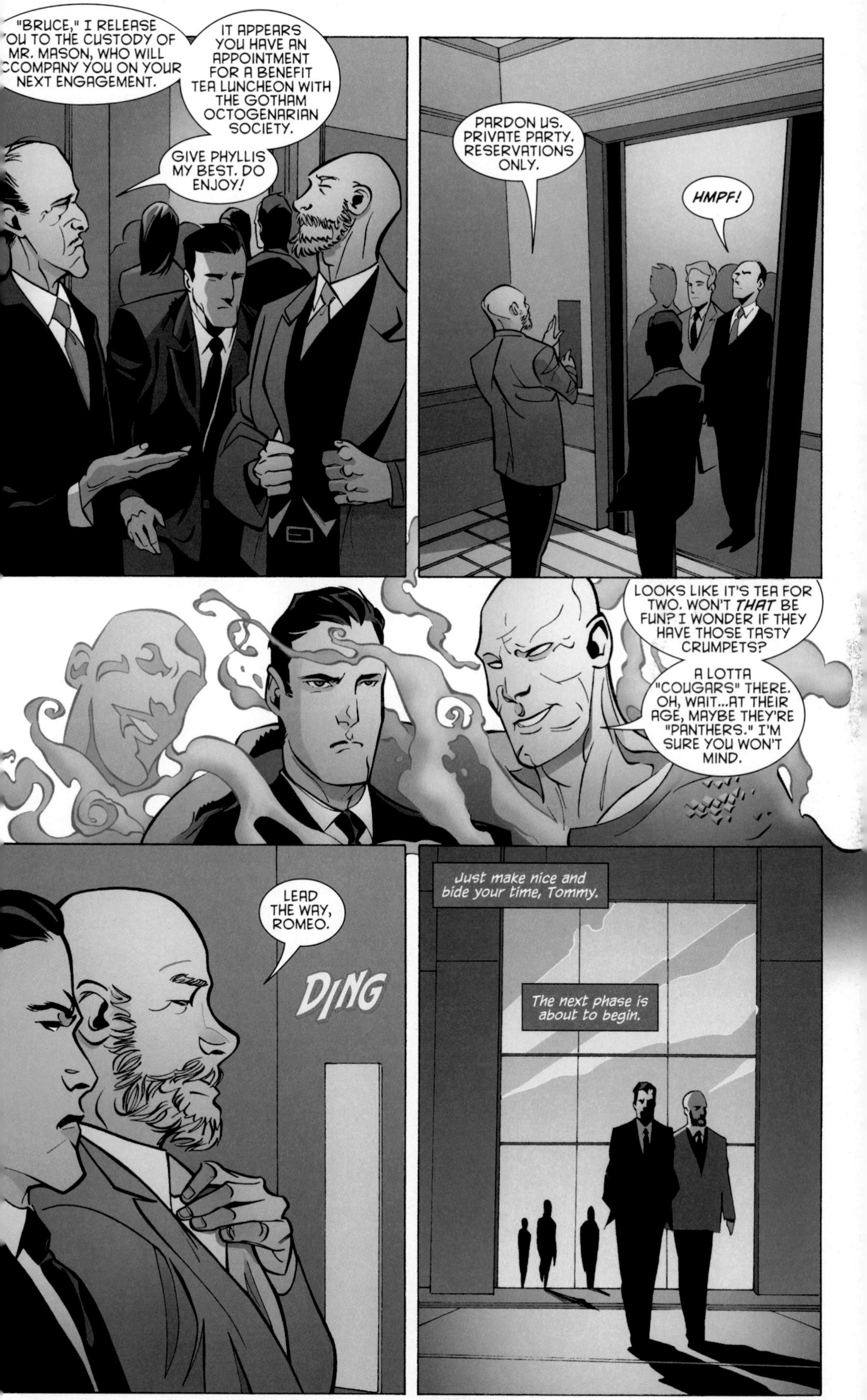
"BRUCE," I RELEASE YOU TO THE CUSTODY OF MR. MASON, WHO WILL ACCOMPANY YOU ON YOUR NEXT ENGAGEMENT.
IT APPEARS YOU HAVE AN APPOINTMENT FOR A BENEFIT TEA LUNCHEON WITH THE GOTHAM OCTOGENARIAN SOCIETY.
GIVE PHYLLIS MY BEST. DO ENJOY!
PARDON US. PRIVATE PARTY. RESERVATIONS ONLY.
HMPF!
LOOKS LIKE IT'S TEA FOR TWO. WON'T THAT BE FUN? I WONDER IF THEY HAVE THOSE TASTY CRUMPETS?
A LOTTA "COUGARS" THERE. OH, WAIT...AT THEIR AGE, MAYBE THEY'RE "PANTHERS." I'M SURE YOU WON'T MIND.
LEAD THE WAY, ROMEO.
DING
Just make nice and bide your time, Tommy.
The next phase is about to begin.

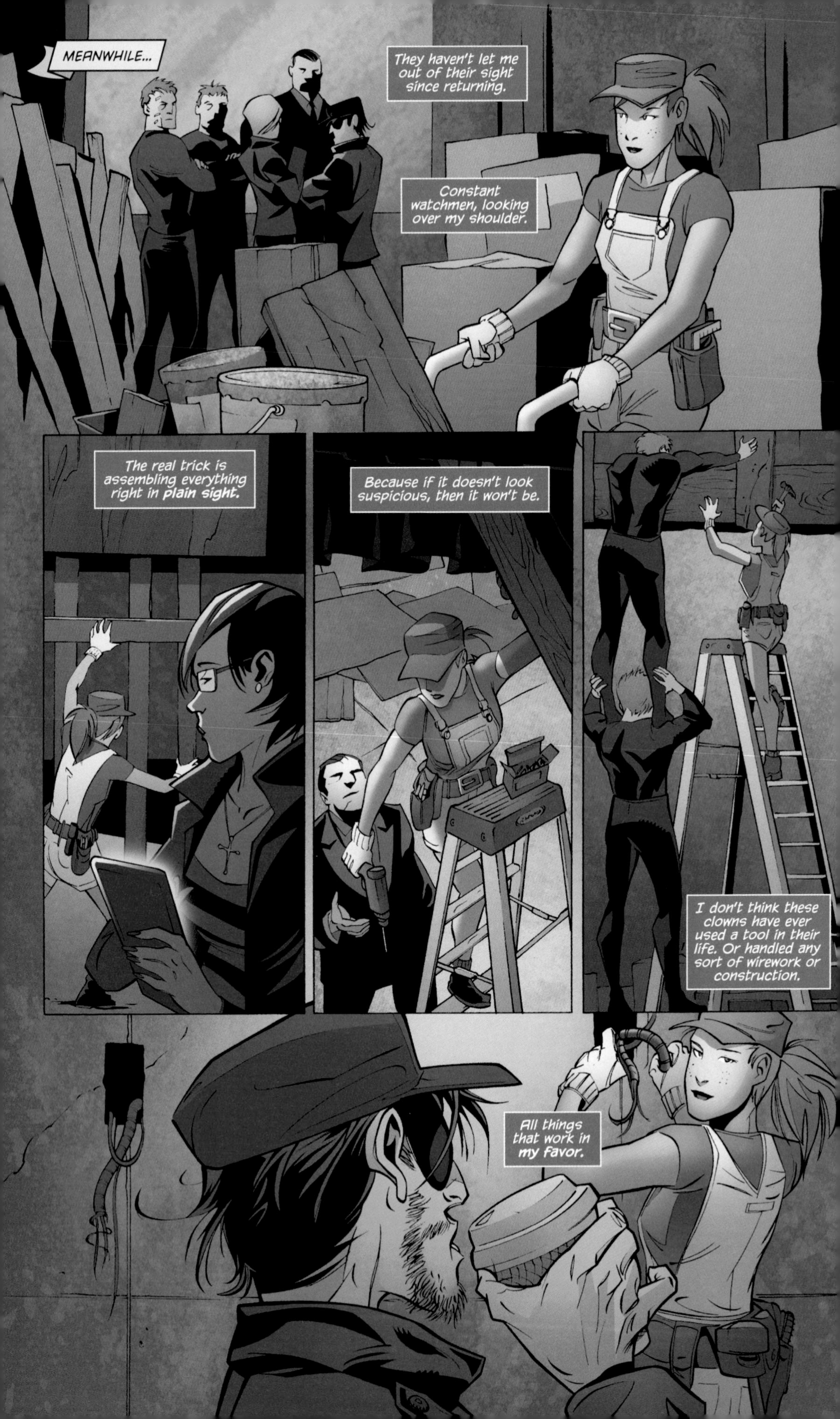
MEANWHILE...
They haven't let me out of their sight since returning.
Constant watchmen, looking over my shoulder.
The real trick is assembling everything right in **plain sight.**
Because if it doesn't look suspicious, then it won't be.
I don't think these clowns have ever used a tool in their life. Or handled any sort of wirework or construction.
All things that work in **my favor.**

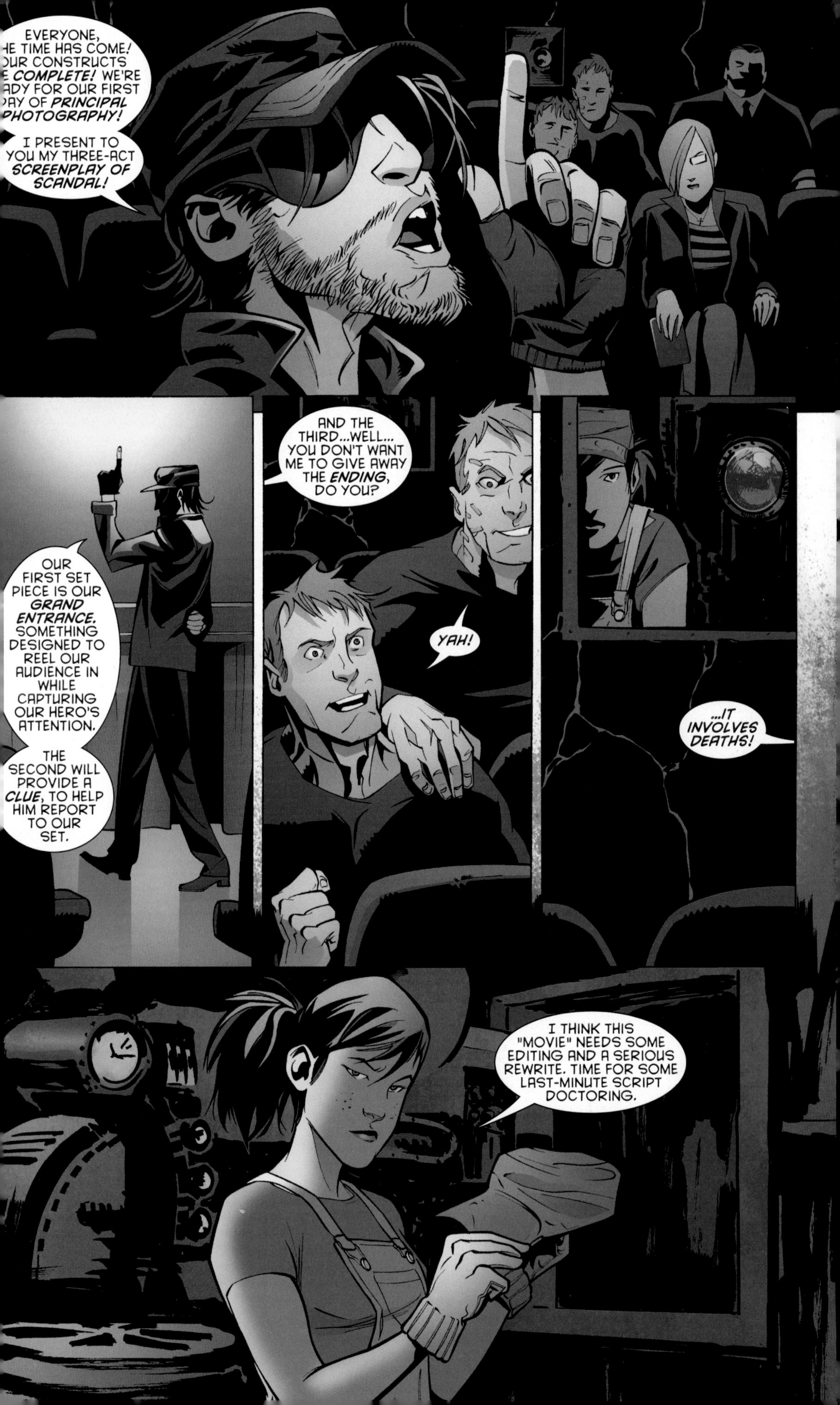
EVERYONE, HE TIME HAS COME! OUR CONSTRUCTS E COMPLETE! WE'RE ADY FOR OUR FIRST AY OF PRINCIPAL PHOTOGRAPHY!
I PRESENT TO YOU MY THREE-ACT SCREENPLAY OF SCANDAL!
OUR FIRST SET PIECE IS OUR GRAND ENTRANCE. SOMETHING DESIGNED TO REEL OUR AUDIENCE IN WHILE CAPTURING OUR HERO'S ATTENTION.
THE SECOND WILL PROVIDE A CLUE, TO HELP HIM REPORT TO OUR SET.
AND THE THIRD...WELL... YOU DON'T WANT ME TO GIVE AWAY THE ENDING, DO YOU?
YAH!
...IT INVOLVES DEATHS!
I THINK THIS "MOVIE" NEEDS SOME EDITING AND A SERIOUS REWRITE. TIME FOR SOME LAST-MINUTE SCRIPT DOCTORING.

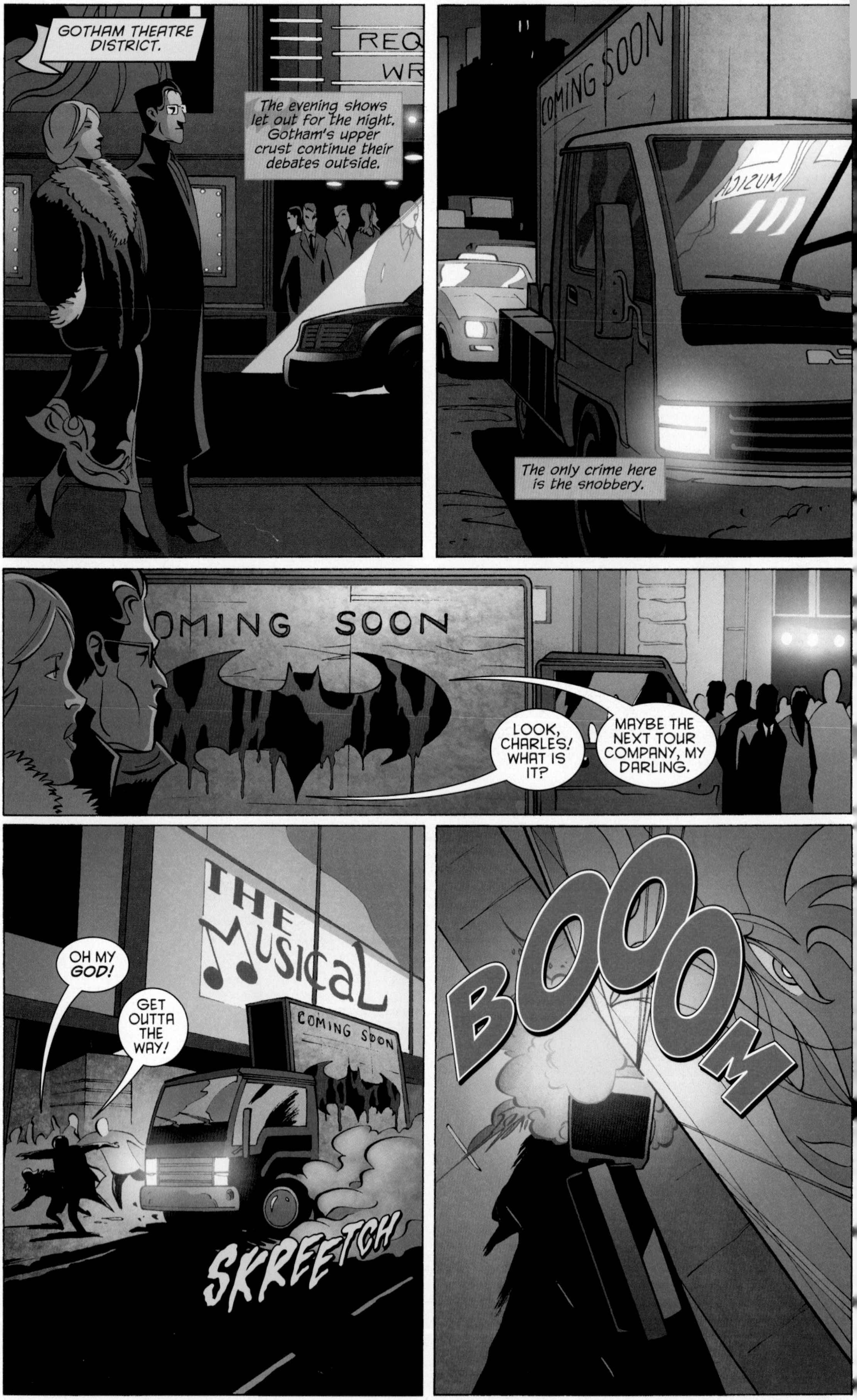

GOTHAM THEATRE DISTRICT.
REQ
WR
The evening shows let out for the night. Gotham's upper crust continue their debates outside.
COMING SOON
The only crime here is the snobbery.
OMING SOON
LOOK, CHARLES! WHAT IS IT?
MAYBE THE NEXT TOUR COMPANY, MY DARLING.
THE MUSICAL
OH MY GOD!
GET OUTTA THE WAY!
COMING SOON
SKREETCH
BOOOOM

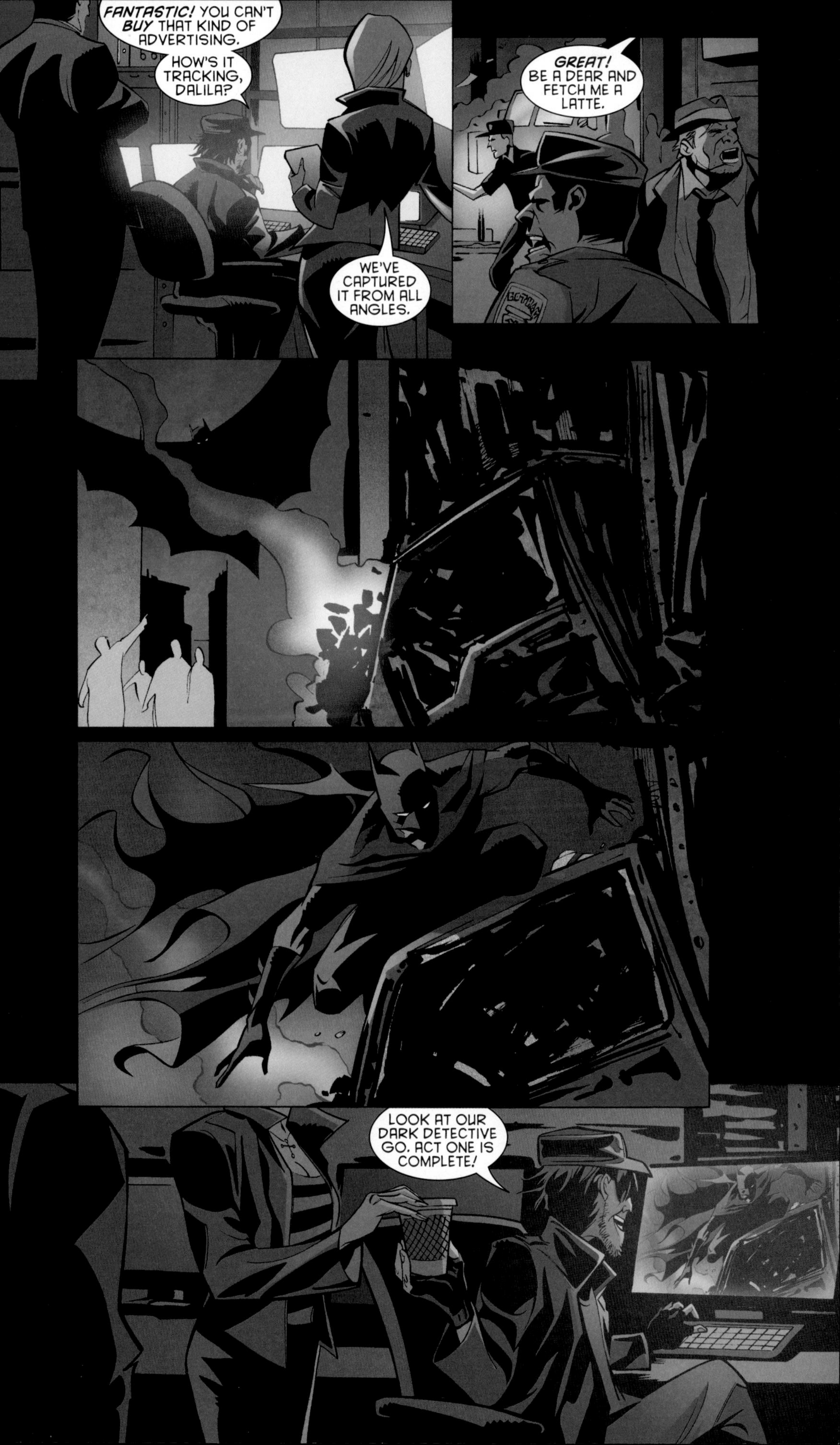
FANTASTIC! YOU CAN'T BUY THAT KIND OF ADVERTISING.
HOW'S IT TRACKING, DALILA?
WE'VE CAPTURED IT FROM ALL ANGLES.
GREAT! BE A DEAR AND FETCH ME A LATTE.
LOOK AT OUR DARK DETECTIVE GO. ACT ONE IS COMPLETE!

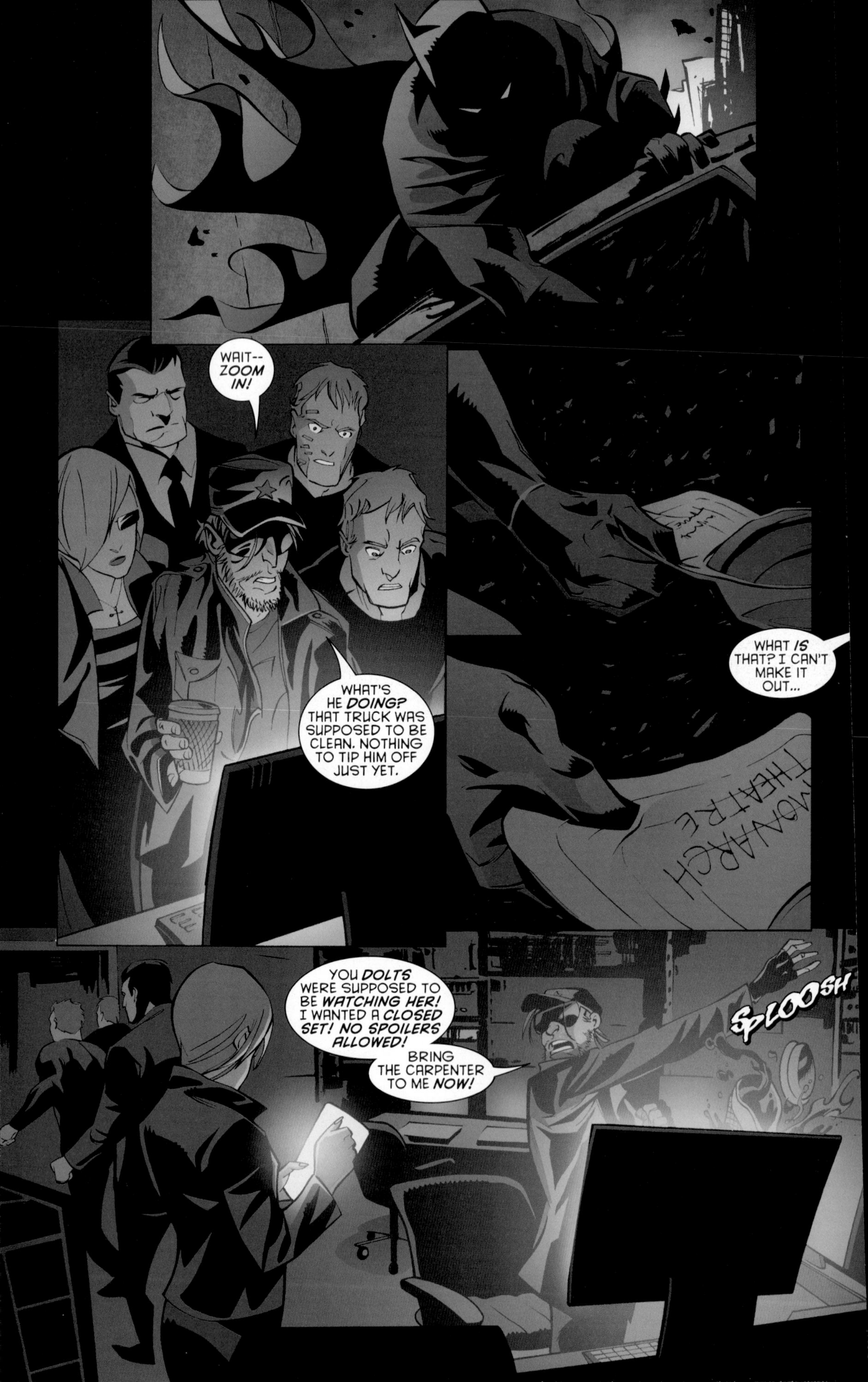
WAIT-- ZOOM IN!
WHAT'S HE DOING? THAT TRUCK WAS SUPPOSED TO BE CLEAN. NOTHING TO TIP HIM OFF JUST YET.
WHAT IS THAT? I CAN'T MAKE IT OUT...
MONARCH THEATRE
YOU DOLTS WERE SUPPOSED TO BE WATCHING HER! I WANTED A CLOSED SET! NO SPOILERS ALLOWED!
BRING THE CARPENTER TO ME NOW!
SPLOOSH

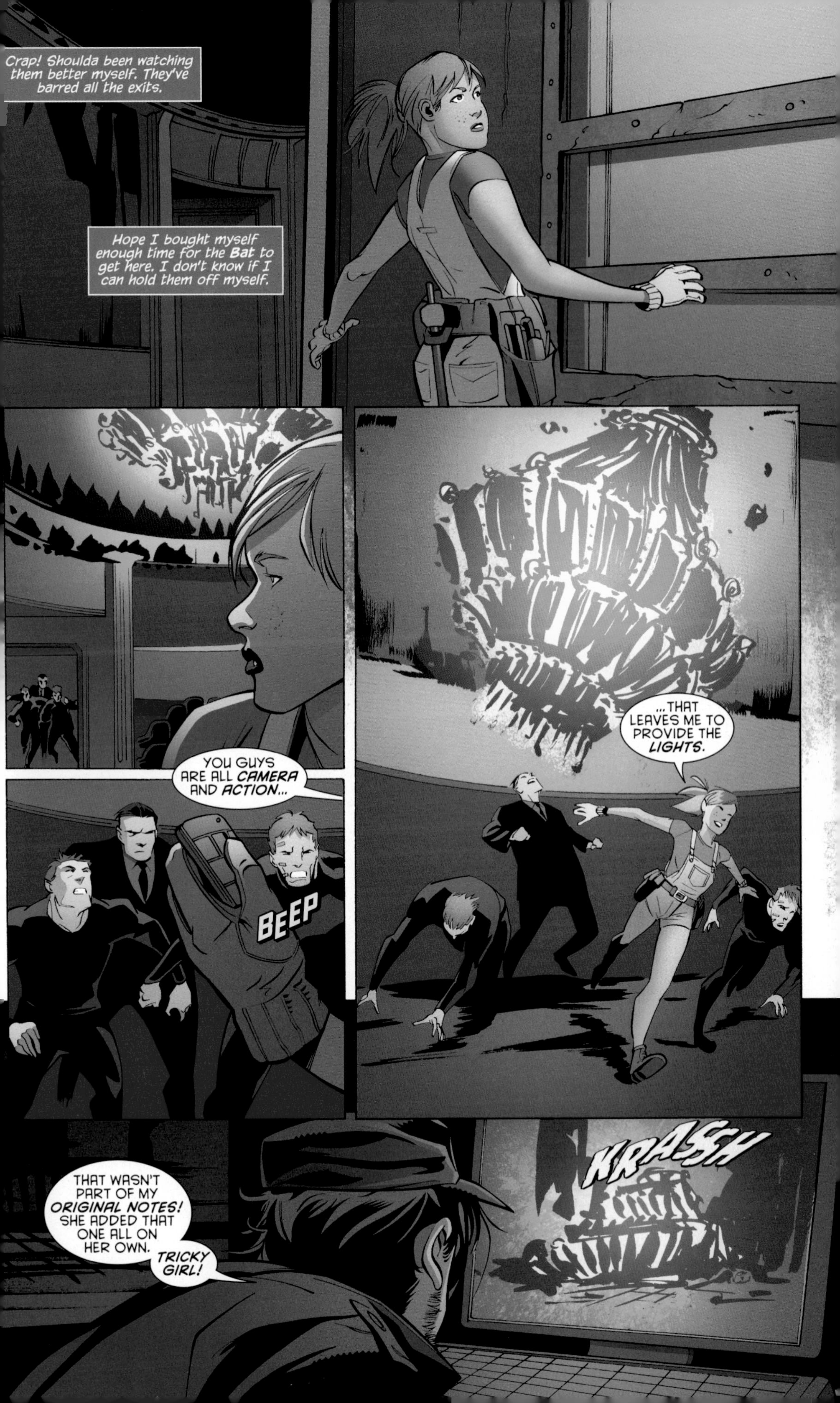
Crap! Shoulda been watching them better myself. They've barred all the exits.
Hope I bought myself enough time for the Bat to get here. I don't know if I can hold them off myself.
YOU GUYS ARE ALL CAMERA AND ACTION...
BEEP
...THAT LEAVES ME TO PROVIDE THE LIGHTS.
KRASH
THAT WASN'T PART OF MY ORIGINAL NOTES! SHE ADDED THAT ONE ALL ON HER OWN.
TRICKY GIRL!

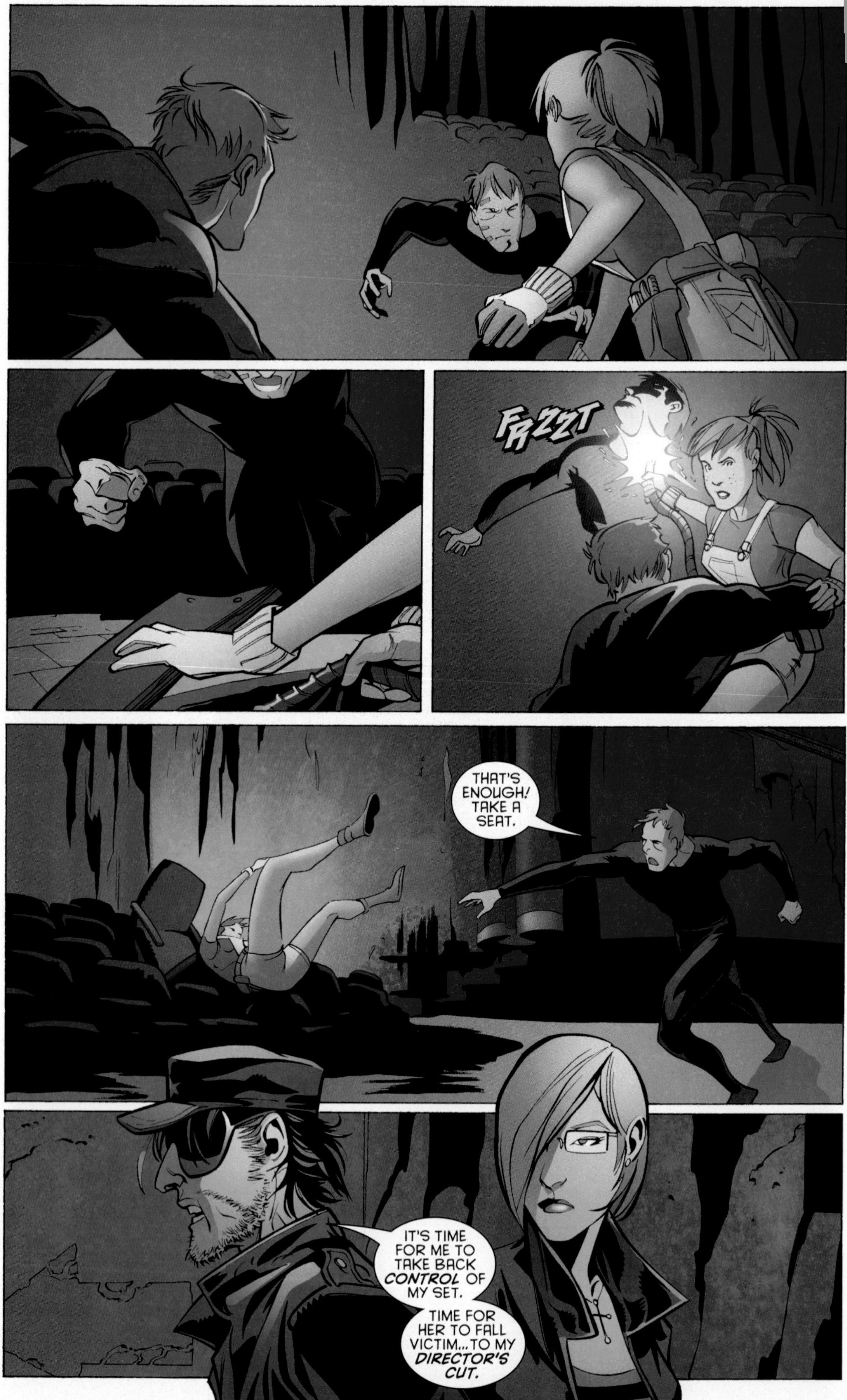
FRZZT
THAT'S ENOUGH! TAKE A SEAT.
IT'S TIME FOR ME TO TAKE BACK CONTROL OF MY SET.
TIME FOR HER TO FALL VICTIM...TO MY DIRECTOR'S CUT.

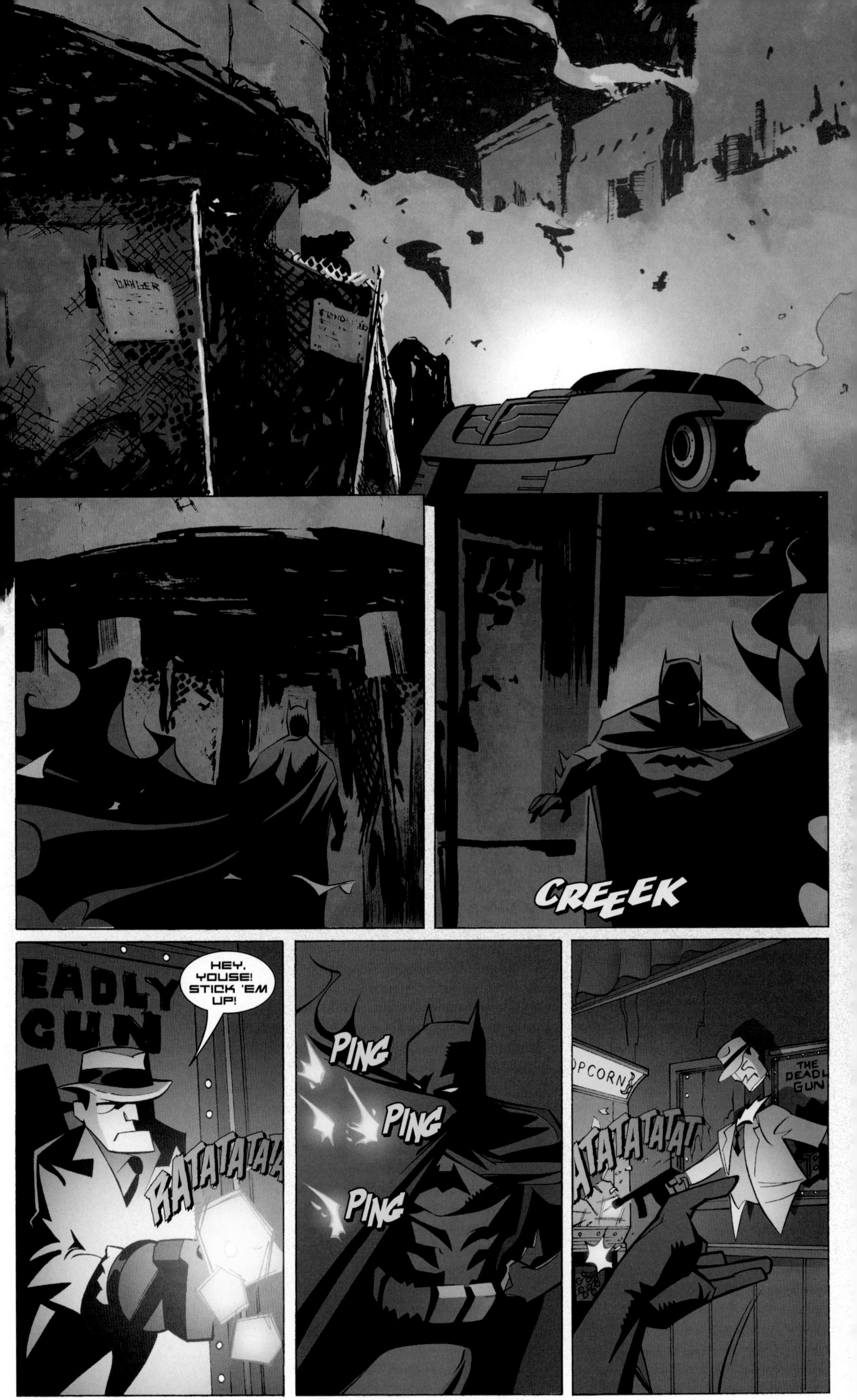

CREEEK
EADLY
GUN
HEY, YOUSE! STICK 'EM UP!
RATATATATA
PING
PING
PING
OPCORN
THE DEADLY GUN
RATATATATAT

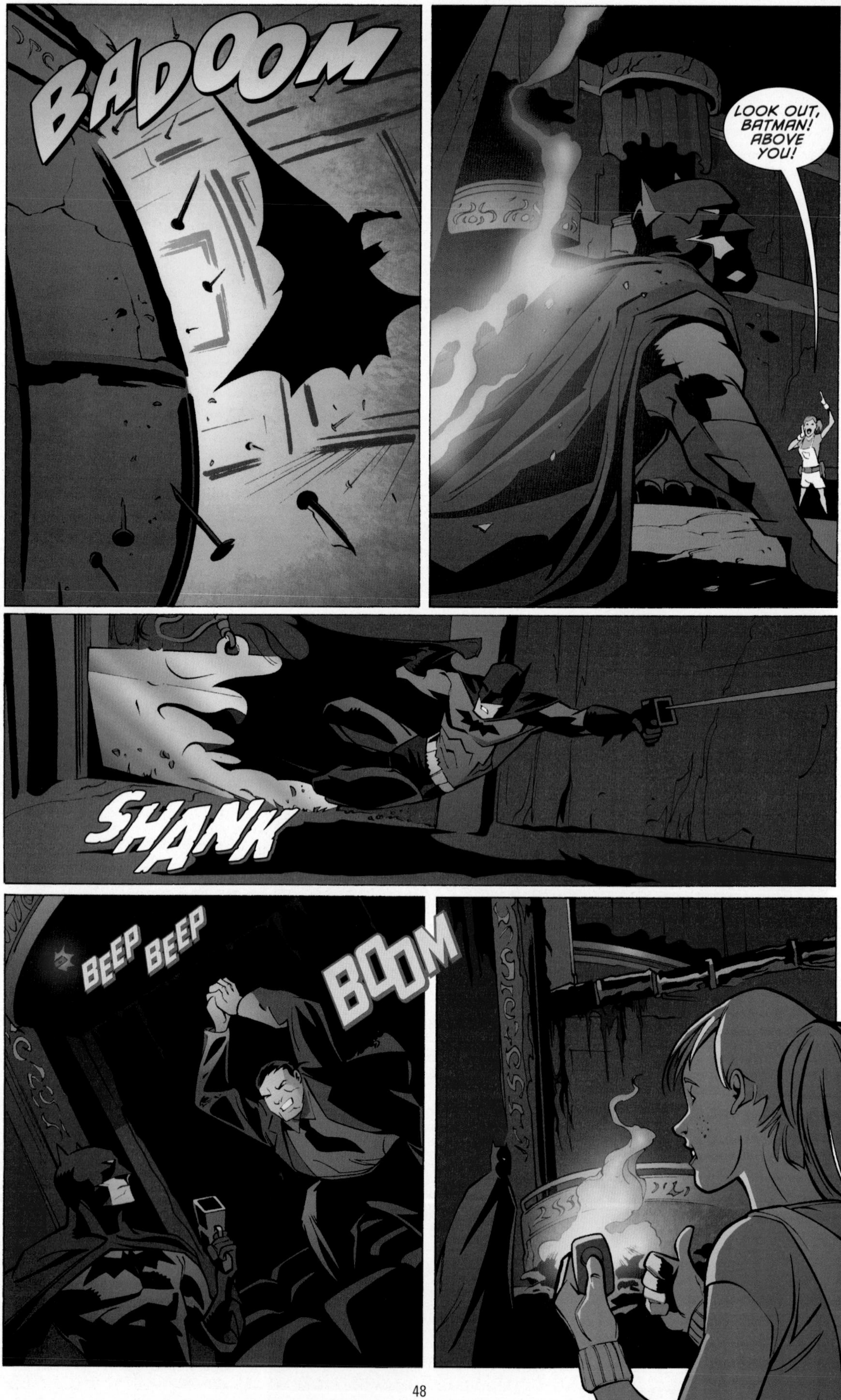
BADOOM
LOOK OUT, BATMAN! ABOVE YOU!
SHANK
BEEP BEEP
BOOM

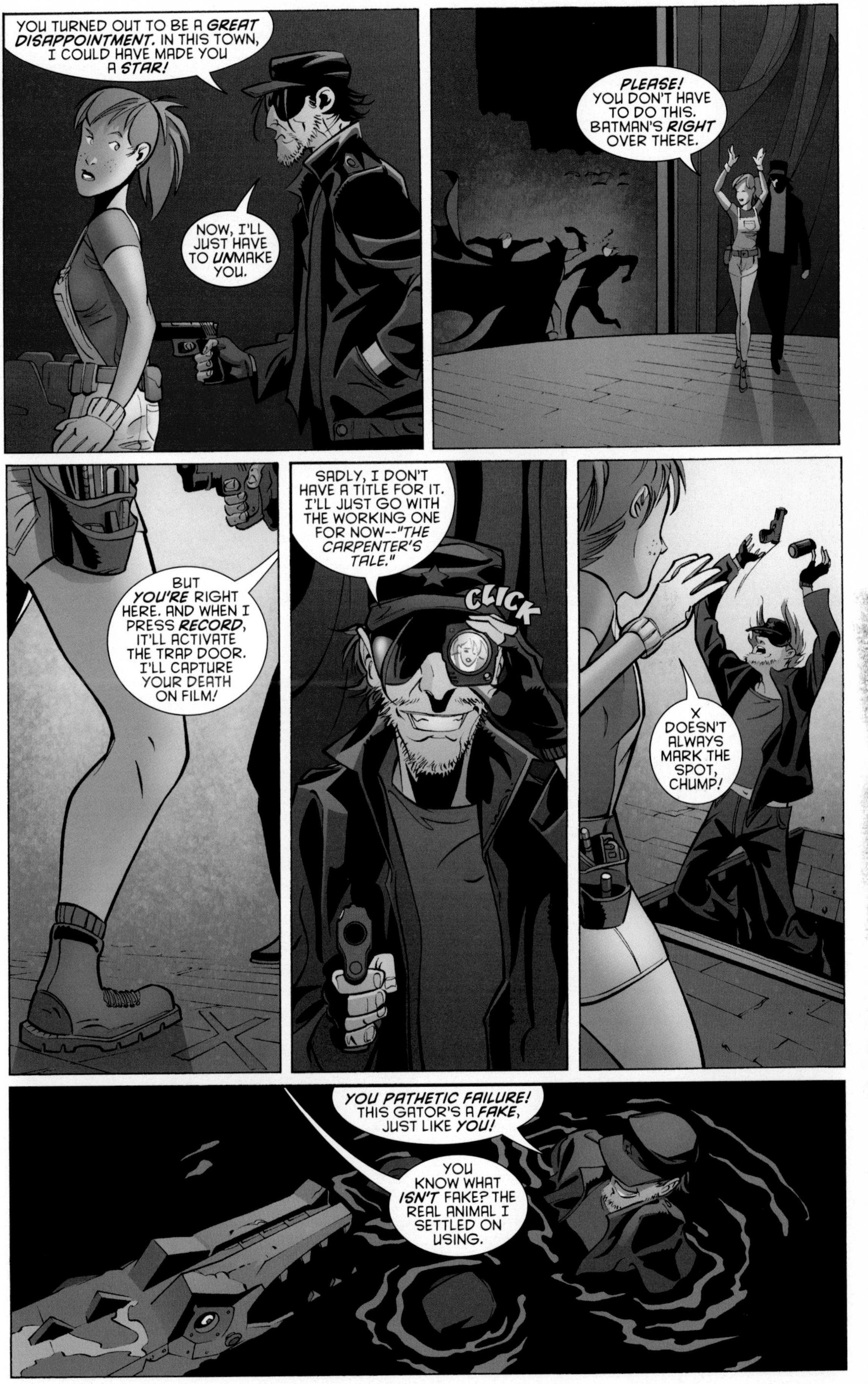
YOU TURNED OUT TO BE A GREAT DISAPPOINTMENT. IN THIS TOWN, I COULD HAVE MADE YOU A STAR!
NOW, I'LL JUST HAVE TO UNMAKE YOU.
PLEASE! YOU DON'T HAVE TO DO THIS. BATMAN'S RIGHT OVER THERE.
BUT YOU'RE RIGHT HERE. AND WHEN I PRESS RECORD, IT'LL ACTIVATE THE TRAP DOOR. I'LL CAPTURE YOUR DEATH ON FILM!
SADLY, I DON'T HAVE A TITLE FOR IT. I'LL JUST GO WITH THE WORKING ONE FOR NOW--"THE CARPENTER'S TALE."
CLICK
X DOESN'T ALWAYS MARK THE SPOT, CHUMP!
YOU PATHETIC FAILURE! THIS GATOR'S A FAKE, JUST LIKE YOU!
YOU KNOW WHAT ISN'T FAKE? THE REAL ANIMAL I SETTLED ON USING.

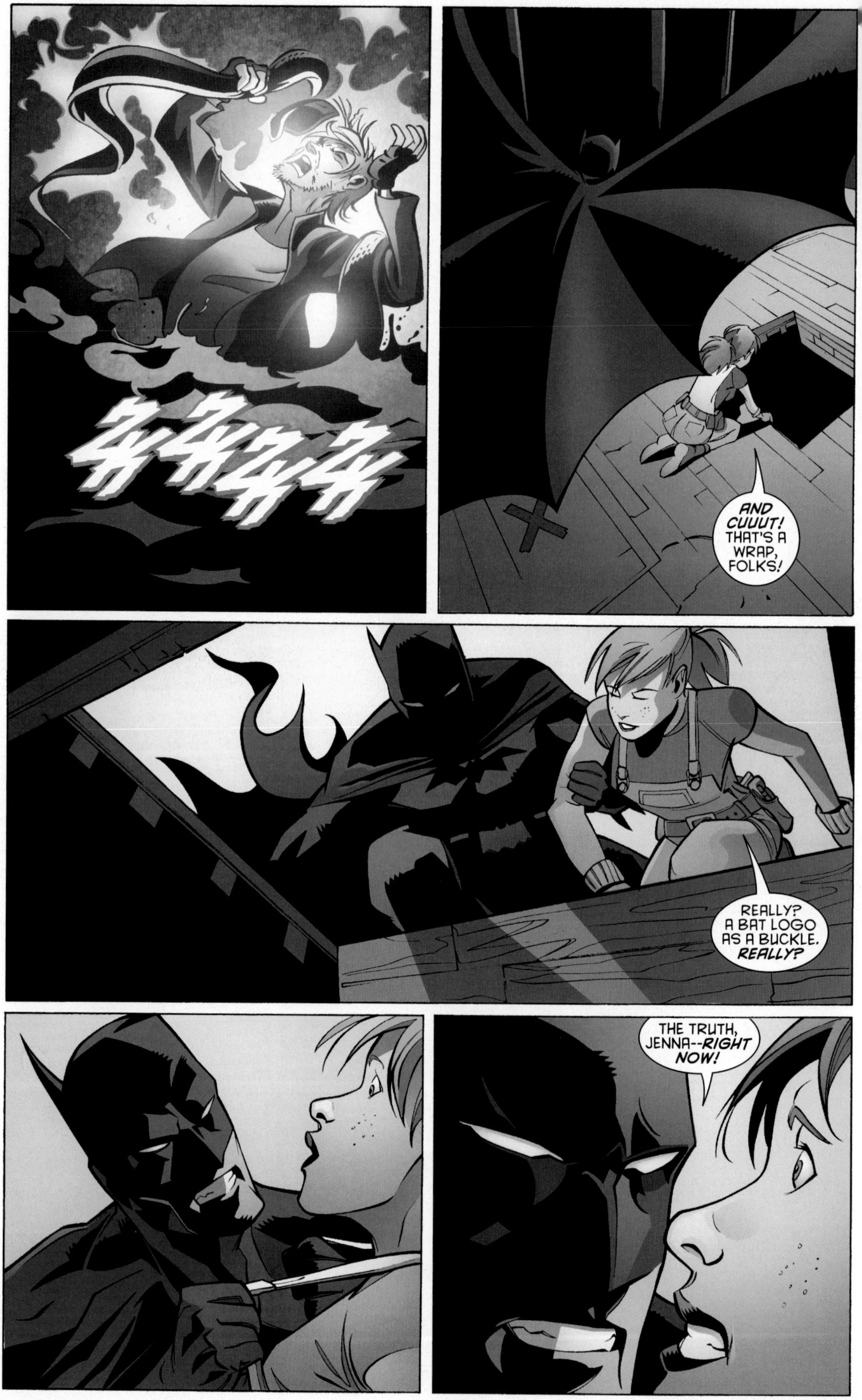
AND CUUUT! THAT'S A WRAP, FOLKS!
REALLY? A BAT LOGO AS A BUCKLE. REALLY?
THE TRUTH, JENNA--RIGHT NOW!

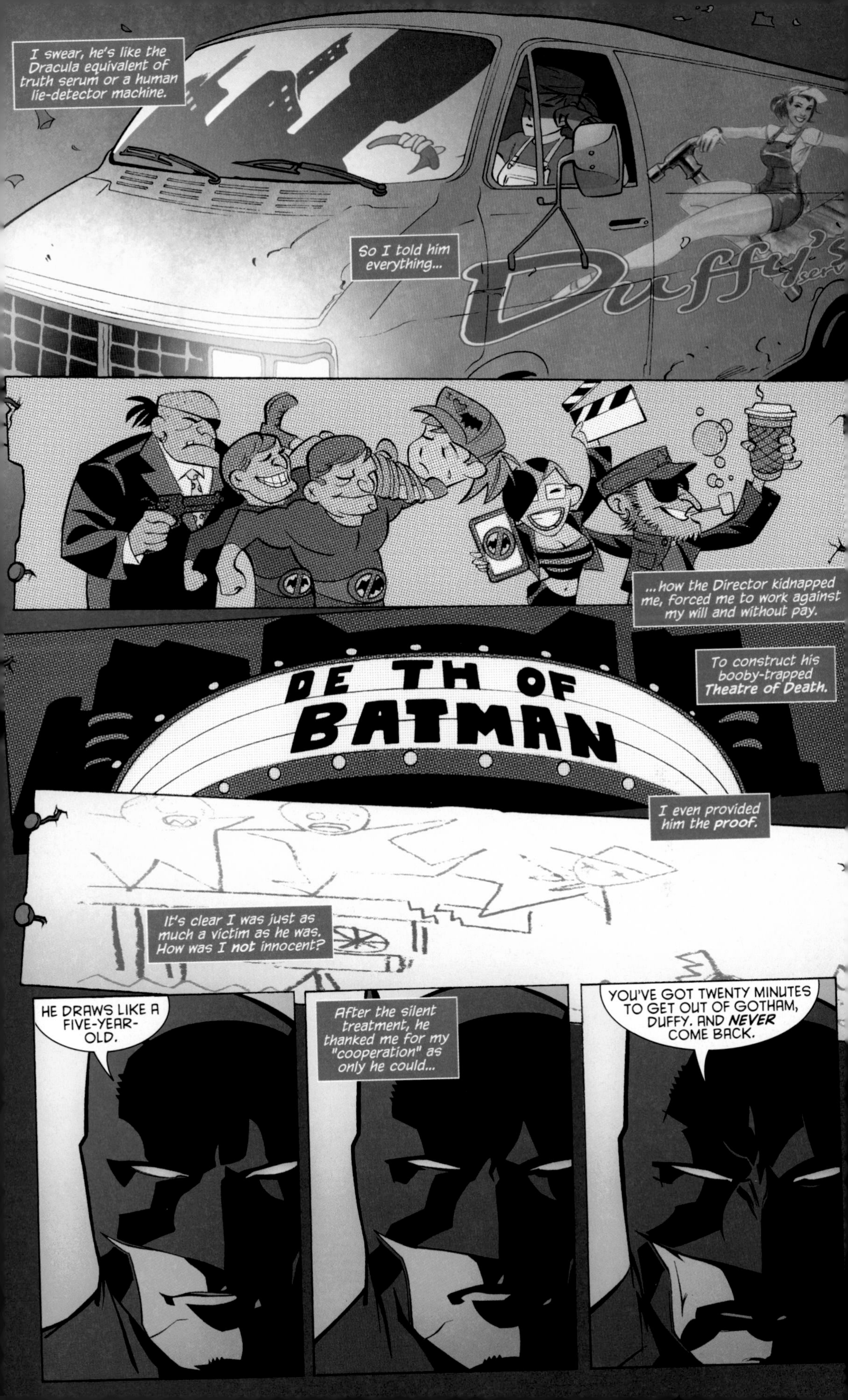
I swear, he's like the Dracula equivalent of truth serum or a human lie-detector machine.
So I told him everything...
Duffy's
...how the Director kidnapped me, forced me to work against my will and without pay.
To construct his booby-trapped Theatre of Death.
DE TH OF BATMAN
I even provided him the proof.
It's clear I was just as much a victim as he was. How was I not innocent?
HE DRAWS LIKE A FIVE-YEAR-OLD.
After the silent treatment, he thanked me for my "cooperation" as only he could...
YOU'VE GOT TWENTY MINUTES TO GET OUT OF GOTHAM, DUFFY. AND NEVER COME BACK.

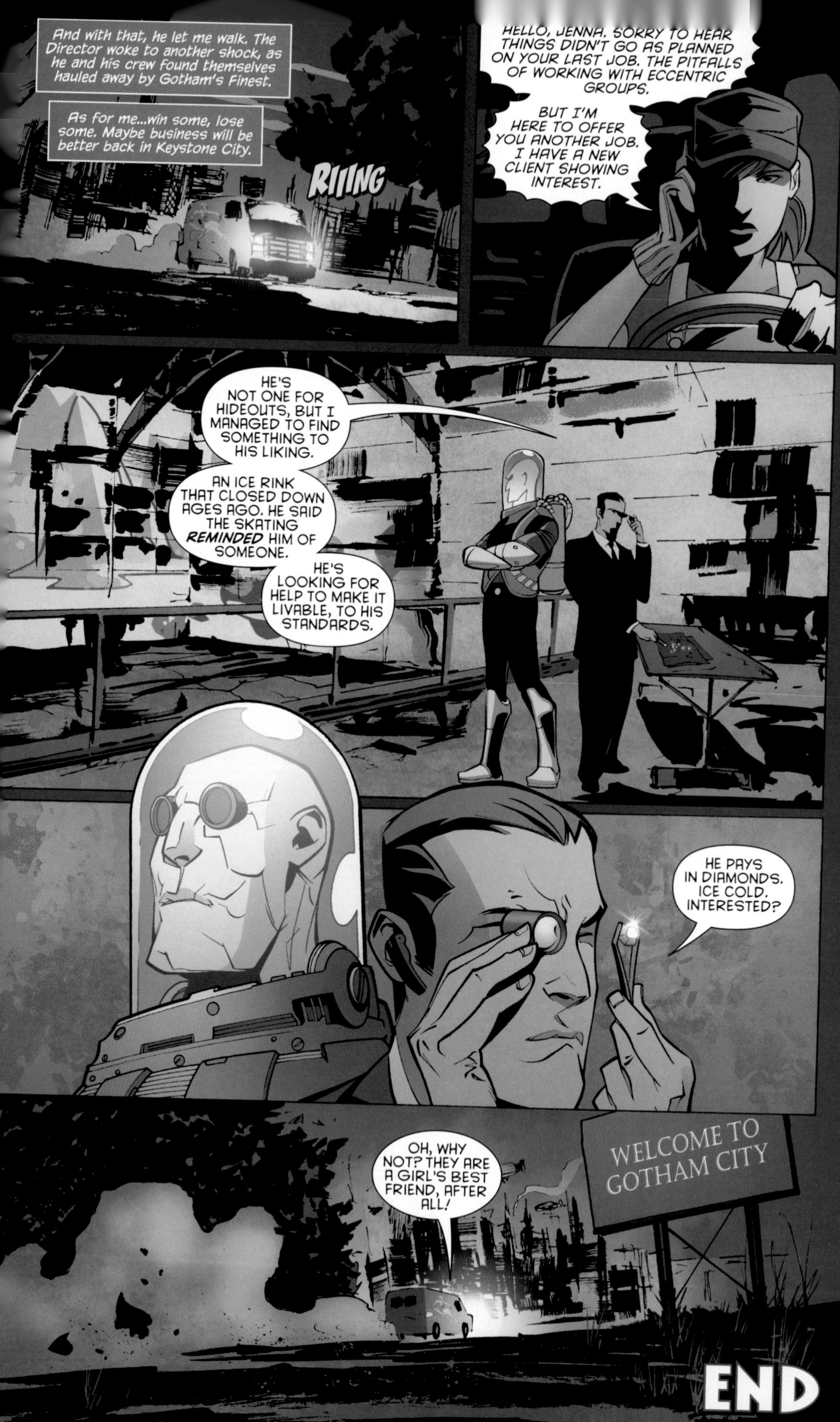
And with that, he let me walk. The Director woke to another shock, as he and his crew found themselves hauled away by Gotham's Finest.
As for me...win some, lose some. Maybe business will be better back in Keystone City.
RIIING
HELLO, JENNA. SORRY TO HEAR THINGS DIDN'T GO AS PLANNED ON YOUR LAST JOB. THE PITFALLS OF WORKING WITH ECCENTRIC GROUPS.
BUT I'M HERE TO OFFER YOU ANOTHER JOB. I HAVE A NEW CLIENT SHOWING INTEREST.
HE'S NOT ONE FOR HIDEOUTS, BUT I MANAGED TO FIND SOMETHING TO HIS LIKING.
AN ICE RINK THAT CLOSED DOWN AGES AGO. HE SAID THE SKATING REMINDED HIM OF SOMEONE.
HE'S LOOKING FOR HELP TO MAKE IT LIVABLE, TO HIS STANDARDS.
HE PAYS IN DIAMONDS. ICE COLD. INTERESTED?
OH, WHY NOT? THEY ARE A GIRL'S BEST FRIEND, AFTER ALL!
WELCOME TO GOTHAM CITY
END

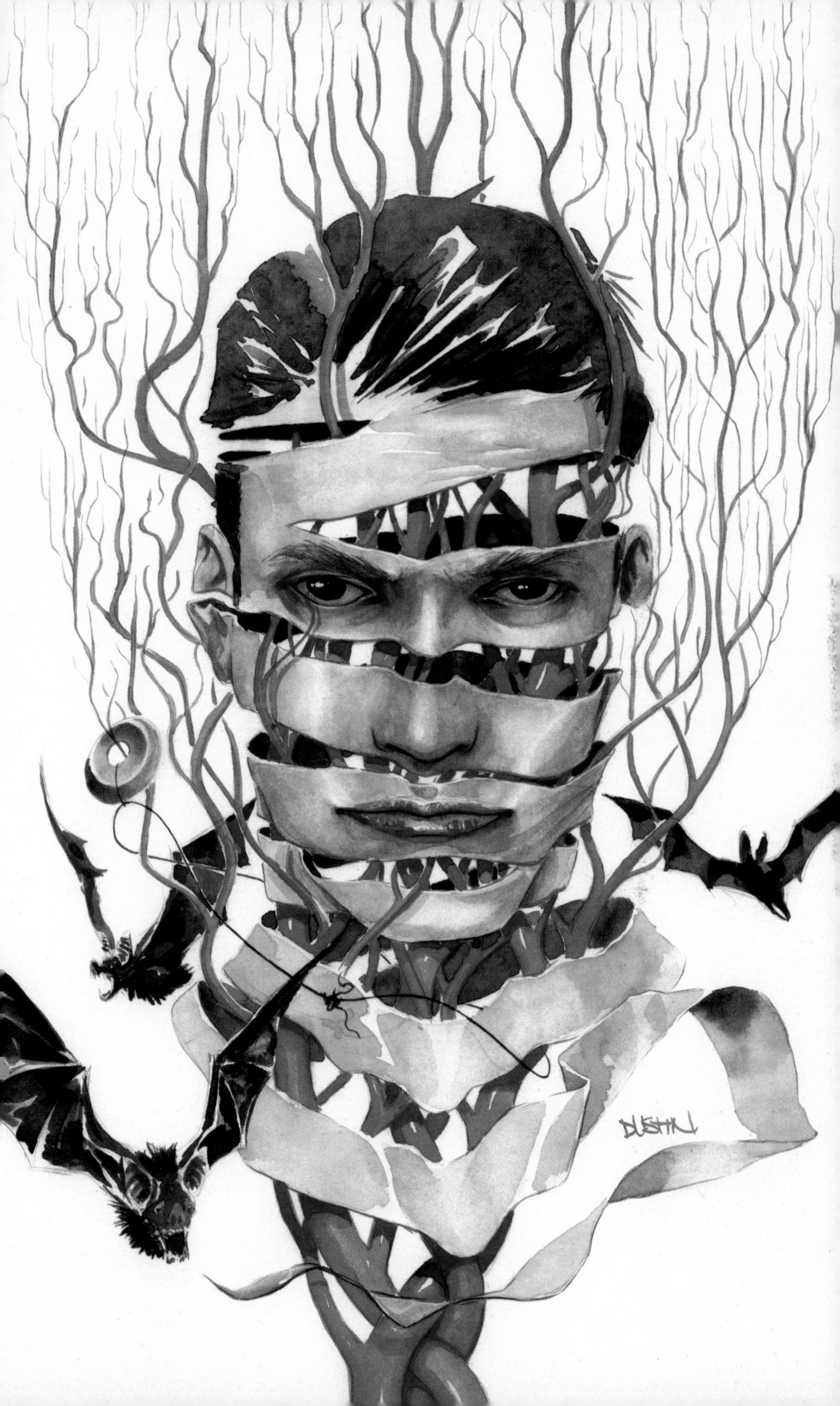
DUSTIN

"Gotham City... I hear crime's a new game now."

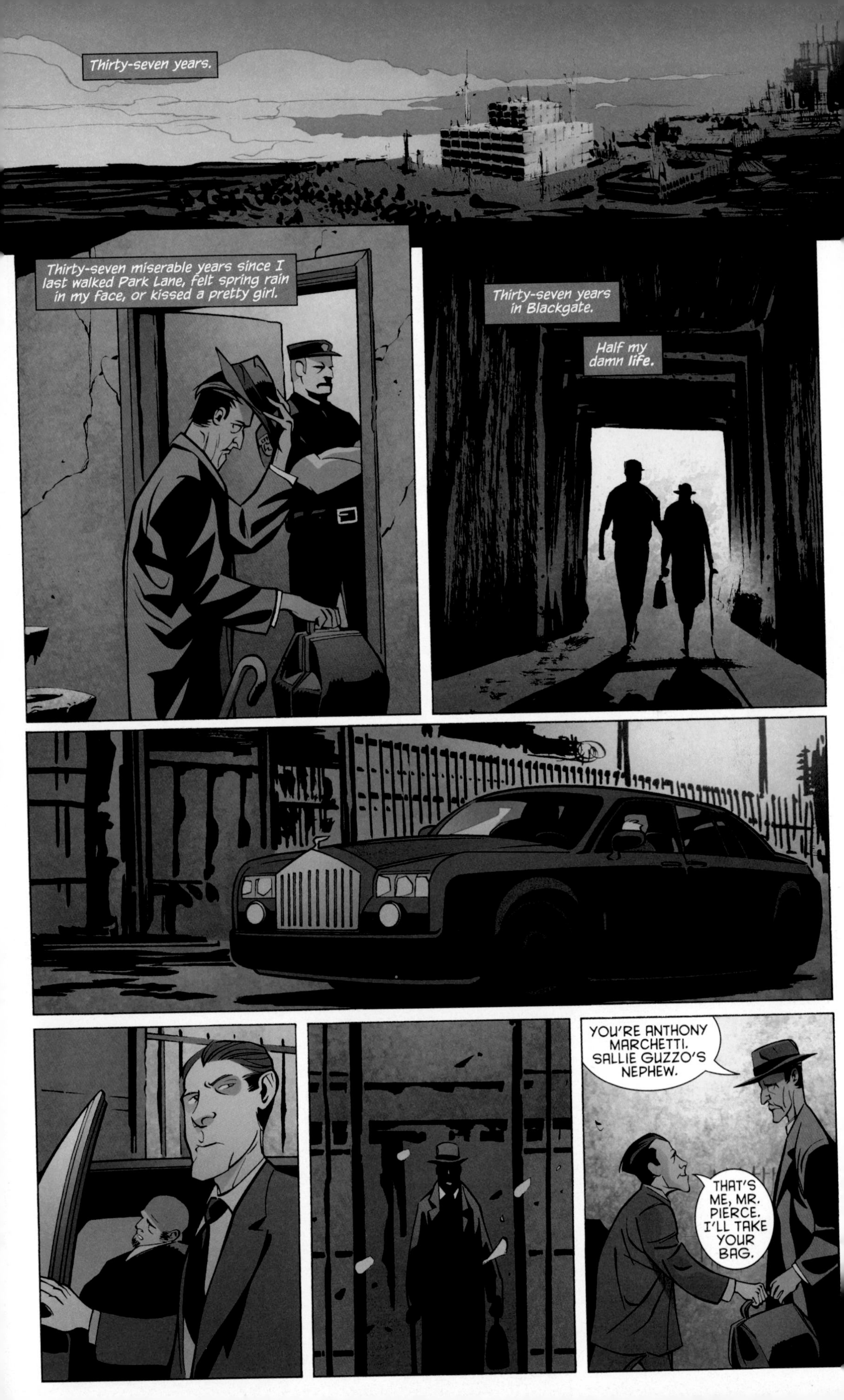
Thirty-seven years.
Thirty-seven miserable years since I last walked Park Lane, felt spring rain in my face, or kissed a pretty girl.
Thirty-seven years in Blackgate.
Half my damn life.
YOU'RE ANTHONY MARCHETTI. SALLIE GUZZO'S NEPHEW.
THAT'S ME, MR. PIERCE. I'LL TAKE YOUR BAG.

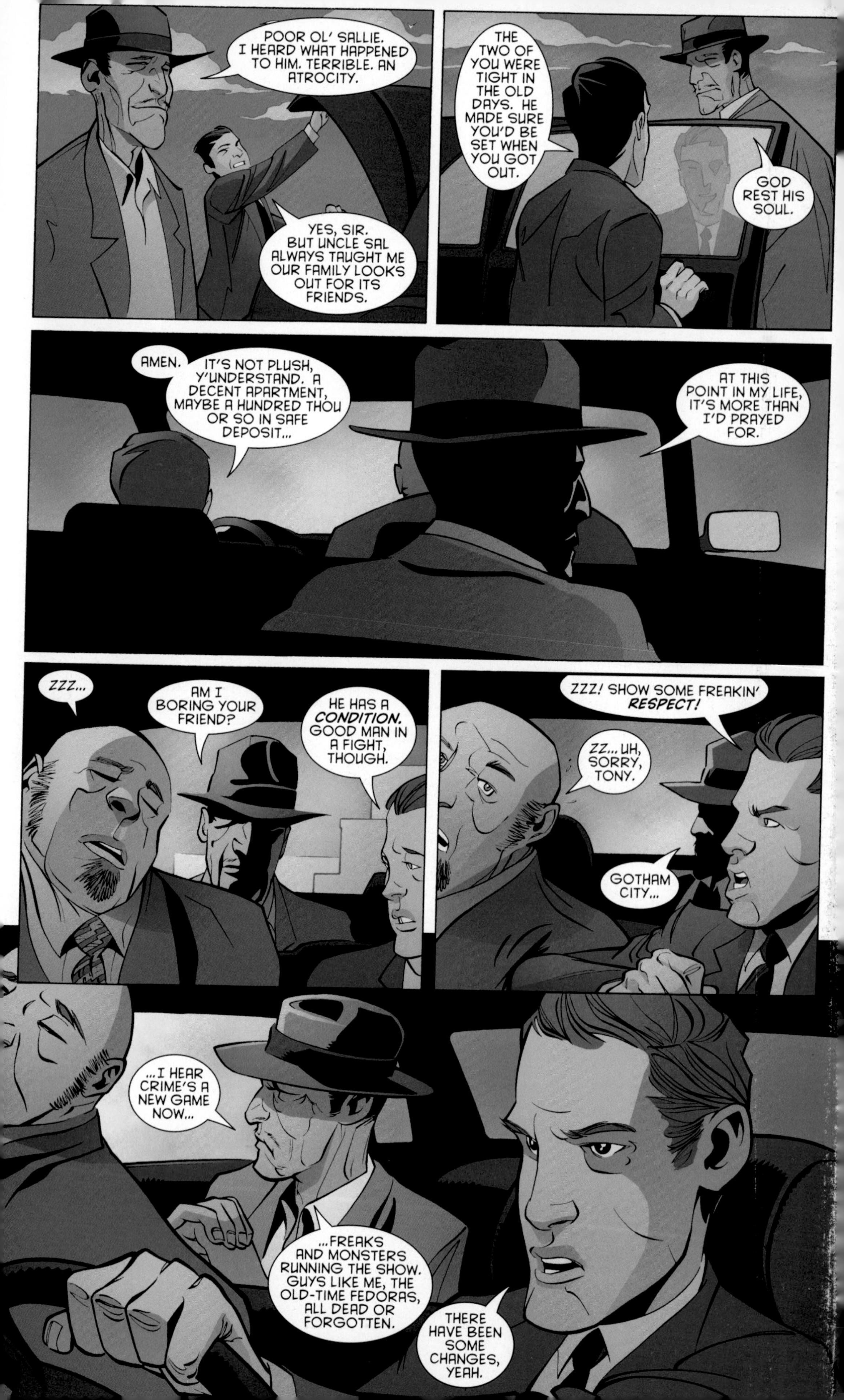
POOR OL' SALLIE. I HEARD WHAT HAPPENED TO HIM. TERRIBLE. AN ATROCITY.
YES, SIR. BUT UNCLE SAL ALWAYS TAUGHT ME OUR FAMILY LOOKS OUT FOR ITS FRIENDS.
THE TWO OF YOU WERE TIGHT IN THE OLD DAYS. HE MADE SURE YOU'D BE SET WHEN YOU GOT OUT.
GOD REST HIS SOUL.
AMEN.
IT'S NOT PLUSH, Y'UNDERSTAND. A DECENT APARTMENT, MAYBE A HUNDRED THOU OR SO IN SAFE DEPOSIT...
AT THIS POINT IN MY LIFE, IT'S MORE THAN I'D PRAYED FOR.
ZZZ...
AM I BORING YOUR FRIEND?
HE HAS A *CONDITION.* GOOD MAN IN A FIGHT, THOUGH.
ZZZ! SHOW SOME FREAKIN' *RESPECT!*
ZZ... UH, SORRY, TONY.
GOTHAM CITY...
...I HEAR CRIME'S A NEW GAME NOW...
...FREAKS AND MONSTERS RUNNING THE SHOW. GUYS LIKE ME, THE OLD-TIME FEDORAS, ALL DEAD OR FORGOTTEN.
THERE HAVE BEEN SOME CHANGES, YEAH.

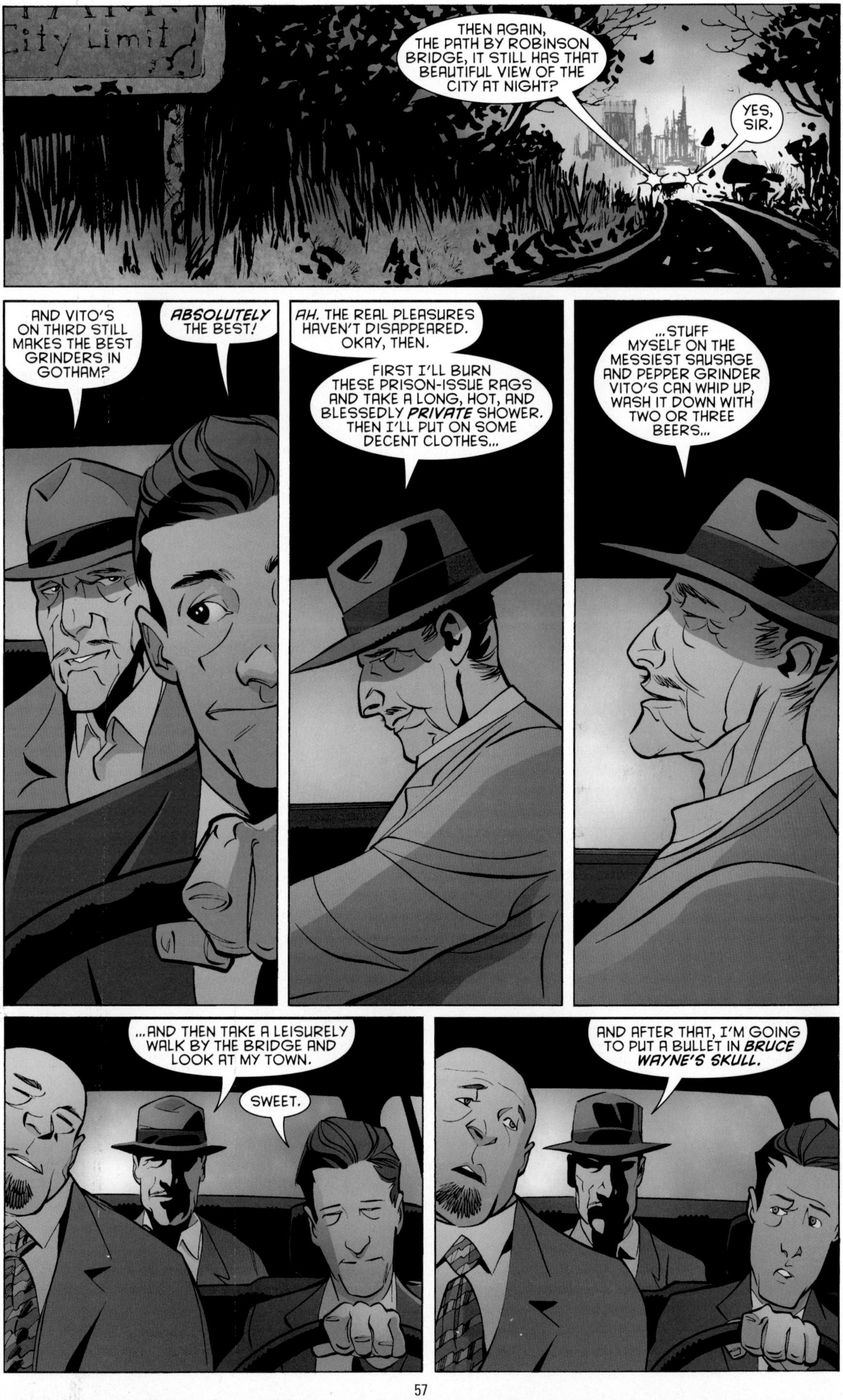
City Limit
THEN AGAIN, THE PATH BY ROBINSON BRIDGE, IT STILL HAS THAT BEAUTIFUL VIEW OF THE CITY AT NIGHT?
YES, SIR.
AND VITO'S ON THIRD STILL MAKES THE BEST GRINDERS IN GOTHAM?
ABSOLUTELY THE BEST!
AH. THE REAL PLEASURES HAVEN'T DISAPPEARED. OKAY, THEN.
FIRST I'LL BURN THESE PRISON-ISSUE RAGS AND TAKE A LONG, HOT, AND BLESSEDLY PRIVATE SHOWER. THEN I'LL PUT ON SOME DECENT CLOTHES...
...STUFF MYSELF ON THE MESSIEST SAUSAGE AND PEPPER GRINDER VITO'S CAN WHIP UP, WASH IT DOWN WITH TWO OR THREE BEERS...
...AND THEN TAKE A LEISURELY WALK BY THE BRIDGE AND LOOK AT MY TOWN.
SWEET.
AND AFTER THAT, I'M GOING TO PUT A BULLET IN BRUCE WAYNE'S SKULL.

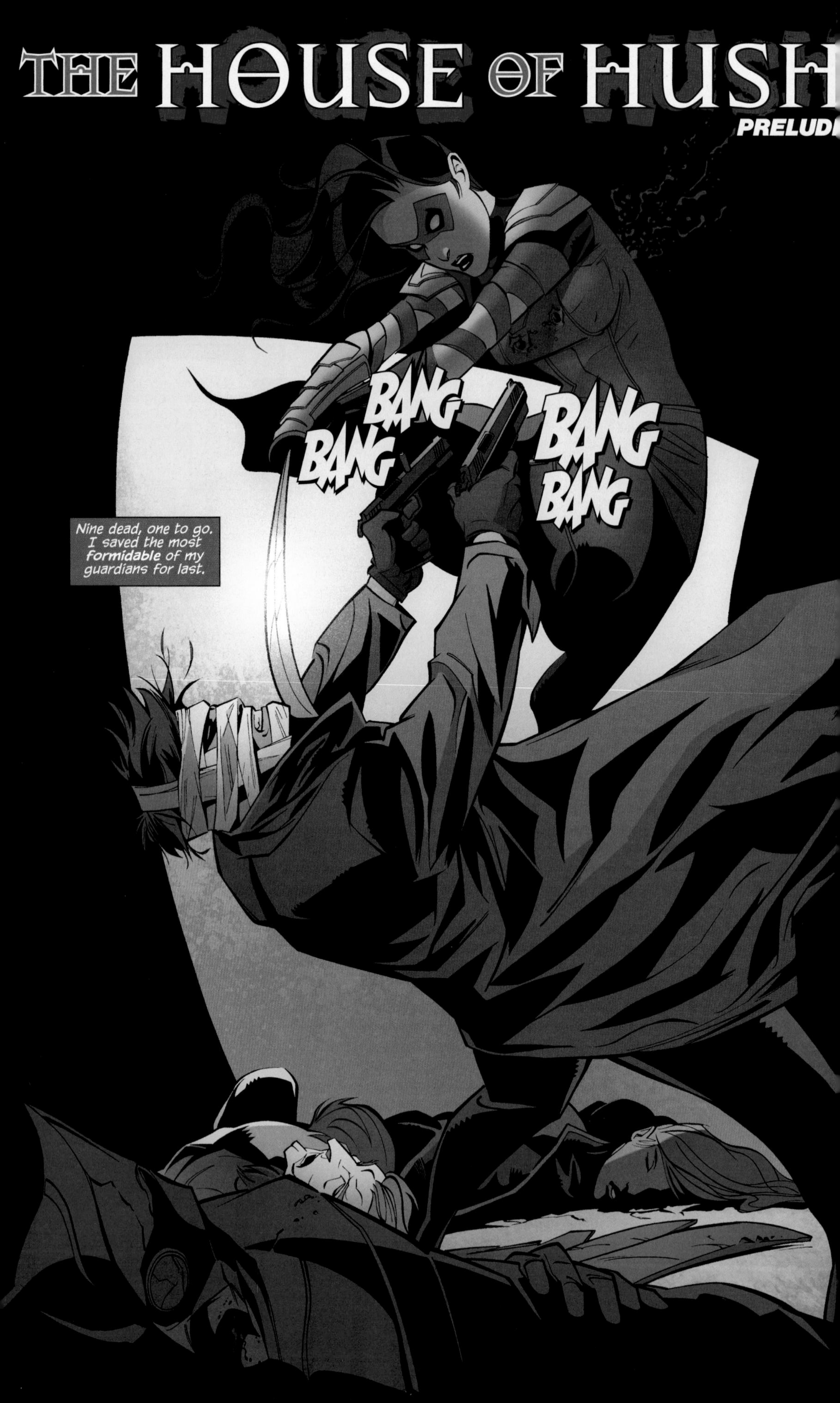
THE HOUSE OF HUSH
PRELUD
BANG
BANG
BANG
BANG
Nine dead, one to go. I saved the most formidable of my guardians for last.

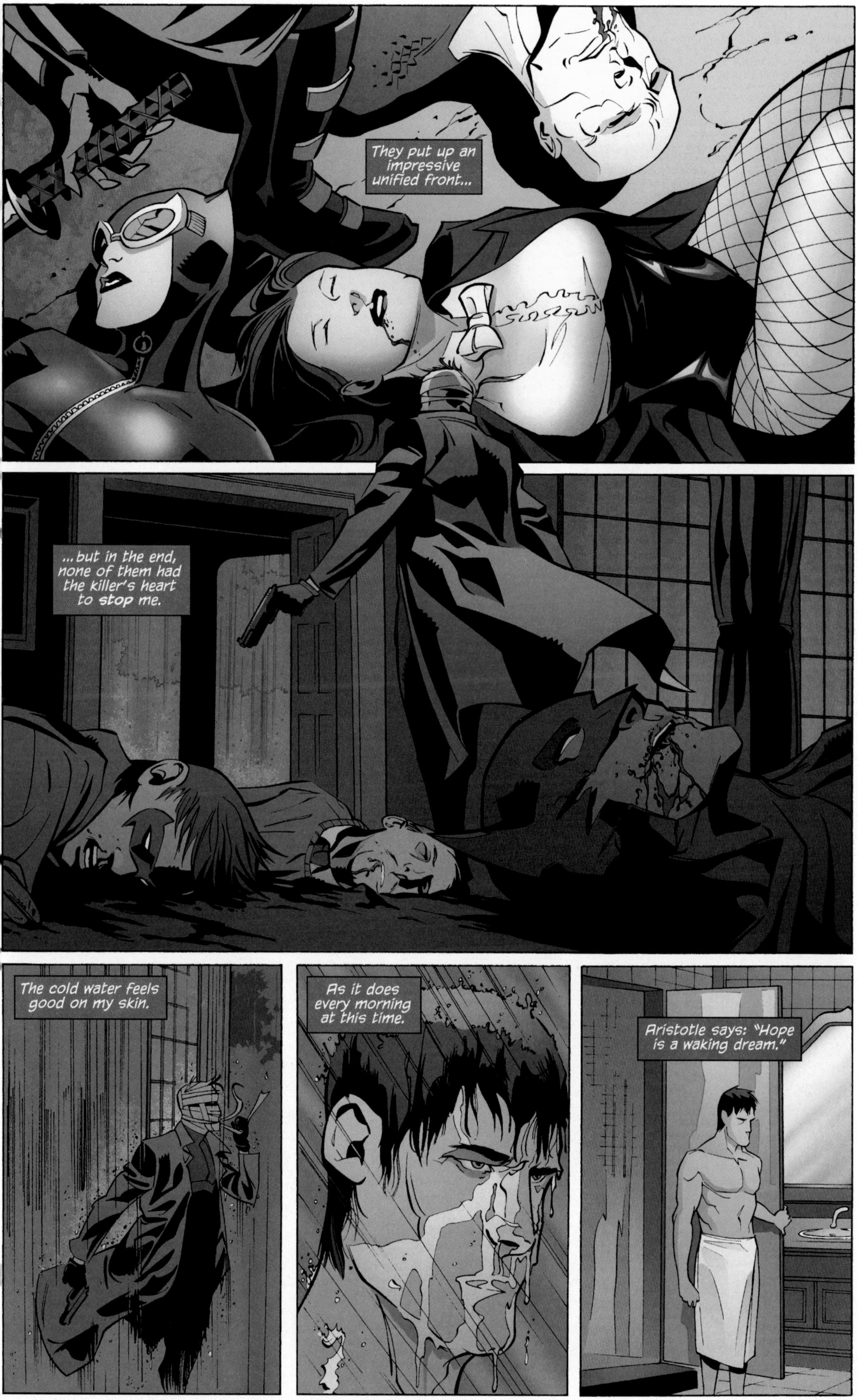
They put up an impressive unified front...
...but in the end, none of them had the killer's heart to stop me.
The cold water feels good on my skin.
As it does every morning at this time.
Aristotle says: "Hope is a waking dream."

I know that to be true, as there has not been a moment, waking or asleep, I have not dreamed of executing my captors.

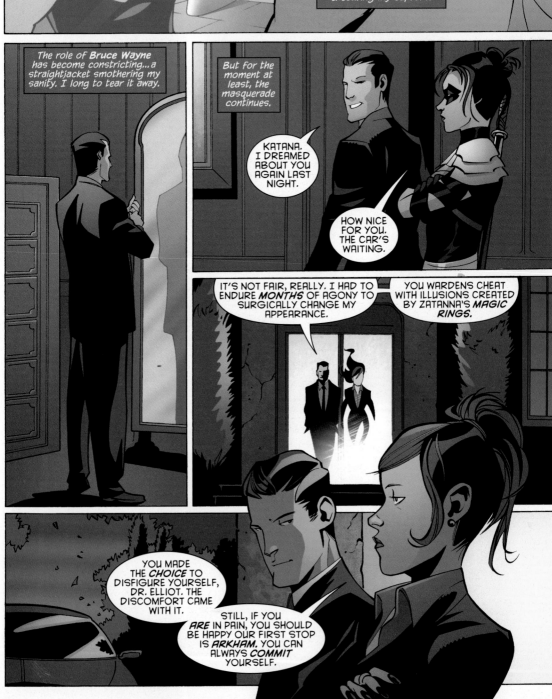

The role of *Bruce Wayne* has become constricting...a straightjacket smothering my sanity. I long to tear it away.

But for the moment at least, the masquerade continues.

KATANA. I DREAMED ABOUT YOU AGAIN LAST NIGHT.

HOW NICE FOR YOU. THE CAR'S WAITING.

IT'S NOT FAIR, REALLY. I HAD TO ENDURE *MONTHS* OF AGONY TO SURGICALLY CHANGE MY APPEARANCE.

YOU WARDENS CHEAT WITH ILLUSIONS CREATED BY ZATANNA'S *MAGIC RINGS.*

YOU MADE THE *CHOICE* TO DISFIGURE YOURSELF, DR. ELLIOT. THE DISCOMFORT CAME WITH IT.

STILL, IF YOU *ARE* IN PAIN, YOU SHOULD BE HAPPY OUR FIRST STOP IS *ARKHAM.* YOU CAN ALWAYS *COMMIT* YOURSELF.

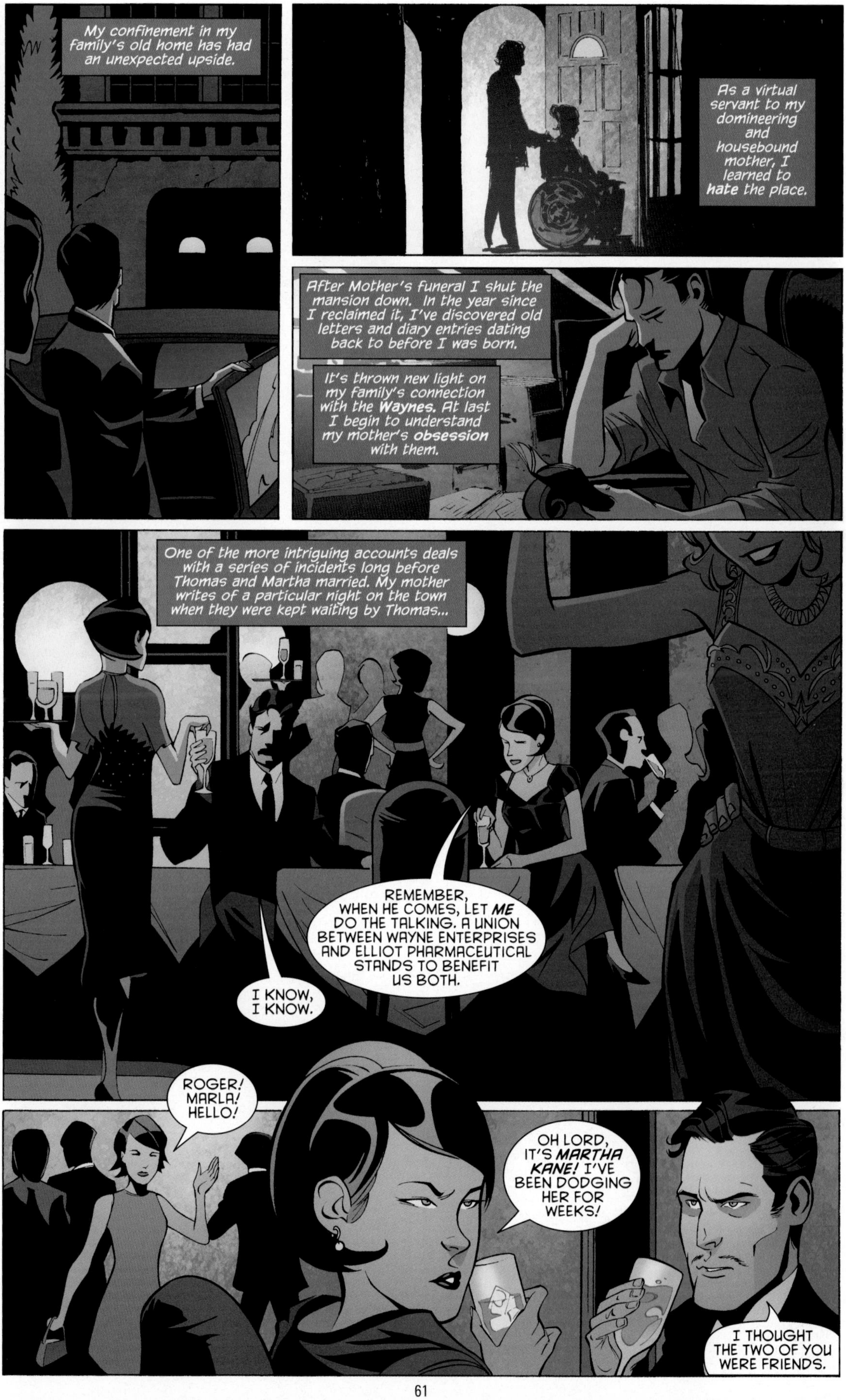

My confinement in my family's old home has had an unexpected upside.
As a virtual servant to my domineering and housebound mother, I learned to hate the place.
After Mother's funeral I shut the mansion down. In the year since I reclaimed it, I've discovered old letters and diary entries dating back to before I was born.
It's thrown new light on my family's connection with the Waynes. At last I begin to understand my mother's obsession with them.
One of the more intriguing accounts deals with a series of incidents long before Thomas and Martha married. My mother writes of a particular night on the town when they were kept waiting by Thomas...
REMEMBER, WHEN HE COMES, LET ME DO THE TALKING. A UNION BETWEEN WAYNE ENTERPRISES AND ELLIOT PHARMACEUTICAL STANDS TO BENEFIT US BOTH.
I KNOW, I KNOW.
ROGER! MARLA! HELLO!
OH LORD, IT'S MARTHA KANE! I'VE BEEN DODGING HER FOR WEEKS!
I THOUGHT THE TWO OF YOU WERE FRIENDS.

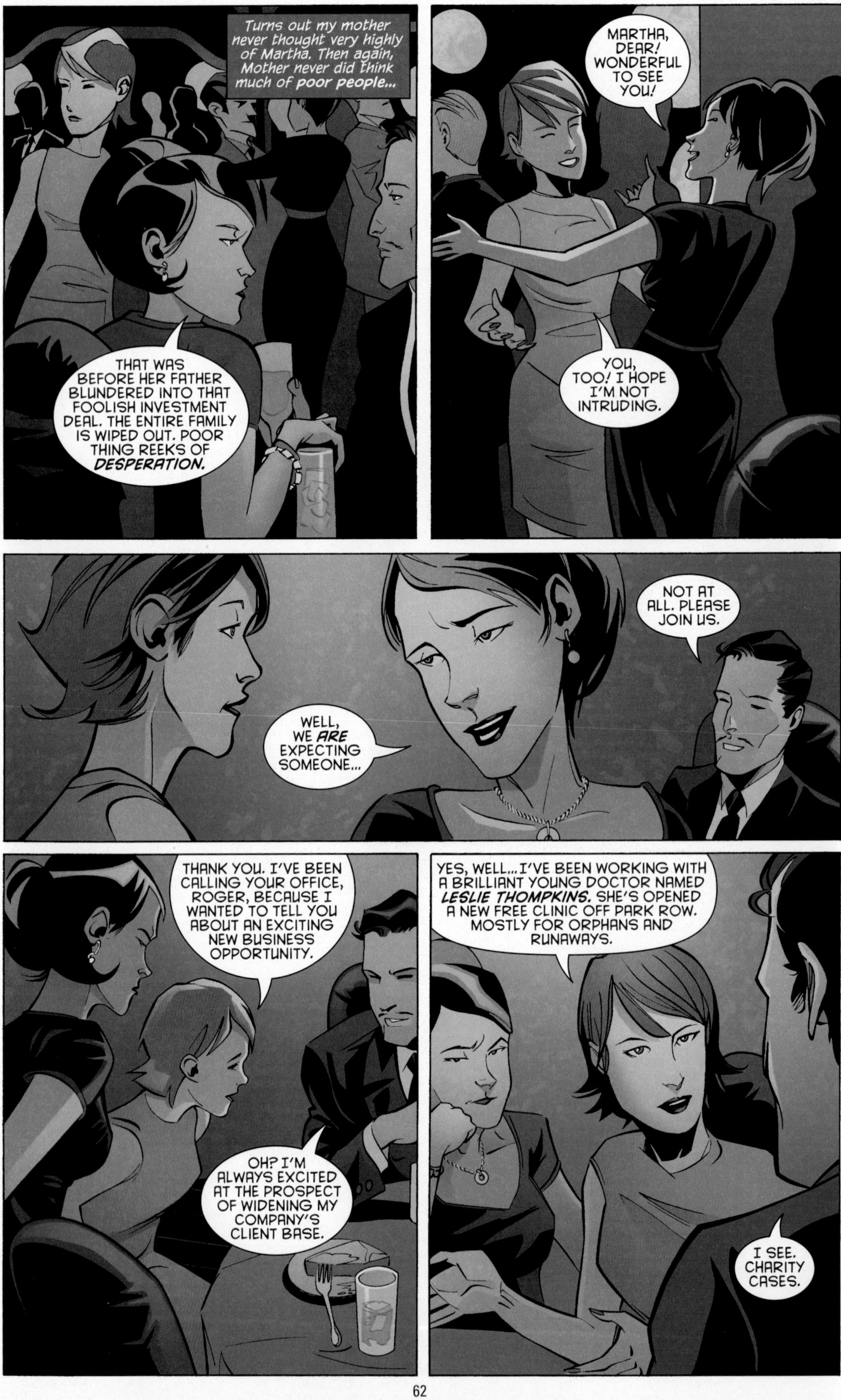

Turns out my mother never thought very highly of Martha. Then again, Mother never did think much of poor people...
THAT WAS BEFORE HER FATHER BLUNDERED INTO THAT FOOLISH INVESTMENT DEAL. THE ENTIRE FAMILY IS WIPED OUT. POOR THING REEKS OF DESPERATION.
MARTHA, DEAR! WONDERFUL TO SEE YOU!
YOU, TOO! I HOPE I'M NOT INTRUDING.
NOT AT ALL. PLEASE JOIN US.
WELL, WE ARE EXPECTING SOMEONE...
THANK YOU. I'VE BEEN CALLING YOUR OFFICE, ROGER, BECAUSE I WANTED TO TELL YOU ABOUT AN EXCITING NEW BUSINESS OPPORTUNITY.
OH? I'M ALWAYS EXCITED AT THE PROSPECT OF WIDENING MY COMPANY'S CLIENT BASE.
YES, WELL...I'VE BEEN WORKING WITH A BRILLIANT YOUNG DOCTOR NAMED LESLIE THOMPKINS. SHE'S OPENED A NEW FREE CLINIC OFF PARK ROW. MOSTLY FOR ORPHANS AND RUNAWAYS.
I SEE. CHARITY CASES.

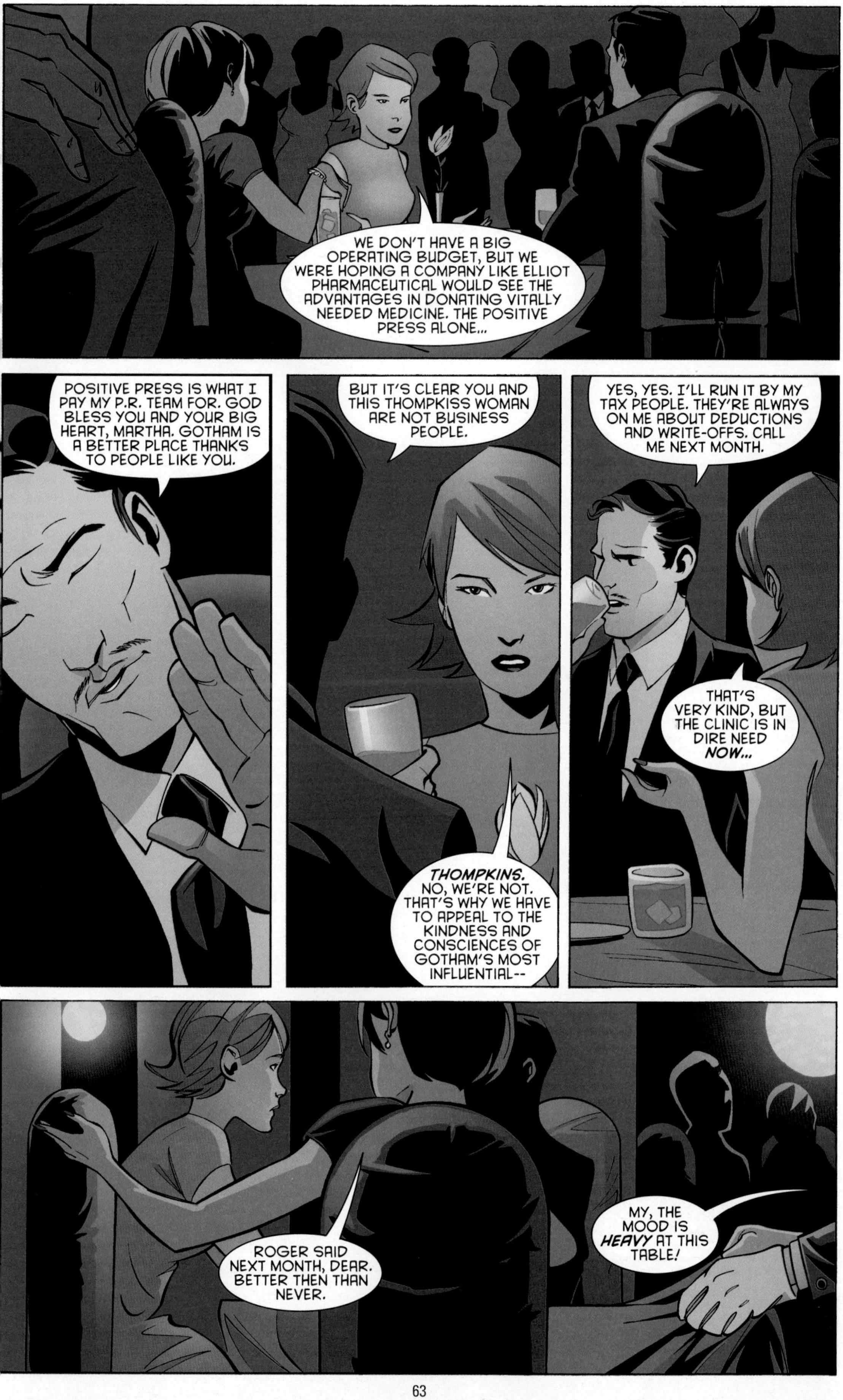
WE DON'T HAVE A BIG OPERATING BUDGET, BUT WE WERE HOPING A COMPANY LIKE ELLIOT PHARMACEUTICAL WOULD SEE THE ADVANTAGES IN DONATING VITALLY NEEDED MEDICINE. THE POSITIVE PRESS ALONE...
POSITIVE PRESS IS WHAT I PAY MY P.R. TEAM FOR. GOD BLESS YOU AND YOUR BIG HEART, MARTHA. GOTHAM IS A BETTER PLACE THANKS TO PEOPLE LIKE YOU.
BUT IT'S CLEAR YOU AND THIS THOMPKISS WOMAN ARE NOT BUSINESS PEOPLE.
THOMPKINS. NO, WE'RE NOT. THAT'S WHY WE HAVE TO APPEAL TO THE KINDNESS AND CONSCIENCES OF GOTHAM'S MOST INFLUENTIAL--
YES, YES. I'LL RUN IT BY MY TAX PEOPLE. THEY'RE ALWAYS ON ME ABOUT DEDUCTIONS AND WRITE-OFFS. CALL ME NEXT MONTH.
THAT'S VERY KIND, BUT THE CLINIC IS IN DIRE NEED *NOW...*
ROGER SAID NEXT MONTH, DEAR. BETTER THEN THAN NEVER.
MY, THE MOOD IS *HEAVY* AT THIS TABLE!

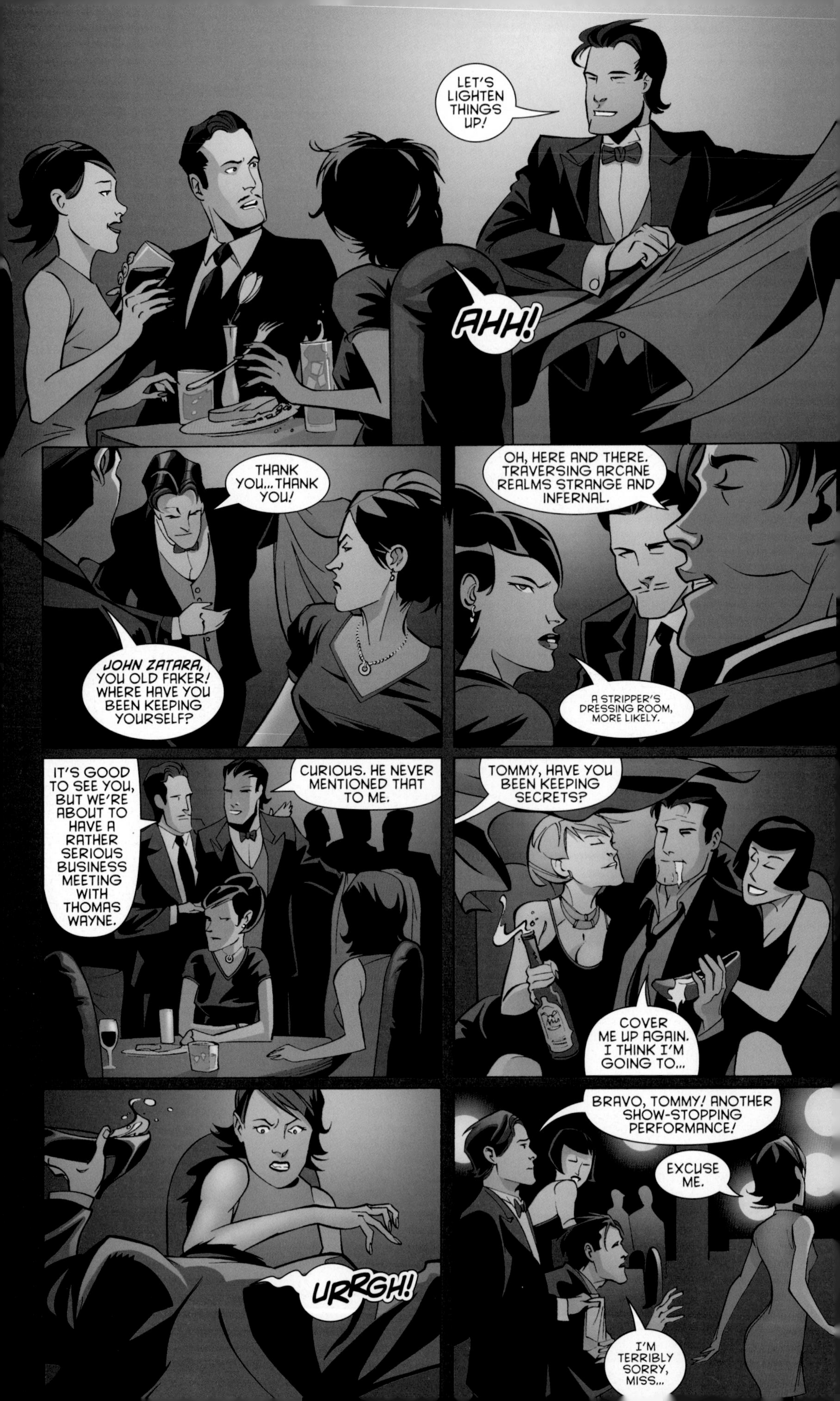
LET'S LIGHTEN THINGS UP!
AHH!
THANK YOU...THANK YOU!
JOHN ZATARA, YOU OLD FAKER! WHERE HAVE YOU BEEN KEEPING YOURSELF?
OH, HERE AND THERE. TRAVERSING ARCANE REALMS STRANGE AND INFERNAL.
A STRIPPER'S DRESSING ROOM, MORE LIKELY.
IT'S GOOD TO SEE YOU, BUT WE'RE ABOUT TO HAVE A RATHER SERIOUS BUSINESS MEETING WITH THOMAS WAYNE.
CURIOUS. HE NEVER MENTIONED THAT TO ME.
TOMMY, HAVE YOU BEEN KEEPING SECRETS?
COVER ME UP AGAIN. I THINK I'M GOING TO...
URRGH!
BRAVO, TOMMY! ANOTHER SHOW-STOPPING PERFORMANCE!
EXCUSE ME.
I'M TERRIBLY SORRY, MISS...

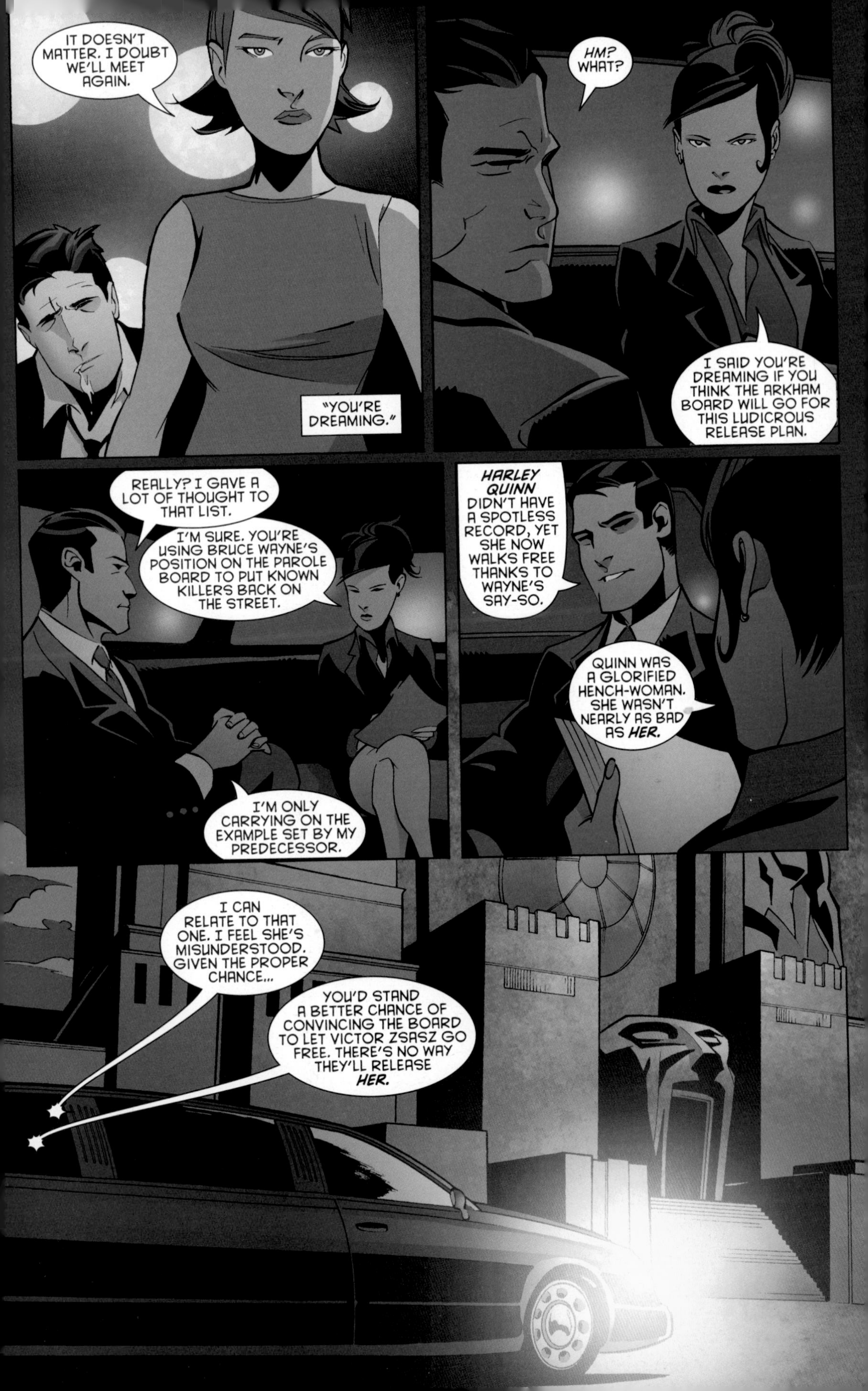

IT DOESN'T MATTER. I DOUBT WE'LL MEET AGAIN.
"YOU'RE DREAMING."
HM? WHAT?
I SAID YOU'RE DREAMING IF YOU THINK THE ARKHAM BOARD WILL GO FOR THIS LUDICROUS RELEASE PLAN.
REALLY? I GAVE A LOT OF THOUGHT TO THAT LIST.
I'M SURE. YOU'RE USING BRUCE WAYNE'S POSITION ON THE PAROLE BOARD TO PUT KNOWN KILLERS BACK ON THE STREET.
I'M ONLY CARRYING ON THE EXAMPLE SET BY MY PREDECESSOR.
HARLEY QUINN DIDN'T HAVE A SPOTLESS RECORD, YET SHE NOW WALKS FREE THANKS TO WAYNE'S SAY-SO.
QUINN WAS A GLORIFIED HENCH-WOMAN. SHE WASN'T NEARLY AS BAD AS HER.
I CAN RELATE TO THAT ONE. I FEEL SHE'S MISUNDERSTOOD. GIVEN THE PROPER CHANCE...
YOU'D STAND A BETTER CHANCE OF CONVINCING THE BOARD TO LET VICTOR ZSASZ GO FREE. THERE'S NO WAY THEY'LL RELEASE HER.

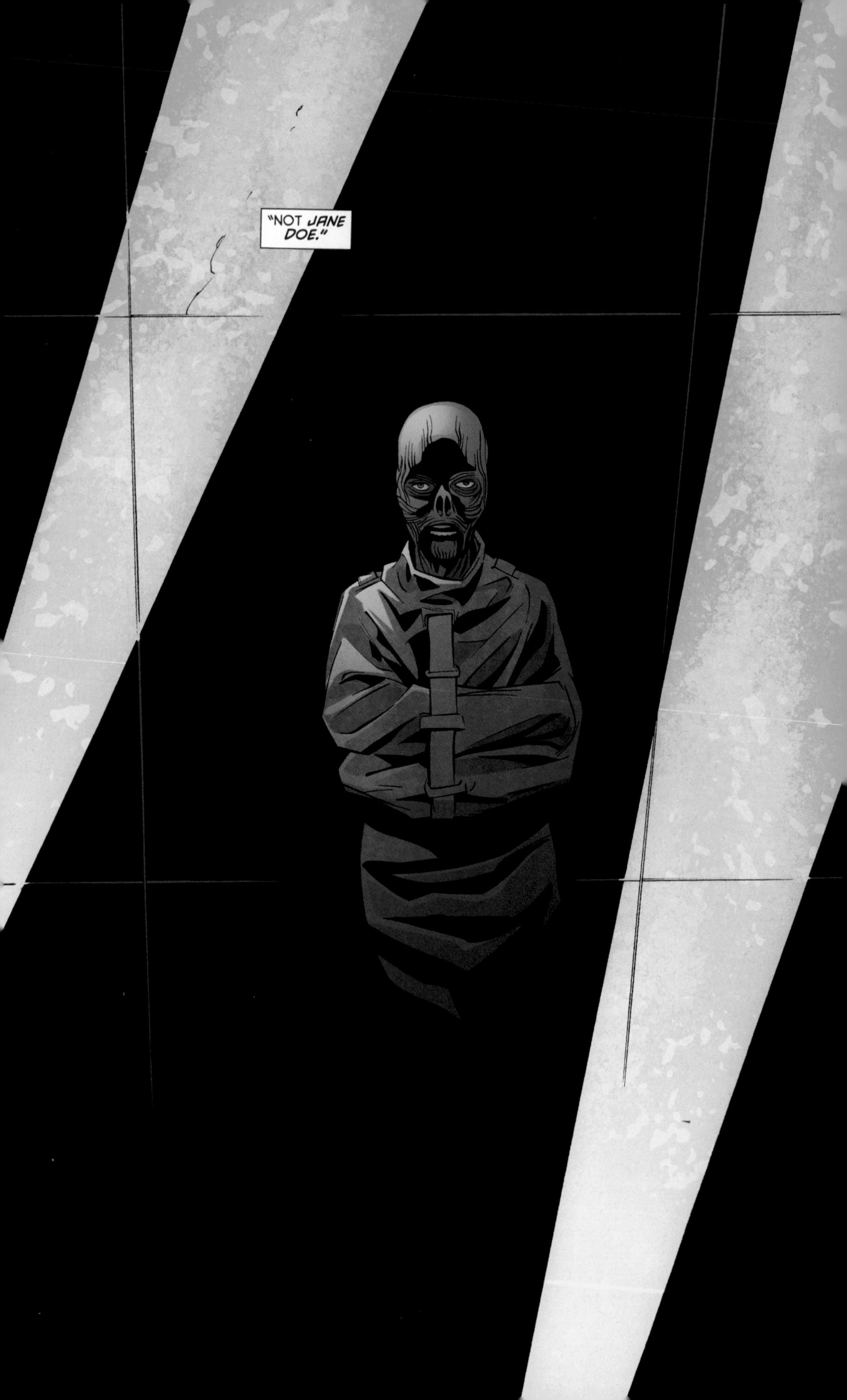
"NOT JANE DOE."

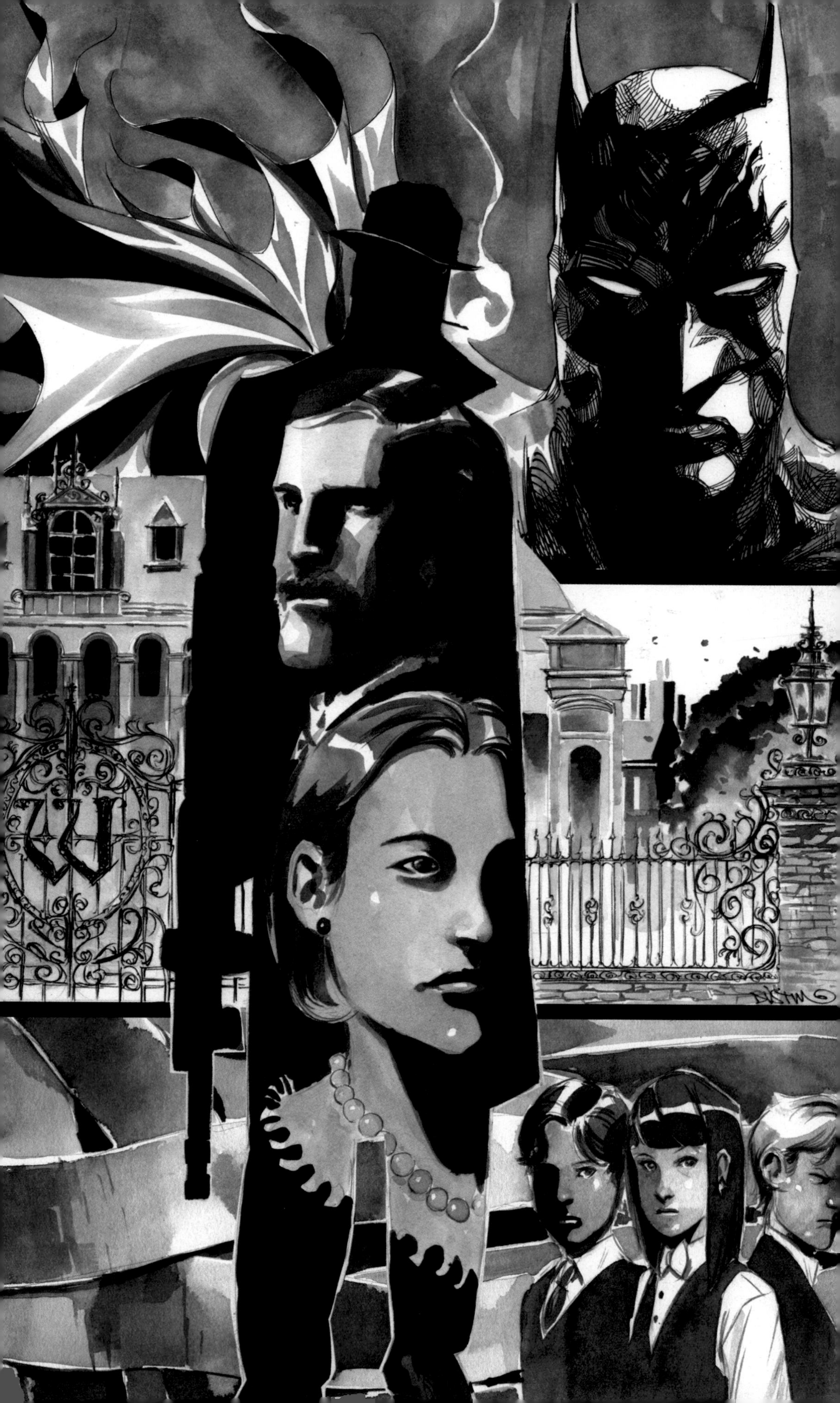

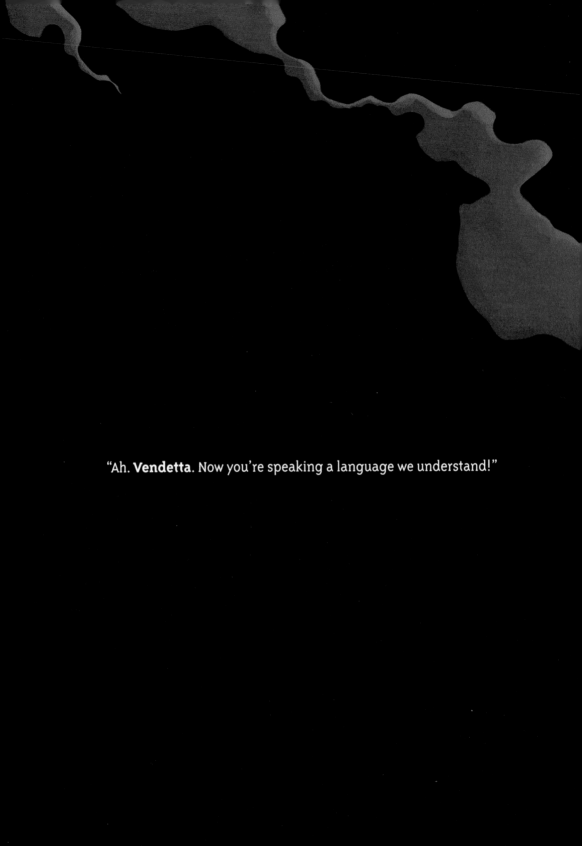

"Ah. **Vendetta**. Now you're speaking a language we understand!"

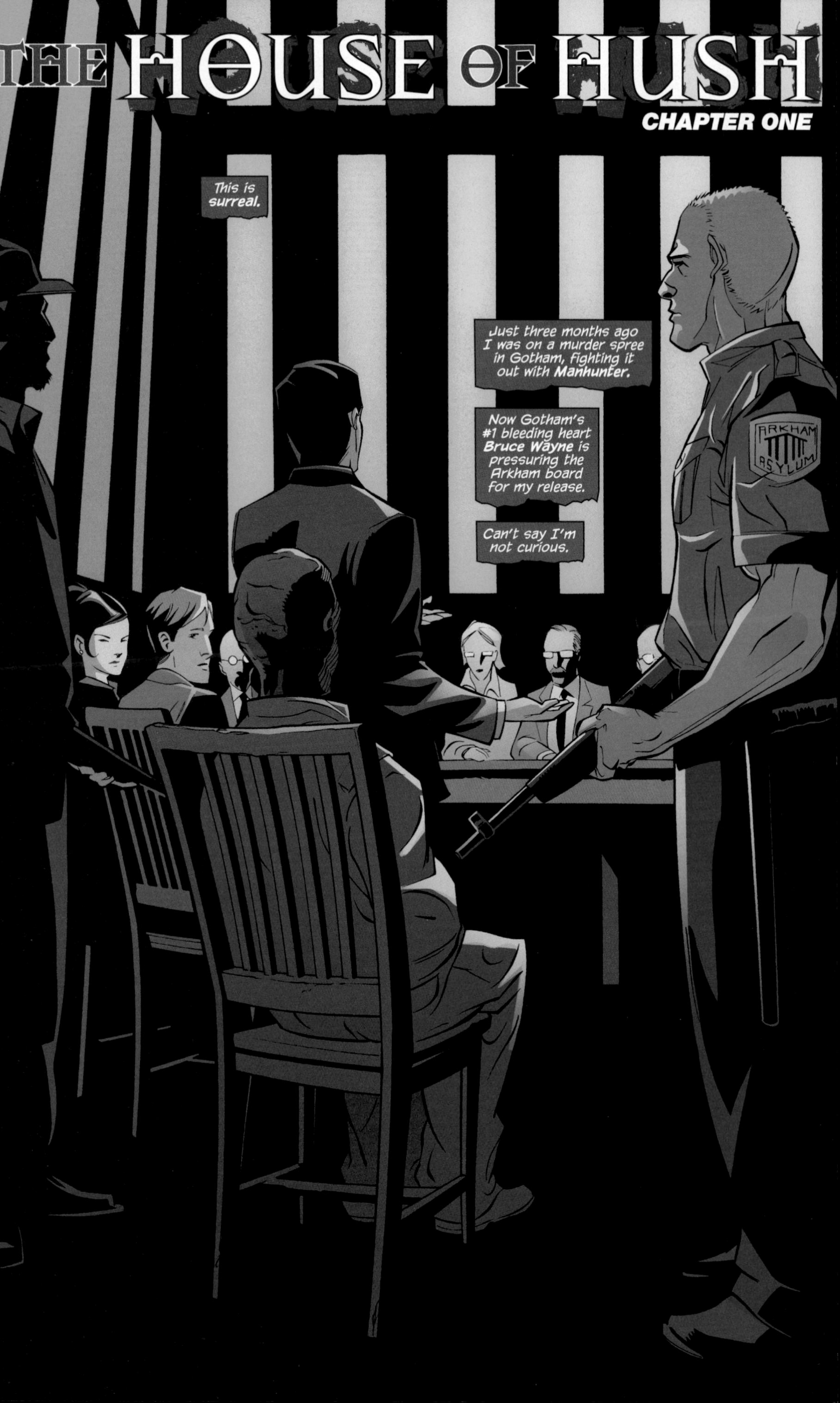

THE HOUSE OF HUSH
CHAPTER ONE
This is surreal.
Just three months ago I was on a murder spree in Gotham, fighting it out with Manhunter.
Now Gotham's #1 bleeding heart Bruce Wayne is pressuring the Arkham board for my release.
Can't say I'm not curious.
ARKHAM ASYLUM

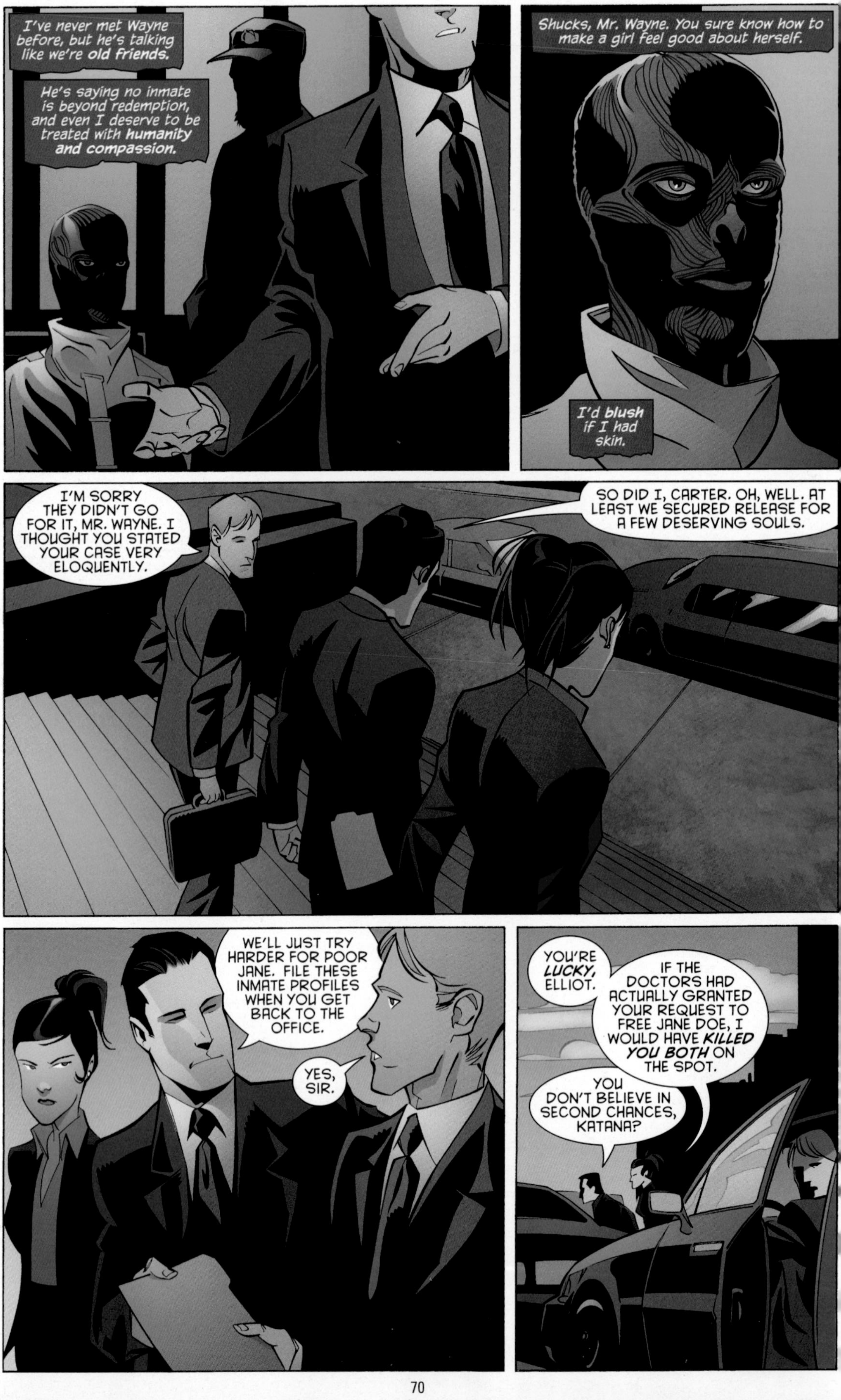

I've never met Wayne before, but he's talking like we're old friends.
He's saying no inmate is beyond redemption, and even I deserve to be treated with humanity and compassion.
Shucks, Mr. Wayne. You sure know how to make a girl feel good about herself.
I'd blush if I had skin.
I'M SORRY THEY DIDN'T GO FOR IT, MR. WAYNE. I THOUGHT YOU STATED YOUR CASE VERY ELOQUENTLY.
SO DID I, CARTER. OH, WELL. AT LEAST WE SECURED RELEASE FOR A FEW DESERVING SOULS.
WE'LL JUST TRY HARDER FOR POOR JANE. FILE THESE INMATE PROFILES WHEN YOU GET BACK TO THE OFFICE.
YES, SIR.
YOU'RE LUCKY, ELLIOT.
IF THE DOCTORS HAD ACTUALLY GRANTED YOUR REQUEST TO FREE JANE DOE, I WOULD HAVE KILLED YOU BOTH ON THE SPOT.
YOU DON'T BELIEVE IN SECOND CHANCES, KATANA?

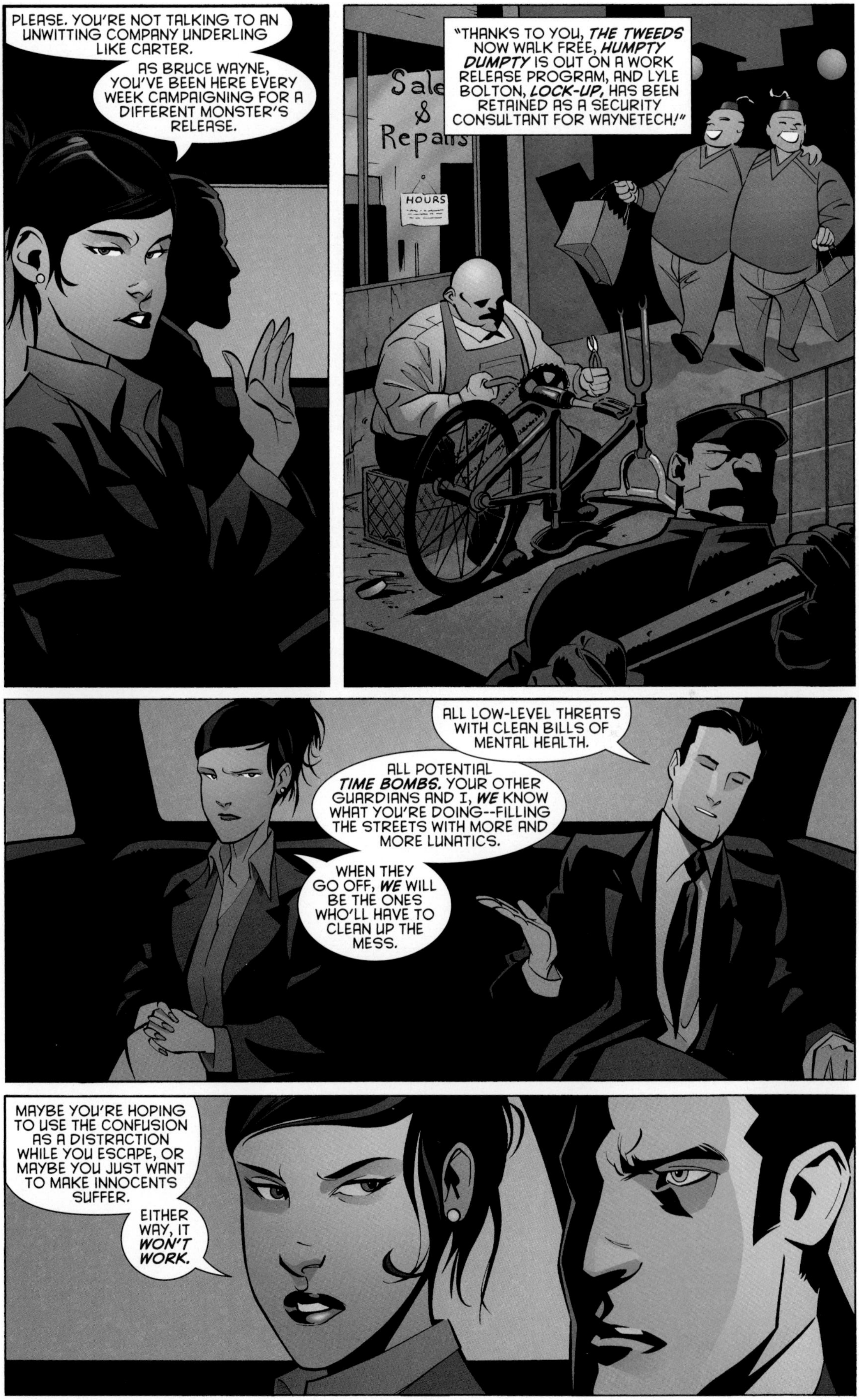
PLEASE. YOU'RE NOT TALKING TO AN UNWITTING COMPANY UNDERLING LIKE CARTER.
AS BRUCE WAYNE, YOU'VE BEEN HERE EVERY WEEK CAMPAIGNING FOR A DIFFERENT MONSTER'S RELEASE.
Sale & Repairs
HOURS
"THANKS TO YOU, THE TWEEDS NOW WALK FREE, HUMPTY DUMPTY IS OUT ON A WORK RELEASE PROGRAM, AND LYLE BOLTON, LOCK-UP, HAS BEEN RETAINED AS A SECURITY CONSULTANT FOR WAYNETECH!"
ALL LOW-LEVEL THREATS WITH CLEAN BILLS OF MENTAL HEALTH.
ALL POTENTIAL TIME BOMBS. YOUR OTHER GUARDIANS AND I, WE KNOW WHAT YOU'RE DOING--FILLING THE STREETS WITH MORE AND MORE LUNATICS.
WHEN THEY GO OFF, WE WILL BE THE ONES WHO'LL HAVE TO CLEAN UP THE MESS.
MAYBE YOU'RE HOPING TO USE THE CONFUSION AS A DISTRACTION WHILE YOU ESCAPE, OR MAYBE YOU JUST WANT TO MAKE INNOCENTS SUFFER.
EITHER WAY, IT WON'T WORK.

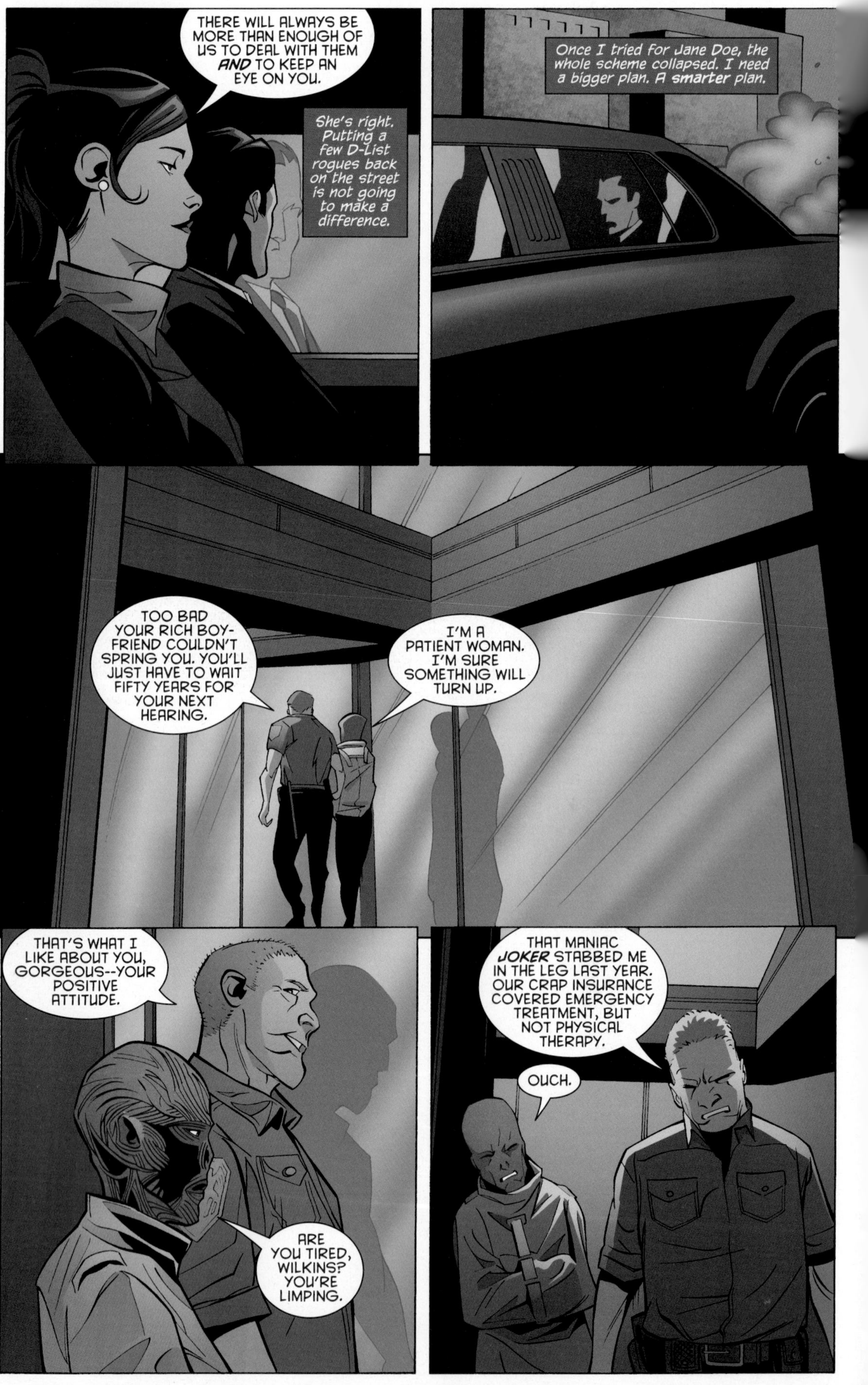

THERE WILL ALWAYS BE MORE THAN ENOUGH OF US TO DEAL WITH THEM *AND* TO KEEP AN EYE ON YOU.
She's right. Putting a few D-List rogues back on the street is not going to make a difference.
Once I tried for Jane Doe, the whole scheme collapsed. I need a bigger plan. A *smarter* plan.
TOO BAD YOUR RICH BOY-FRIEND COULDN'T SPRING YOU. YOU'LL JUST HAVE TO WAIT FIFTY YEARS FOR YOUR NEXT HEARING.
I'M A PATIENT WOMAN. I'M SURE SOMETHING WILL TURN UP.
THAT'S WHAT I LIKE ABOUT YOU, GORGEOUS--YOUR POSITIVE ATTITUDE.
ARE YOU TIRED, WILKINS? YOU'RE LIMPING.
THAT MANIAC *JOKER* STABBED ME IN THE LEG LAST YEAR. OUR CRAP INSURANCE COVERED EMERGENCY TREATMENT, BUT NOT PHYSICAL THERAPY.
OUCH.

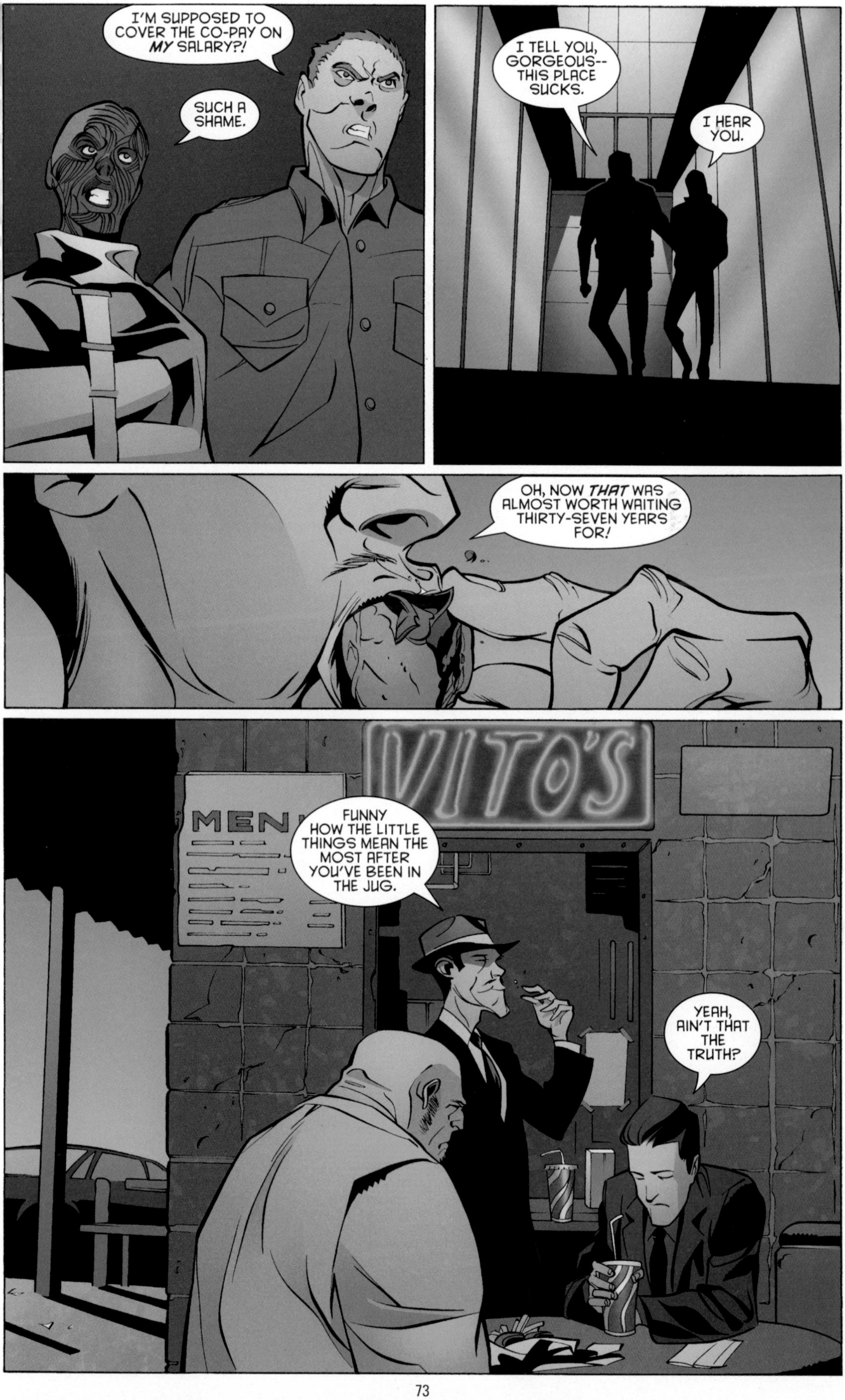
I'M SUPPOSED TO COVER THE CO-PAY ON MY SALARY?!
SUCH A SHAME.
I TELL YOU, GORGEOUS-- THIS PLACE SUCKS.
I HEAR YOU.
OH, NOW THAT WAS ALMOST WORTH WAITING THIRTY-SEVEN YEARS FOR!
VITO'S
MEN
FUNNY HOW THE LITTLE THINGS MEAN THE MOST AFTER YOU'VE BEEN IN THE JUG.
YEAH, AIN'T THAT THE TRUTH?

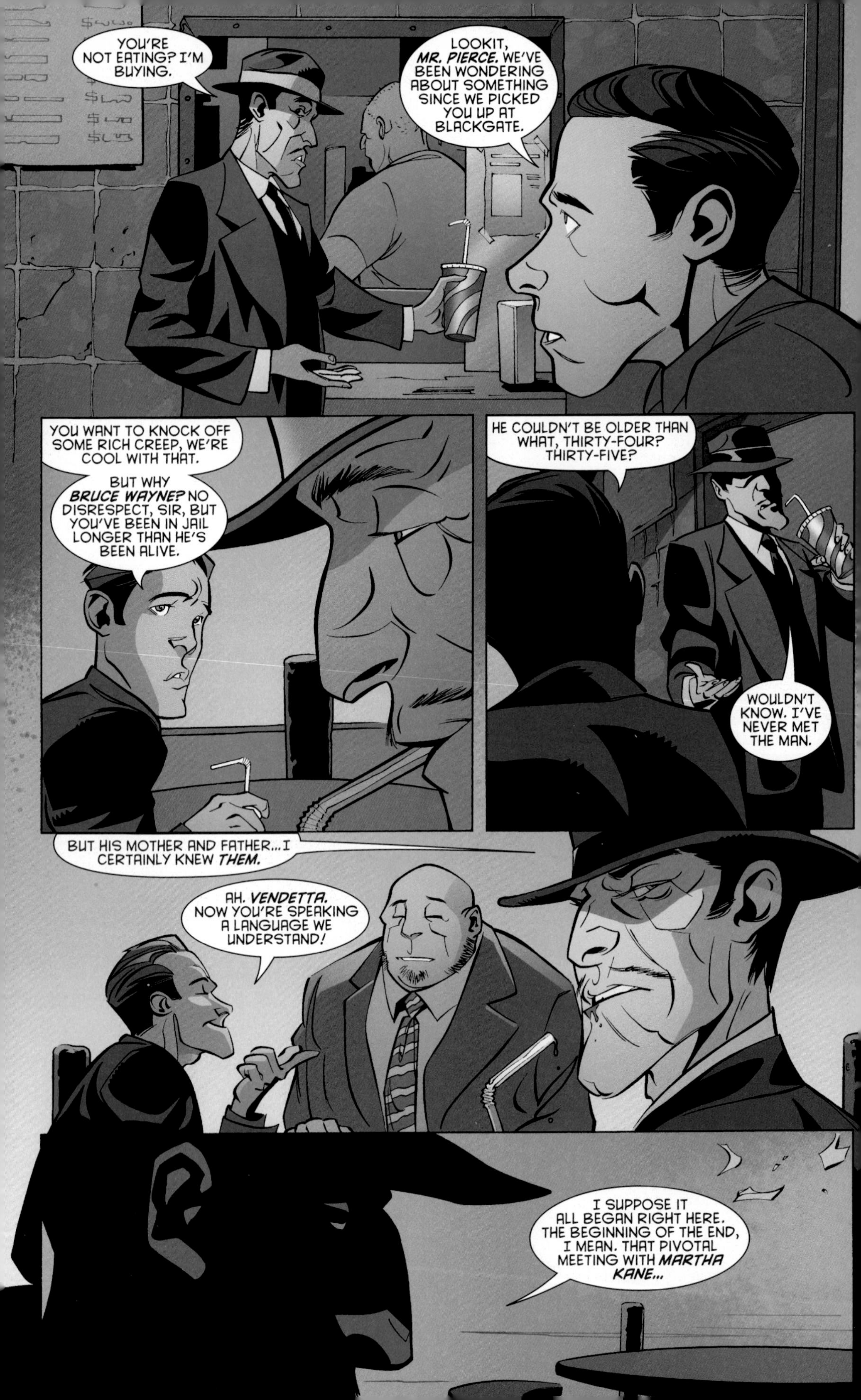
YOU'RE NOT EATING? I'M BUYING.
LOOKIT, MR. PIERCE. WE'VE BEEN WONDERING ABOUT SOMETHING SINCE WE PICKED YOU UP AT BLACKGATE.
YOU WANT TO KNOCK OFF SOME RICH CREEP, WE'RE COOL WITH THAT.
BUT WHY BRUCE WAYNE? NO DISRESPECT, SIR, BUT YOU'VE BEEN IN JAIL LONGER THAN HE'S BEEN ALIVE.
HE COULDN'T BE OLDER THAN WHAT, THIRTY-FOUR? THIRTY-FIVE?
WOULDN'T KNOW. I'VE NEVER MET THE MAN.
BUT HIS MOTHER AND FATHER...I CERTAINLY KNEW THEM.
AH. VENDETTA. NOW YOU'RE SPEAKING A LANGUAGE WE UNDERSTAND!
I SUPPOSE IT ALL BEGAN RIGHT HERE. THE BEGINNING OF THE END, I MEAN. THAT PIVOTAL MEETING WITH MARTHA KANE...

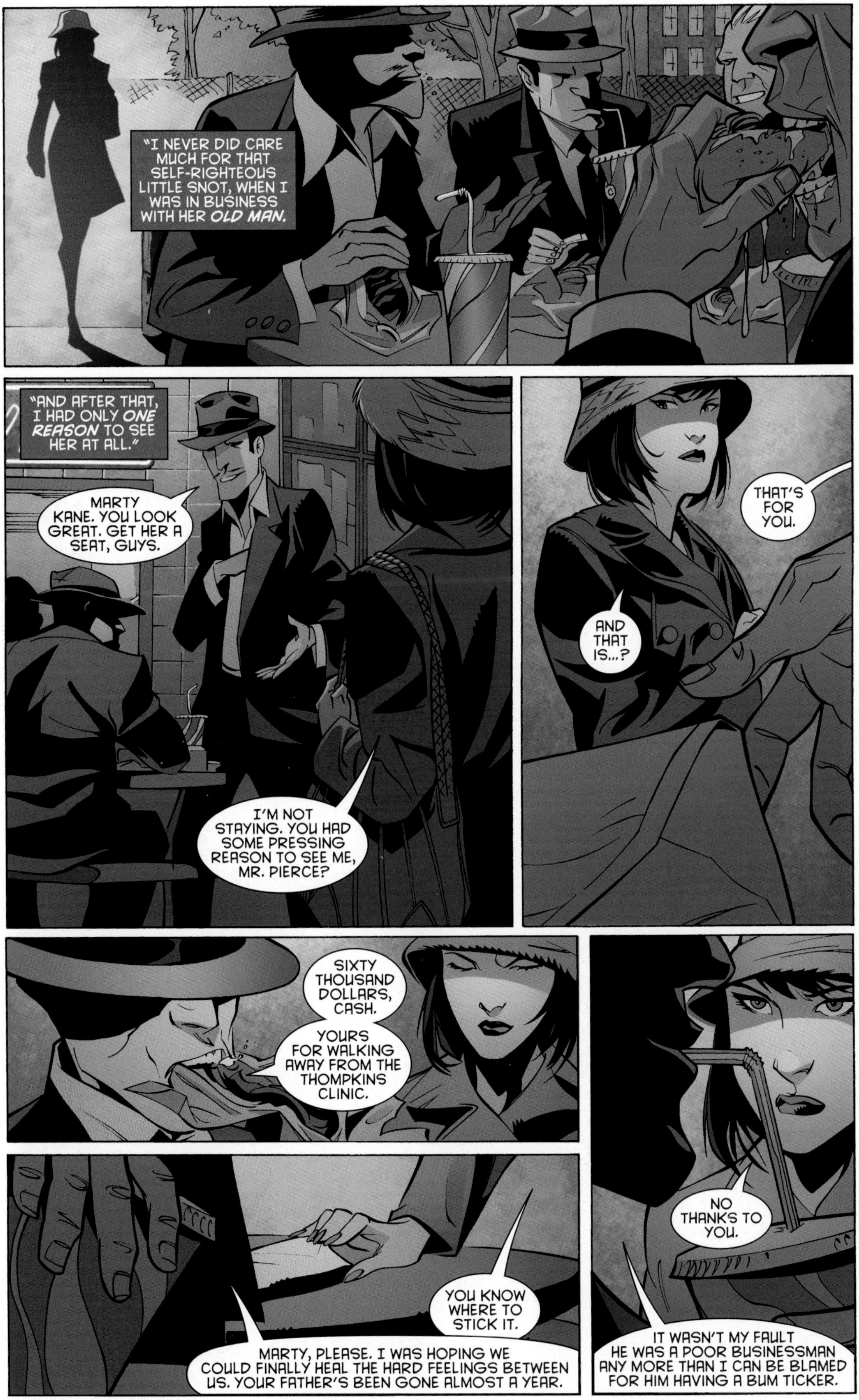
"I NEVER DID CARE MUCH FOR THAT SELF-RIGHTEOUS LITTLE SNOT, WHEN I WAS IN BUSINESS WITH HER OLD MAN.
"AND AFTER THAT, I HAD ONLY ONE REASON TO SEE HER AT ALL."
MARTY KANE. YOU LOOK GREAT. GET HER A SEAT, GUYS.
I'M NOT STAYING. YOU HAD SOME PRESSING REASON TO SEE ME, MR. PIERCE?
THAT'S FOR YOU.
AND THAT IS...?
SIXTY THOUSAND DOLLARS, CASH.
YOURS FOR WALKING AWAY FROM THE THOMPKINS CLINIC.
YOU KNOW WHERE TO STICK IT.
MARTY, PLEASE. I WAS HOPING WE COULD FINALLY HEAL THE HARD FEELINGS BETWEEN US. YOUR FATHER'S BEEN GONE ALMOST A YEAR.
NO THANKS TO YOU.
IT WASN'T MY FAULT HE WAS A POOR BUSINESSMAN ANY MORE THAN I CAN BE BLAMED FOR HIM HAVING A BUM TICKER.

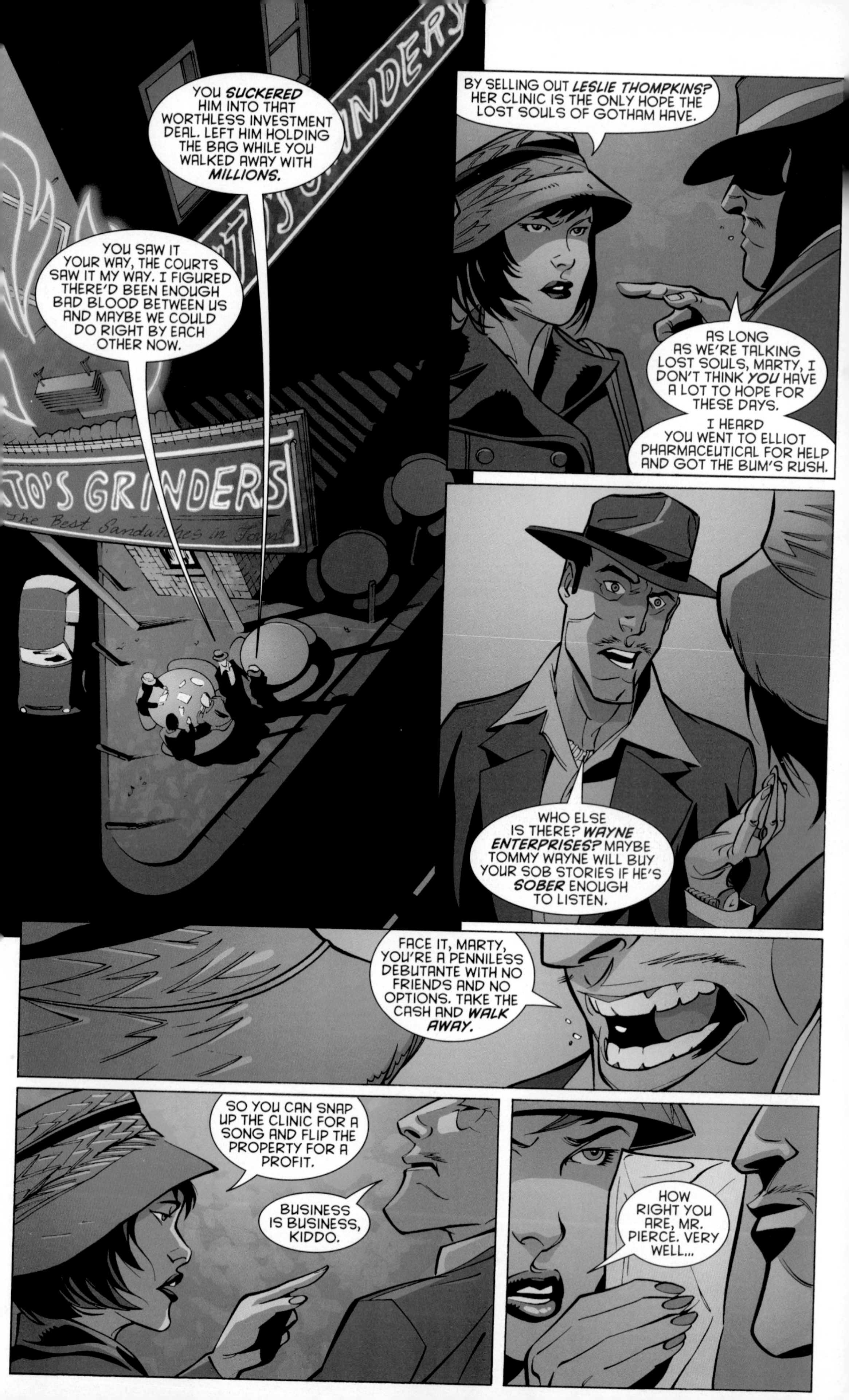

YOU SUCKERED HIM INTO THAT WORTHLESS INVESTMENT DEAL. LEFT HIM HOLDING THE BAG WHILE YOU WALKED AWAY WITH MILLIONS.
YOU SAW IT YOUR WAY, THE COURTS SAW IT MY WAY. I FIGURED THERE'D BEEN ENOUGH BAD BLOOD BETWEEN US AND MAYBE WE COULD DO RIGHT BY EACH OTHER NOW.
TO'S GRINDERS
The Best Sandwiches in Town
BY SELLING OUT LESLIE THOMPKINS? HER CLINIC IS THE ONLY HOPE THE LOST SOULS OF GOTHAM HAVE.
AS LONG AS WE'RE TALKING LOST SOULS, MARTY, I DON'T THINK YOU HAVE A LOT TO HOPE FOR THESE DAYS.
I HEARD YOU WENT TO ELLIOT PHARMACEUTICAL FOR HELP AND GOT THE BUM'S RUSH.
WHO ELSE IS THERE? WAYNE ENTERPRISES? MAYBE TOMMY WAYNE WILL BUY YOUR SOB STORIES IF HE'S SOBER ENOUGH TO LISTEN.
FACE IT, MARTY, YOU'RE A PENNILESS DEBUTANTE WITH NO FRIENDS AND NO OPTIONS. TAKE THE CASH AND WALK AWAY.
SO YOU CAN SNAP UP THE CLINIC FOR A SONG AND FLIP THE PROPERTY FOR A PROFIT.
BUSINESS IS BUSINESS, KIDDO.
HOW RIGHT YOU ARE, MR. PIERCE. VERY WELL...

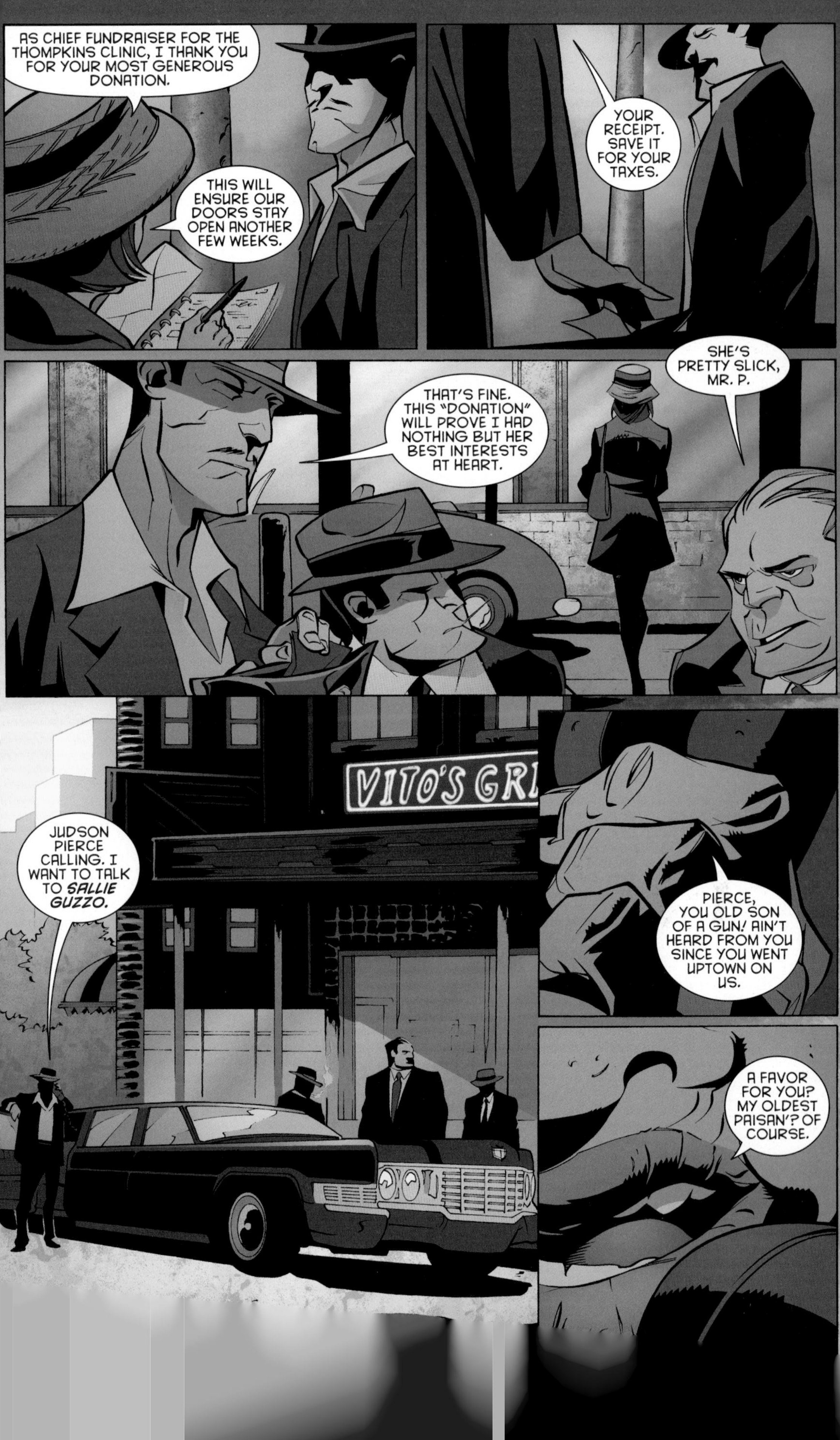
AS CHIEF FUNDRAISER FOR THE THOMPKINS CLINIC, I THANK YOU FOR YOUR MOST GENEROUS DONATION.
THIS WILL ENSURE OUR DOORS STAY OPEN ANOTHER FEW WEEKS.
YOUR RECEIPT. SAVE IT FOR YOUR TAXES.
THAT'S FINE. THIS "DONATION" WILL PROVE I HAD NOTHING BUT HER BEST INTERESTS AT HEART.
SHE'S PRETTY SLICK, MR. P.
VITO'S GRI
JUDSON PIERCE CALLING. I WANT TO TALK TO *SALLIE GUZZO.*
PIERCE, YOU OLD SON OF A GUN! AIN'T HEARD FROM YOU SINCE YOU WENT UPTOWN ON US.
A FAVOR FOR YOU? MY OLDEST PAISAN'? OF COURSE.

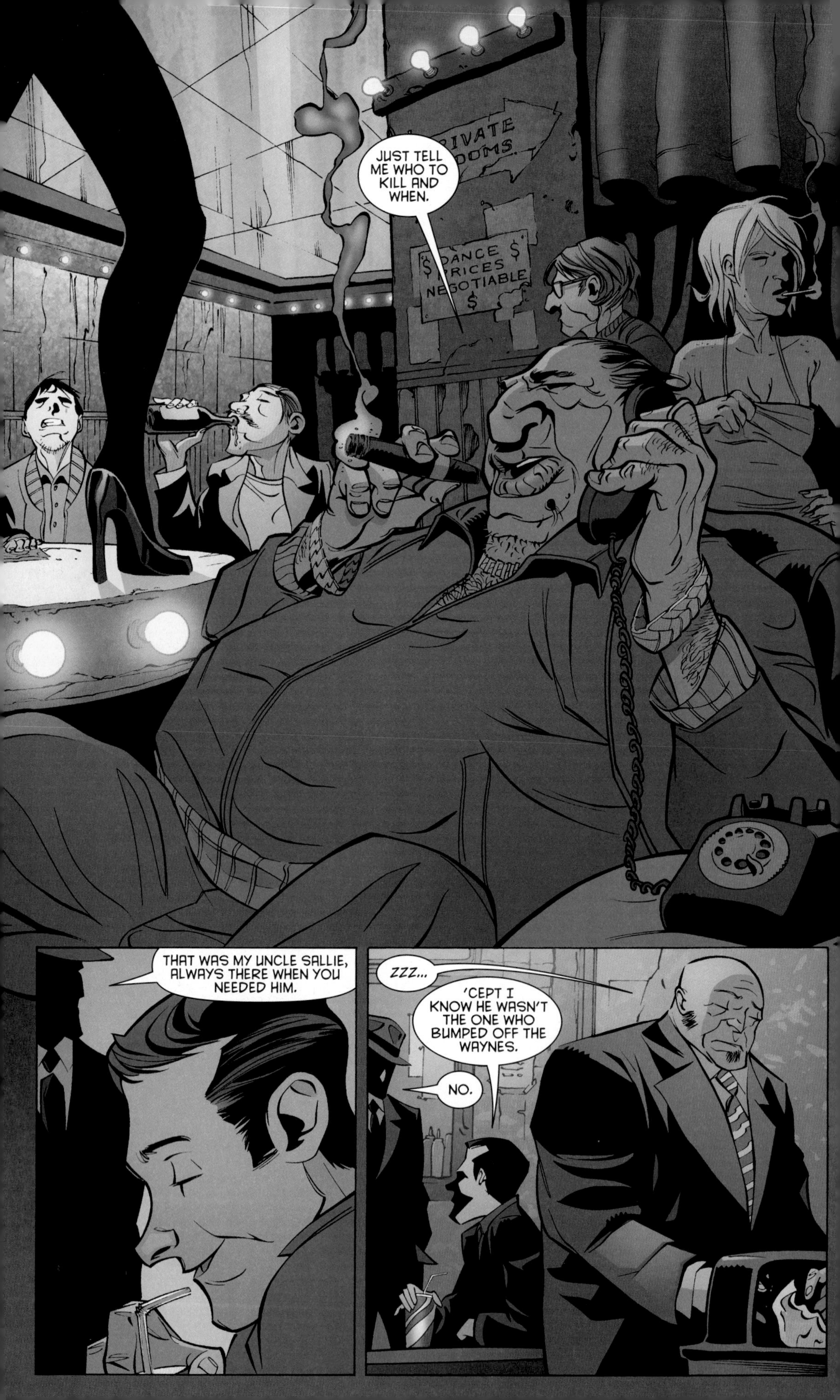
PRIVATE ROOMS
JUST TELL ME WHO TO KILL AND WHEN.
$ DANCE $ PRICES NEGOTIABLE $
THAT WAS MY UNCLE SALLIE, ALWAYS THERE WHEN YOU NEEDED HIM.
ZZZ...
'CEPT I KNOW HE WASN'T THE ONE WHO BUMPED OFF THE WAYNES.
NO.

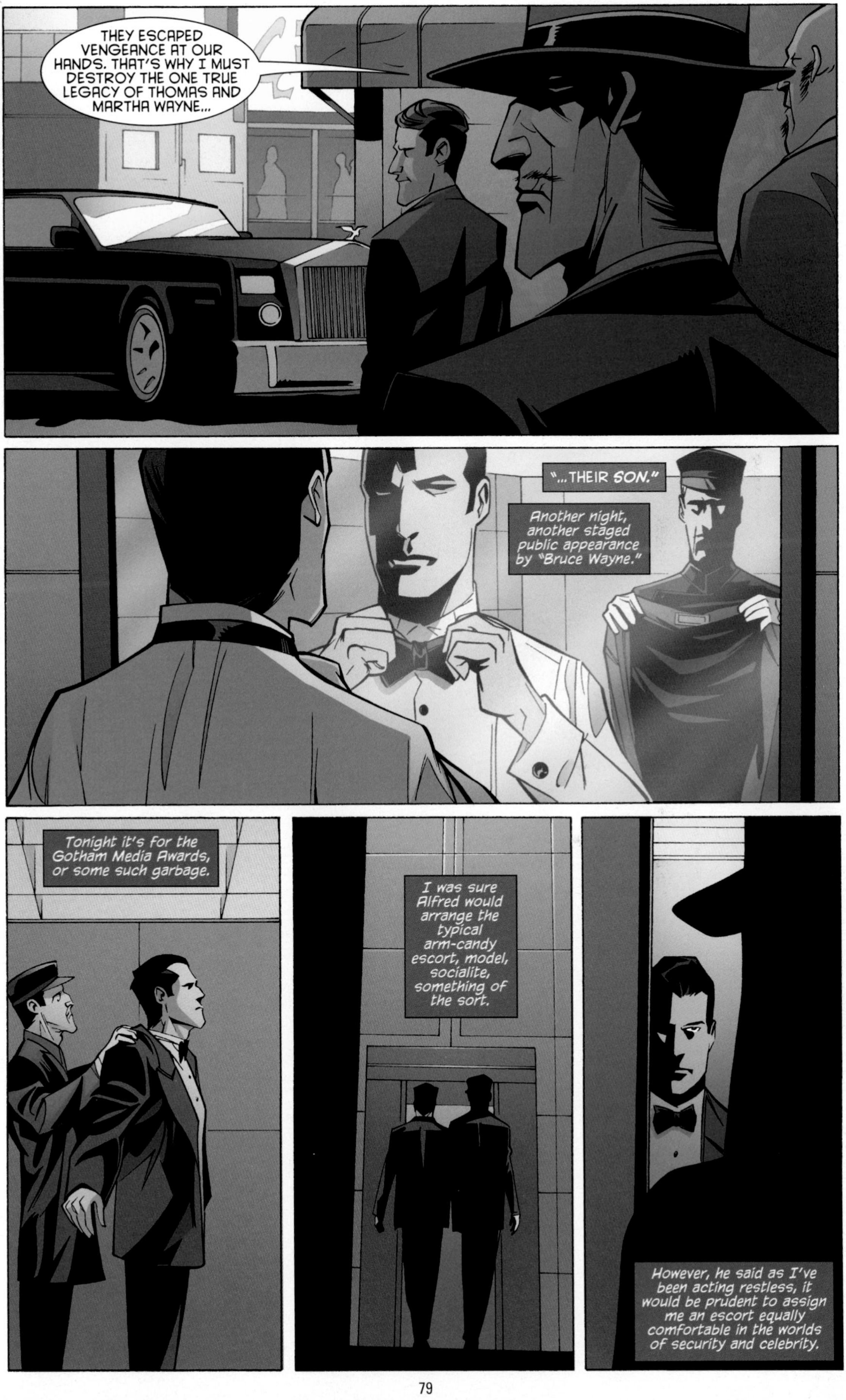
THEY ESCAPED VENGEANCE AT OUR HANDS. THAT'S WHY I MUST DESTROY THE ONE TRUE LEGACY OF THOMAS AND MARTHA WAYNE...
"...THEIR SON."
Another night, another staged public appearance by "Bruce Wayne."
Tonight it's for the Gotham Media Awards, or some such garbage.
I was sure Alfred would arrange the typical arm-candy escort, model, socialite, something of the sort.
However, he said as I've been acting restless, it would be prudent to assign me an escort equally comfortable in the worlds of security and celebrity.

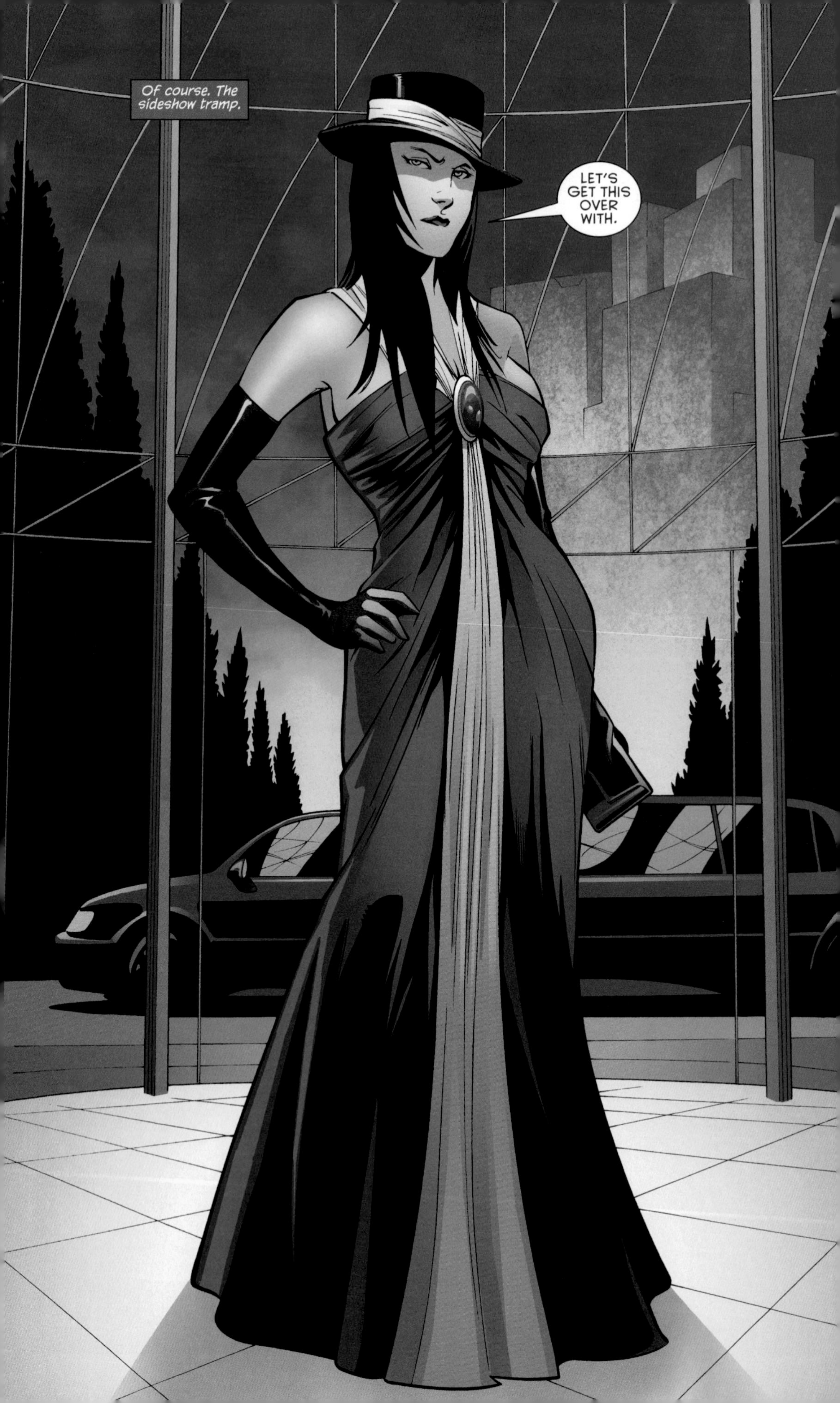
Of course. The sideshow tramp.
LET'S GET THIS OVER WITH.

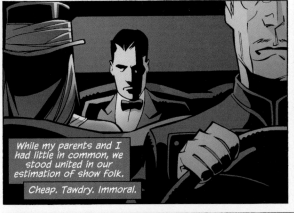

While my parents and I had little in common, we stood united in our estimation of show folk.

Cheap. Tawdry. Immoral.

This filthy gypsy may stand shoulder to shoulder with Earth's greatest heroes, but to me she will always reek of greasepaint and carnivals.

Even as children she sickened me with her father's attempts to ingratiate themselves among decent families.

Poor Bruce. So eager to be dazzled by the commonplace.

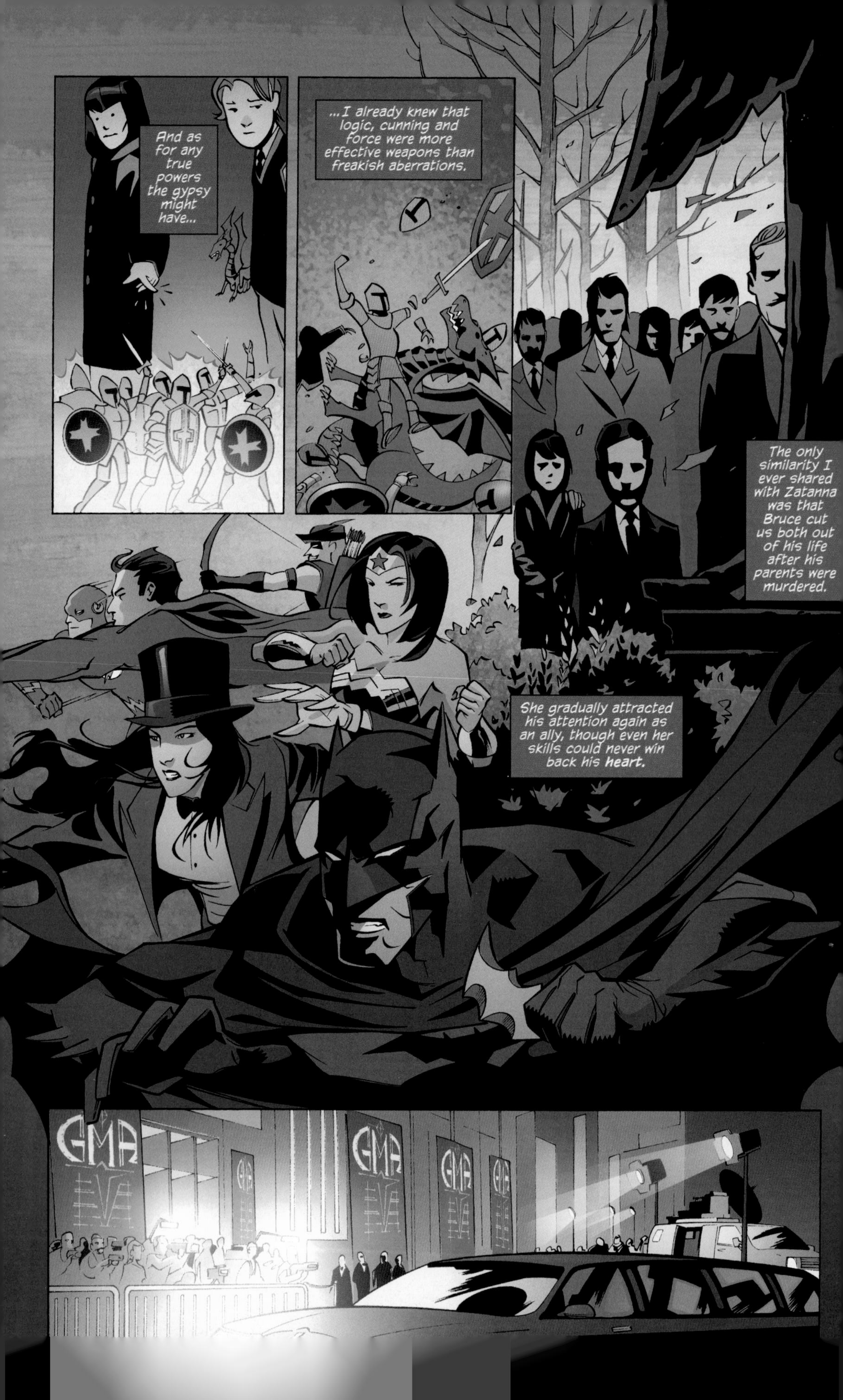
And as for any true powers the gypsy might have...
...I already knew that logic, cunning and force were more effective weapons than freakish aberrations.
The only similarity I ever shared with Zatanna was that Bruce cut us both out of his life after his parents were murdered.
She gradually attracted his attention again as an ally, though even her skills could never win back his heart.
GMA
GMA
GMA
GMA
GMA

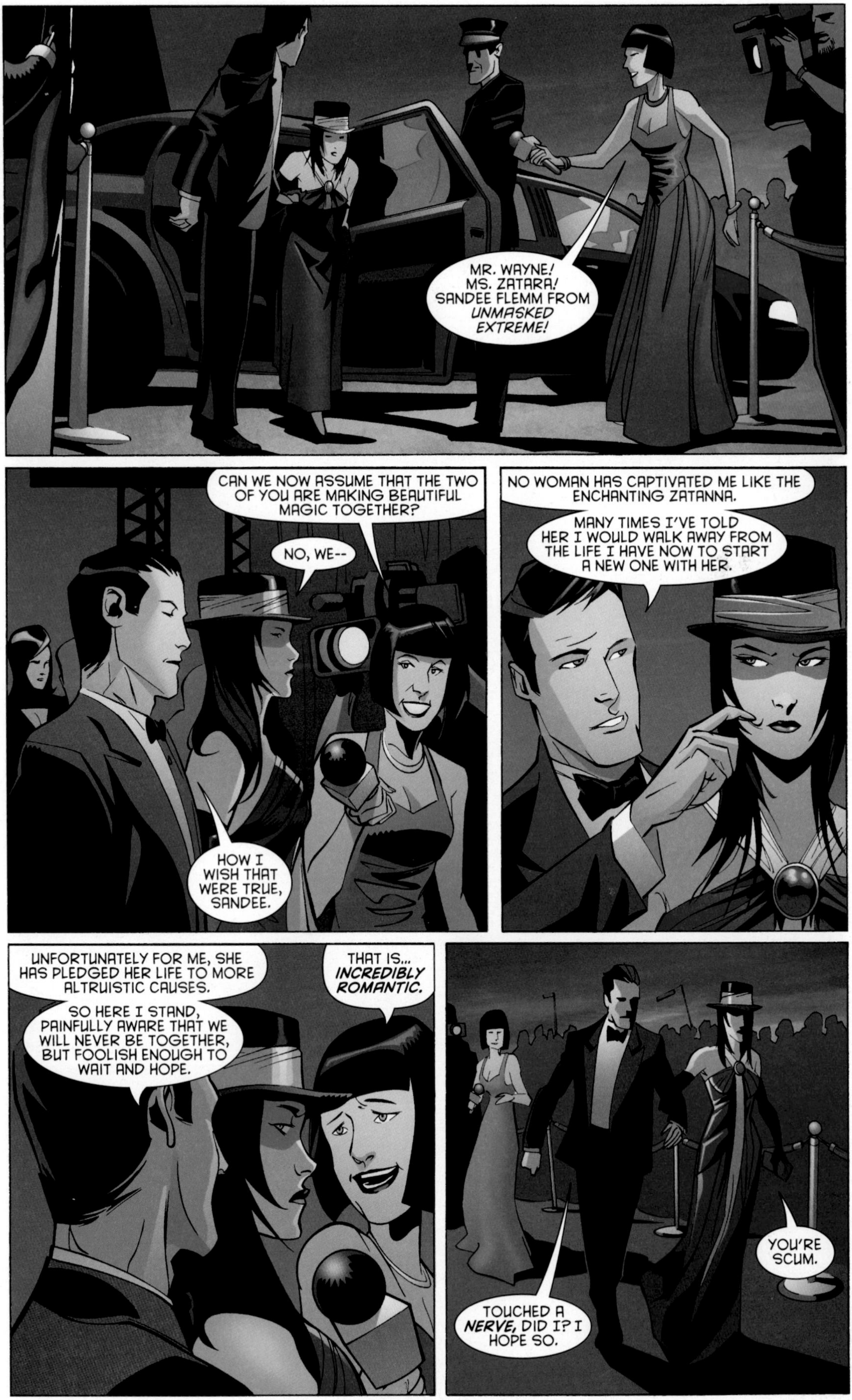
MR. WAYNE! MS. ZATARA! SANDEE FLEMM FROM *UNMASKED EXTREME!*
CAN WE NOW ASSUME THAT THE TWO OF YOU ARE MAKING BEAUTIFUL MAGIC TOGETHER?
NO, WE--
HOW I WISH THAT WERE TRUE, SANDEE.
NO WOMAN HAS CAPTIVATED ME LIKE THE ENCHANTING ZATANNA.
MANY TIMES I'VE TOLD HER I WOULD WALK AWAY FROM THE LIFE I HAVE NOW TO START A NEW ONE WITH HER.
UNFORTUNATELY FOR ME, SHE HAS PLEDGED HER LIFE TO MORE ALTRUISTIC CAUSES.
SO HERE I STAND, PAINFULLY AWARE THAT WE WILL NEVER BE TOGETHER, BUT FOOLISH ENOUGH TO WAIT AND HOPE.
THAT IS... *INCREDIBLY ROMANTIC.*
YOU'RE SCUM.
TOUCHED A *NERVE,* DID I? I HOPE SO.

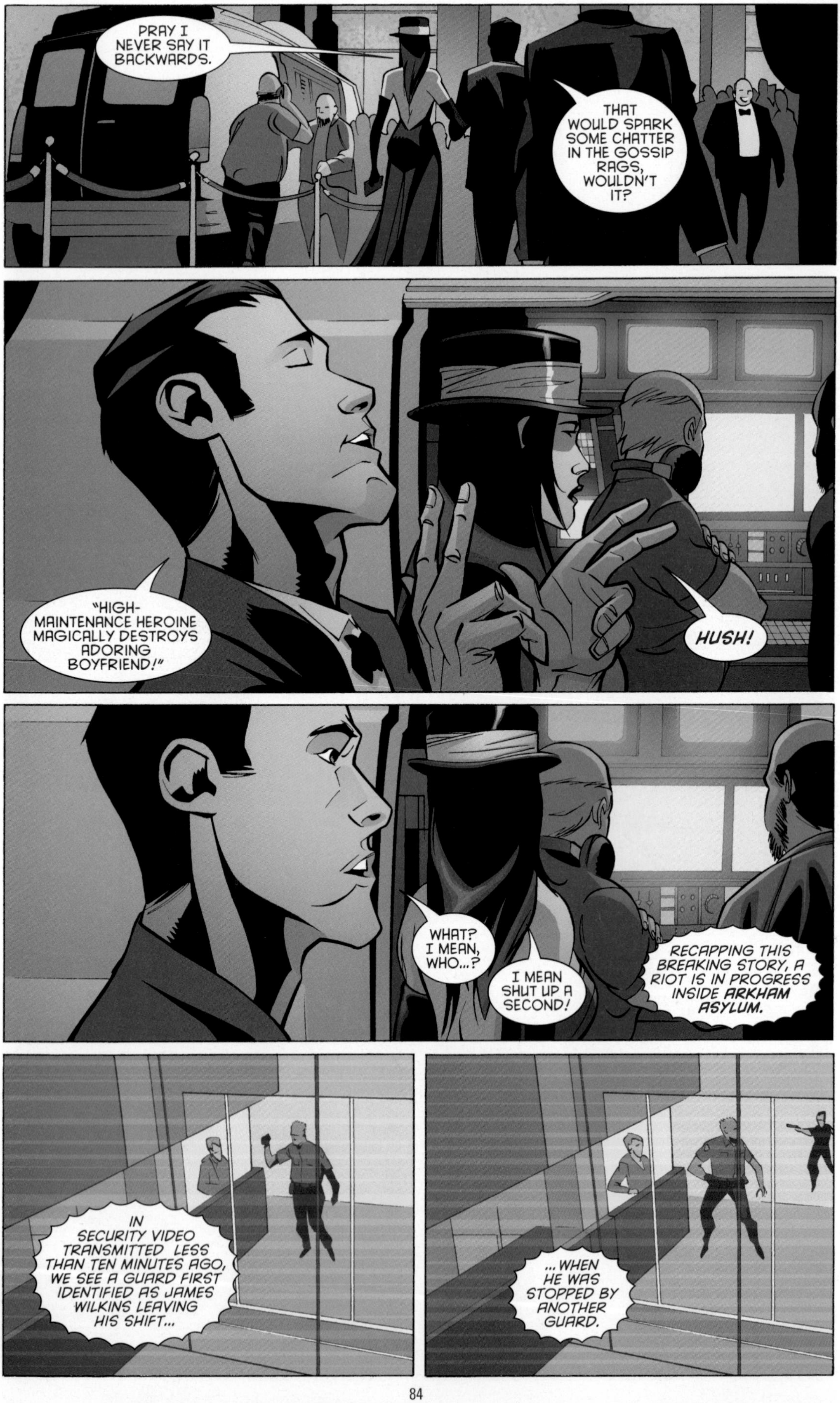

PRAY I NEVER SAY IT BACKWARDS.
THAT WOULD SPARK SOME CHATTER IN THE GOSSIP RAGS, WOULDN'T IT?
"HIGH-MAINTENANCE HEROINE MAGICALLY DESTROYS ADORING BOYFRIEND!"
HUSH!
WHAT? I MEAN, WHO...?
I MEAN SHUT UP A SECOND!
RECAPPING THIS BREAKING STORY, A RIOT IS IN PROGRESS INSIDE ARKHAM ASYLUM.
IN SECURITY VIDEO TRANSMITTED LESS THAN TEN MINUTES AGO, WE SEE A GUARD FIRST IDENTIFIED AS JAMES WILKINS LEAVING HIS SHIFT...
...WHEN HE WAS STOPPED BY ANOTHER GUARD.

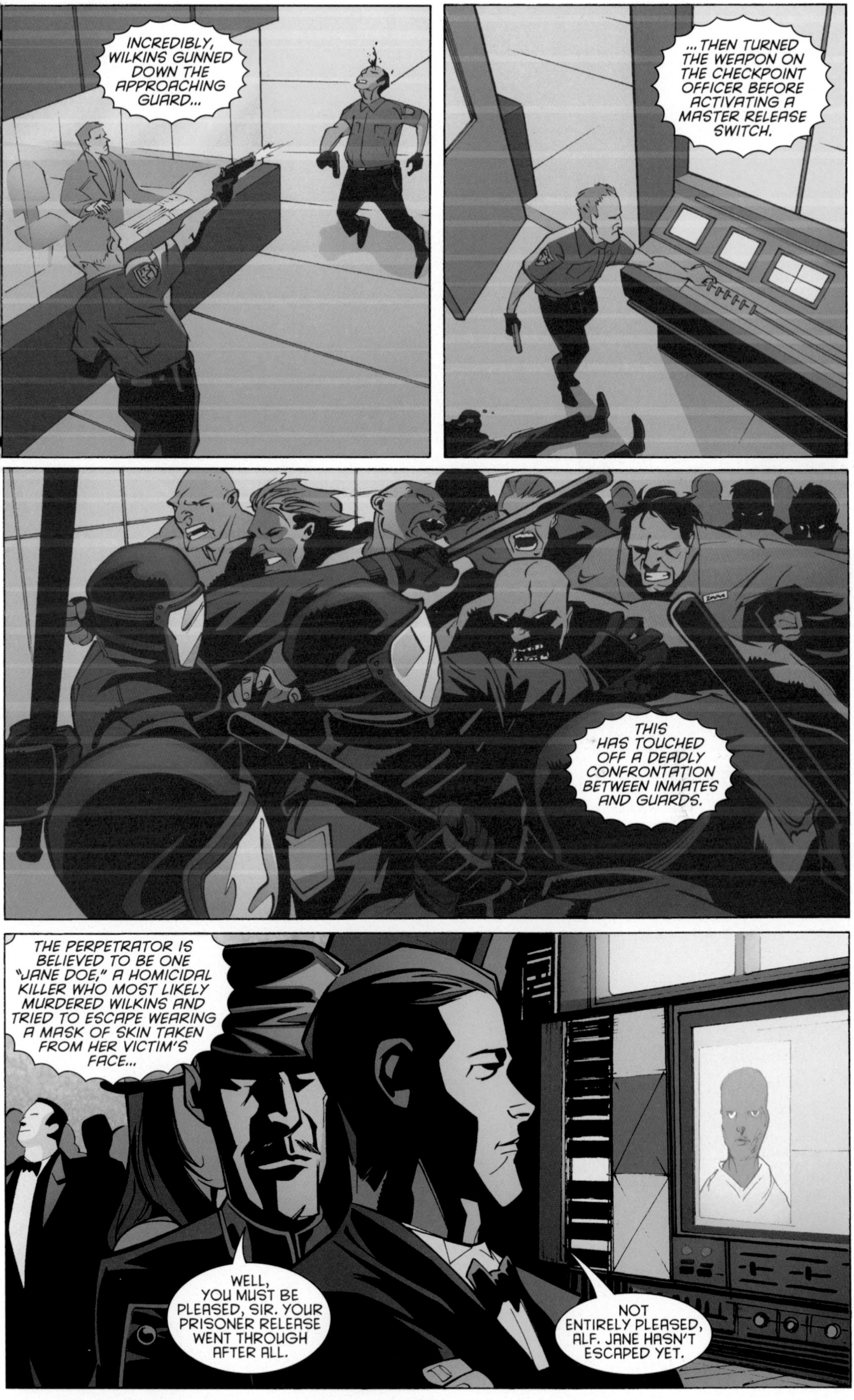
INCREDIBLY, WILKINS GUNNED DOWN THE APPROACHING GUARD...
...THEN TURNED THE WEAPON ON THE CHECKPOINT OFFICER BEFORE ACTIVATING A MASTER RELEASE SWITCH.
THIS HAS TOUCHED OFF A DEADLY CONFRONTATION BETWEEN INMATES AND GUARDS.
THE PERPETRATOR IS BELIEVED TO BE ONE "JANE DOE," A HOMICIDAL KILLER WHO MOST LIKELY MURDERED WILKINS AND TRIED TO ESCAPE WEARING A MASK OF SKIN TAKEN FROM HER VICTIM'S FACE...
WELL, YOU MUST BE PLEASED, SIR. YOUR PRISONER RELEASE WENT THROUGH AFTER ALL.
NOT ENTIRELY PLEASED, ALF. JANE HASN'T ESCAPED YET.

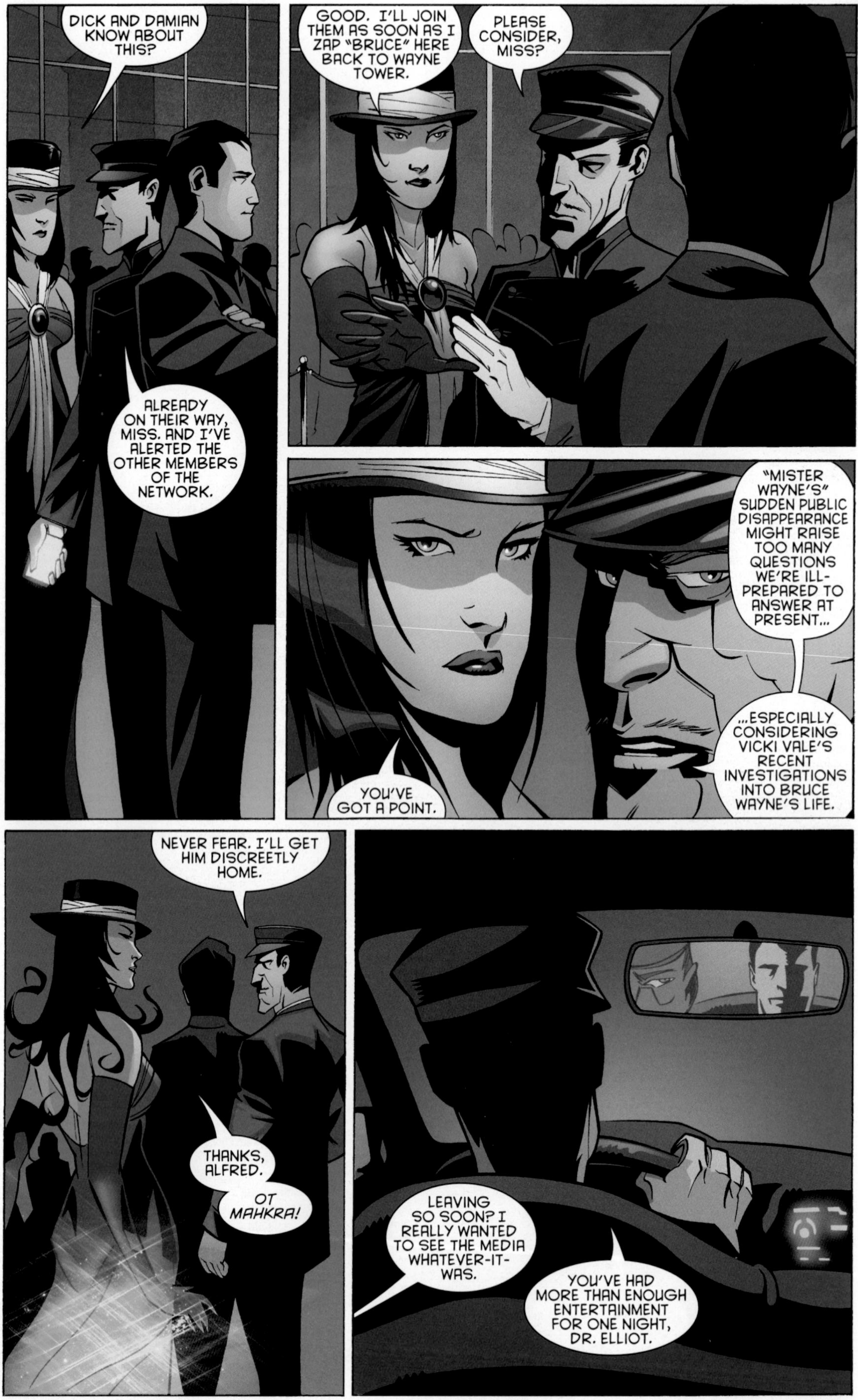
DICK AND DAMIAN KNOW ABOUT THIS?
ALREADY ON THEIR WAY, MISS. AND I'VE ALERTED THE OTHER MEMBERS OF THE NETWORK.
GOOD. I'LL JOIN THEM AS SOON AS I ZAP "BRUCE" HERE BACK TO WAYNE TOWER.
PLEASE CONSIDER, MISS?
"MISTER WAYNE'S" SUDDEN PUBLIC DISAPPEARANCE MIGHT RAISE TOO MANY QUESTIONS WE'RE ILL-PREPARED TO ANSWER AT PRESENT...
...ESPECIALLY CONSIDERING VICKI VALE'S RECENT INVESTIGATIONS INTO BRUCE WAYNE'S LIFE.
YOU'VE GOT A POINT.
NEVER FEAR. I'LL GET HIM DISCREETLY HOME.
THANKS, ALFRED.
OT MAHKRA!
LEAVING SO SOON? I REALLY WANTED TO SEE THE MEDIA WHATEVER-IT-WAS.
YOU'VE HAD MORE THAN ENOUGH ENTERTAINMENT FOR ONE NIGHT, DR. ELLIOT.

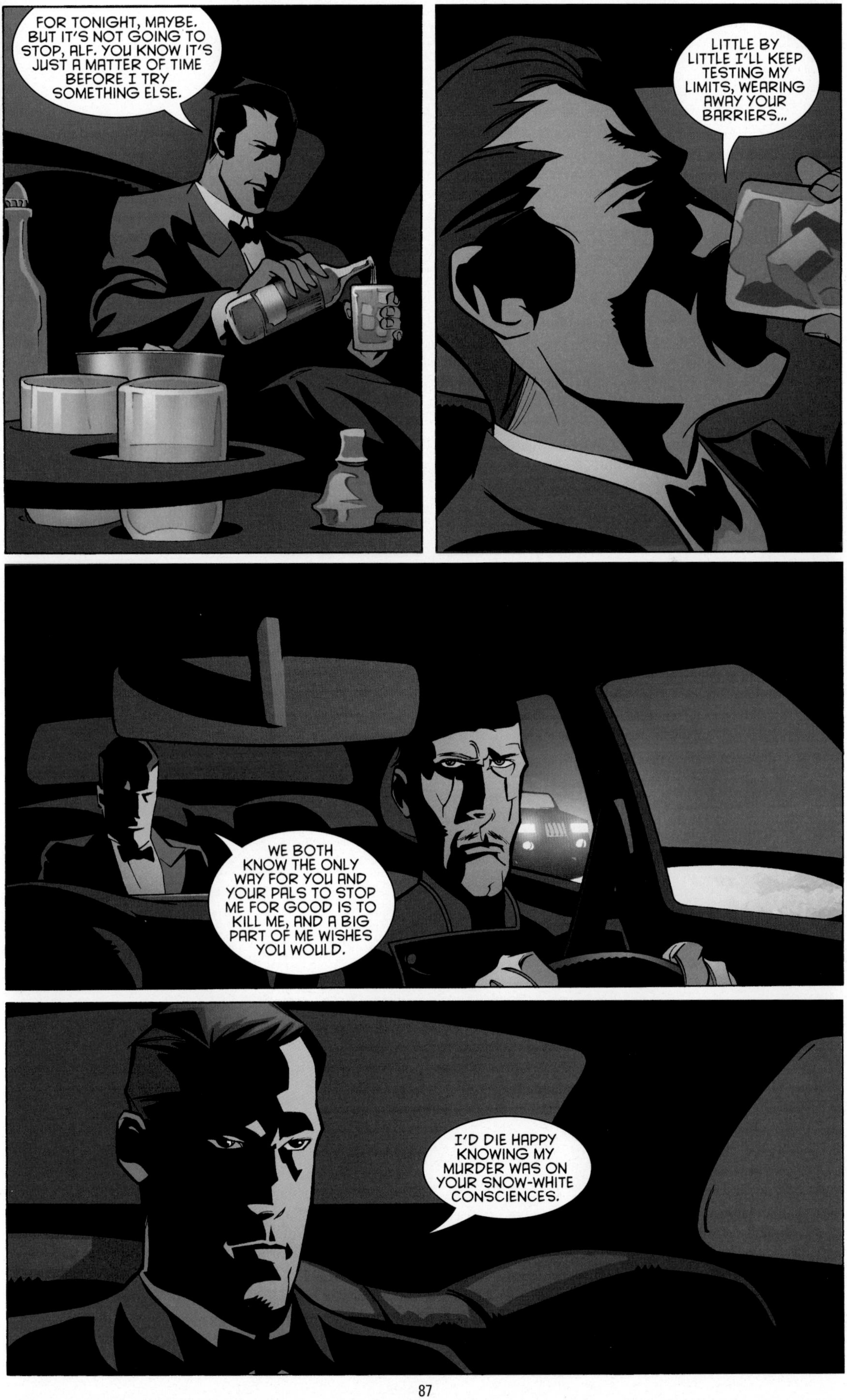
FOR TONIGHT, MAYBE. BUT IT'S NOT GOING TO STOP, ALF. YOU KNOW IT'S JUST A MATTER OF TIME BEFORE I TRY SOMETHING ELSE.
LITTLE BY LITTLE I'LL KEEP TESTING MY LIMITS, WEARING AWAY YOUR BARRIERS...
WE BOTH KNOW THE ONLY WAY FOR YOU AND YOUR PALS TO STOP ME FOR GOOD IS TO KILL ME, AND A BIG PART OF ME WISHES YOU WOULD.
I'D DIE HAPPY KNOWING MY MURDER WAS ON YOUR SNOW-WHITE CONSCIENCES.

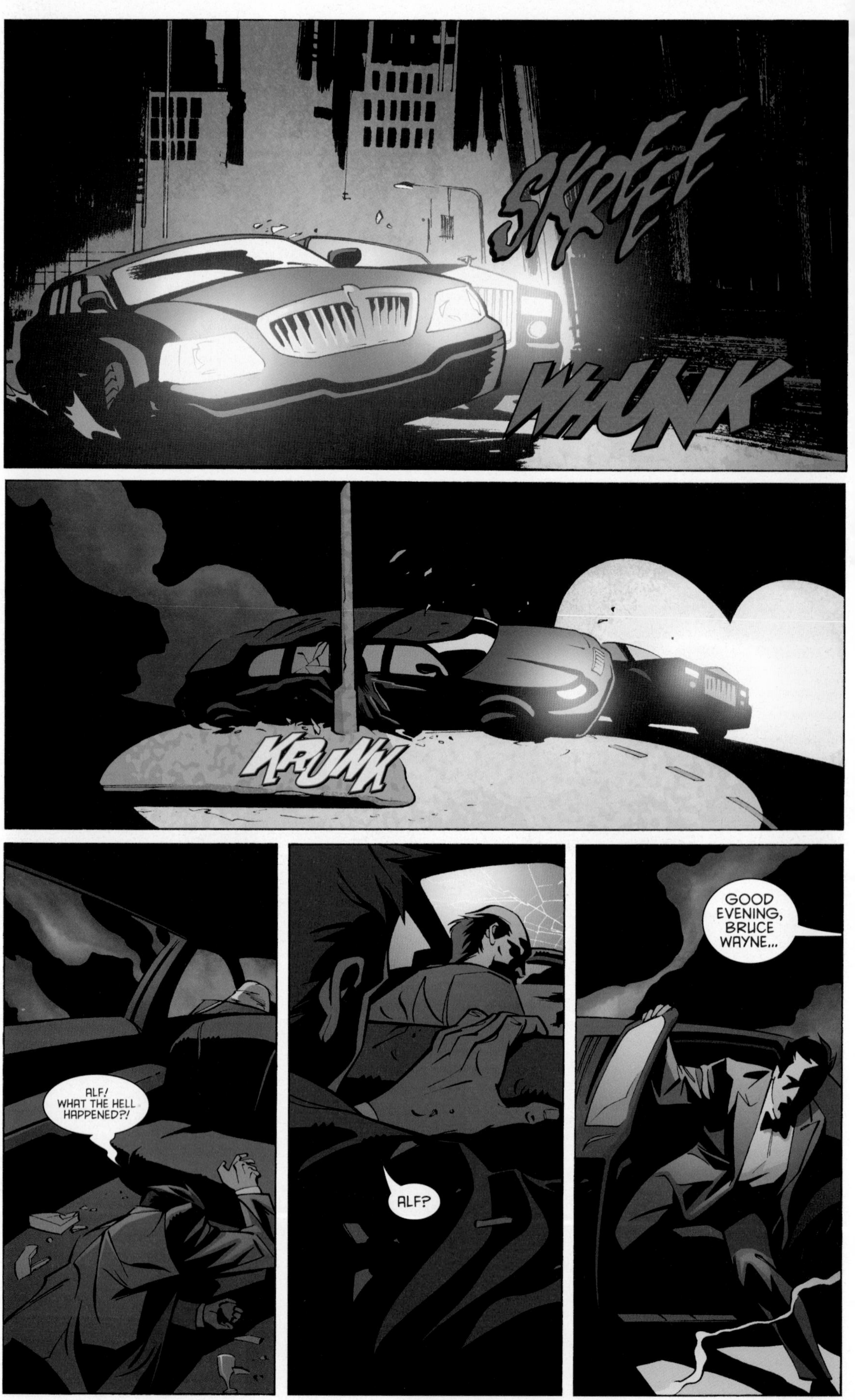
SKREEE
WHUNK
KRUNK
ALF! WHAT THE HELL HAPPENED?!
ALF?
GOOD EVENING, BRUCE WAYNE...

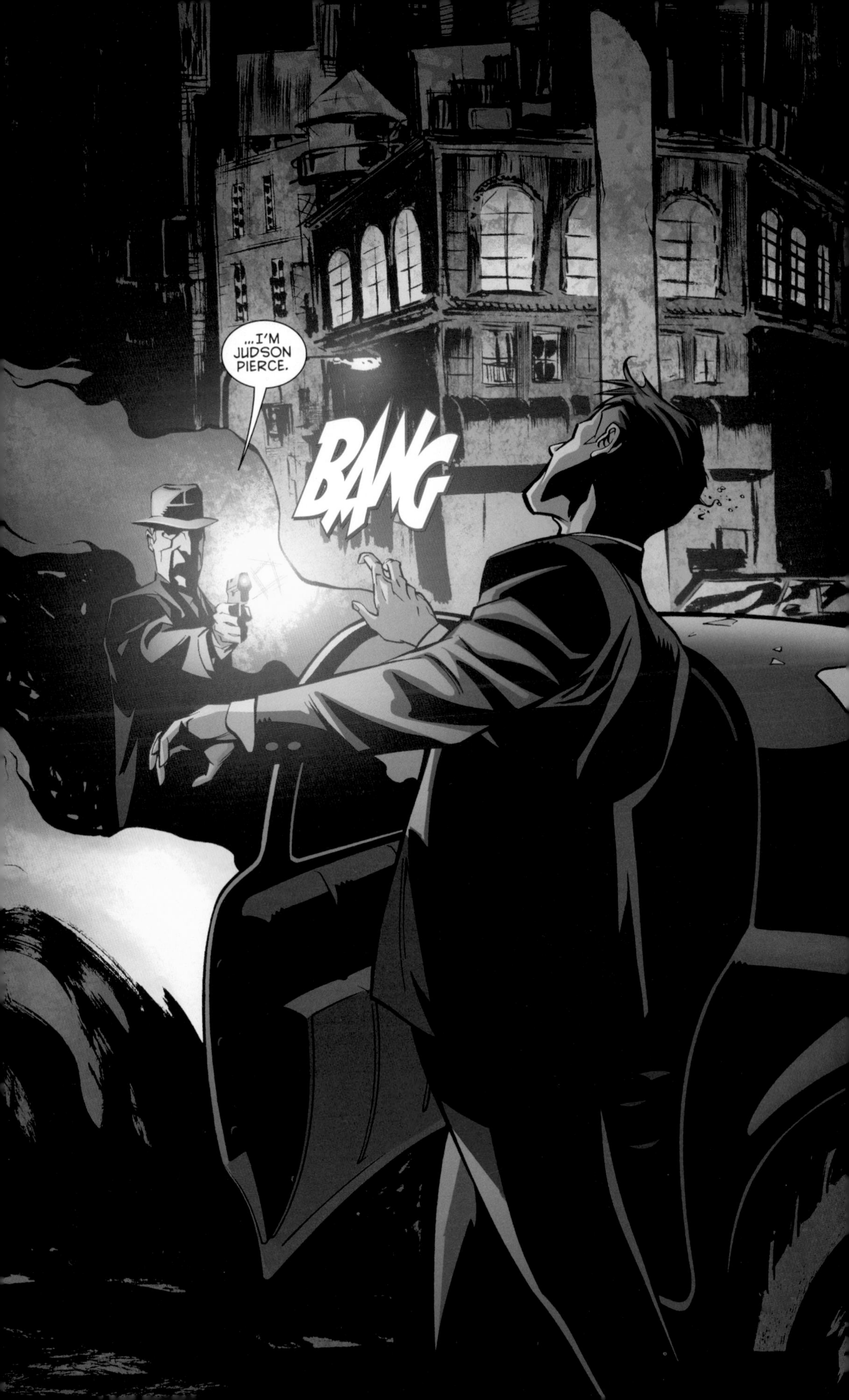
...I'M JUDSON PIERCE.
BANG

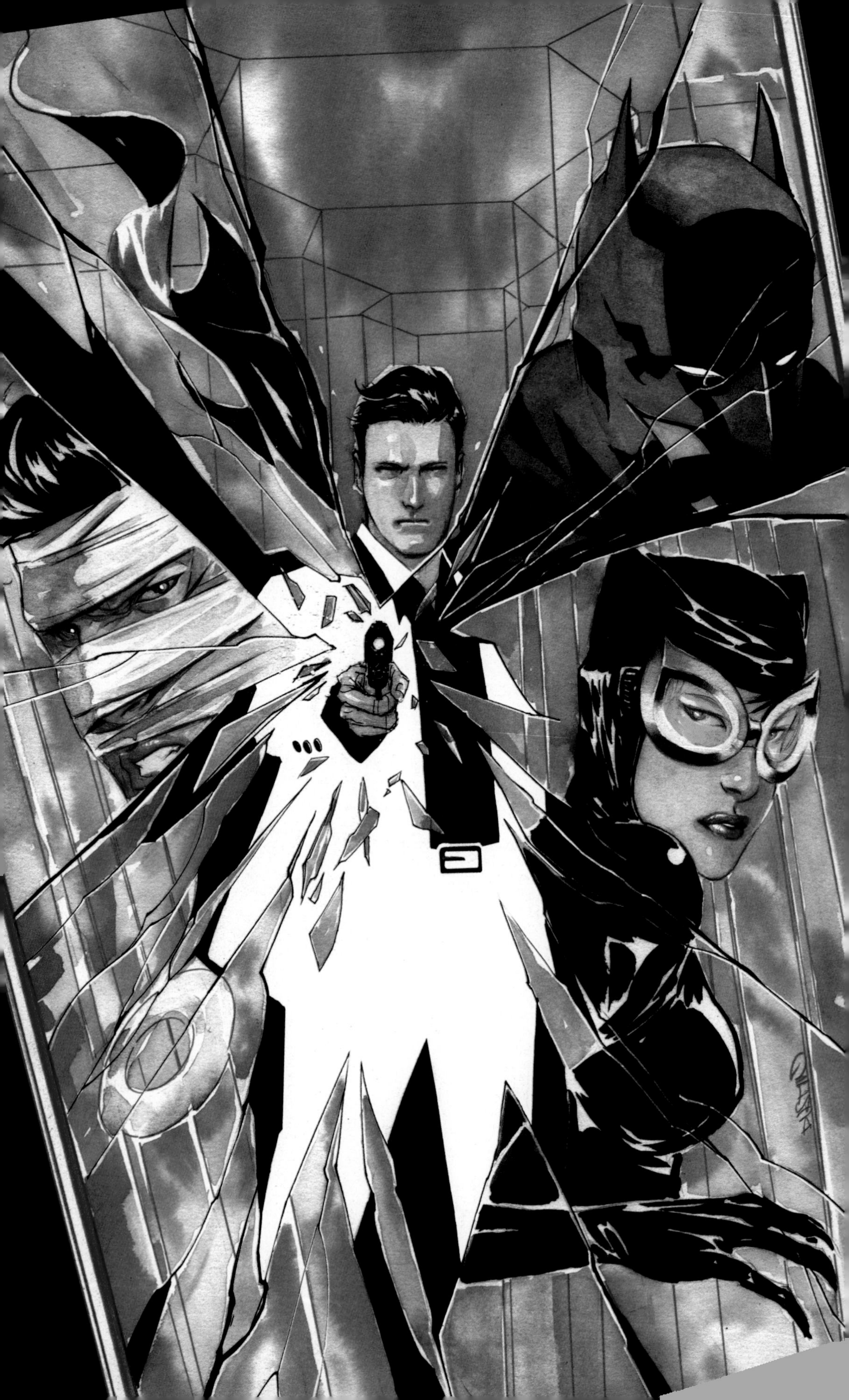

"You Waynes are hard to kill, I'll say that much for you."

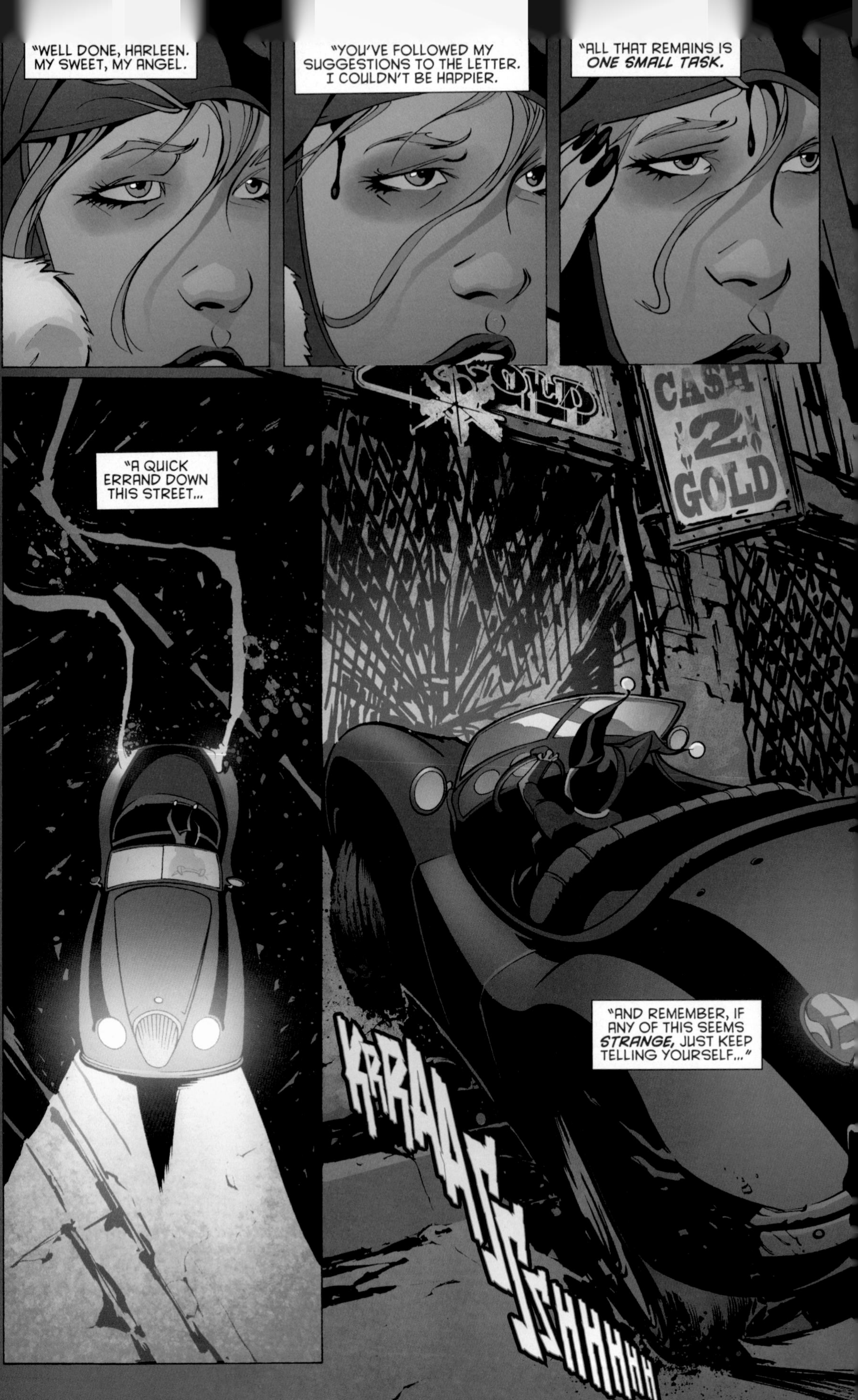
"WELL DONE, HARLEEN. MY SWEET, MY ANGEL.
"YOU'VE FOLLOWED MY SUGGESTIONS TO THE LETTER. I COULDN'T BE HAPPIER.
"ALL THAT REMAINS IS *ONE SMALL TASK.*
"A QUICK ERRAND DOWN THIS STREET...
CASH 2 GOLD
GOLD
"AND REMEMBER, IF ANY OF THIS SEEMS *STRANGE,* JUST KEEP TELLING YOURSELF..."
KRRAAASSHHHHHH

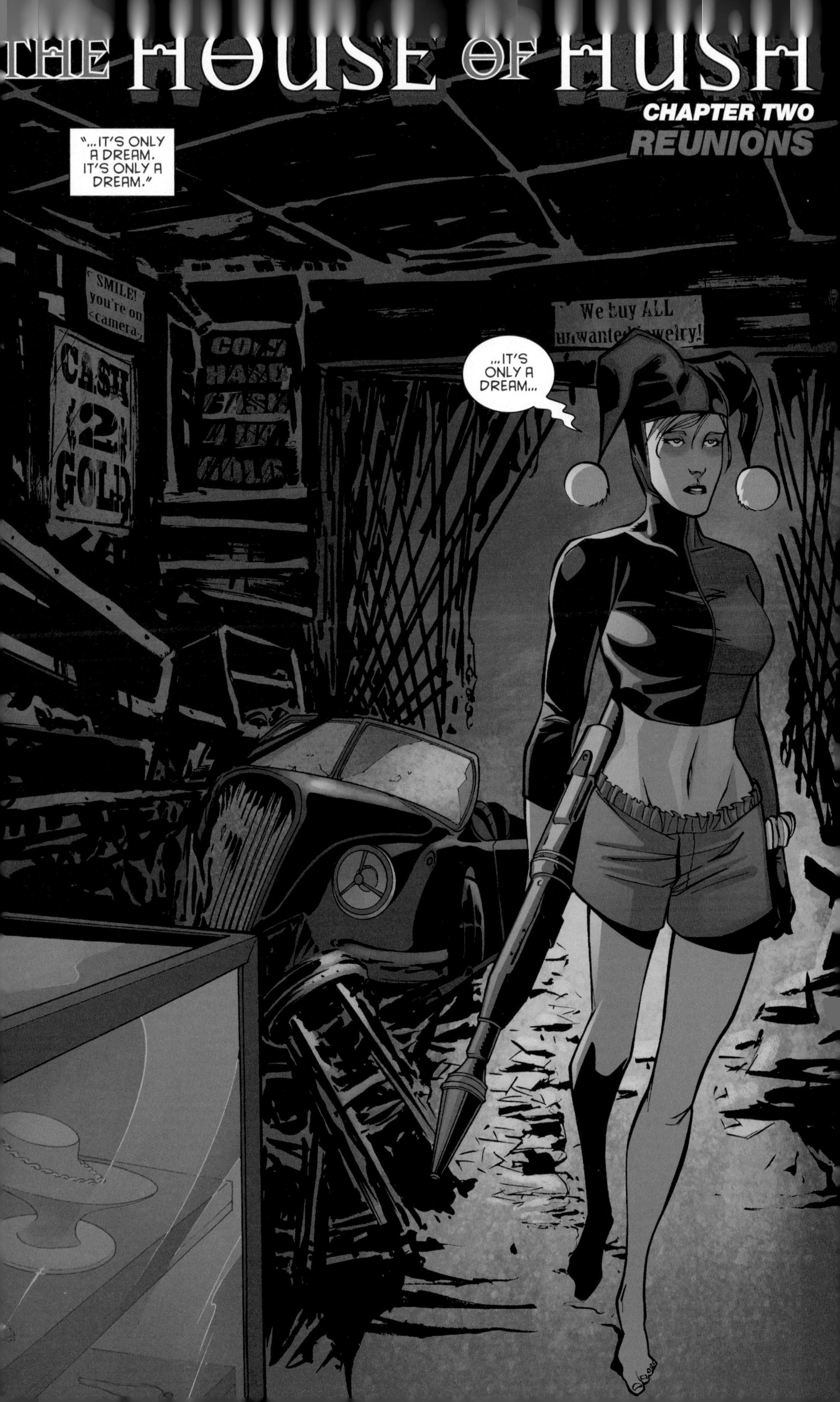
THE HOUSE OF HUSH
CHAPTER TWO
REUNIONS
"...IT'S ONLY A DREAM. IT'S ONLY A DREAM."
SMILE! you're on camera.
CASH 2 GOLD
We buy ALL
...IT'S ONLY A DREAM...

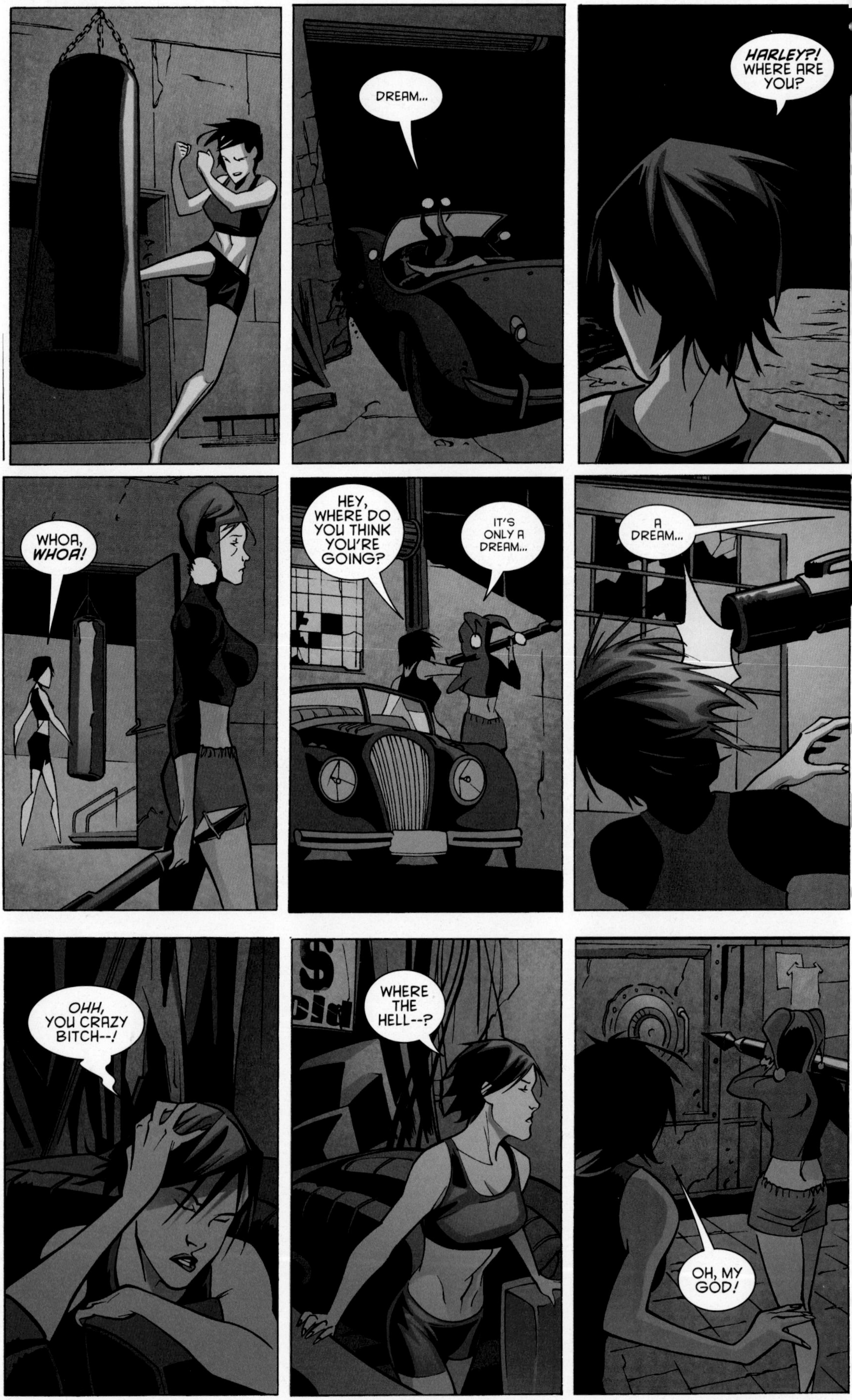
DREAM...
HARLEY?! WHERE ARE YOU?
WHOA, WHOA!
HEY, WHERE DO YOU THINK YOU'RE GOING?
IT'S ONLY A DREAM...
A DREAM...
OHH, YOU CRAZY BITCH--!
WHERE THE HELL--?
OH, MY GOD!

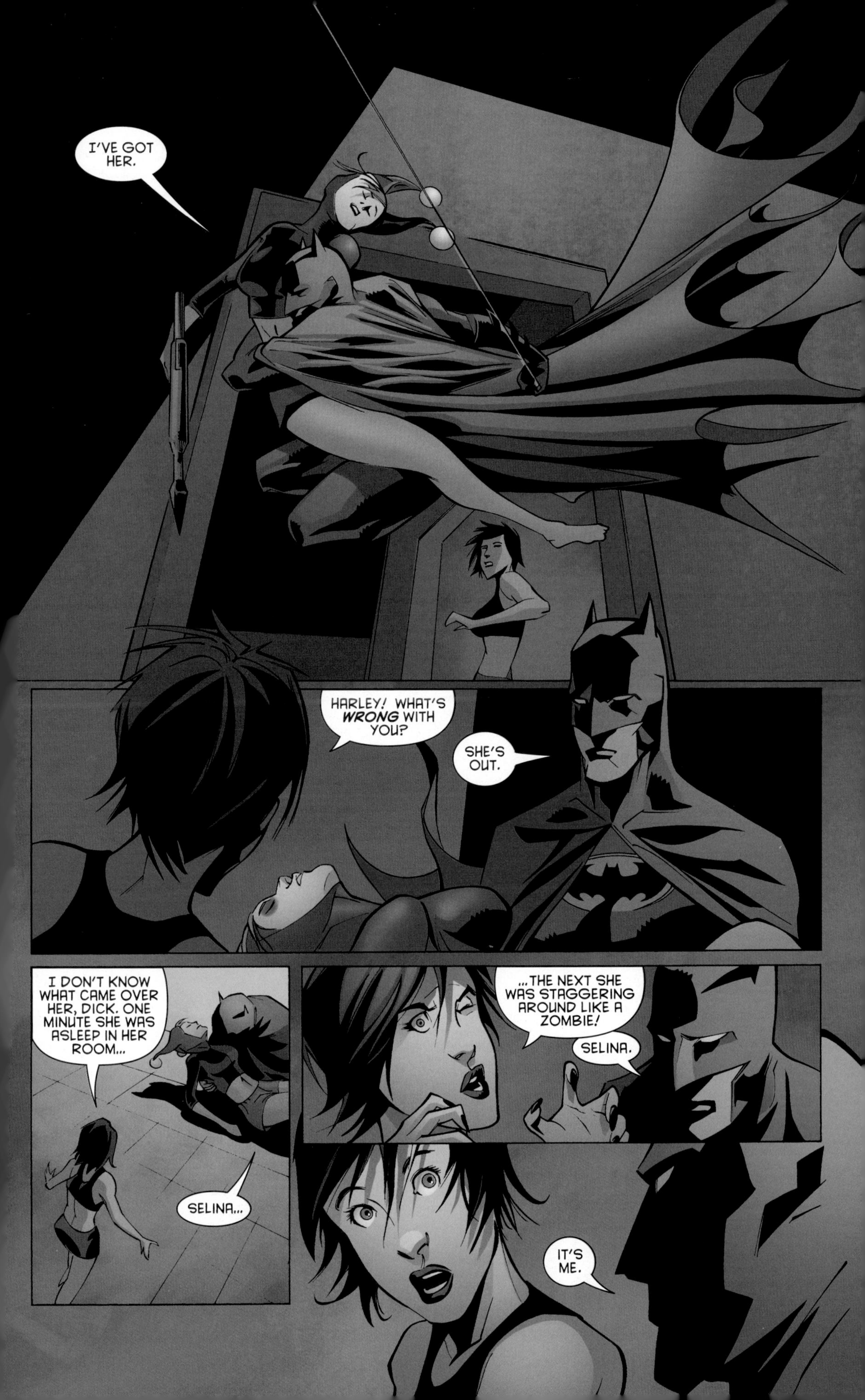
I'VE GOT HER.
HARLEY! WHAT'S *WRONG* WITH YOU?
SHE'S OUT.
I DON'T KNOW WHAT CAME OVER HER, DICK. ONE MINUTE SHE WAS ASLEEP IN HER ROOM...
SELINA...
...THE NEXT SHE WAS STAGGERING AROUND LIKE A ZOMBIE!
SELINA.
IT'S ME.

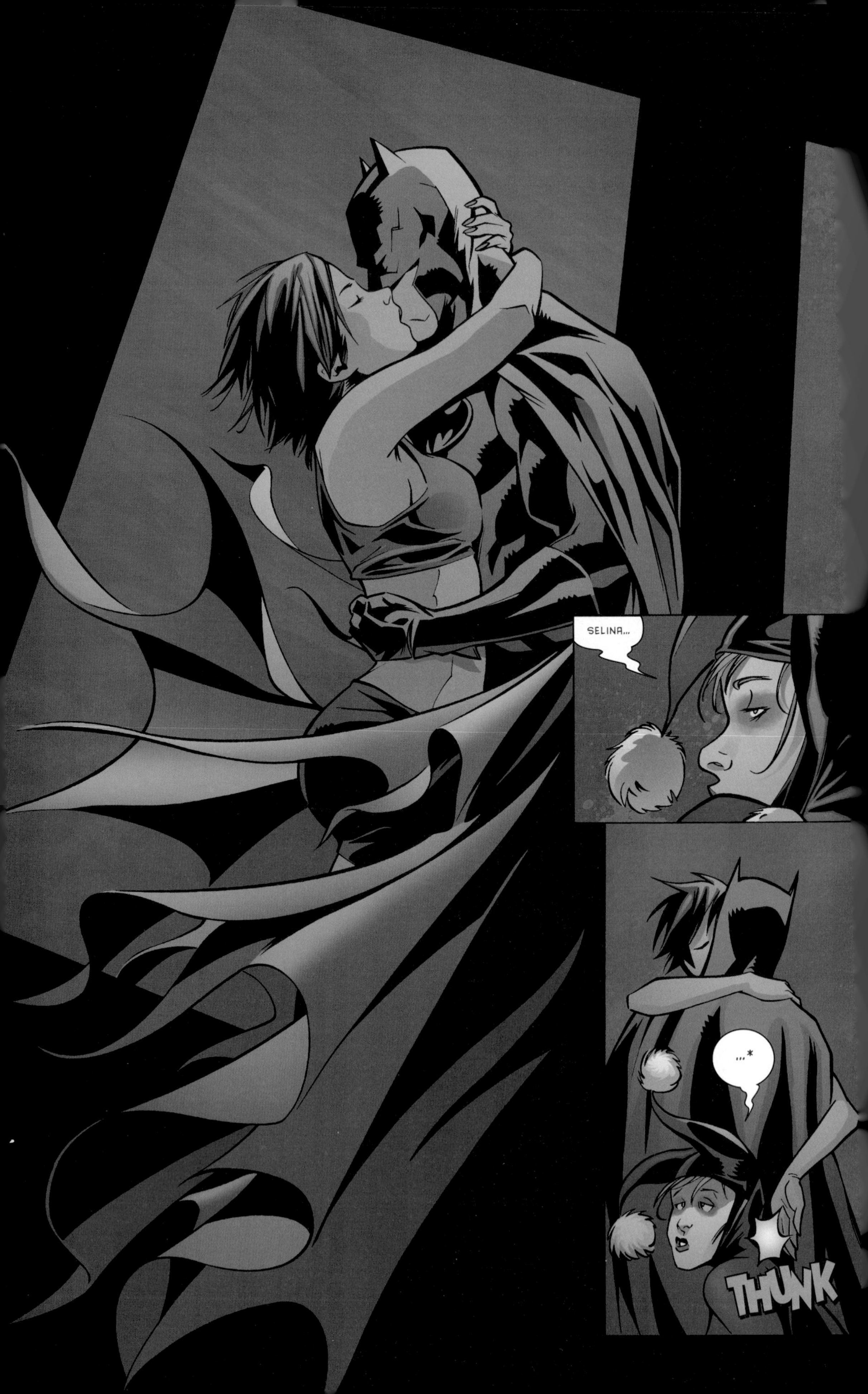
SELINA...
...*
THUNK

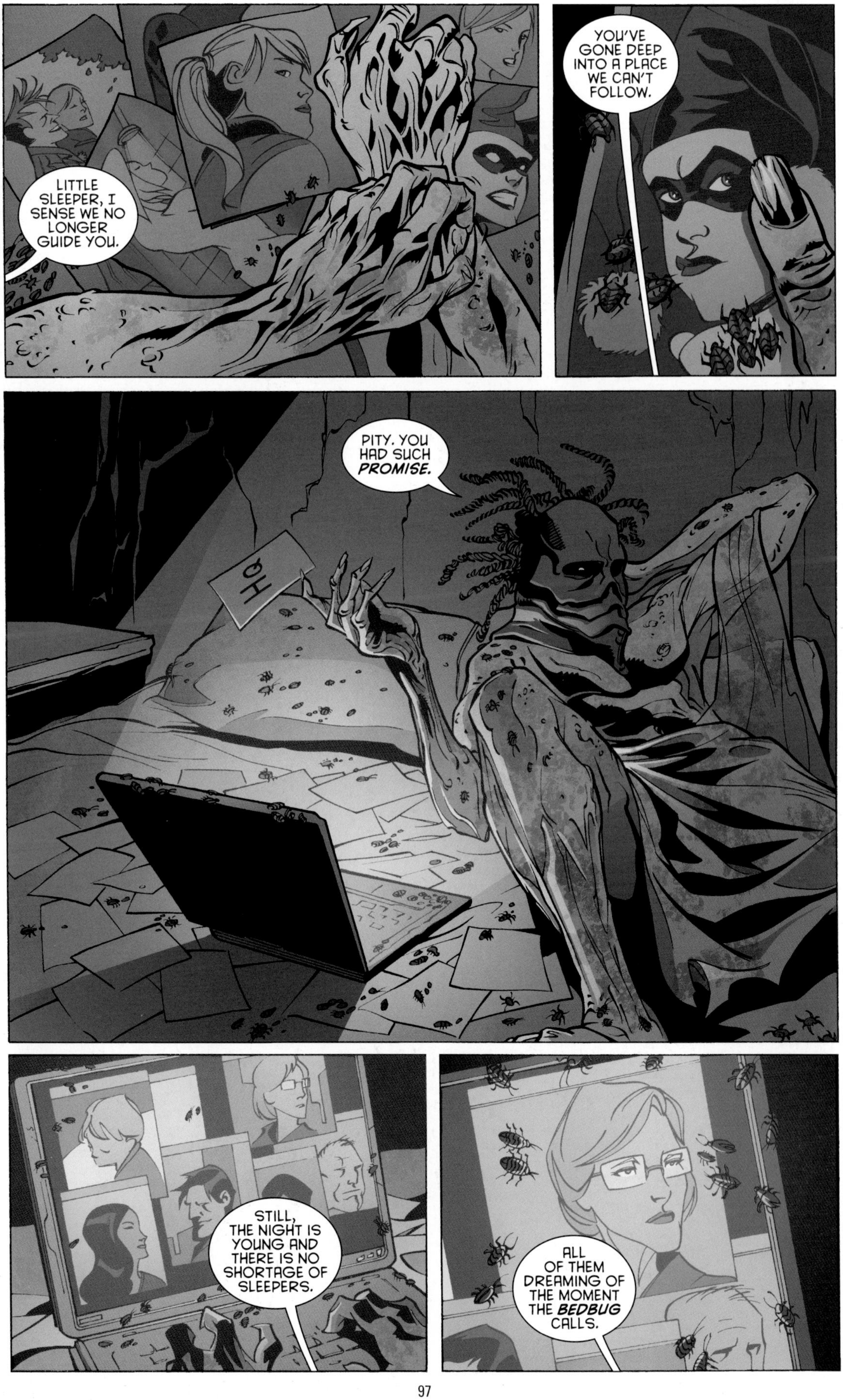
LITTLE SLEEPER, I SENSE WE NO LONGER GUIDE YOU.
YOU'VE GONE DEEP INTO A PLACE WE CAN'T FOLLOW.
PITY. YOU HAD SUCH PROMISE.
STILL, THE NIGHT IS YOUNG AND THERE IS NO SHORTAGE OF SLEEPERS.
ALL OF THEM DREAMING OF THE MOMENT THE BEDBUG CALLS.

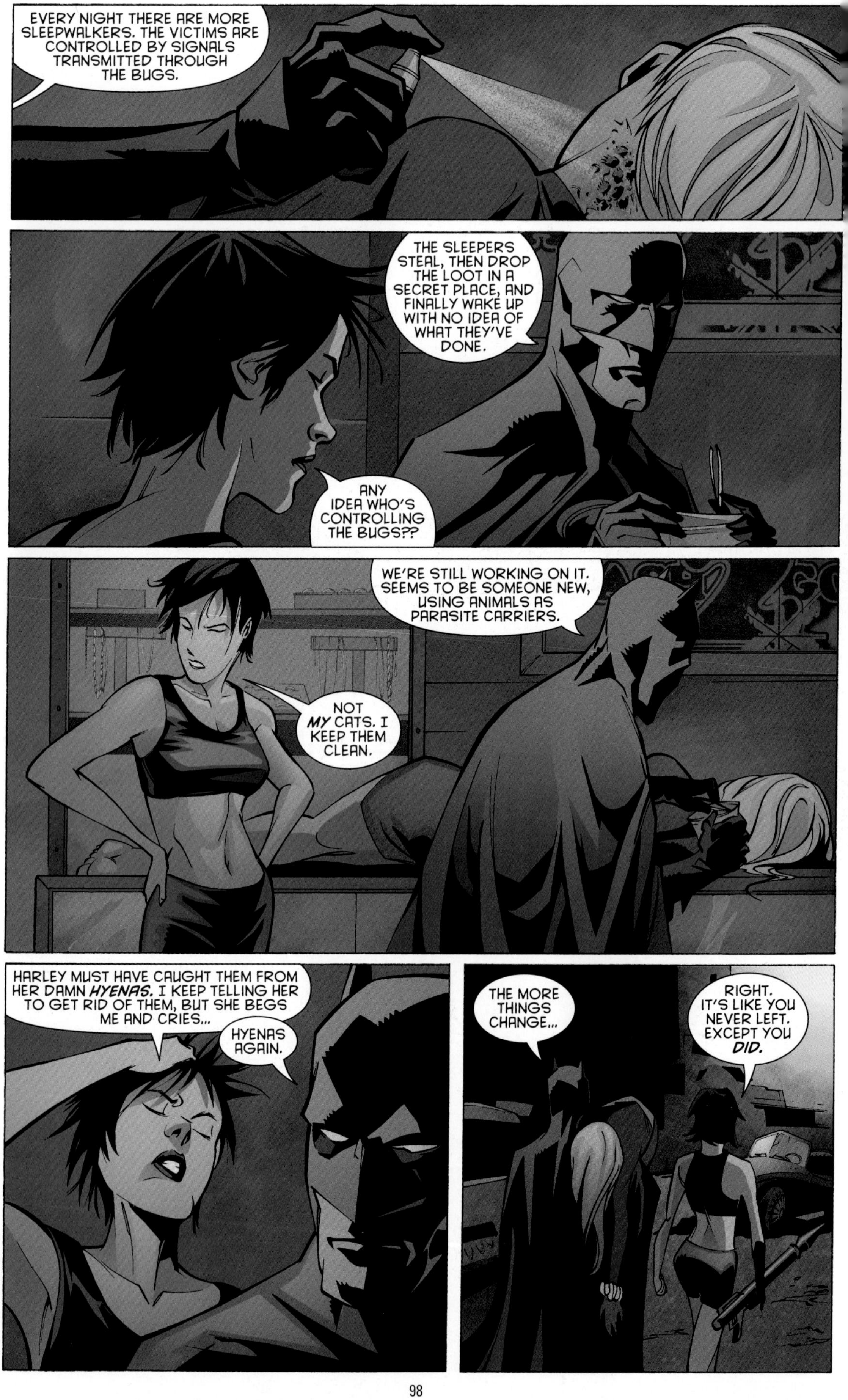
EVERY NIGHT THERE ARE MORE SLEEPWALKERS. THE VICTIMS ARE CONTROLLED BY SIGNALS TRANSMITTED THROUGH THE BUGS.
THE SLEEPERS STEAL, THEN DROP THE LOOT IN A SECRET PLACE, AND FINALLY WAKE UP WITH NO IDEA OF WHAT THEY'VE DONE.
ANY IDEA WHO'S CONTROLLING THE BUGS??
WE'RE STILL WORKING ON IT. SEEMS TO BE SOMEONE NEW, USING ANIMALS AS PARASITE CARRIERS.
NOT *MY* CATS. I KEEP THEM CLEAN.
HARLEY MUST HAVE CAUGHT THEM FROM HER DAMN *HYENAS.* I KEEP TELLING HER TO GET RID OF THEM, BUT SHE BEGS ME AND CRIES...
HYENAS AGAIN.
THE MORE THINGS CHANGE...
RIGHT. IT'S LIKE YOU NEVER LEFT. EXCEPT YOU *DID.*

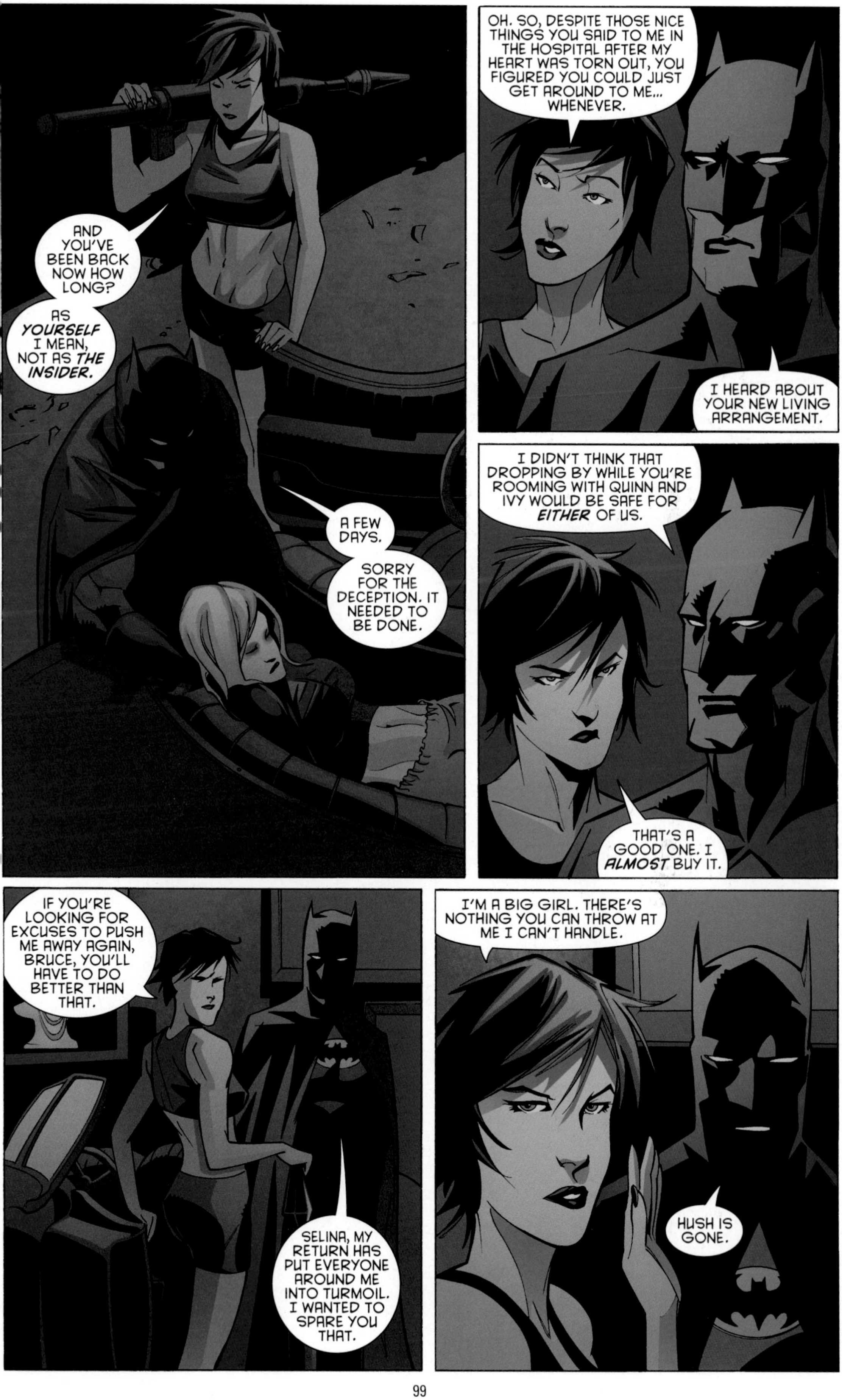
AND YOU'VE BEEN BACK NOW HOW LONG?
AS *YOURSELF* I MEAN, NOT AS *THE INSIDER.*
A FEW DAYS.
SORRY FOR THE DECEPTION. IT NEEDED TO BE DONE.
OH. SO, DESPITE THOSE NICE THINGS YOU SAID TO ME IN THE HOSPITAL AFTER MY HEART WAS TORN OUT, YOU FIGURED YOU COULD JUST GET AROUND TO ME... WHENEVER.
I HEARD ABOUT YOUR NEW LIVING ARRANGEMENT.
I DIDN'T THINK THAT DROPPING BY WHILE YOU'RE ROOMING WITH QUINN AND IVY WOULD BE SAFE FOR *EITHER* OF US.
THAT'S A GOOD ONE. I *ALMOST* BUY IT.
IF YOU'RE LOOKING FOR EXCUSES TO PUSH ME AWAY AGAIN, BRUCE, YOU'LL HAVE TO DO BETTER THAN THAT.
SELINA, MY RETURN HAS PUT EVERYONE AROUND ME INTO TURMOIL. I WANTED TO SPARE YOU THAT.
I'M A BIG GIRL. THERE'S NOTHING YOU CAN THROW AT ME I CAN'T HANDLE.
HUSH IS GONE.

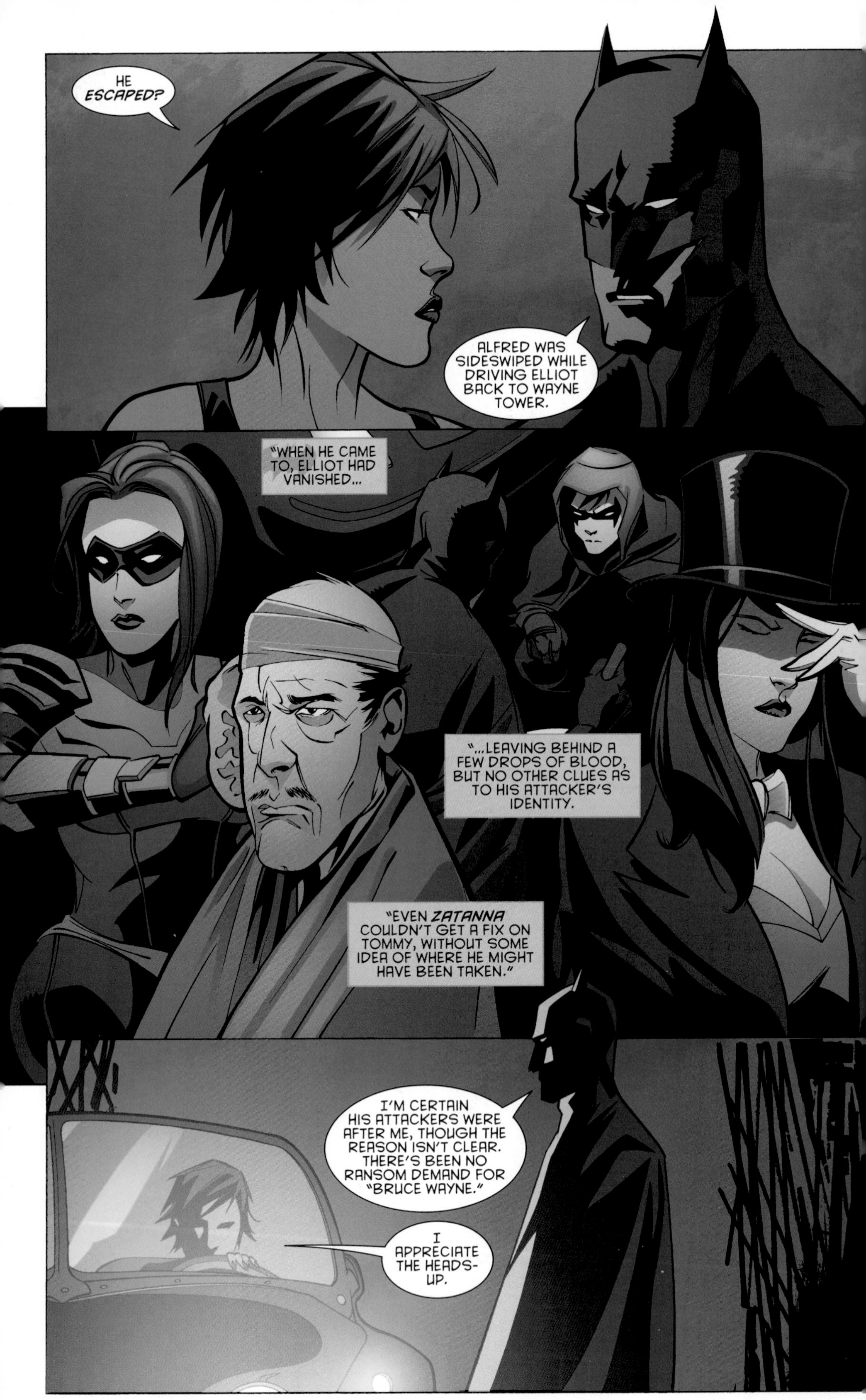
HE ESCAPED?
ALFRED WAS SIDESWIPED WHILE DRIVING ELLIOT BACK TO WAYNE TOWER.
"WHEN HE CAME TO, ELLIOT HAD VANISHED...
"...LEAVING BEHIND A FEW DROPS OF BLOOD, BUT NO OTHER CLUES AS TO HIS ATTACKER'S IDENTITY.
"EVEN ZATANNA COULDN'T GET A FIX ON TOMMY, WITHOUT SOME IDEA OF WHERE HE MIGHT HAVE BEEN TAKEN."
I'M CERTAIN HIS ATTACKERS WERE AFTER ME, THOUGH THE REASON ISN'T CLEAR. THERE'S BEEN NO RANSOM DEMAND FOR "BRUCE WAYNE."
I APPRECIATE THE HEADS-UP.

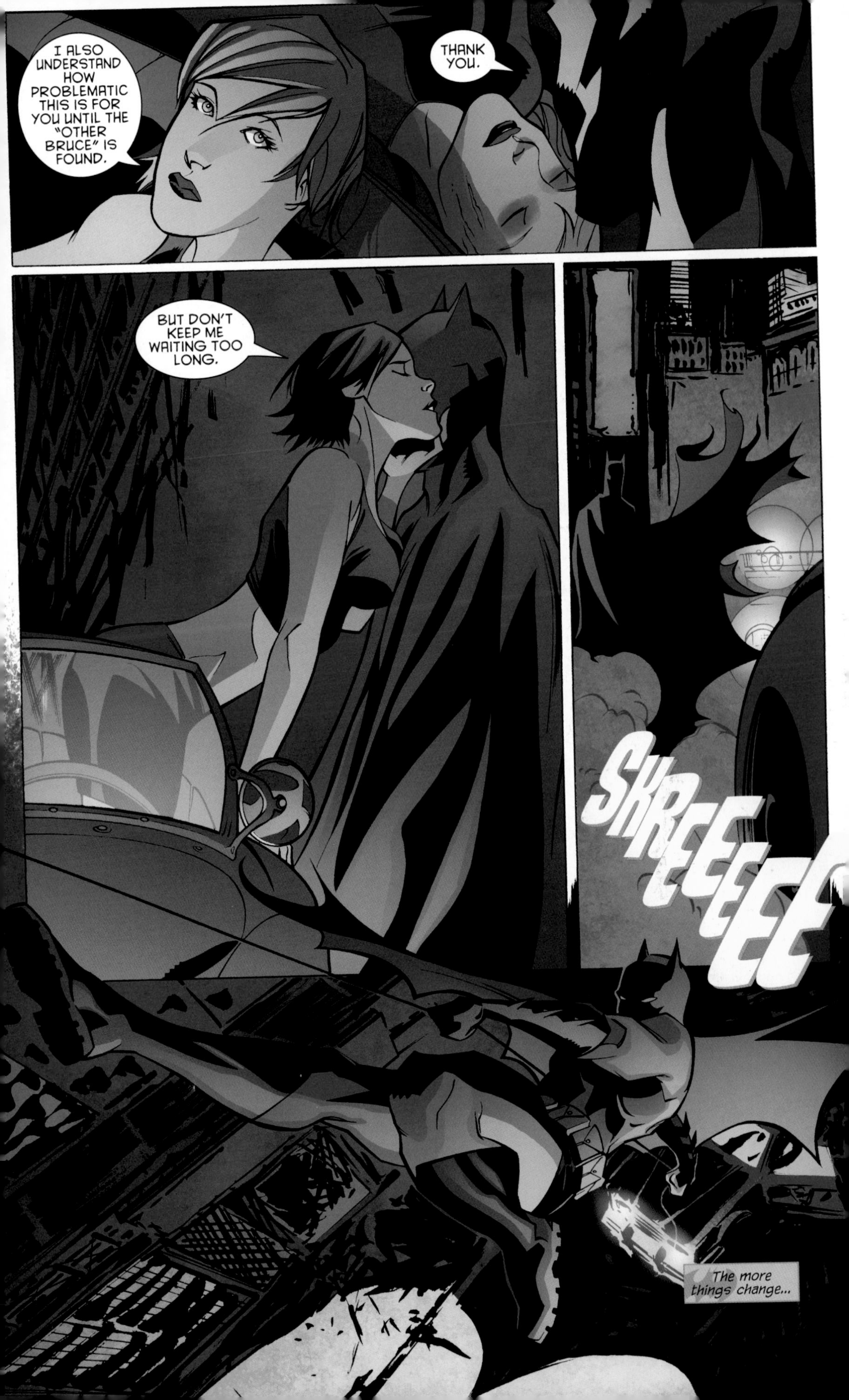
I ALSO UNDERSTAND HOW PROBLEMATIC THIS IS FOR YOU UNTIL THE "OTHER BRUCE" IS FOUND.
THANK YOU.
BUT DON'T KEEP ME WAITING TOO LONG.
SKREEEEEEE
The more things change...

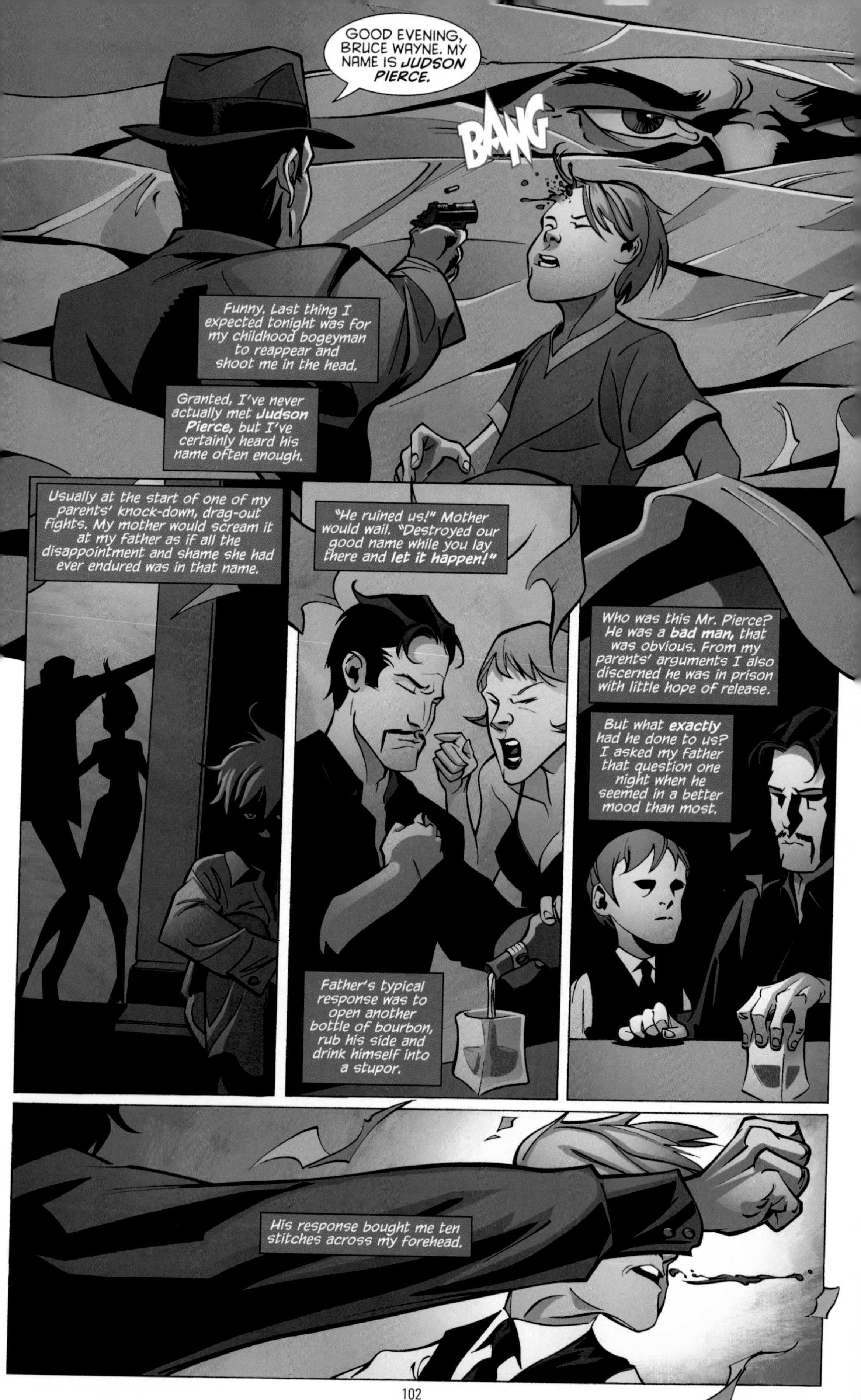
GOOD EVENING, BRUCE WAYNE. MY NAME IS JUDSON PIERCE.
BANG
Funny. Last thing I expected tonight was for my childhood bogeyman to reappear and shoot me in the head.
Granted, I've never actually met Judson Pierce, but I've certainly heard his name often enough.
Usually at the start of one of my parents' knock-down, drag-out fights. My mother would scream it at my father as if all the disappointment and shame she had ever endured was in that name.
"He ruined us!" Mother would wail. "Destroyed our good name while you lay there and let it happen!"
Father's typical response was to open another bottle of bourbon, rub his side and drink himself into a stupor.
Who was this Mr. Pierce? He was a bad man, that was obvious. From my parents' arguments I also discerned he was in prison with little hope of release.
But what exactly had he done to us? I asked my father that question one night when he seemed in a better mood than most.
His response bought me ten stitches across my forehead.

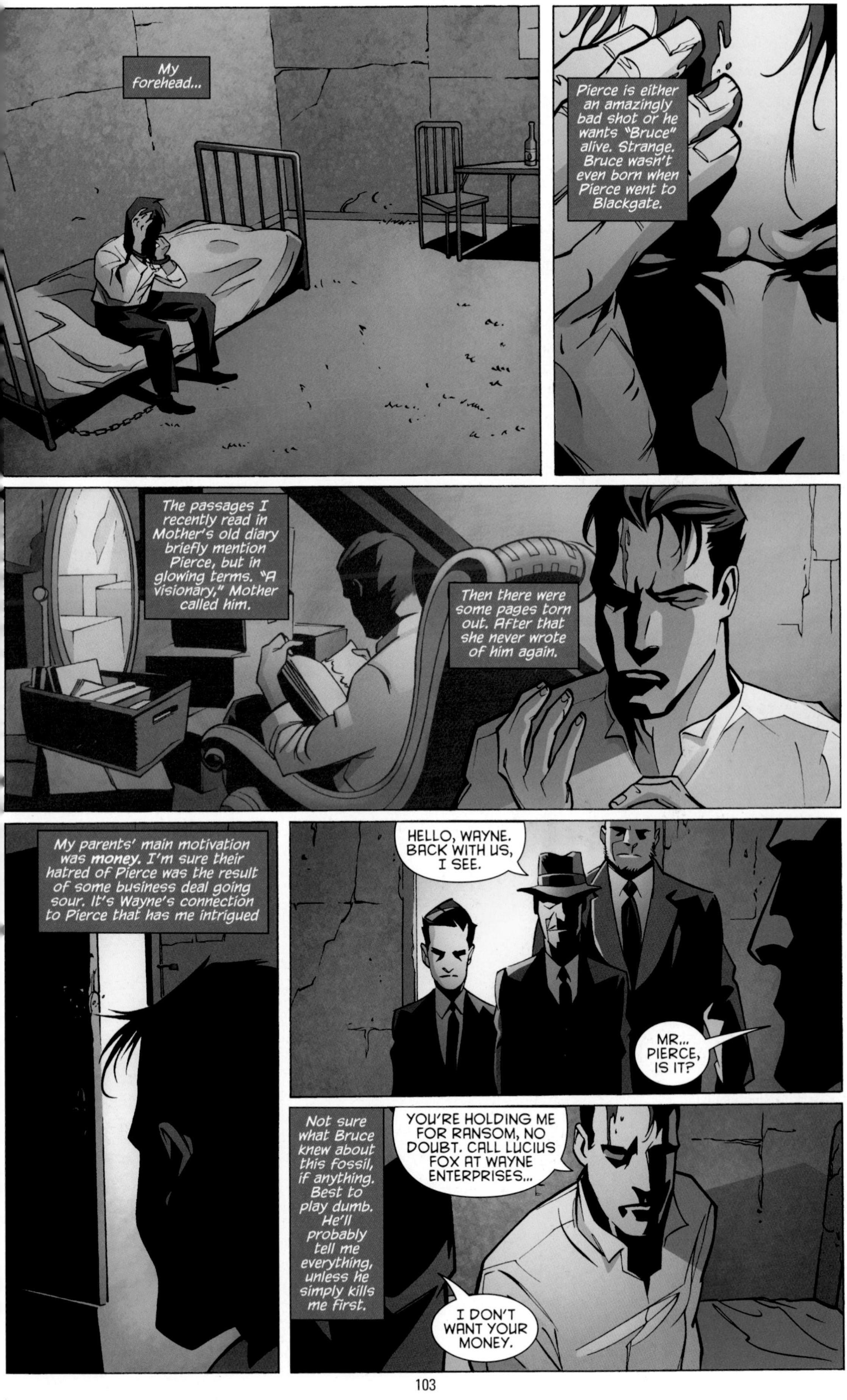

My forehead...
Pierce is either an amazingly bad shot or he wants "Bruce" alive. Strange. Bruce wasn't even born when Pierce went to Blackgate.
The passages I recently read in Mother's old diary briefly mention Pierce, but in glowing terms. "A visionary," Mother called him.
Then there were some pages torn out. After that she never wrote of him again.
My parents' main motivation was **money**. I'm sure their hatred of Pierce was the result of some business deal going sour. It's Wayne's connection to Pierce that has me intrigued
HELLO, WAYNE. BACK WITH US, I SEE.
MR... PIERCE, IS IT?
Not sure what Bruce knew about this fossil, if anything. Best to play dumb. He'll probably tell me everything, unless he simply kills me first.
YOU'RE HOLDING ME FOR RANSOM, NO DOUBT. CALL LUCIUS FOX AT WAYNE ENTERPRISES...
I DON'T WANT YOUR MONEY.

I'M AN OLD MAN. SICK. DYING WITHIN THE YEAR, OR SO THE PRISON DOCS TOLD ME.

AND THIS RELATES TO ME *HOW?*

HEY. SHOW SOME RESPECT!

YOU WANT ME TO BEAT SOME *MANNERS* INTO HIM?

NO POINT. HE AND I WON'T BE ALIVE LONG ENOUGH TO MATTER.

YOU WAYNES ARE HARD TO KILL, I'LL SAY THAT MUCH FOR YOU. YOUR FOLKS EVER MENTION ME?

I DON'T REMEMBER. THOMAS WAYNE WAS A WEALTHY MAN. MY BUTLER TOLD ME HE ATTRACTED AS MANY ENEMIES AS HE DID FRIENDS.

WELL THEN YOU DIDN'T HEAR MUCH, BECAUSE AT FIRST MY BEEF WAS WITH YOUR MA, NOT YOUR PA.

Here it comes.

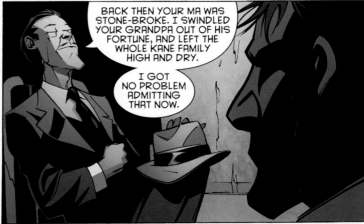

BACK THEN YOUR MA WAS STONE-BROKE. I SWINDLED YOUR GRANDPA OUT OF HIS FORTUNE, AND LEFT THE WHOLE KANE FAMILY HIGH AND DRY.

I GOT NO PROBLEM ADMITTING THAT NOW.

YOU'RE ALL CLASS, PIERCE.

I FIGURED YOUR MA COULD JUST SPREAD HER LEGS FOR SOME WEALTHY SAP AND BE IN THE GREEN AGAIN. THAT WORKED OUT OKAY FOR HER PAL, MARLA WHAT'S-ER-NAME.

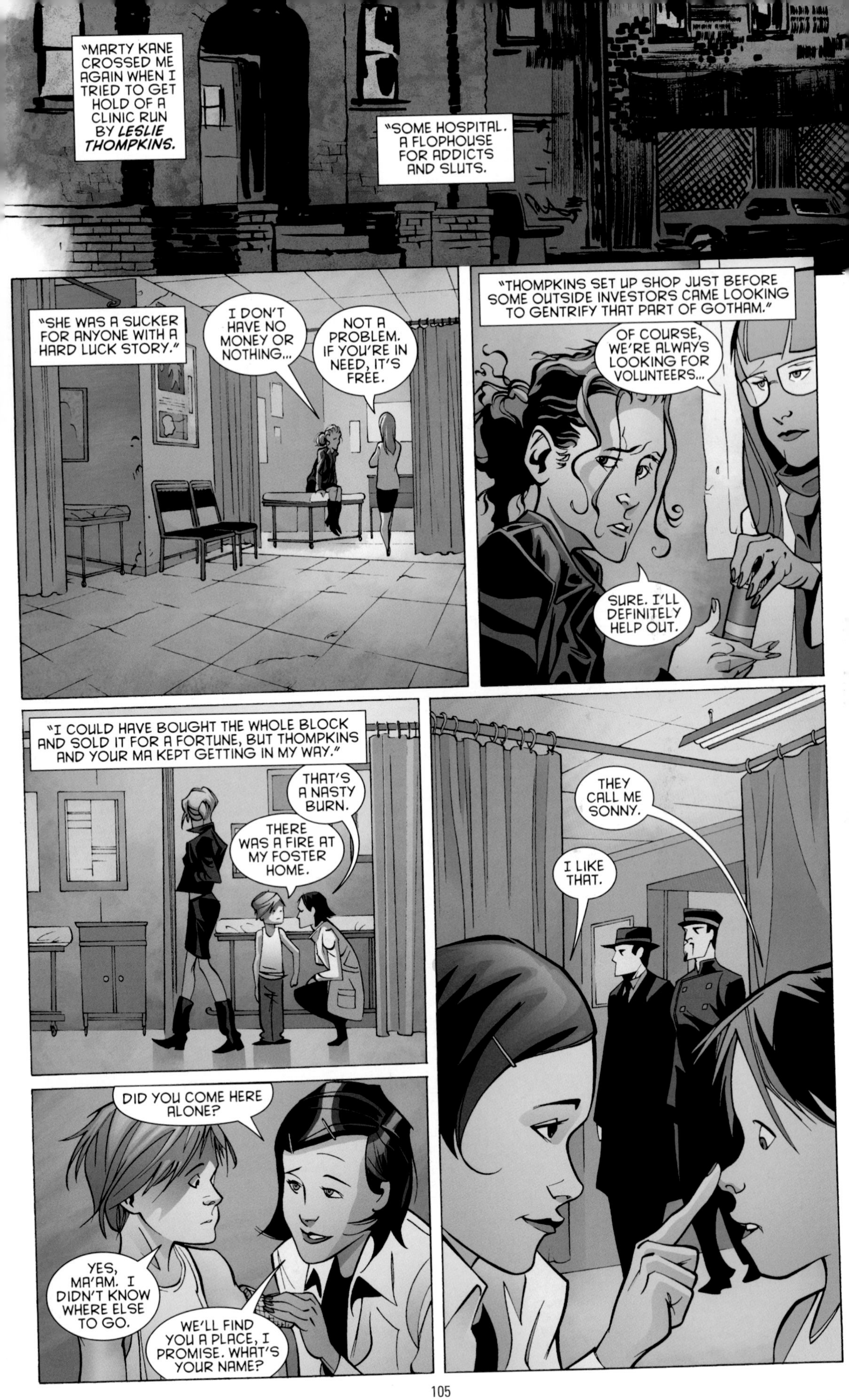
"MARTY KANE CROSSED ME AGAIN WHEN I TRIED TO GET HOLD OF A CLINIC RUN BY LESLIE THOMPKINS.
"SOME HOSPITAL. A FLOPHOUSE FOR ADDICTS AND SLUTS.
"SHE WAS A SUCKER FOR ANYONE WITH A HARD LUCK STORY."
I DON'T HAVE NO MONEY OR NOTHING...
NOT A PROBLEM. IF YOU'RE IN NEED, IT'S FREE.
"THOMPKINS SET UP SHOP JUST BEFORE SOME OUTSIDE INVESTORS CAME LOOKING TO GENTRIFY THAT PART OF GOTHAM."
OF COURSE, WE'RE ALWAYS LOOKING FOR VOLUNTEERS...
SURE. I'LL DEFINITELY HELP OUT.
"I COULD HAVE BOUGHT THE WHOLE BLOCK AND SOLD IT FOR A FORTUNE, BUT THOMPKINS AND YOUR MA KEPT GETTING IN MY WAY."
THAT'S A NASTY BURN.
THERE WAS A FIRE AT MY FOSTER HOME.
DID YOU COME HERE ALONE?
YES, MA'AM. I DIDN'T KNOW WHERE ELSE TO GO.
WE'LL FIND YOU A PLACE, I PROMISE. WHAT'S YOUR NAME?
THEY CALL ME SONNY.
I LIKE THAT.

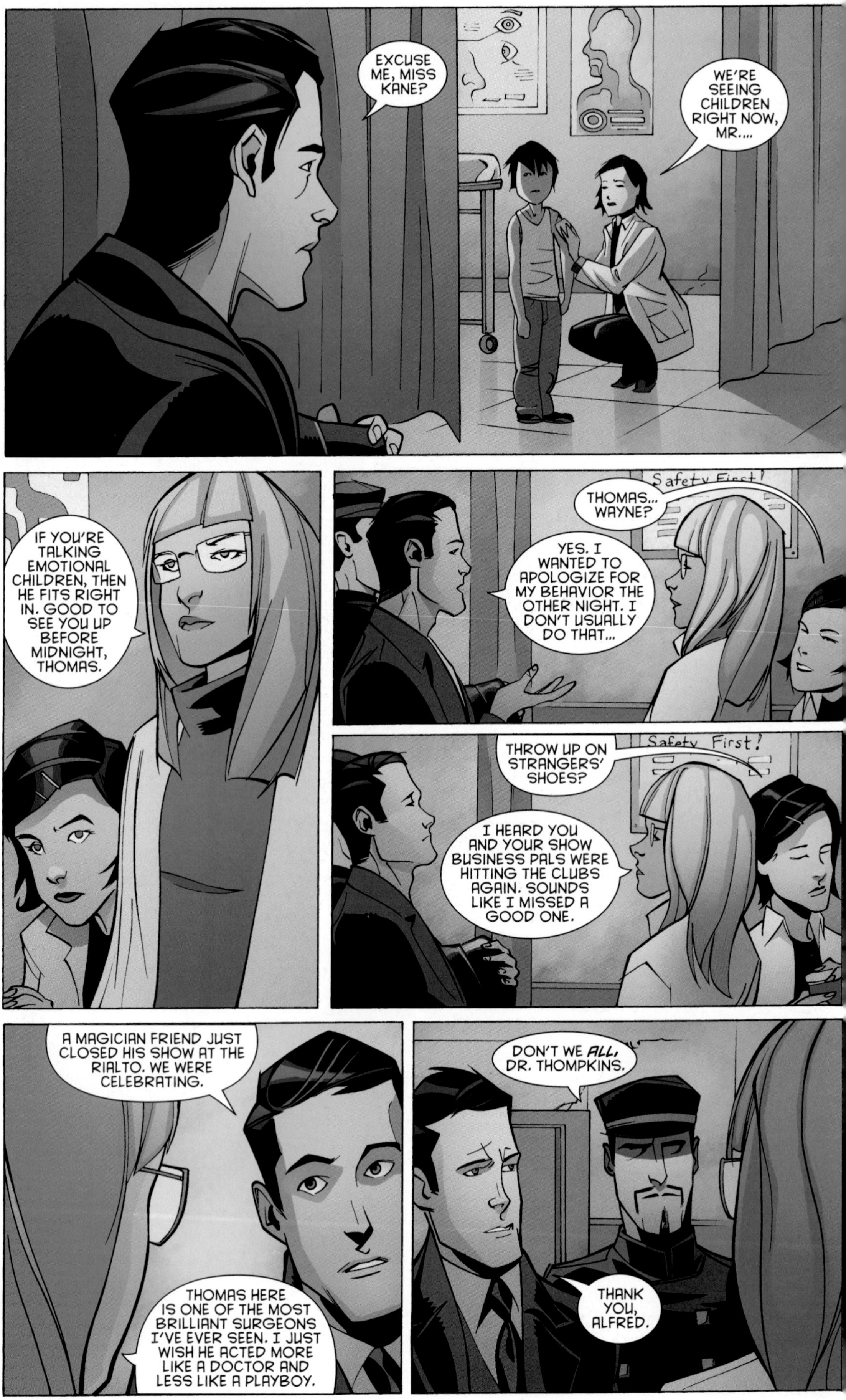
EXCUSE ME, MISS KANE?
WE'RE SEEING CHILDREN RIGHT NOW, MR....
IF YOU'RE TALKING EMOTIONAL CHILDREN, THEN HE FITS RIGHT IN. GOOD TO SEE YOU UP BEFORE MIDNIGHT, THOMAS.
Safety First!
THOMAS... WAYNE?
YES. I WANTED TO APOLOGIZE FOR MY BEHAVIOR THE OTHER NIGHT. I DON'T USUALLY DO THAT...
Safety First!
THROW UP ON STRANGERS' SHOES?
I HEARD YOU AND YOUR SHOW BUSINESS PALS WERE HITTING THE CLUBS AGAIN. SOUNDS LIKE I MISSED A GOOD ONE.
A MAGICIAN FRIEND JUST CLOSED HIS SHOW AT THE RIALTO. WE WERE CELEBRATING.
THOMAS HERE IS ONE OF THE MOST BRILLIANT SURGEONS I'VE EVER SEEN. I JUST WISH HE ACTED MORE LIKE A DOCTOR AND LESS LIKE A PLAYBOY.
DON'T WE *ALL*, DR. THOMPKINS.
THANK YOU, ALFRED.

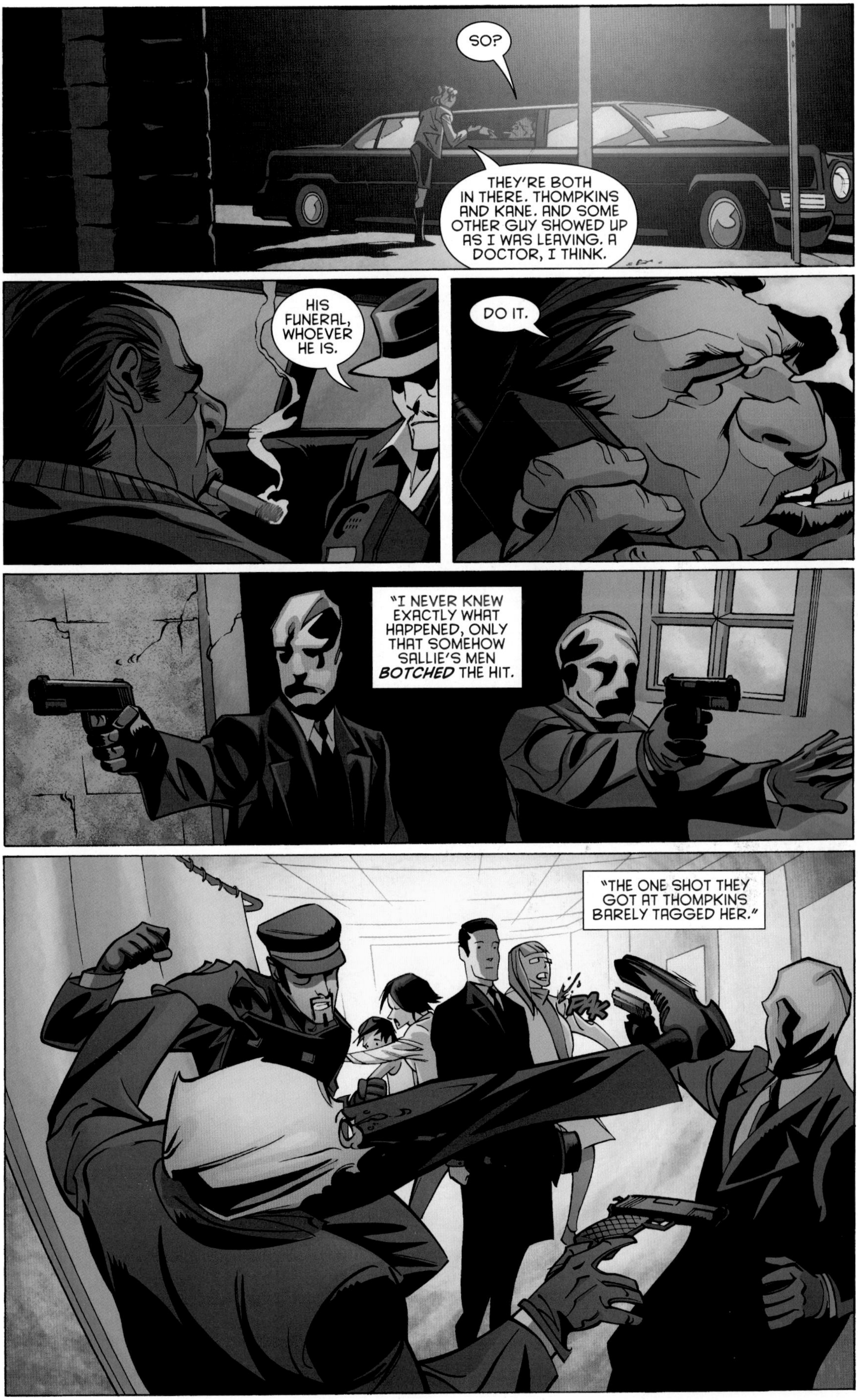
SO?
THEY'RE BOTH IN THERE. THOMPKINS AND KANE. AND SOME OTHER GUY SHOWED UP AS I WAS LEAVING. A DOCTOR, I THINK.
HIS FUNERAL, WHOEVER HE IS.
DO IT.
"I NEVER KNEW EXACTLY WHAT HAPPENED, ONLY THAT SOMEHOW SALLIE'S MEN ***BOTCHED*** THE HIT.
"THE ONE SHOT THEY GOT AT THOMPKINS BARELY TAGGED HER."

"I LATER HEARD SALLIE'S MEN WERE NEARLY BEATEN TO DEATH.

"I GUESS YOUR OLD MAN HAD MORE GUTS THAN ANYONE THOUGHT."

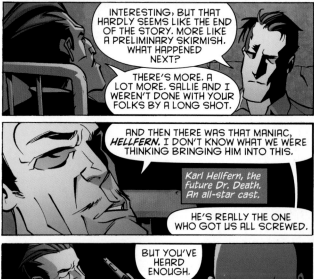

INTERESTING, BUT THAT HARDLY SEEMS LIKE THE END OF THE STORY. MORE LIKE A PRELIMINARY SKIRMISH. WHAT HAPPENED NEXT?

THERE'S MORE. A LOT MORE. SALLIE AND I WEREN'T DONE WITH YOUR FOLKS BY A LONG SHOT.

AND THEN THERE WAS THAT MANIAC, *HELLFERN.* I DON'T KNOW WHAT WE WERE THINKING BRINGING HIM INTO THIS.

Karl Hellfern, the future Dr. Death. An all-star cast.

HE'S REALLY THE ONE WHO GOT US ALL SCREWED.

BUT YOU'VE HEARD ENOUGH.

STAND HIM UP.

YOU CAN ASK YOUR QUESTIONS IN HELL.

OH, WELL. THERE'S ONE LAST LITTLE THING.

OOPS.

KKAK

108

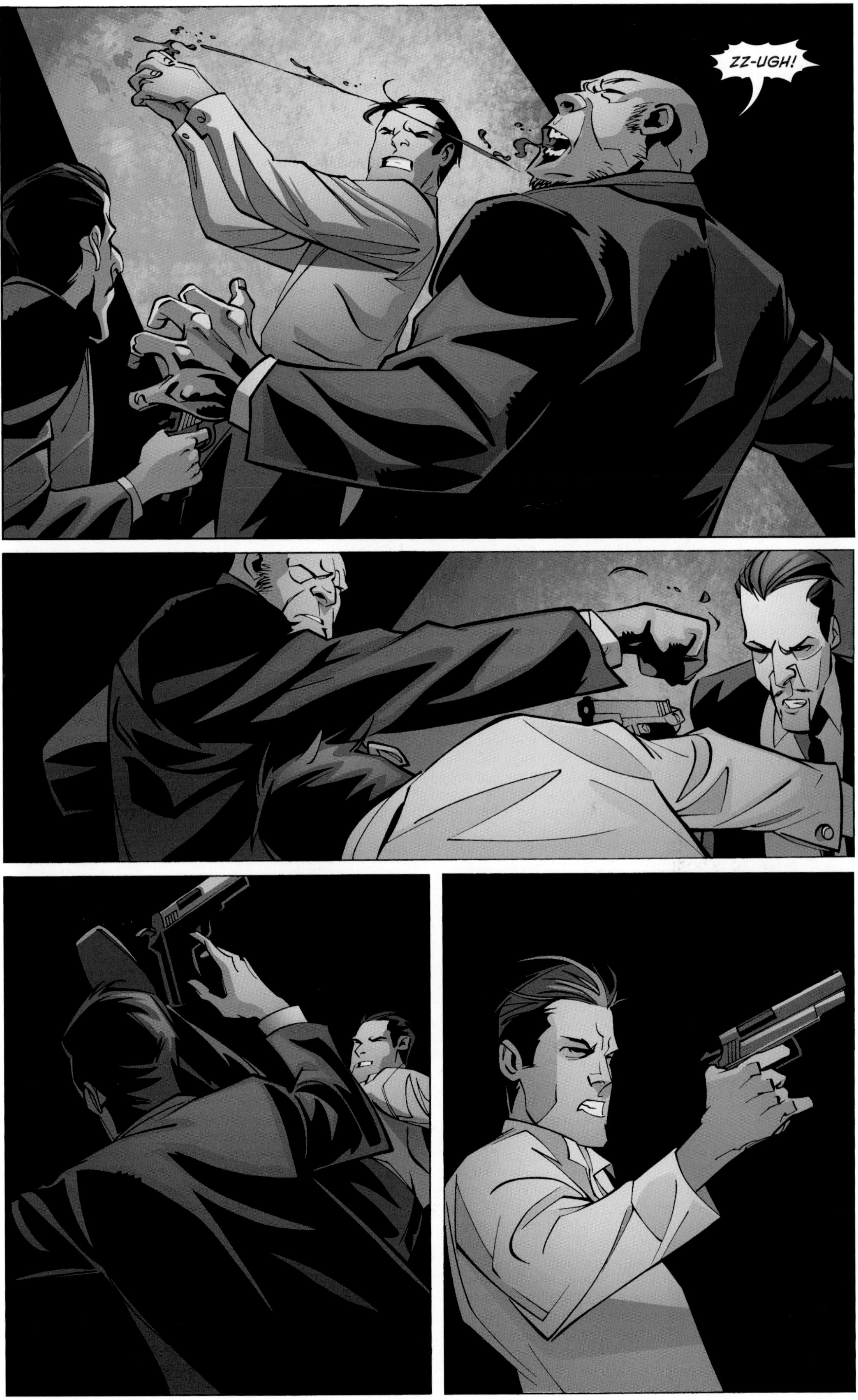
ZZ-UGH!

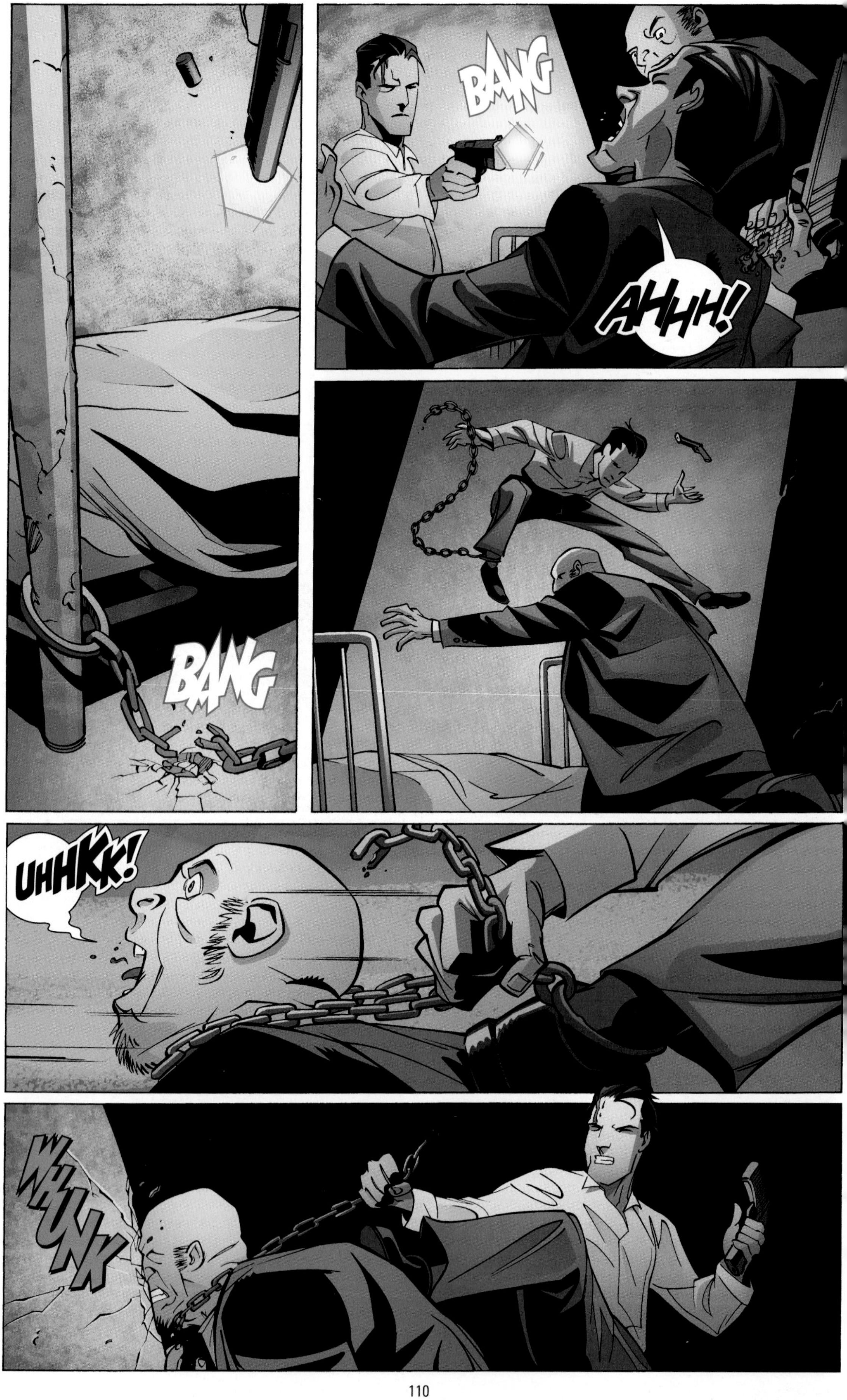
BANG
BANG
AHHH!
UHHKK!
WHUNK

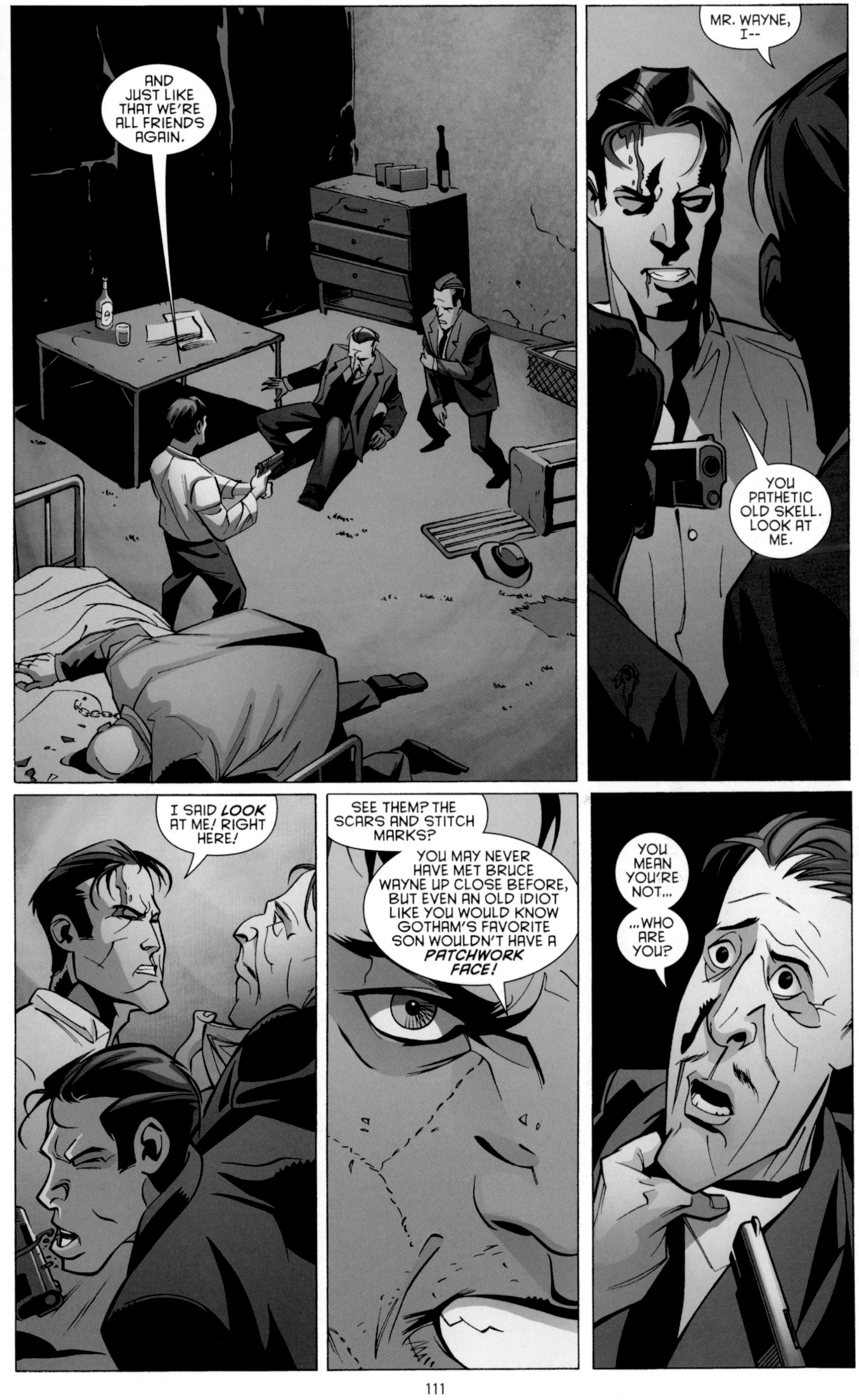
AND JUST LIKE THAT WE'RE ALL FRIENDS AGAIN.
MR. WAYNE, I--
YOU PATHETIC OLD SKELL. LOOK AT ME.
I SAID *LOOK* AT ME! RIGHT HERE!
SEE THEM? THE SCARS AND STITCH MARKS?
YOU MAY NEVER HAVE MET BRUCE WAYNE UP CLOSE BEFORE, BUT EVEN AN OLD IDIOT LIKE YOU WOULD KNOW GOTHAM'S FAVORITE SON WOULDN'T HAVE A *PATCHWORK FACE!*
YOU MEAN YOU'RE NOT...
...WHO ARE YOU?

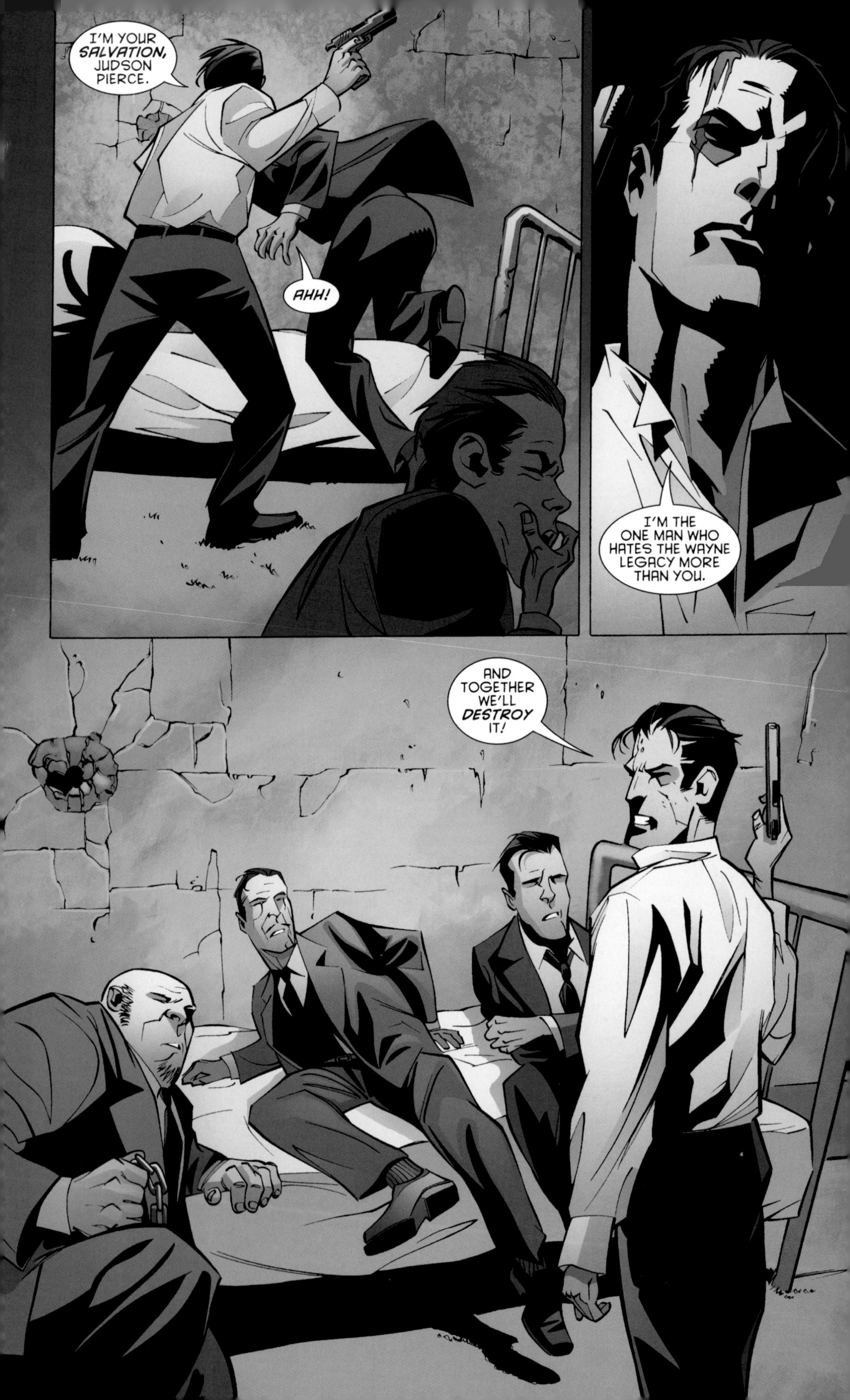
I'M YOUR SALVATION, JUDSON PIERCE.
AHH!
I'M THE ONE MAN WHO HATES THE WAYNE LEGACY MORE THAN YOU.
AND TOGETHER WE'LL DESTROY IT!

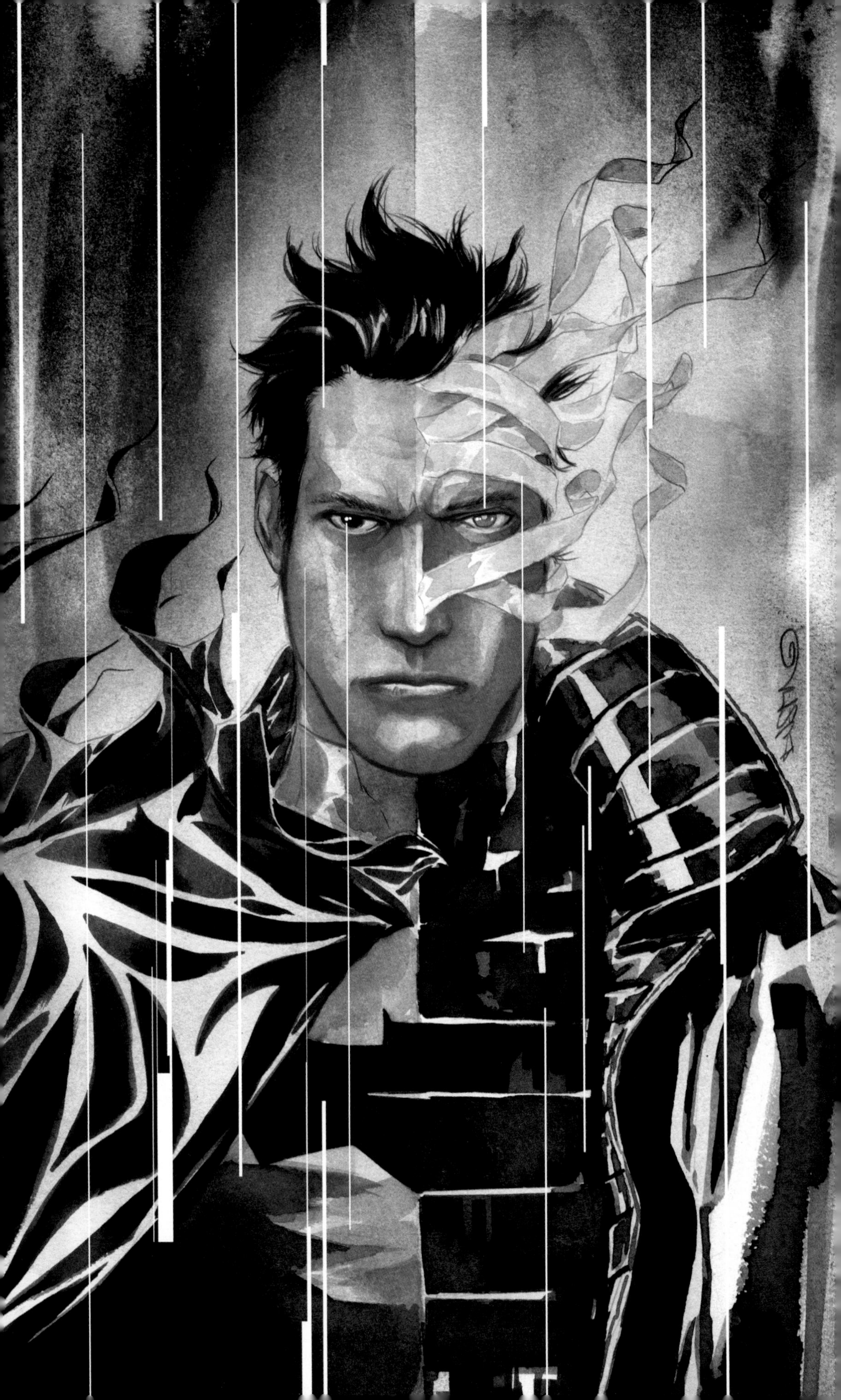

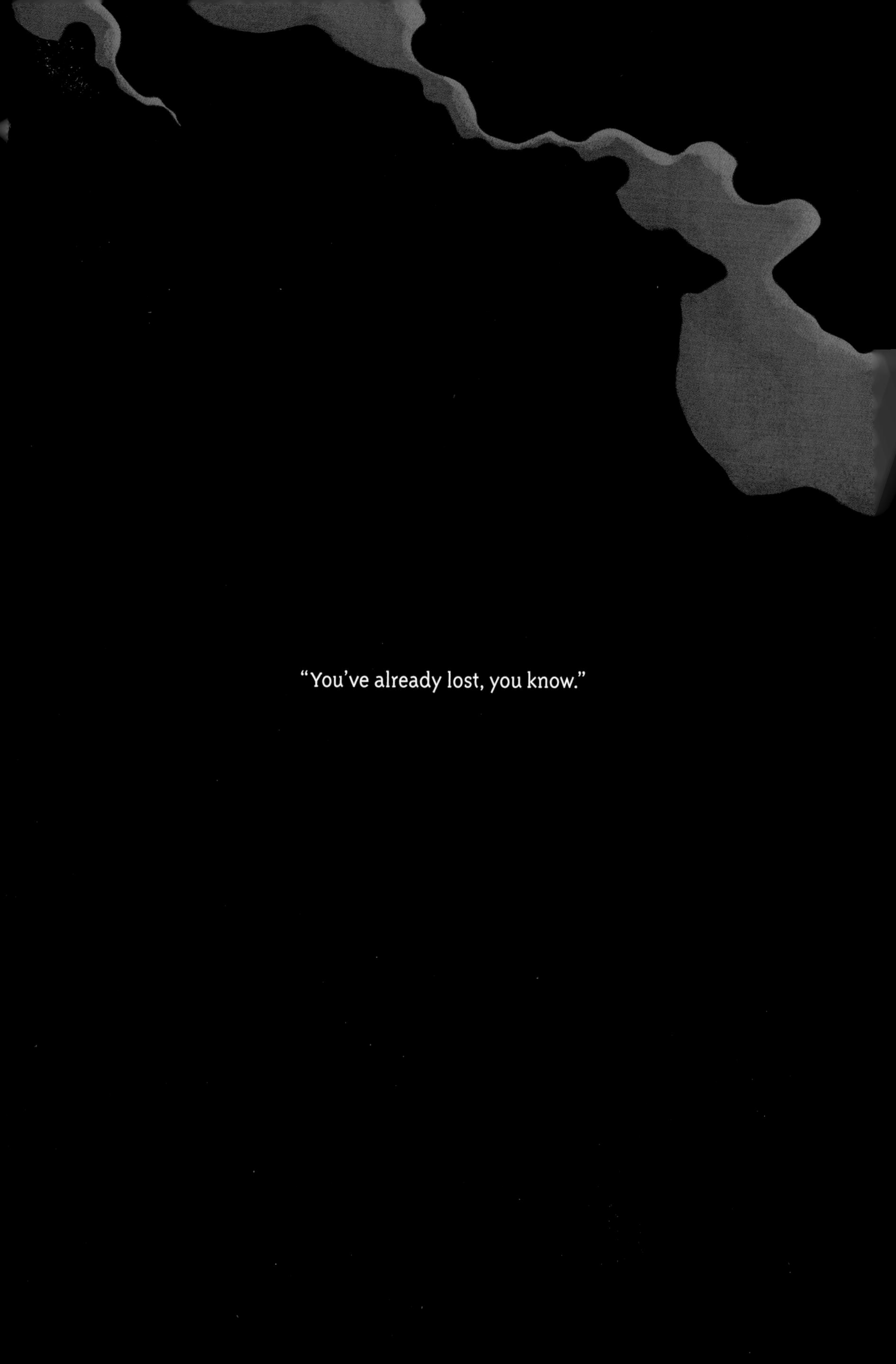
"You've already lost, you know."

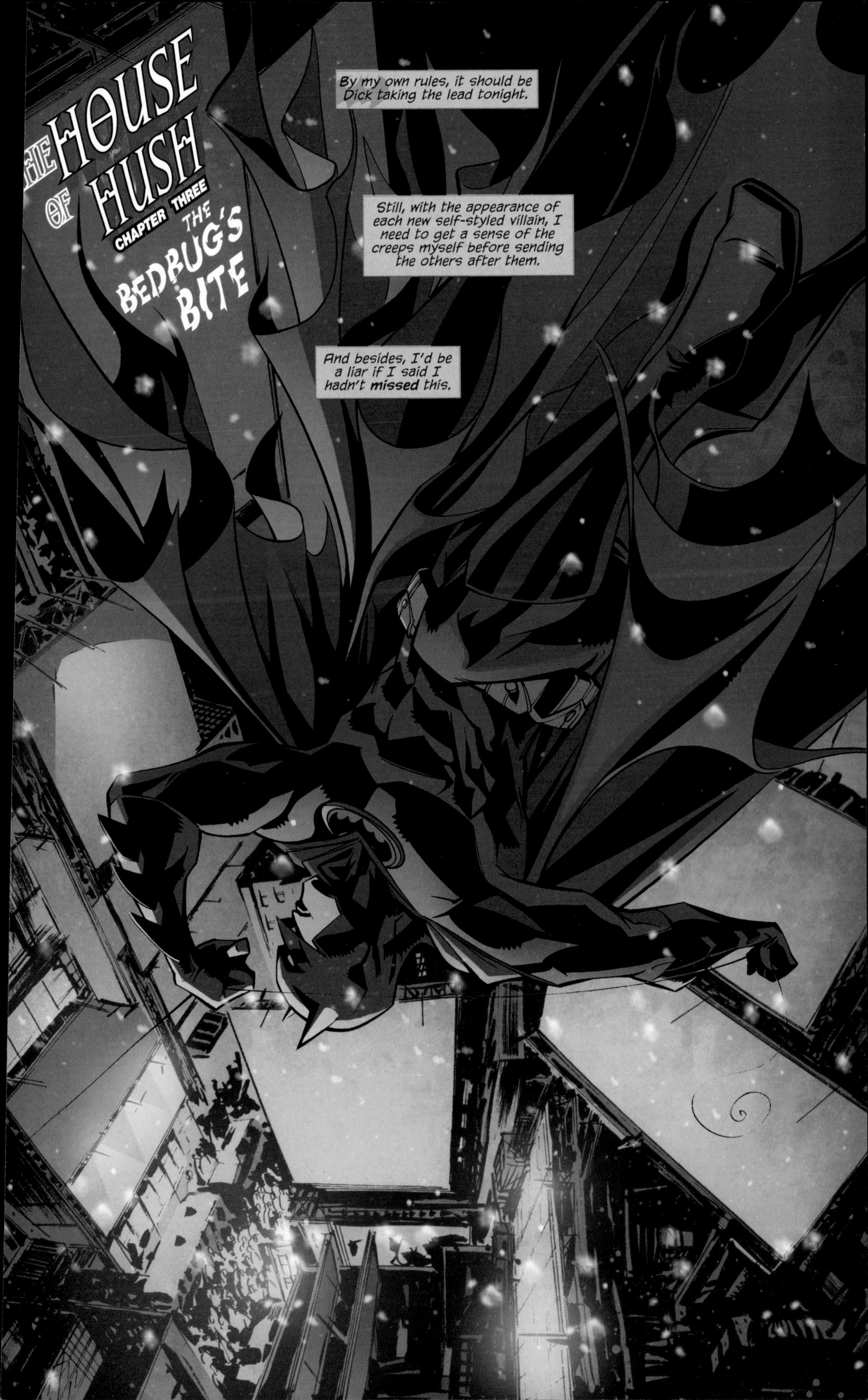
THE HOUSE OF HUSH
CHAPTER THREE
THE BEDBUG'S BITE
By my own rules, it should be Dick taking the lead tonight.
Still, with the appearance of each new self-styled villain, I need to get a sense of the creeps myself before sending the others after them.
And besides, I'd be a liar if I said I hadn't **missed** this.

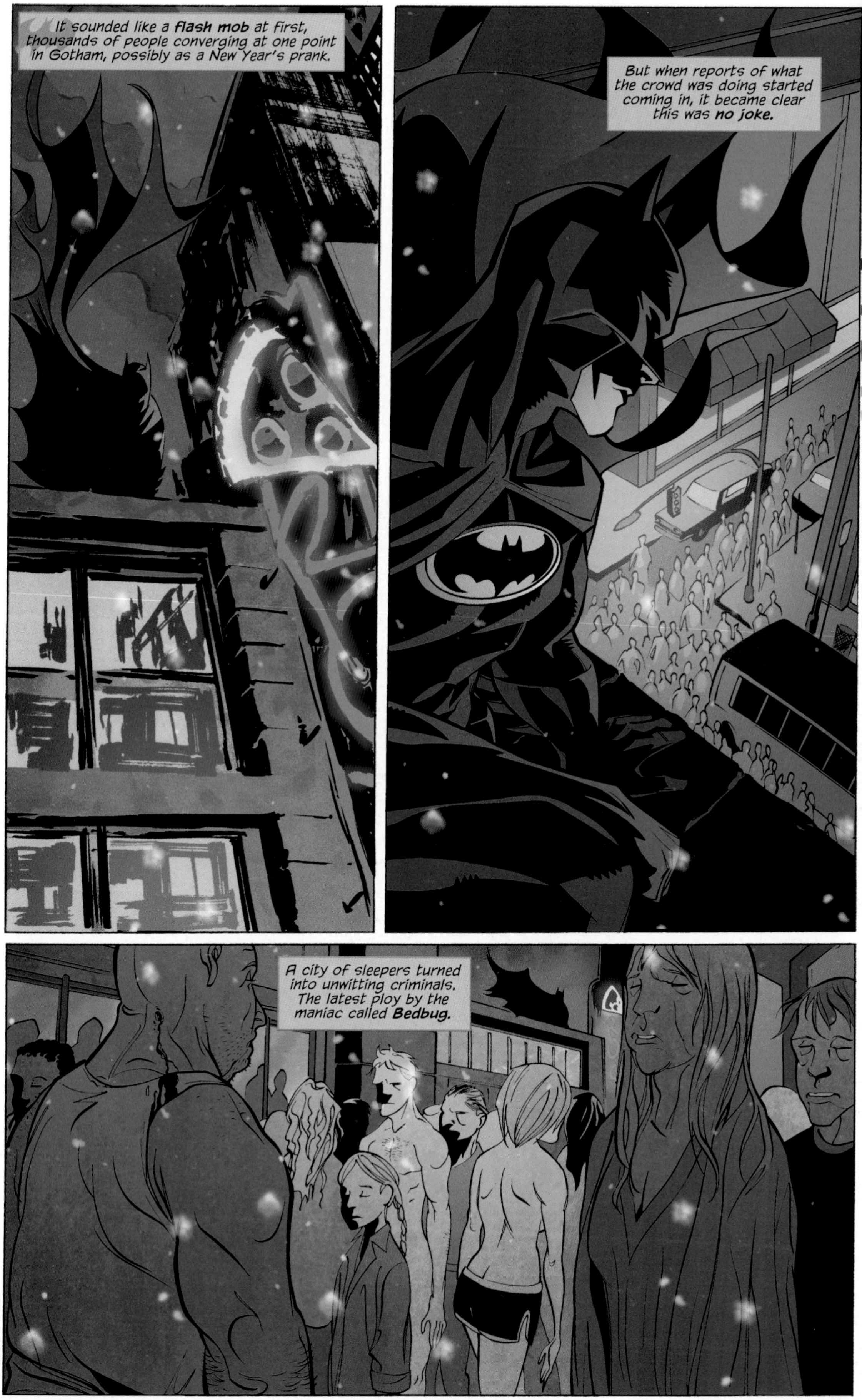
It sounded like a **flash mob** at first, thousands of people converging at one point in Gotham, possibly as a New Year's prank.
But when reports of what the crowd was doing started coming in, it became clear this was **no joke.**
A city of sleepers turned into unwitting criminals. The latest ploy by the maniac called **Bedbug.**

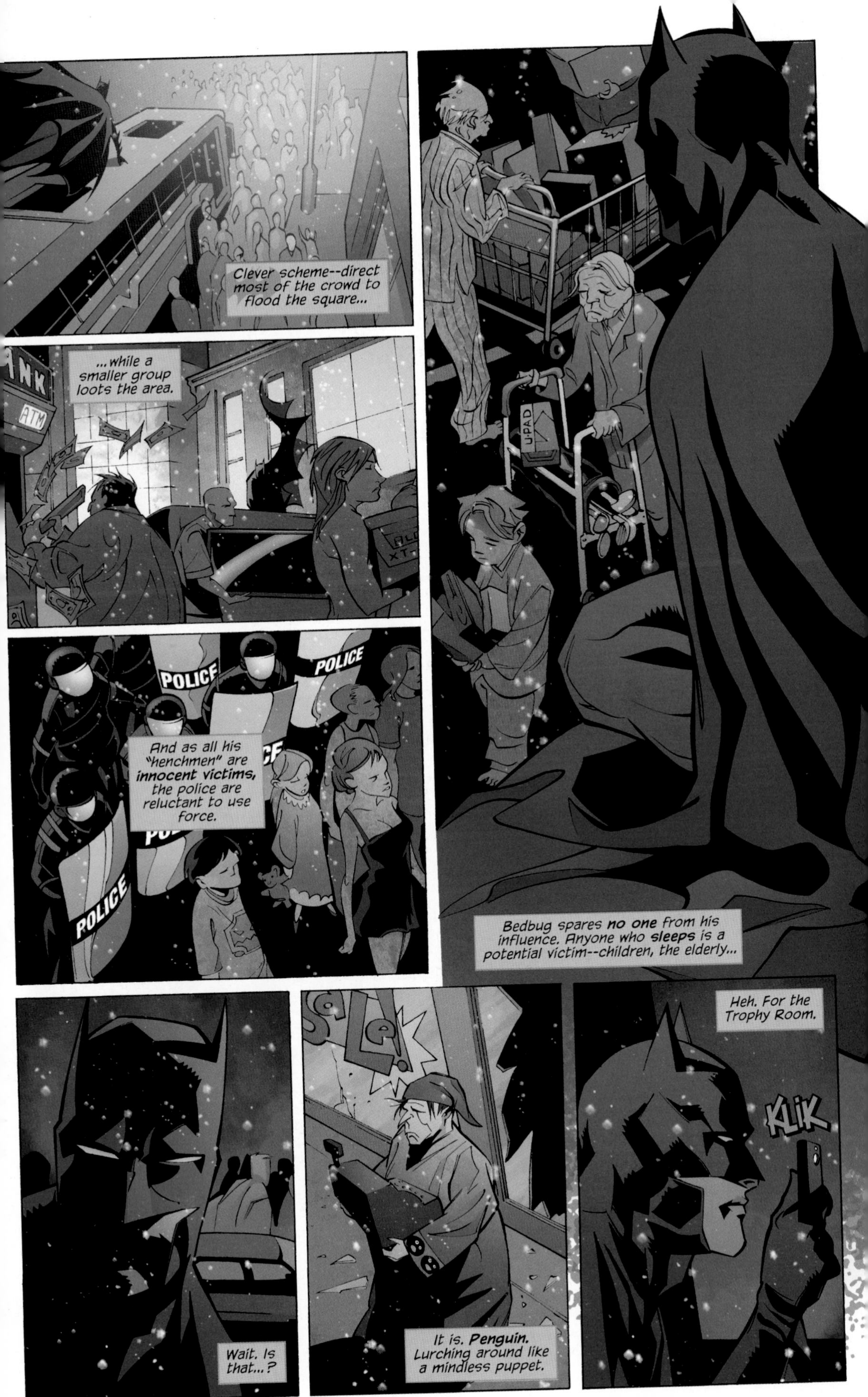
Clever scheme--direct most of the crowd to flood the square...
...while a smaller group loots the area.
And as all his "henchmen" are **innocent victims,** the police are reluctant to use force.
POLICE
Bedbug spares **no one** from his influence. Anyone who **sleeps** is a potential victim--children, the elderly...
Wait. Is that...?
It is. **Penguin.** Lurching around like a mindless puppet.
Heh. For the Trophy Room.
KLIK

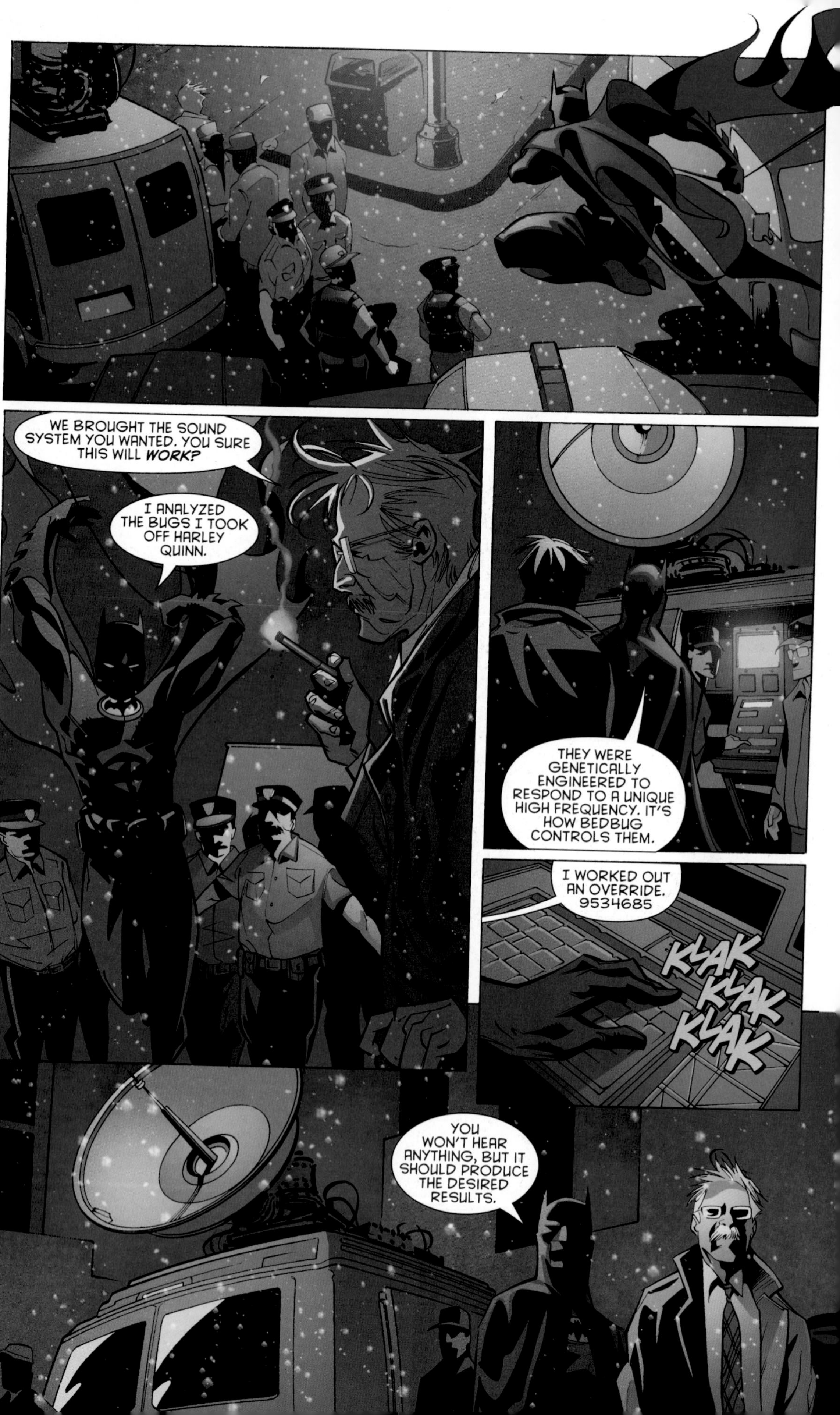
WE BROUGHT THE SOUND SYSTEM YOU WANTED. YOU SURE THIS WILL *WORK?*
I ANALYZED THE BUGS I TOOK OFF HARLEY QUINN.
THEY WERE GENETICALLY ENGINEERED TO RESPOND TO A UNIQUE HIGH FREQUENCY. IT'S HOW BEDBUG CONTROLS THEM.
I WORKED OUT AN OVERRIDE. 9534685
KLAK KLAK KLAK
YOU WON'T HEAR ANYTHING, BUT IT SHOULD PRODUCE THE DESIRED RESULTS.

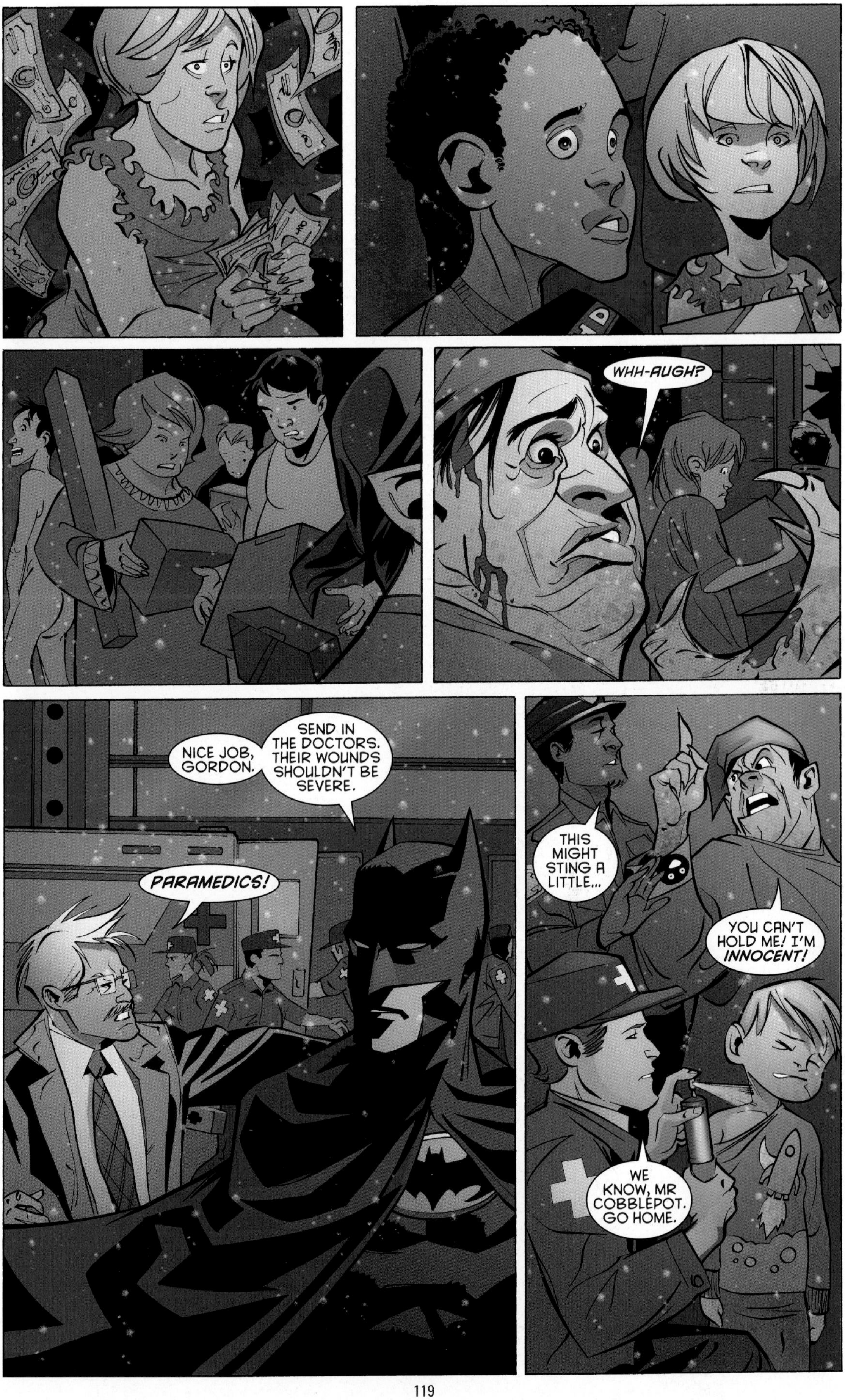
WHH-AUGH?
NICE JOB, GORDON.
SEND IN THE DOCTORS. THEIR WOUNDS SHOULDN'T BE SEVERE.
PARAMEDICS!
THIS MIGHT STING A LITTLE...
YOU CAN'T HOLD ME! I'M INNOCENT!
WE KNOW, MR COBBLEPOT. GO HOME.

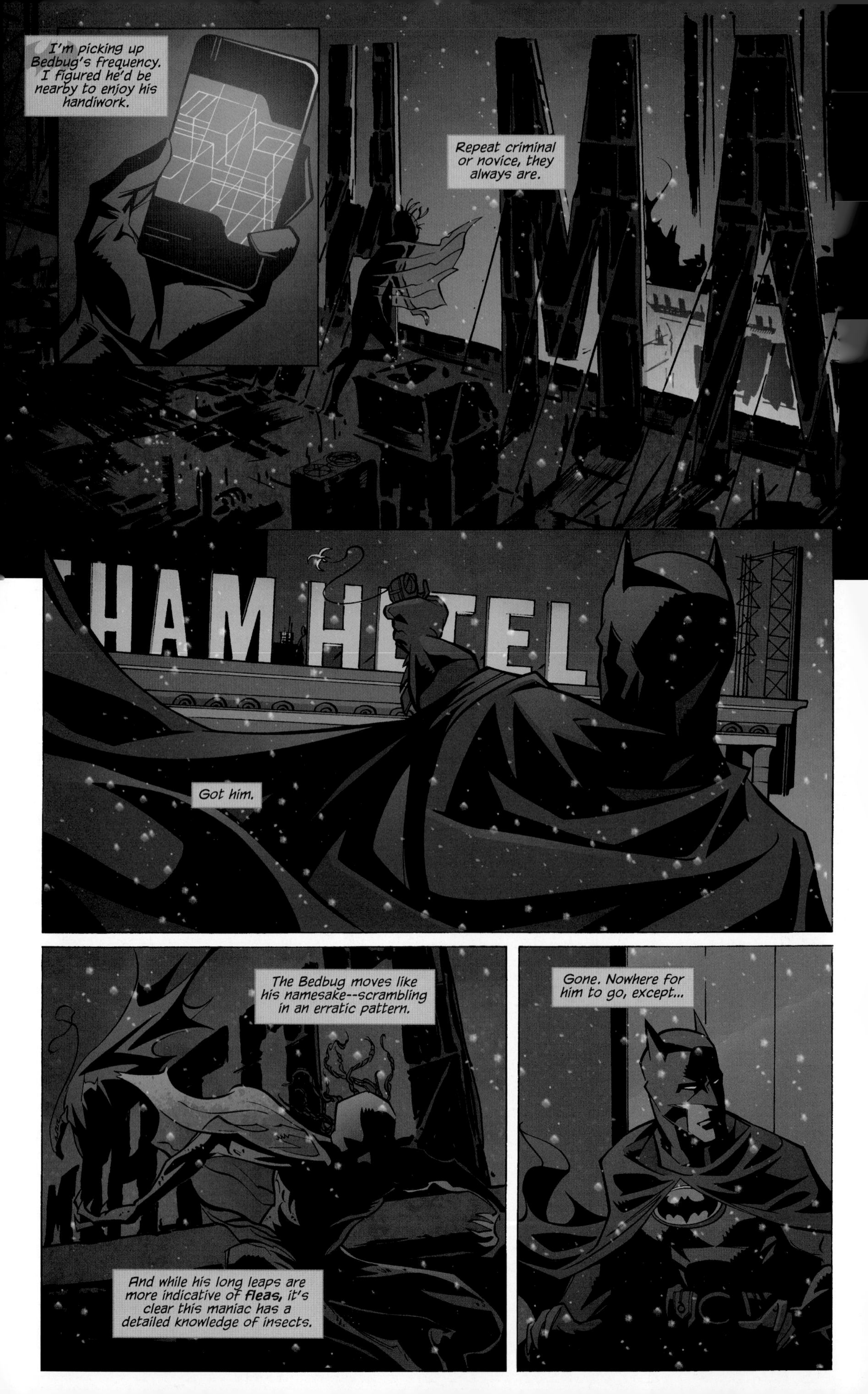
I'm picking up Bedbug's frequency. I figured he'd be nearby to enjoy his handiwork.
Repeat criminal or novice, they always are.
HAM HOTEL
Got him.
The Bedbug moves like his namesake--scrambling in an erratic pattern.
And while his long leaps are more indicative of fleas, it's clear this maniac has a detailed knowledge of insects.
Gone. Nowhere for him to go, except...

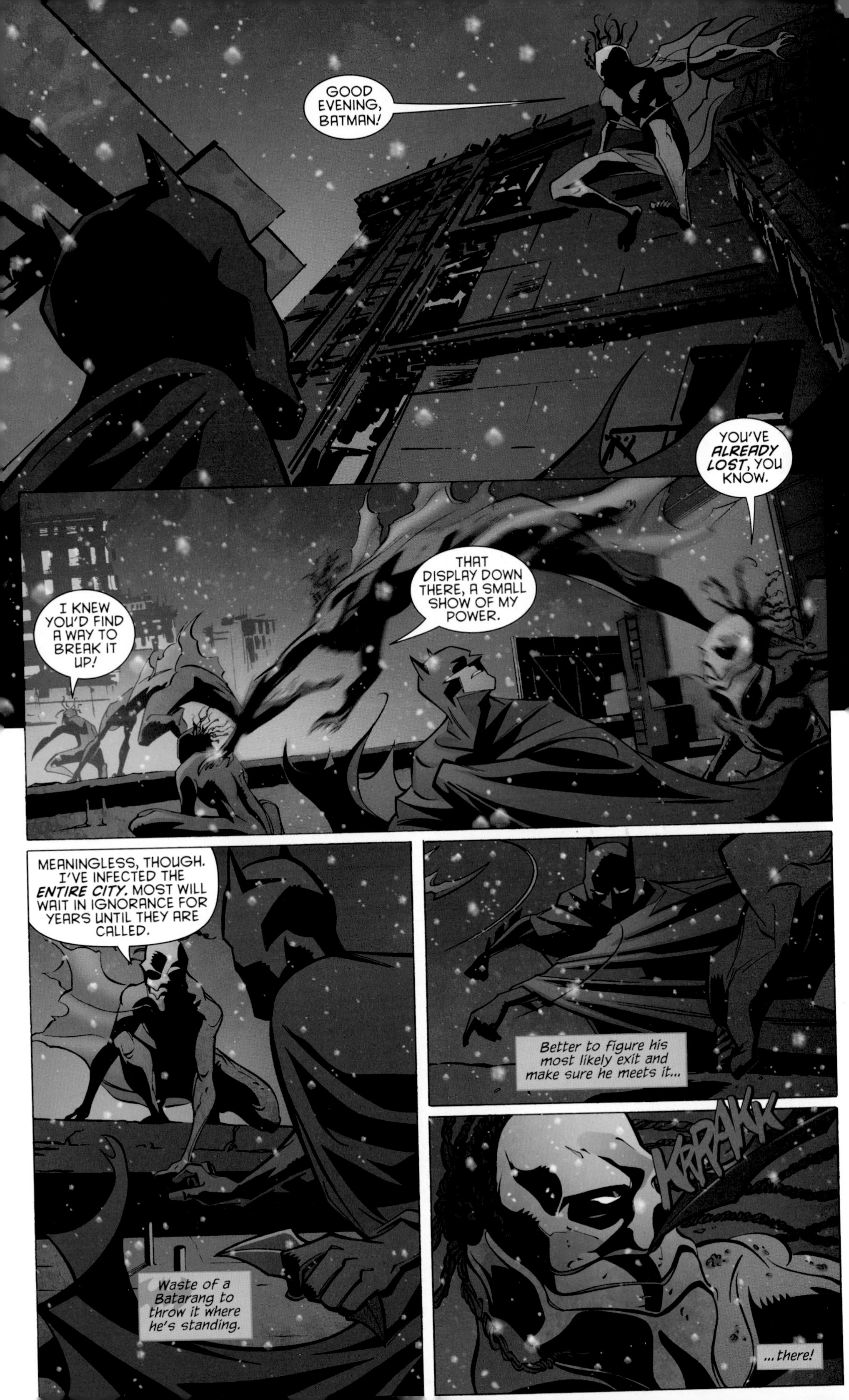
GOOD EVENING, BATMAN!
YOU'VE ALREADY LOST, YOU KNOW.
THAT DISPLAY DOWN THERE, A SMALL SHOW OF MY POWER.
I KNEW YOU'D FIND A WAY TO BREAK IT UP!
MEANINGLESS, THOUGH. I'VE INFECTED THE ENTIRE CITY. MOST WILL WAIT IN IGNORANCE FOR YEARS UNTIL THEY ARE CALLED.
Waste of a Batarang to throw it where he's standing.
Better to figure his most likely exit and make sure he meets it...
KRAKK
...there!

NO, *PLEASE.* NOT MY *MASK!*

TRIED TO WARN YOU.

NOW YOU'LL JOIN MY SLEEPERS!

FAREWELL UNTIL YOU *DREAM,* BATMAN!

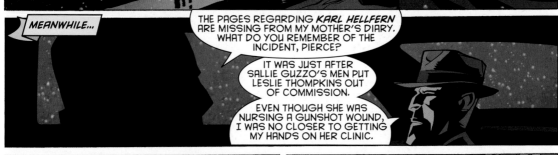

MEANWHILE...

THE PAGES REGARDING *KARL HELLFERN* ARE MISSING FROM MY MOTHER'S DIARY. WHAT DO YOU REMEMBER OF THE INCIDENT, PIERCE?

IT WAS JUST AFTER SALLIE GUZZO'S MEN PUT LESLIE THOMPKINS OUT OF COMMISSION.

EVEN THOUGH SHE WAS NURSING A GUNSHOT WOUND, I WAS NO CLOSER TO GETTING MY HANDS ON HER CLINIC.

"SEEMS *THOMAS WAYNE* HAD SOBERED UP AND GROWN A CONSCIENCE ALL OF A SUDDEN.

"NOT ONLY WAS HE FILLING IN FOR THOMPKINS AS DOC-ON-CALL, BUT HE STARTED PUMPING SERIOUS *CASH* INTO THE PLACE AS WELL.

"'COURSE THE FACT THAT HE HAD FALLEN HARD FOR SWEET, SELFLESS *MARTY KANE* DIDN'T HELP ME ANY."

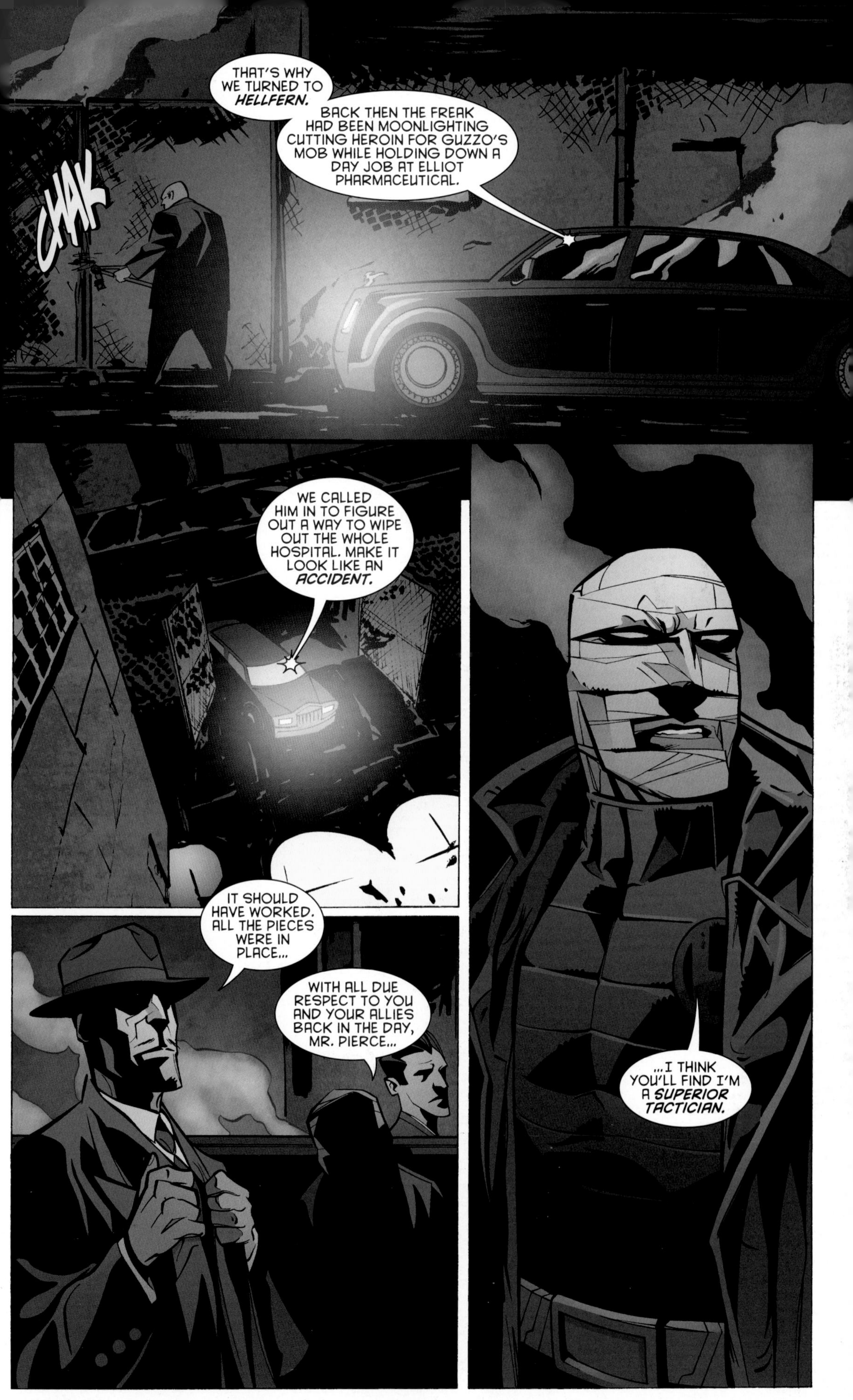
THAT'S WHY WE TURNED TO *HELLFERN.*
BACK THEN THE FREAK HAD BEEN MOONLIGHTING CUTTING HEROIN FOR GUZZO'S MOB WHILE HOLDING DOWN A DAY JOB AT ELLIOT PHARMACEUTICAL.
CHAK
WE CALLED HIM IN TO FIGURE OUT A WAY TO WIPE OUT THE WHOLE HOSPITAL. MAKE IT LOOK LIKE AN *ACCIDENT.*
IT SHOULD HAVE WORKED. ALL THE PIECES WERE IN PLACE...
WITH ALL DUE RESPECT TO YOU AND YOUR ALLIES BACK IN THE DAY, MR. PIERCE...
...I THINK YOU'LL FIND I'M A *SUPERIOR TACTICIAN.*

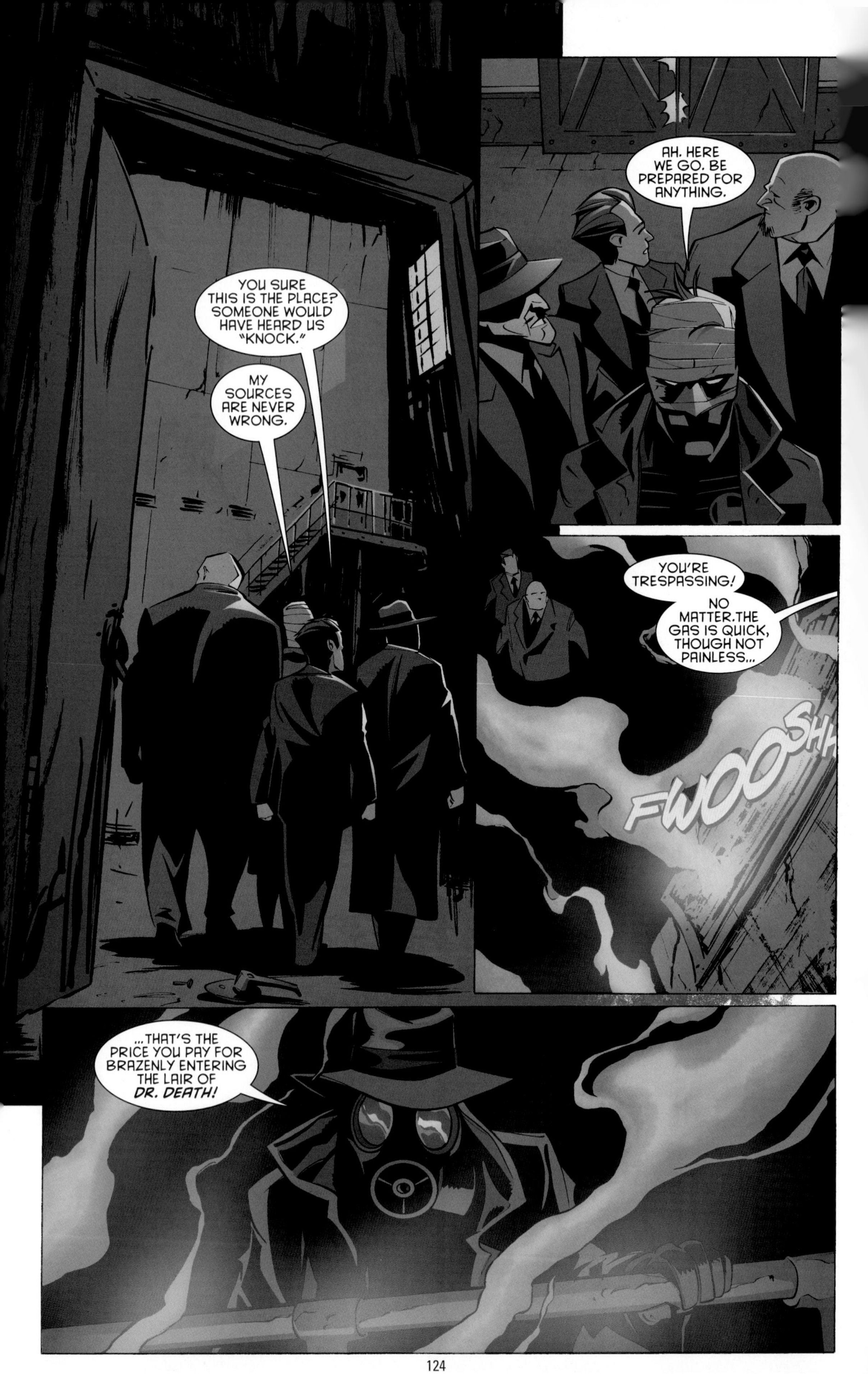
YOU SURE THIS IS THE PLACE? SOMEONE WOULD HAVE HEARD US "KNOCK."
MY SOURCES ARE NEVER WRONG.
AH. HERE WE GO. BE PREPARED FOR ANYTHING.
YOU'RE TRESPASSING!
NO MATTER. THE GAS IS QUICK, THOUGH NOT PAINLESS...
FWOOSH
...THAT'S THE PRICE YOU PAY FOR BRAZENLY ENTERING THE LAIR OF *DR. DEATH!*

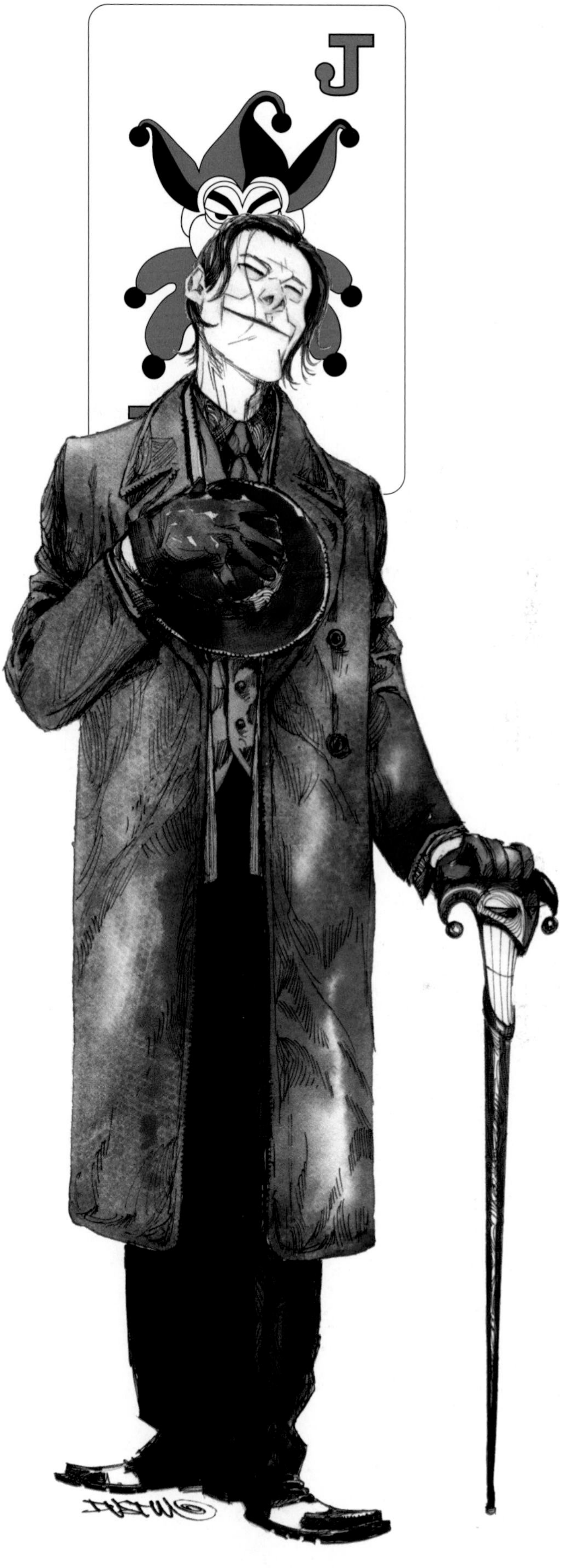
J

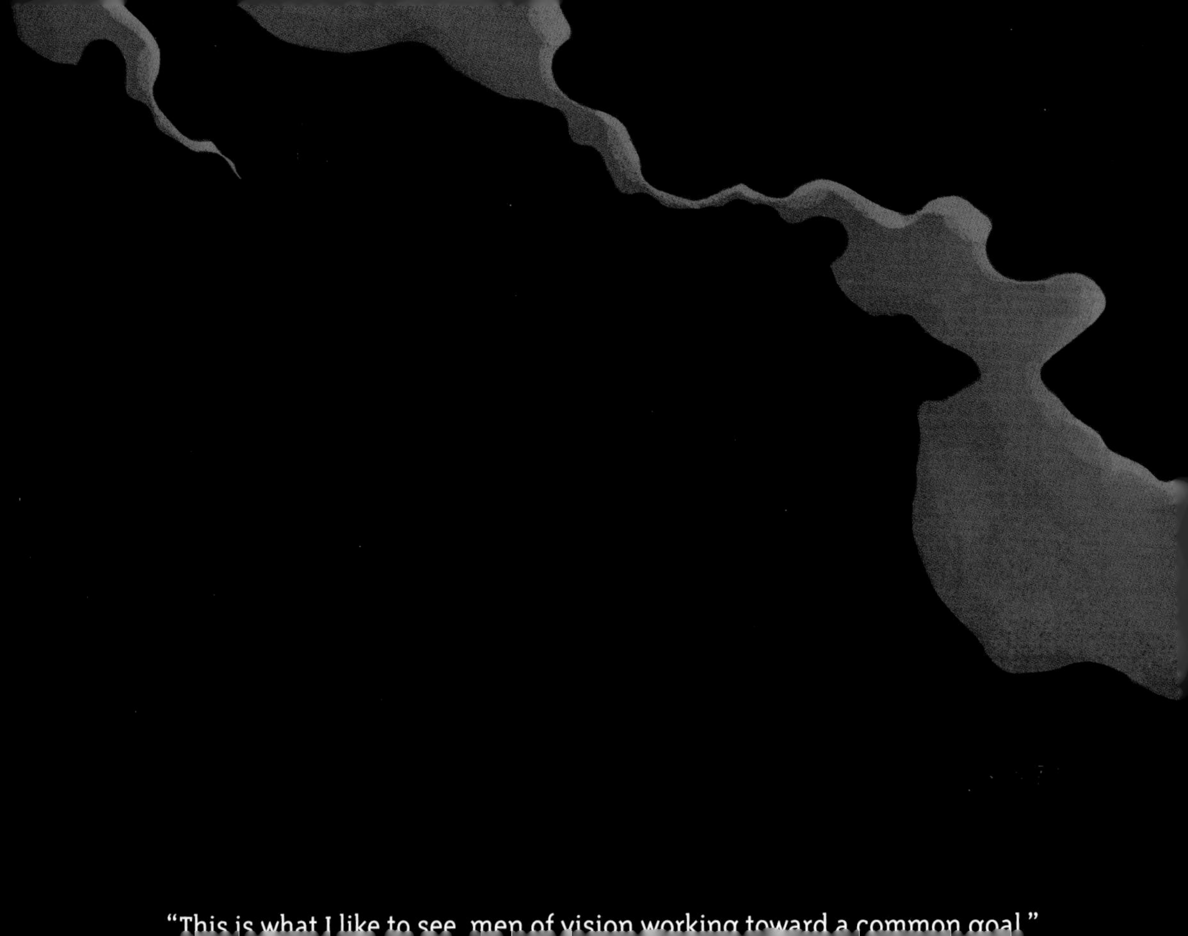
“This is what I like to see, men of vision working toward a common goal.”

ARISTOTLE SAYS, "THE SECRET TO HUMOR IS SURPRISE."
AND WHILE YOU MAY NOT SEE ANYTHING FUNNY ABOUT YOUR PRESENT SITUATION, DR. DEATH, I ASSURE YOU WE'RE ALL SMILING BEHIND OUR MASKS.
THE HOUSE OF HUSH
CHAPTER FOUR
THE REASON FOR HYENAS

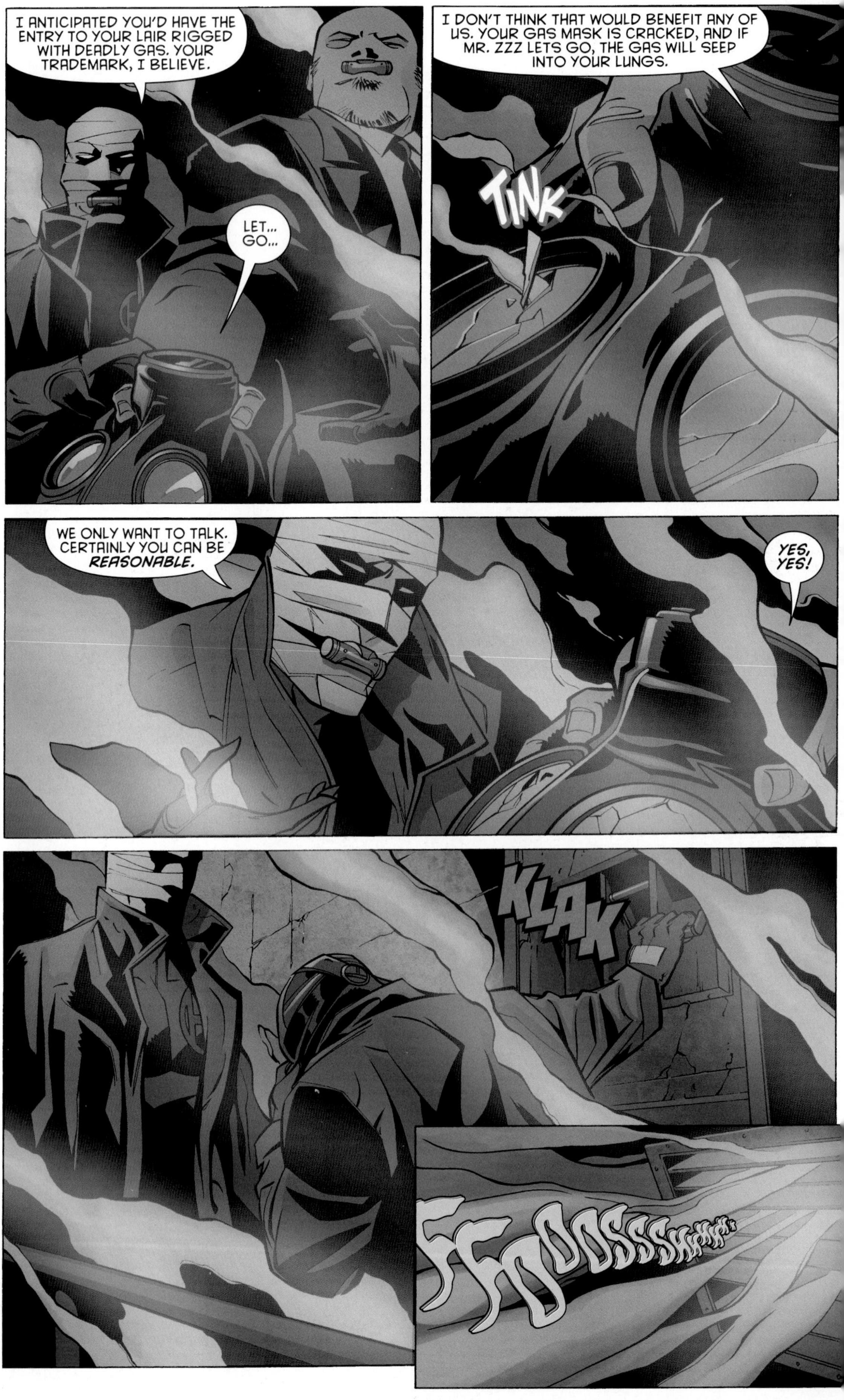

I ANTICIPATED YOU'D HAVE THE ENTRY TO YOUR LAIR RIGGED WITH DEADLY GAS. YOUR TRADEMARK, I BELIEVE.
LET... GO...
I DON'T THINK THAT WOULD BENEFIT ANY OF US. YOUR GAS MASK IS CRACKED, AND IF MR. ZZZ LETS GO, THE GAS WILL SEEP INTO YOUR LUNGS.
TINK
WE ONLY WANT TO TALK. CERTAINLY YOU CAN BE *REASONABLE.*
YES, YES!
KLAK
FFOOOSSSSHHHH

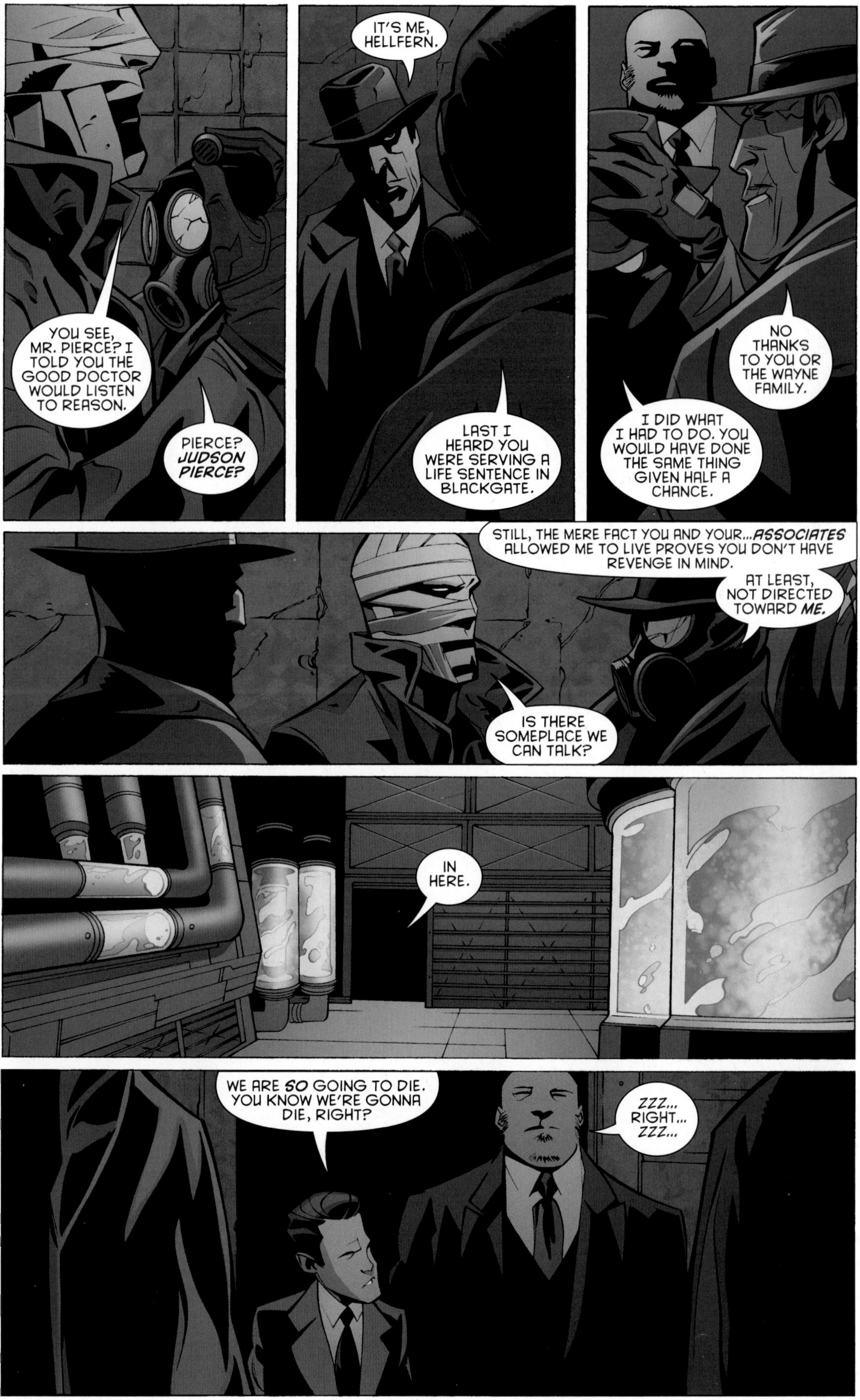

YOU SEE, MR. PIERCE? I TOLD YOU THE GOOD DOCTOR WOULD LISTEN TO REASON.
PIERCE? JUDSON PIERCE?
IT'S ME, HELLFERN.
LAST I HEARD YOU WERE SERVING A LIFE SENTENCE IN BLACKGATE.
I DID WHAT I HAD TO DO. YOU WOULD HAVE DONE THE SAME THING GIVEN HALF A CHANCE.
NO THANKS TO YOU OR THE WAYNE FAMILY.
STILL, THE MERE FACT YOU AND YOUR...ASSOCIATES ALLOWED ME TO LIVE PROVES YOU DON'T HAVE REVENGE IN MIND.
AT LEAST, NOT DIRECTED TOWARD ME.
IS THERE SOMEPLACE WE CAN TALK?
IN HERE.
WE ARE SO GOING TO DIE. YOU KNOW WE'RE GONNA DIE, RIGHT?
ZZZ... RIGHT... ZZZ...

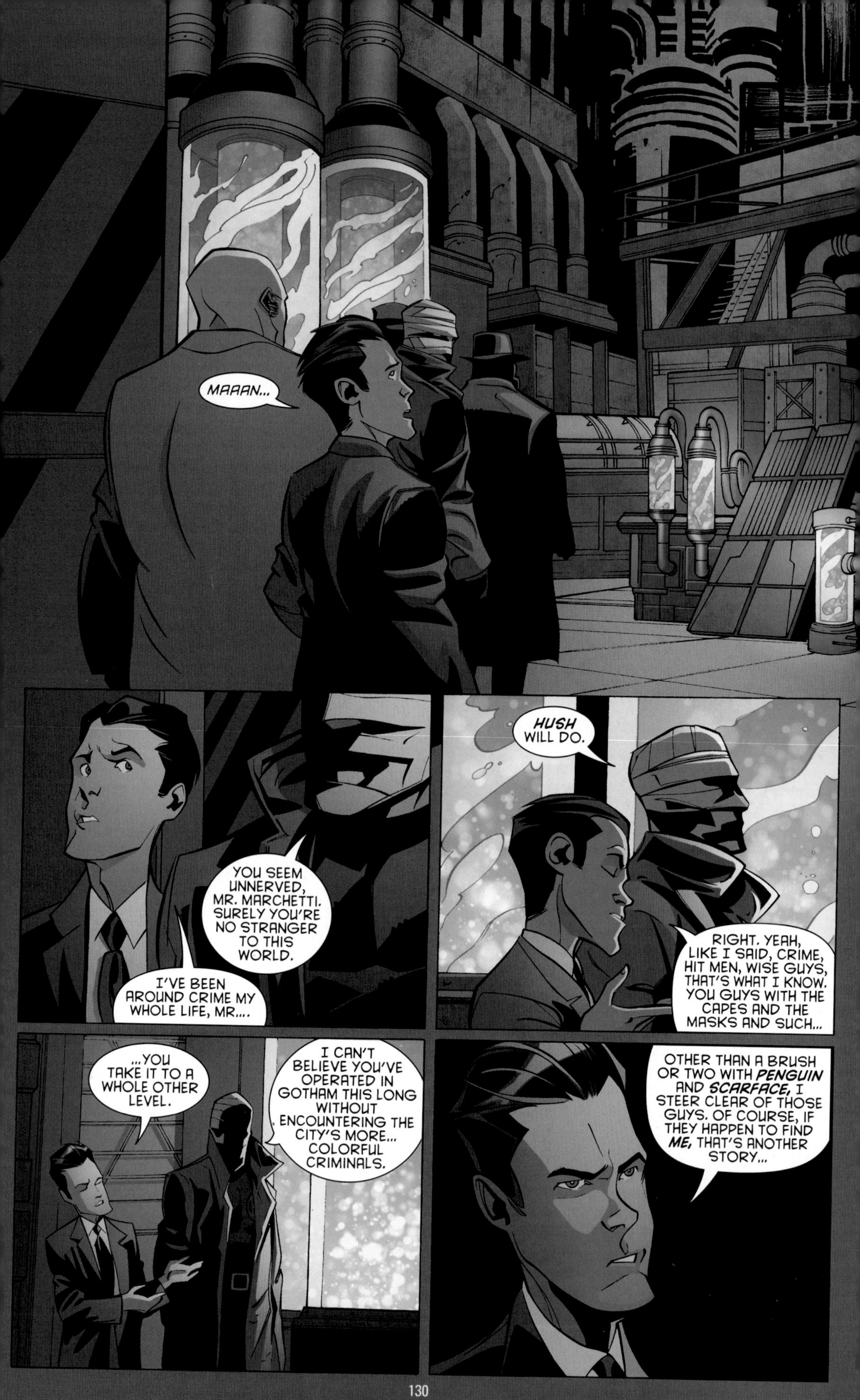

MAAAN...
YOU SEEM UNNERVED, MR. MARCHETTI. SURELY YOU'RE NO STRANGER TO THIS WORLD.
I'VE BEEN AROUND CRIME MY WHOLE LIFE, MR....
HUSH WILL DO.
RIGHT. YEAH, LIKE I SAID, CRIME, HIT MEN, WISE GUYS, THAT'S WHAT I KNOW. YOU GUYS WITH THE CAPES AND THE MASKS AND SUCH...
...YOU TAKE IT TO A WHOLE OTHER LEVEL.
I CAN'T BELIEVE YOU'VE OPERATED IN GOTHAM THIS LONG WITHOUT ENCOUNTERING THE CITY'S MORE... COLORFUL CRIMINALS.
OTHER THAN A BRUSH OR TWO WITH PENGUIN AND SCARFACE, I STEER CLEAR OF THOSE GUYS. OF COURSE, IF THEY HAPPEN TO FIND ME, THAT'S ANOTHER STORY...

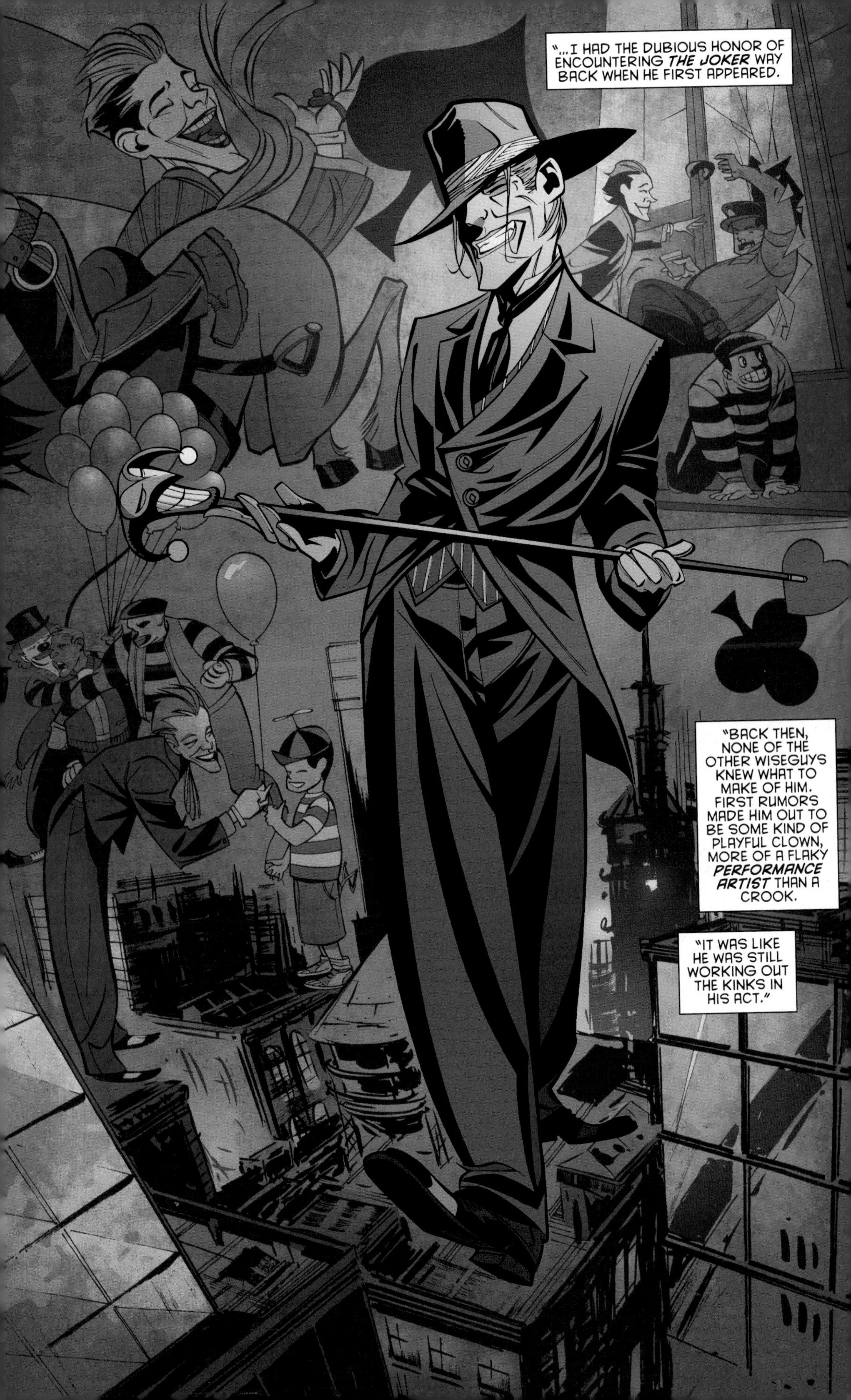
"...I HAD THE DUBIOUS HONOR OF ENCOUNTERING *THE JOKER* WAY BACK WHEN HE FIRST APPEARED.
"BACK THEN, NONE OF THE OTHER WISEGUYS KNEW WHAT TO MAKE OF HIM. FIRST RUMORS MADE HIM OUT TO BE SOME KIND OF PLAYFUL CLOWN, MORE OF A FLAKY *PERFORMANCE ARTIST* THAN A CROOK.
"IT WAS LIKE HE WAS STILL WORKING OUT THE KINKS IN HIS ACT."

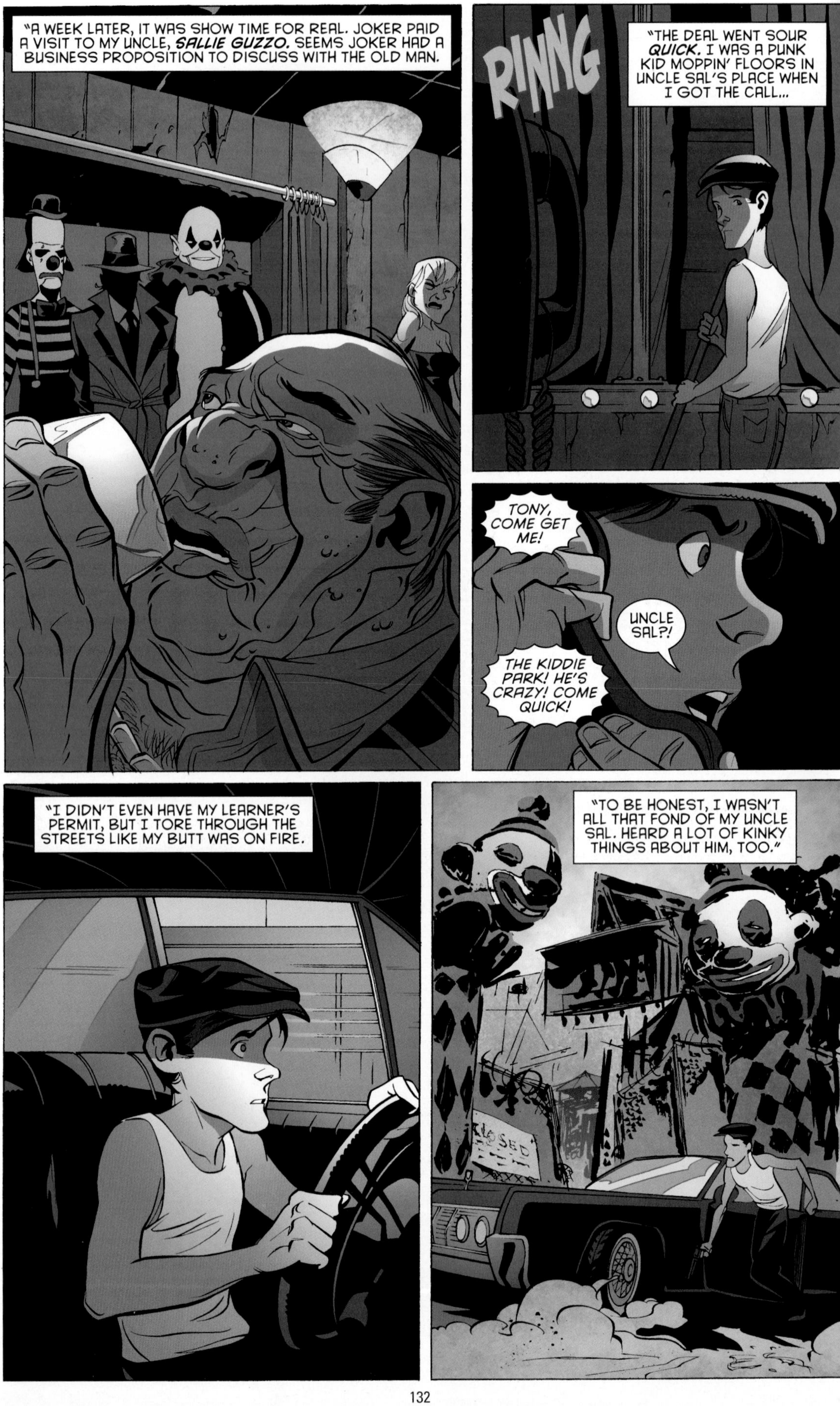

"A WEEK LATER, IT WAS SHOW TIME FOR REAL. JOKER PAID A VISIT TO MY UNCLE, *SALLIE GUZZO.* SEEMS JOKER HAD A BUSINESS PROPOSITION TO DISCUSS WITH THE OLD MAN.
RINNG
"THE DEAL WENT SOUR *QUICK.* I WAS A PUNK KID MOPPIN' FLOORS IN UNCLE SAL'S PLACE WHEN I GOT THE CALL...
TONY, COME GET ME!
UNCLE SAL?!
THE KIDDIE PARK! HE'S CRAZY! COME QUICK!
"I DIDN'T EVEN HAVE MY LEARNER'S PERMIT, BUT I TORE THROUGH THE STREETS LIKE MY BUTT WAS ON FIRE.
"TO BE HONEST, I WASN'T ALL THAT FOND OF MY UNCLE SAL. HEARD A LOT OF KINKY THINGS ABOUT HIM, TOO."
CLOSED

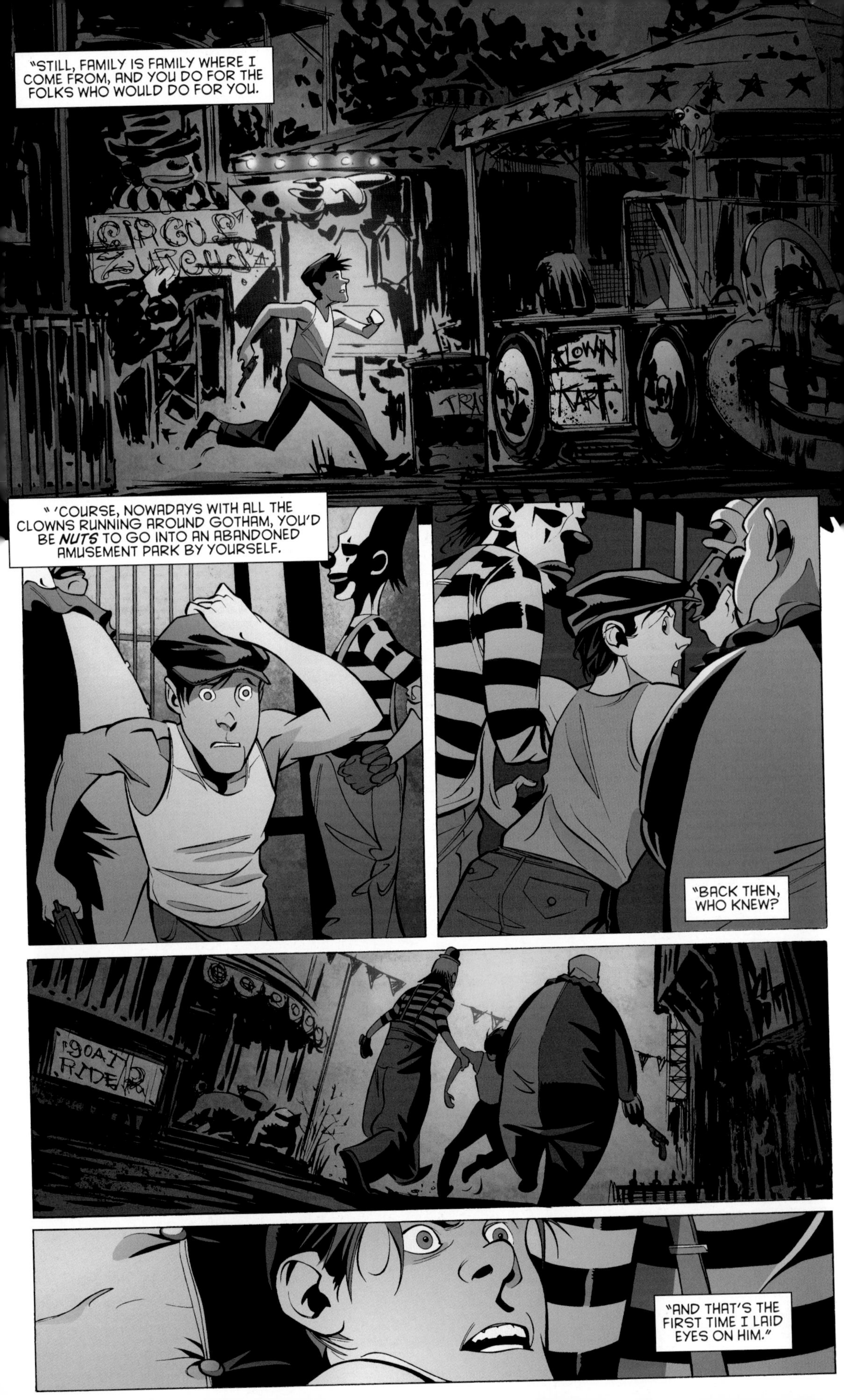
"STILL, FAMILY IS FAMILY WHERE I COME FROM, AND YOU DO FOR THE FOLKS WHO WOULD DO FOR YOU.
CLOWN KART
"'COURSE, NOWADAYS WITH ALL THE CLOWNS RUNNING AROUND GOTHAM, YOU'D BE NUTS TO GO INTO AN ABANDONED AMUSEMENT PARK BY YOURSELF.
"BACK THEN, WHO KNEW?
GOAT RIDE
"AND THAT'S THE FIRST TIME I LAID EYES ON HIM."

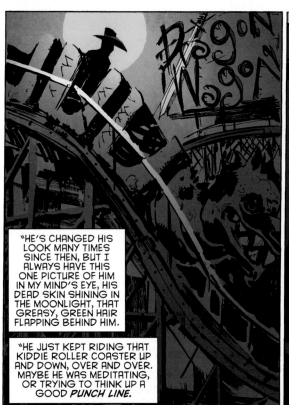

"HE'S CHANGED HIS LOOK MANY TIMES SINCE THEN, BUT I ALWAYS HAVE THIS ONE PICTURE OF HIM IN MY MIND'S EYE, HIS DEAD SKIN SHINING IN THE MOONLIGHT, THAT GREASY, GREEN HAIR FLAPPING BEHIND HIM.

"HE JUST KEPT RIDING THAT KIDDIE ROLLER COASTER UP AND DOWN, OVER AND OVER. MAYBE HE WAS MEDITATING, OR TRYING TO THINK UP A GOOD *PUNCH LINE.*

"OR MAYBE THERE'S *ALWAYS* BEEN A PART OF HIM THAT NEVER GREW UP. WHO THE HELL KNOWS, RIGHT?"

I'M SORRY, BIG MAN...

WHACK

→UFF!←

MUST BE THIS ↓ TALL ↓ TO RIDE THE Drag Wago

...BUT YOU MUST BE *THIS* TALL TO RIDE.

HEH.

FREAK....!

WHERE'S MY UNCLE?

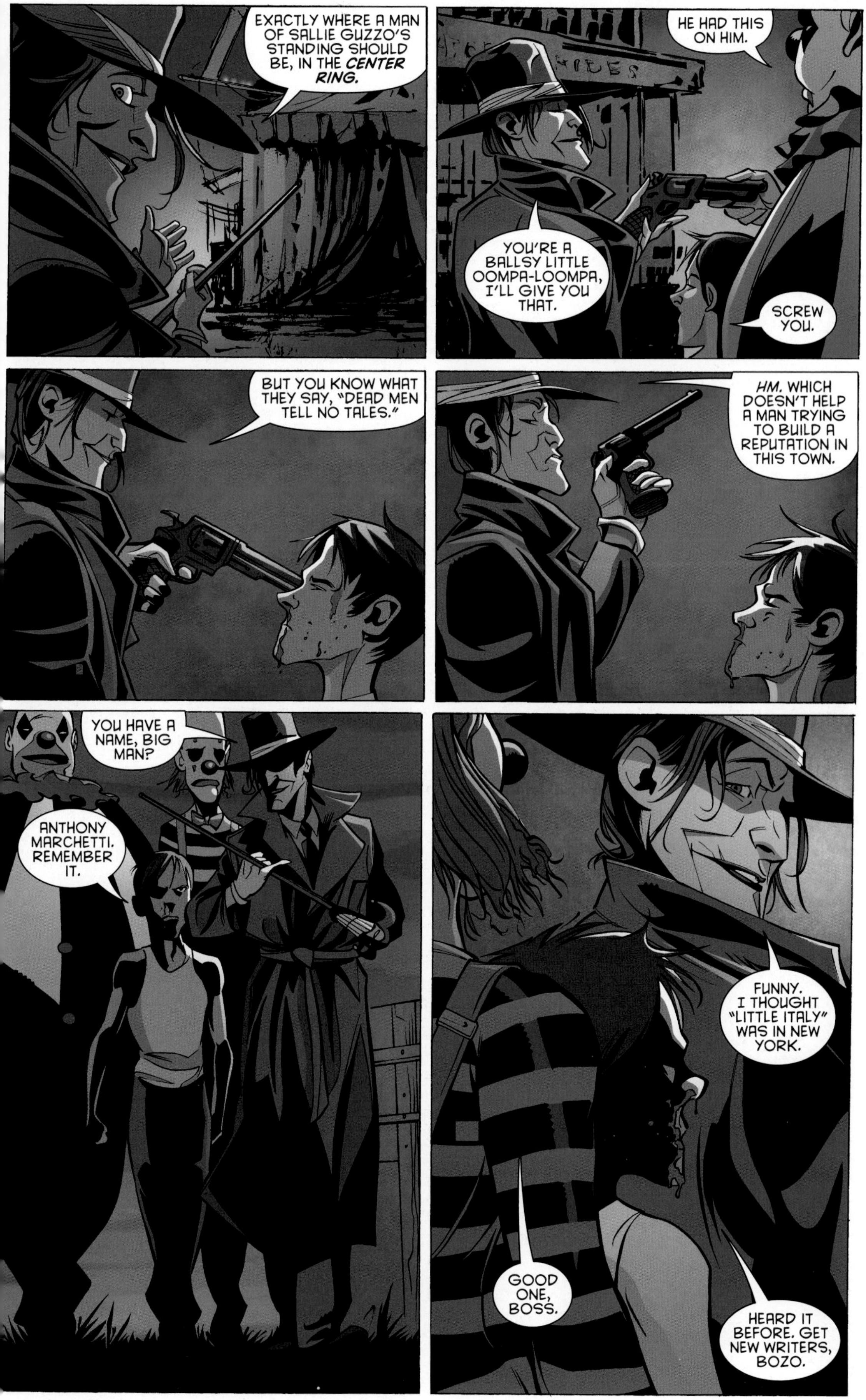
EXACTLY WHERE A MAN OF SALLIE GUZZO'S STANDING SHOULD BE, IN THE *CENTER RING.*
HE HAD THIS ON HIM.
YOU'RE A BALLSY LITTLE OOMPA-LOOMPA, I'LL GIVE YOU THAT.
SCREW YOU.
BUT YOU KNOW WHAT THEY SAY, "DEAD MEN TELL NO TALES."
HM. WHICH DOESN'T HELP A MAN TRYING TO BUILD A REPUTATION IN THIS TOWN.
YOU HAVE A NAME, BIG MAN?
ANTHONY MARCHETTI. REMEMBER IT.
FUNNY. I THOUGHT "LITTLE ITALY" WAS IN NEW YORK.
GOOD ONE, BOSS.
HEARD IT BEFORE. GET NEW WRITERS, BOZO.

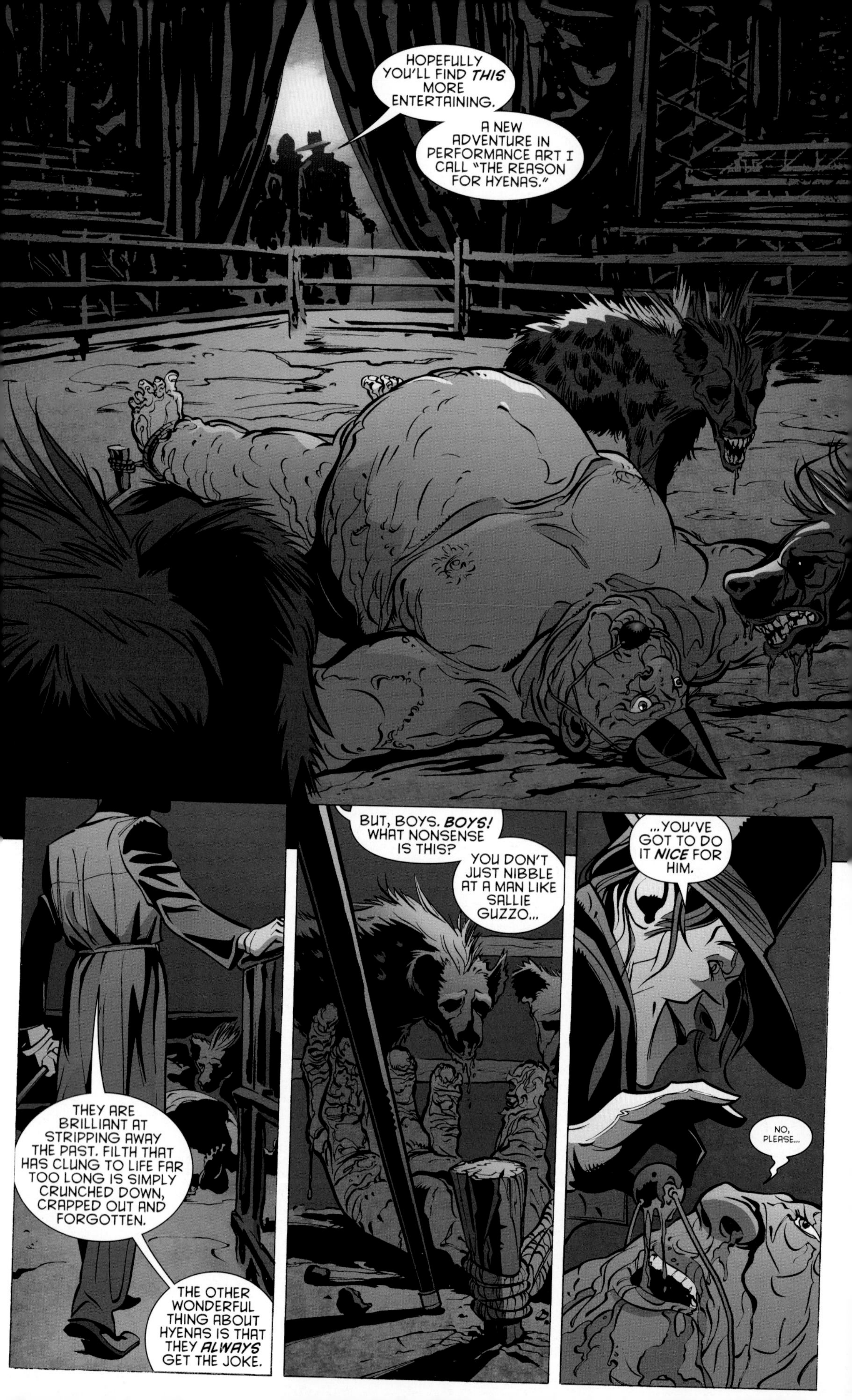
HOPEFULLY YOU'LL FIND THIS MORE ENTERTAINING.
A NEW ADVENTURE IN PERFORMANCE ART I CALL "THE REASON FOR HYENAS."
THEY ARE BRILLIANT AT STRIPPING AWAY THE PAST. FILTH THAT HAS CLUNG TO LIFE FAR TOO LONG IS SIMPLY CRUNCHED DOWN, CRAPPED OUT AND FORGOTTEN.
THE OTHER WONDERFUL THING ABOUT HYENAS IS THAT THEY ALWAYS GET THE JOKE.
BUT, BOYS. BOYS! WHAT NONSENSE IS THIS?
YOU DON'T JUST NIBBLE AT A MAN LIKE SALLIE GUZZO...
...YOU'VE GOT TO DO IT NICE FOR HIM.
NO, PLEASE...

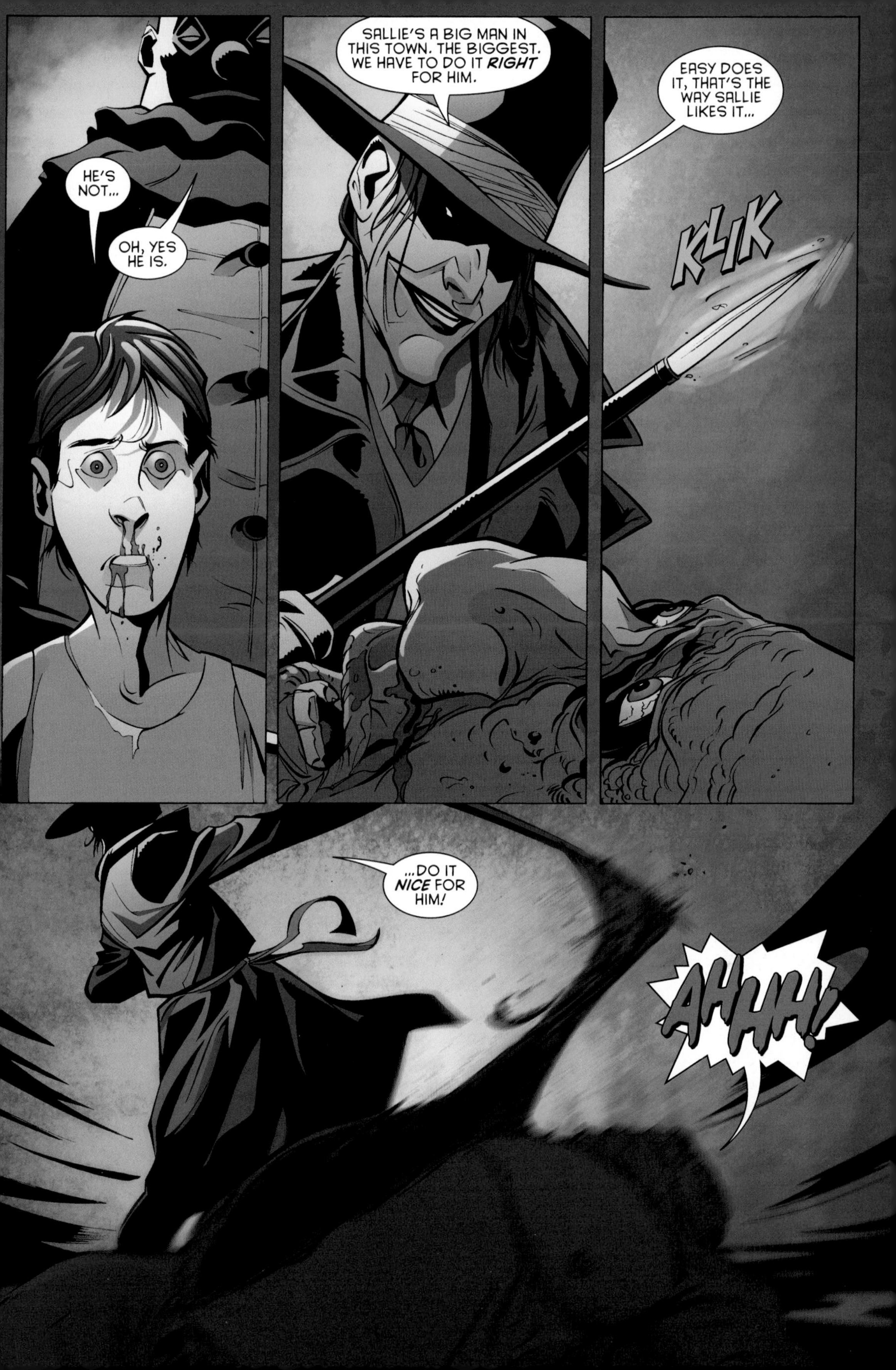
HE'S NOT...
OH, YES HE IS.
SALLIE'S A BIG MAN IN THIS TOWN. THE BIGGEST. WE HAVE TO DO IT *RIGHT* FOR HIM.
EASY DOES IT, THAT'S THE WAY SALLIE LIKES IT...
KLIK
...DO IT *NICE* FOR HIM!
AHHH!

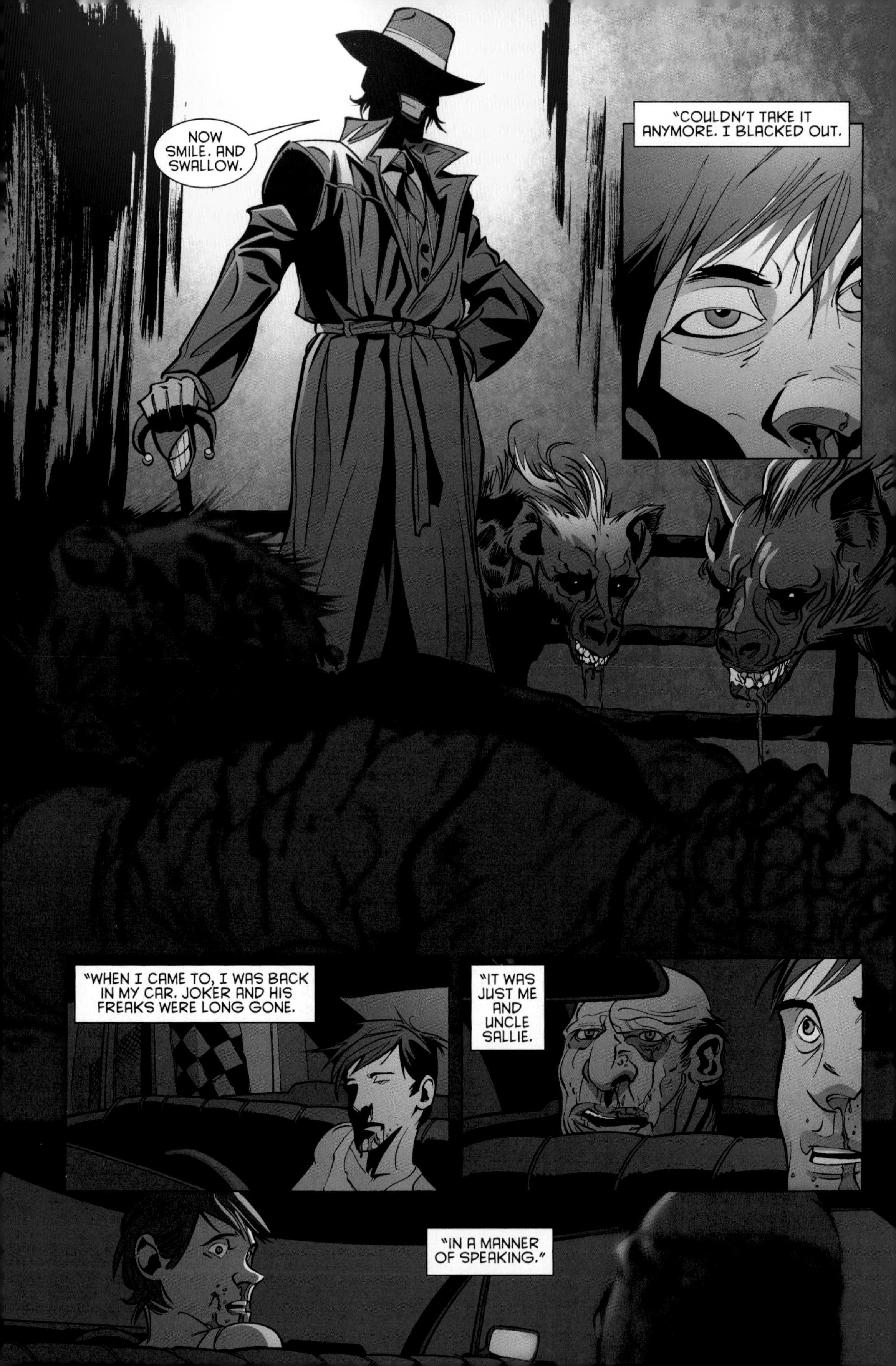
NOW SMILE. AND SWALLOW.
"COULDN'T TAKE IT ANYMORE. I BLACKED OUT.
"WHEN I CAME TO, I WAS BACK IN MY CAR. JOKER AND HIS FREAKS WERE LONG GONE.
"IT WAS JUST ME AND UNCLE SALLIE.
"IN A MANNER OF SPEAKING."

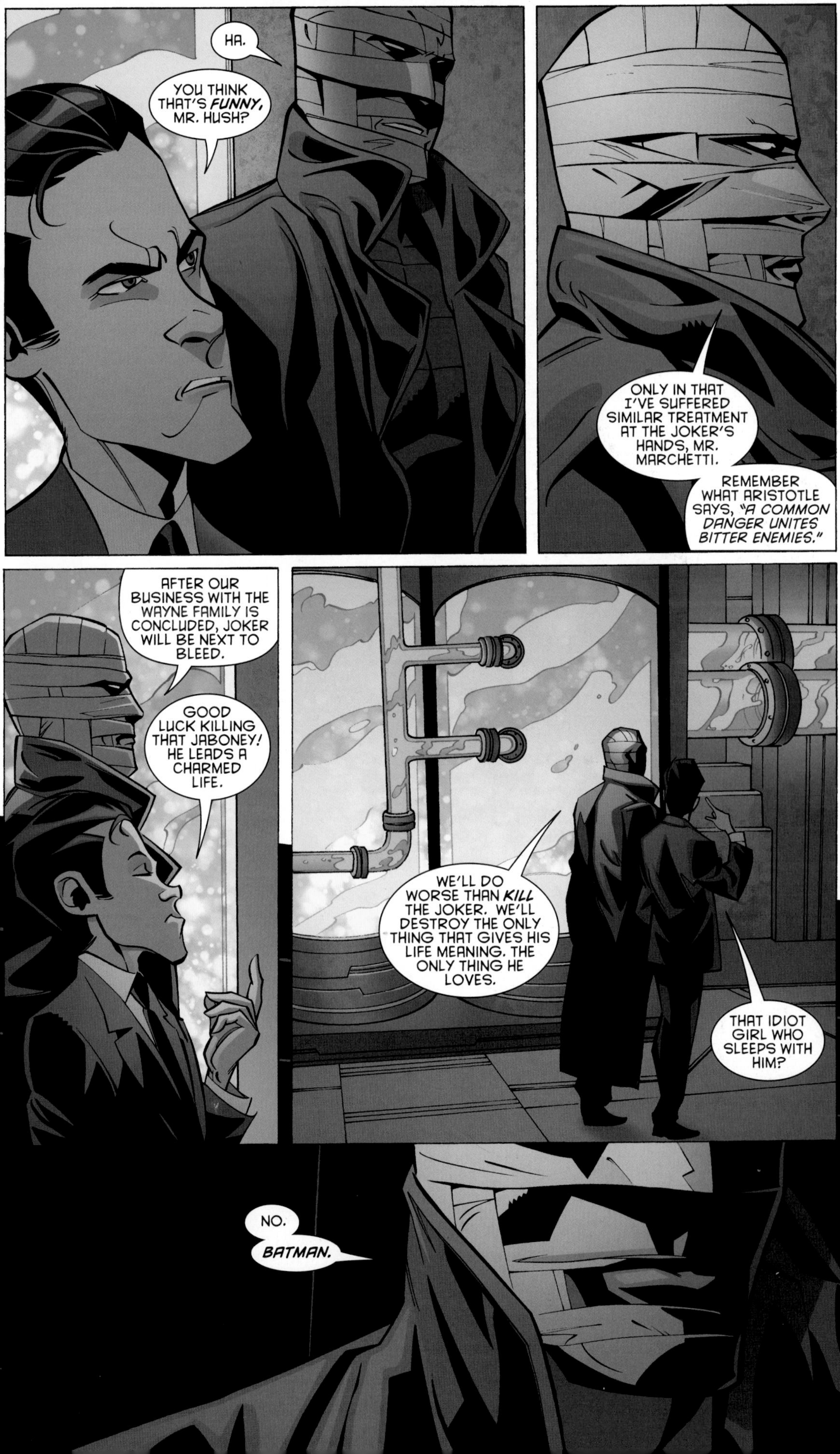
HA.
YOU THINK THAT'S *FUNNY,* MR. HUSH?
ONLY IN THAT I'VE SUFFERED SIMILAR TREATMENT AT THE JOKER'S HANDS, MR. MARCHETTI.
REMEMBER WHAT ARISTOTLE SAYS, *"A COMMON DANGER UNITES BITTER ENEMIES."*
AFTER OUR BUSINESS WITH THE WAYNE FAMILY IS CONCLUDED, JOKER WILL BE NEXT TO BLEED.
GOOD LUCK KILLING THAT JABONEY! HE LEADS A CHARMED LIFE.
WE'LL DO WORSE THAN *KILL* THE JOKER. WE'LL DESTROY THE ONLY THING THAT GIVES HIS LIFE MEANING. THE ONLY THING HE LOVES.
THAT IDIOT GIRL WHO SLEEPS WITH HIM?
NO.
BATMAN.

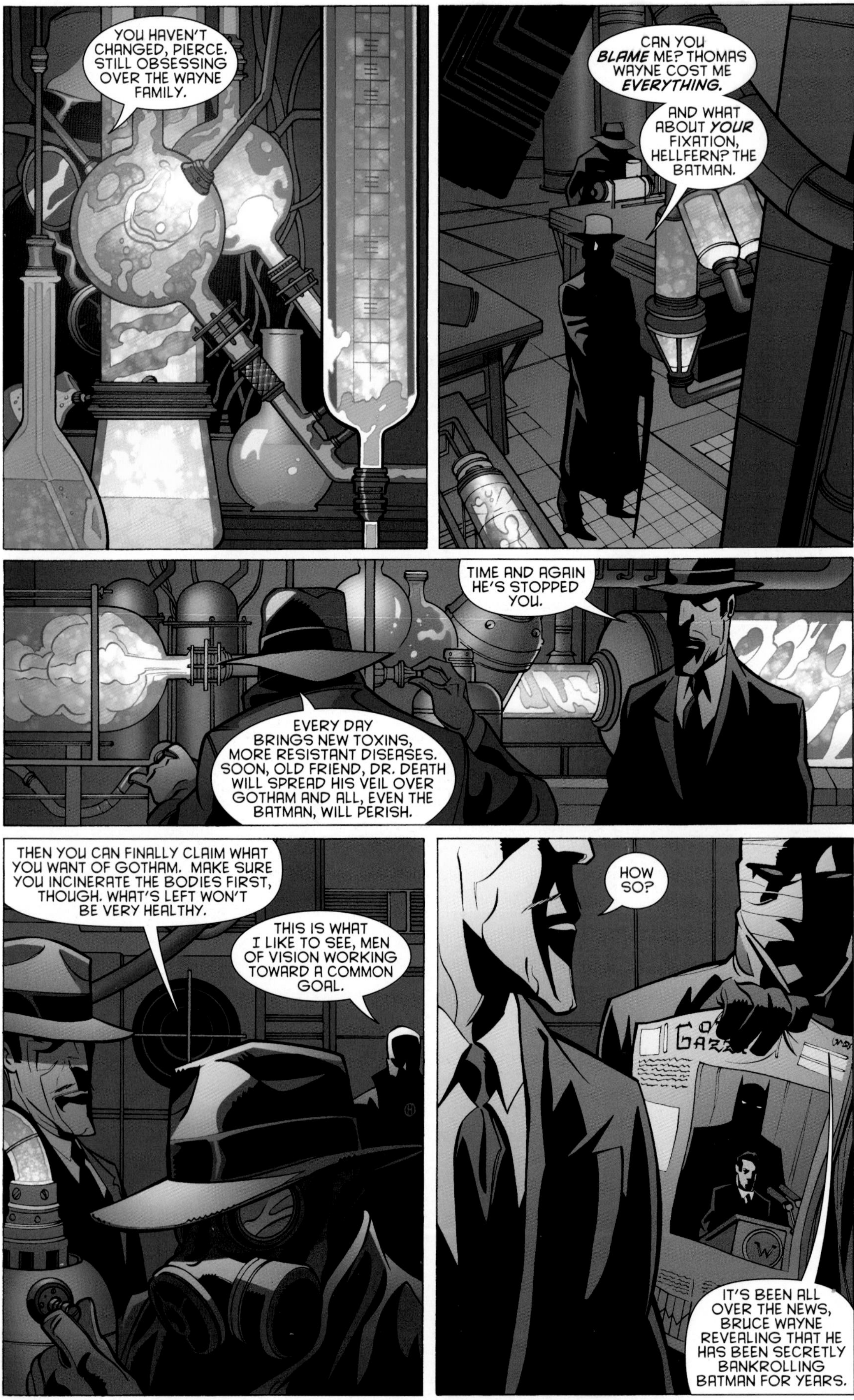

YOU HAVEN'T CHANGED, PIERCE. STILL OBSESSING OVER THE WAYNE FAMILY.
CAN YOU BLAME ME? THOMAS WAYNE COST ME EVERYTHING.
AND WHAT ABOUT YOUR FIXATION, HELLFERN? THE BATMAN.
TIME AND AGAIN HE'S STOPPED YOU.
EVERY DAY BRINGS NEW TOXINS, MORE RESISTANT DISEASES. SOON, OLD FRIEND, DR. DEATH WILL SPREAD HIS VEIL OVER GOTHAM AND ALL, EVEN THE BATMAN, WILL PERISH.
THEN YOU CAN FINALLY CLAIM WHAT YOU WANT OF GOTHAM. MAKE SURE YOU INCINERATE THE BODIES FIRST, THOUGH. WHAT'S LEFT WON'T BE VERY HEALTHY.
THIS IS WHAT I LIKE TO SEE, MEN OF VISION WORKING TOWARD A COMMON GOAL.
HOW SO?
IT'S BEEN ALL OVER THE NEWS, BRUCE WAYNE REVEALING THAT HE HAS BEEN SECRETLY BANKROLLING BATMAN FOR YEARS.

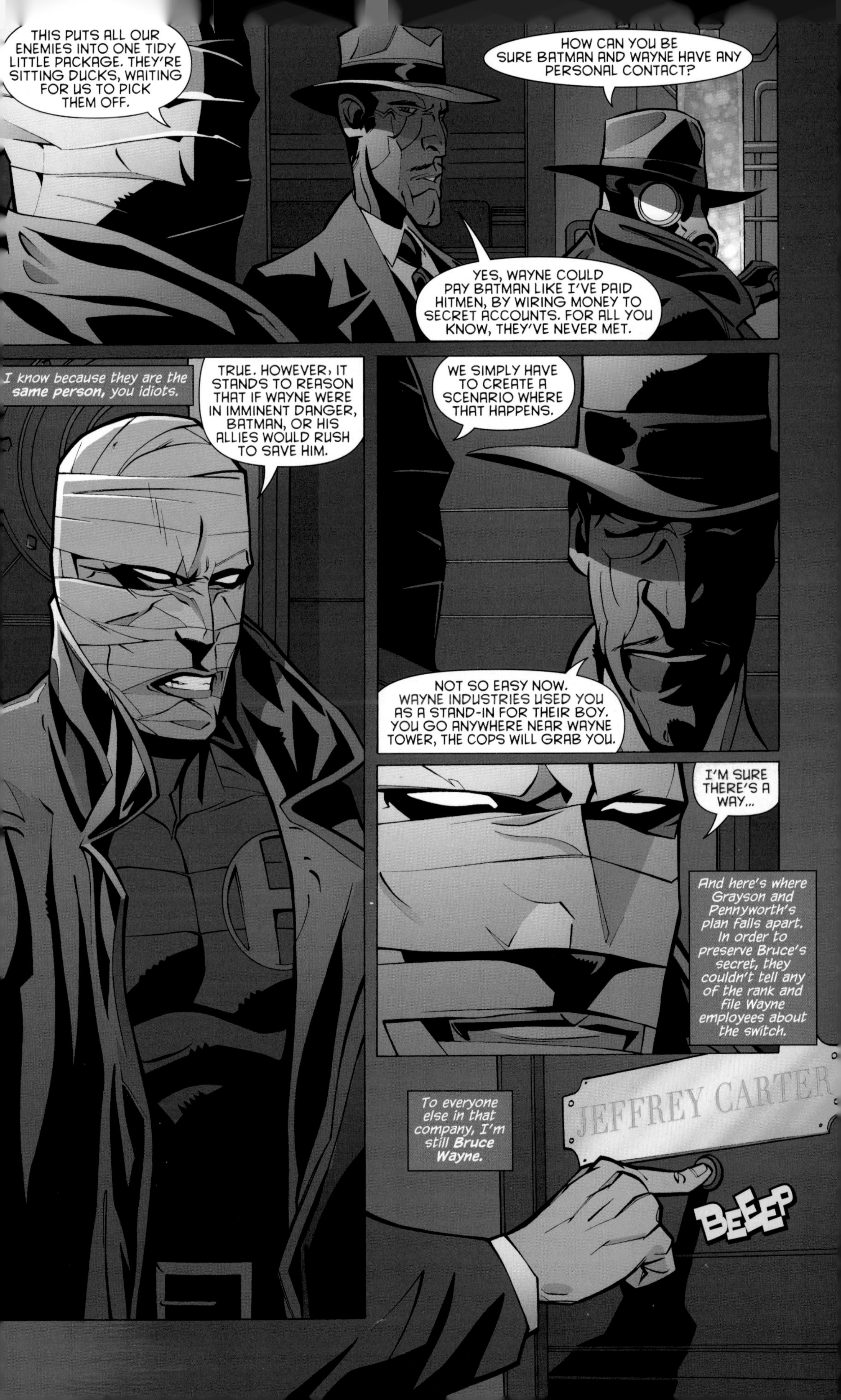
THIS PUTS ALL OUR ENEMIES INTO ONE TIDY LITTLE PACKAGE. THEY'RE SITTING DUCKS, WAITING FOR US TO PICK THEM OFF.
HOW CAN YOU BE SURE BATMAN AND WAYNE HAVE ANY PERSONAL CONTACT?
YES, WAYNE COULD PAY BATMAN LIKE I'VE PAID HITMEN, BY WIRING MONEY TO SECRET ACCOUNTS. FOR ALL YOU KNOW, THEY'VE NEVER MET.
I know because they are the same person, you idiots.
TRUE. HOWEVER, IT STANDS TO REASON THAT IF WAYNE WERE IN IMMINENT DANGER, BATMAN, OR HIS ALLIES WOULD RUSH TO SAVE HIM.
WE SIMPLY HAVE TO CREATE A SCENARIO WHERE THAT HAPPENS.
NOT SO EASY NOW. WAYNE INDUSTRIES USED YOU AS A STAND-IN FOR THEIR BOY. YOU GO ANYWHERE NEAR WAYNE TOWER, THE COPS WILL GRAB YOU.
I'M SURE THERE'S A WAY...
And here's where Grayson and Pennyworth's plan falls apart. In order to preserve Bruce's secret, they couldn't tell any of the rank and file Wayne employees about the switch.
To everyone else in that company, I'm still Bruce Wayne.
JEFFREY CARTER
BEEEP

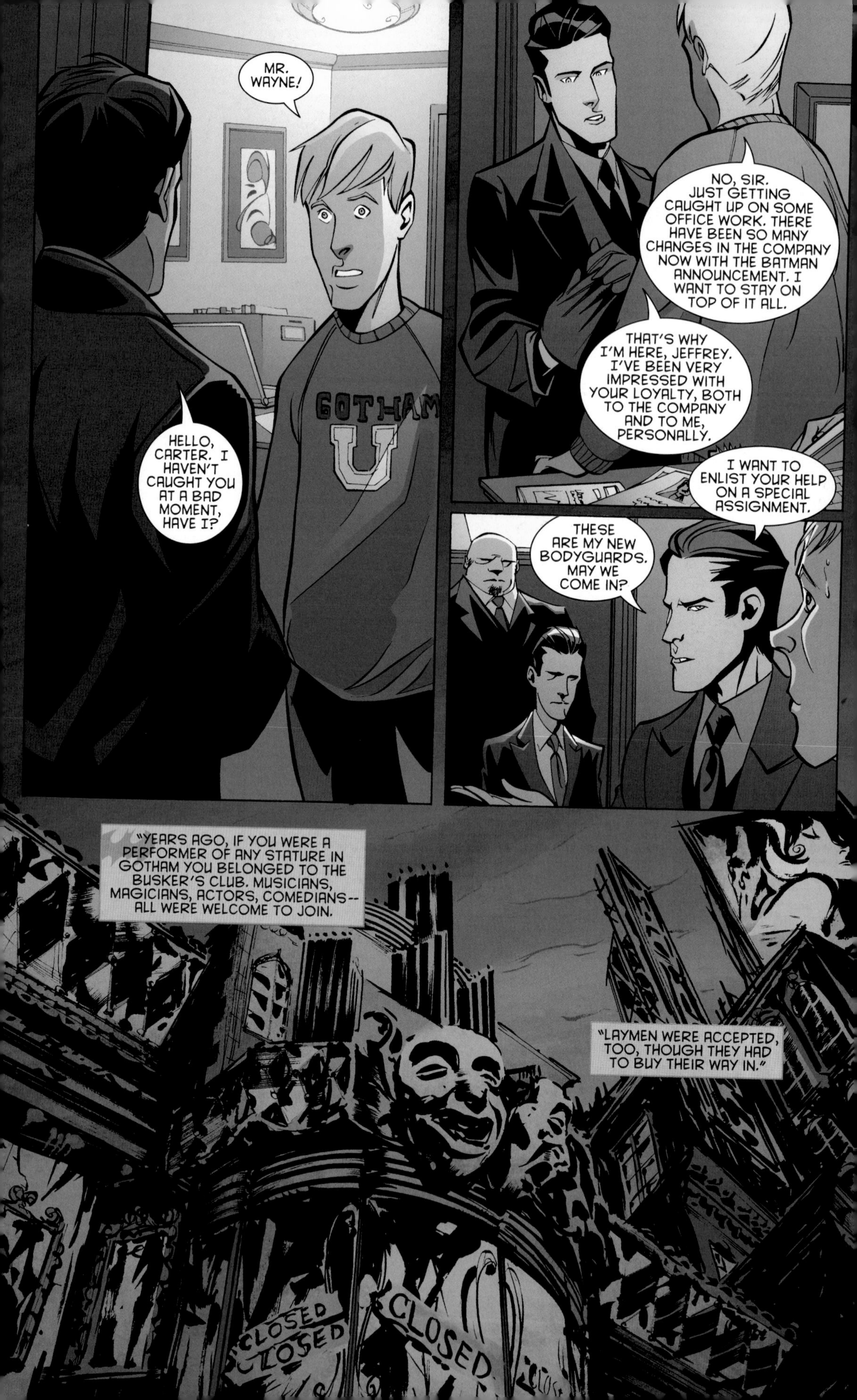
MR. WAYNE!
HELLO, CARTER. I HAVEN'T CAUGHT YOU AT A BAD MOMENT, HAVE I?
NO, SIR. JUST GETTING CAUGHT UP ON SOME OFFICE WORK. THERE HAVE BEEN SO MANY CHANGES IN THE COMPANY NOW WITH THE BATMAN ANNOUNCEMENT. I WANT TO STAY ON TOP OF IT ALL.
THAT'S WHY I'M HERE, JEFFREY. I'VE BEEN VERY IMPRESSED WITH YOUR LOYALTY, BOTH TO THE COMPANY AND TO ME, PERSONALLY.
I WANT TO ENLIST YOUR HELP ON A SPECIAL ASSIGNMENT.
THESE ARE MY NEW BODYGUARDS. MAY WE COME IN?
"YEARS AGO, IF YOU WERE A PERFORMER OF ANY STATURE IN GOTHAM YOU BELONGED TO THE BUSKER'S CLUB. MUSICIANS, MAGICIANS, ACTORS, COMEDIANS--ALL WERE WELCOME TO JOIN.
"LAYMEN WERE ACCEPTED, TOO, THOUGH THEY HAD TO BUY THEIR WAY IN."
CLOSED
CLOSED
CLOSED

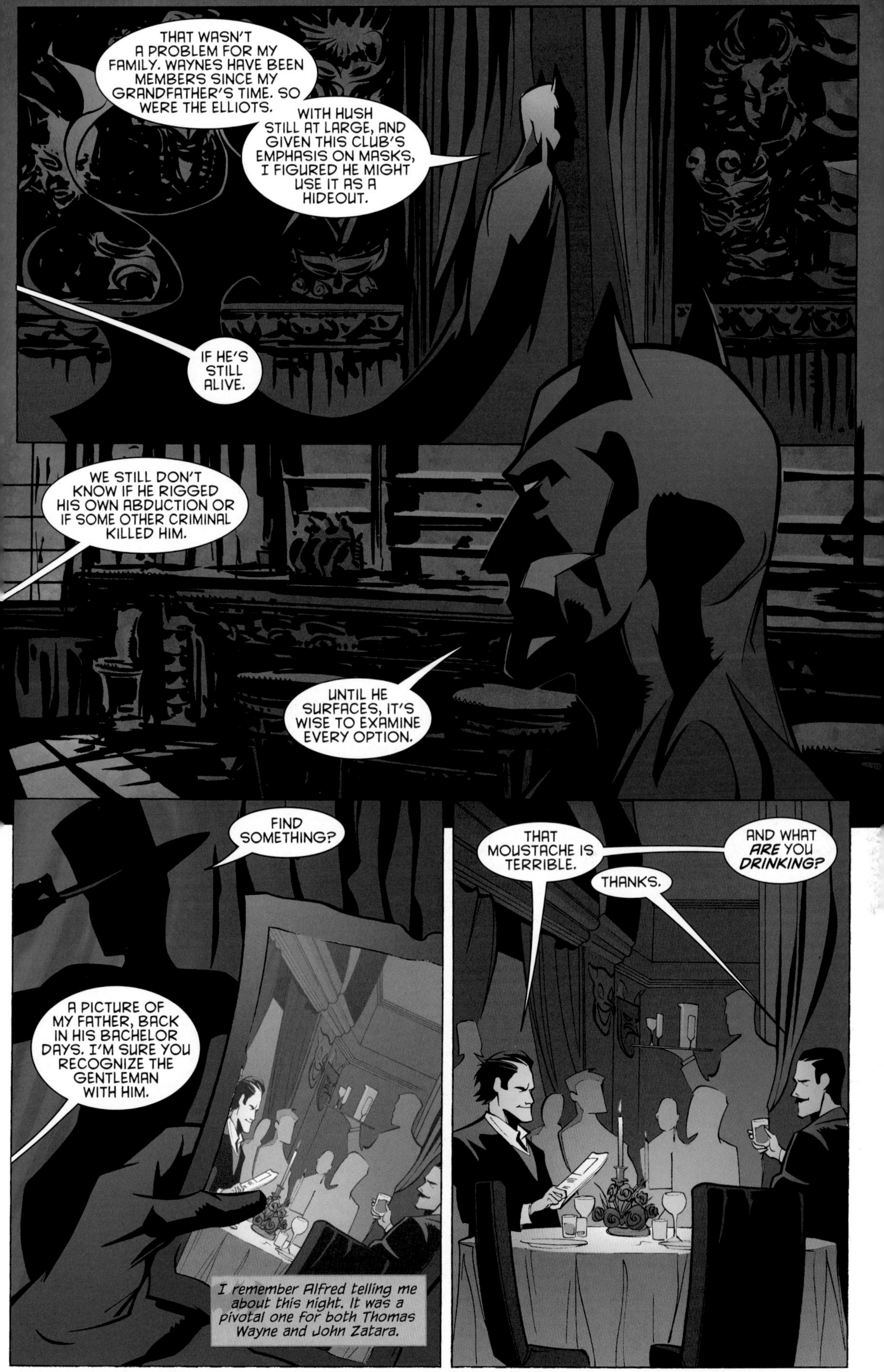
THAT WASN'T A PROBLEM FOR MY FAMILY. WAYNES HAVE BEEN MEMBERS SINCE MY GRANDFATHER'S TIME. SO WERE THE ELLIOTS.
WITH HUSH STILL AT LARGE, AND GIVEN THIS CLUB'S EMPHASIS ON MASKS, I FIGURED HE MIGHT USE IT AS A HIDEOUT.
IF HE'S STILL ALIVE.
WE STILL DON'T KNOW IF HE RIGGED HIS OWN ABDUCTION OR IF SOME OTHER CRIMINAL KILLED HIM.
UNTIL HE SURFACES, IT'S WISE TO EXAMINE EVERY OPTION.
FIND SOMETHING?
A PICTURE OF MY FATHER, BACK IN HIS BACHELOR DAYS. I'M SURE YOU RECOGNIZE THE GENTLEMAN WITH HIM.
I remember Alfred telling me about this night. It was a pivotal one for both Thomas Wayne and John Zatara.
THAT MOUSTACHE IS TERRIBLE.
THANKS.
AND WHAT *ARE* YOU *DRINKING?*

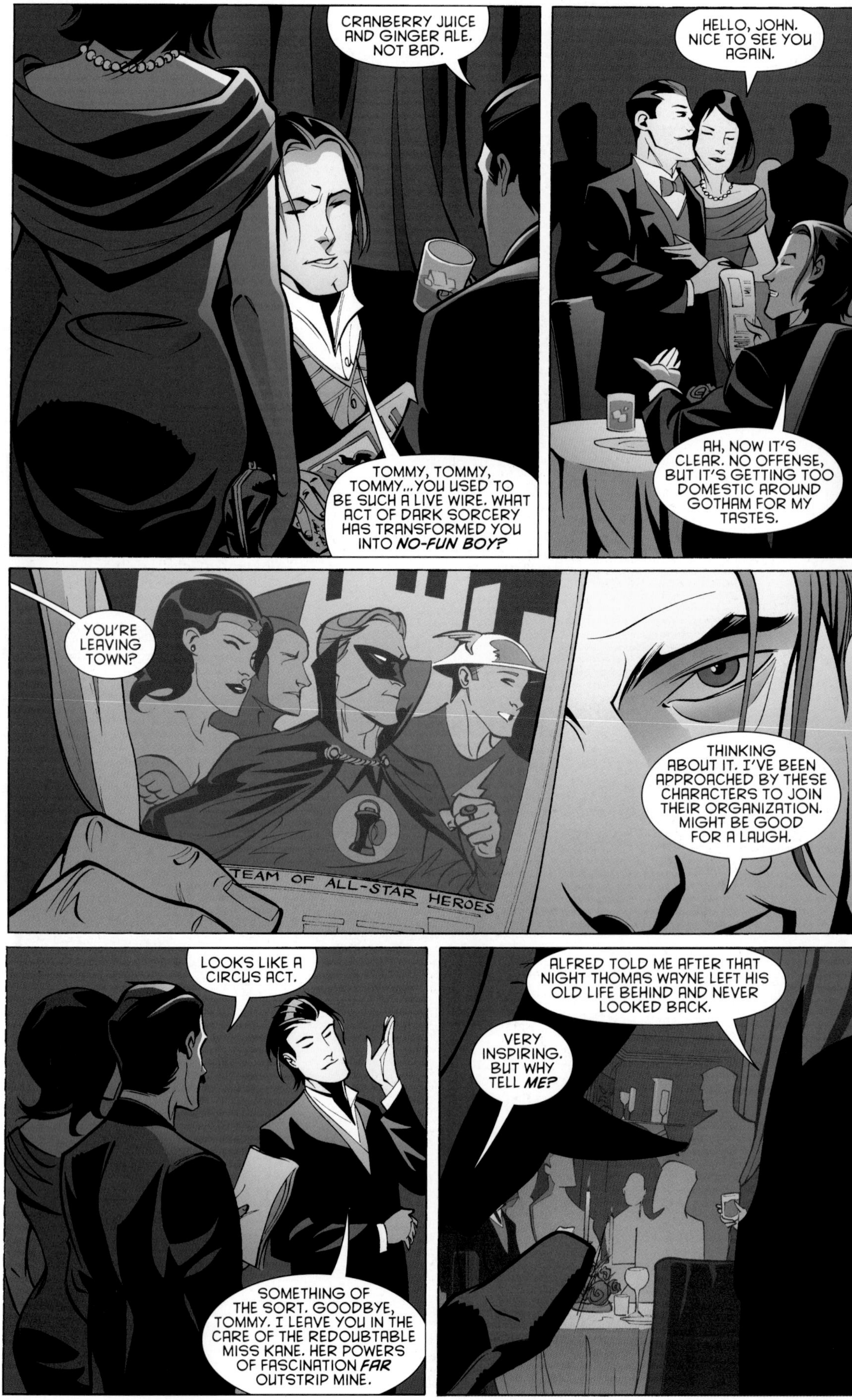

CRANBERRY JUICE AND GINGER ALE. NOT BAD.
TOMMY, TOMMY, TOMMY...YOU USED TO BE SUCH A LIVE WIRE. WHAT ACT OF DARK SORCERY HAS TRANSFORMED YOU INTO *NO-FUN BOY?*
HELLO, JOHN. NICE TO SEE YOU AGAIN.
AH, NOW IT'S CLEAR. NO OFFENSE, BUT IT'S GETTING TOO DOMESTIC AROUND GOTHAM FOR MY TASTES.
YOU'RE LEAVING TOWN?
TEAM OF ALL-STAR HEROES
THINKING ABOUT IT. I'VE BEEN APPROACHED BY THESE CHARACTERS TO JOIN THEIR ORGANIZATION. MIGHT BE GOOD FOR A LAUGH.
LOOKS LIKE A CIRCUS ACT.
SOMETHING OF THE SORT. GOODBYE, TOMMY. I LEAVE YOU IN THE CARE OF THE REDOUBTABLE MISS KANE. HER POWERS OF FASCINATION *FAR* OUTSTRIP MINE.
ALFRED TOLD ME AFTER THAT NIGHT THOMAS WAYNE LEFT HIS OLD LIFE BEHIND AND NEVER LOOKED BACK.
VERY INSPIRING. BUT WHY TELL *ME?*

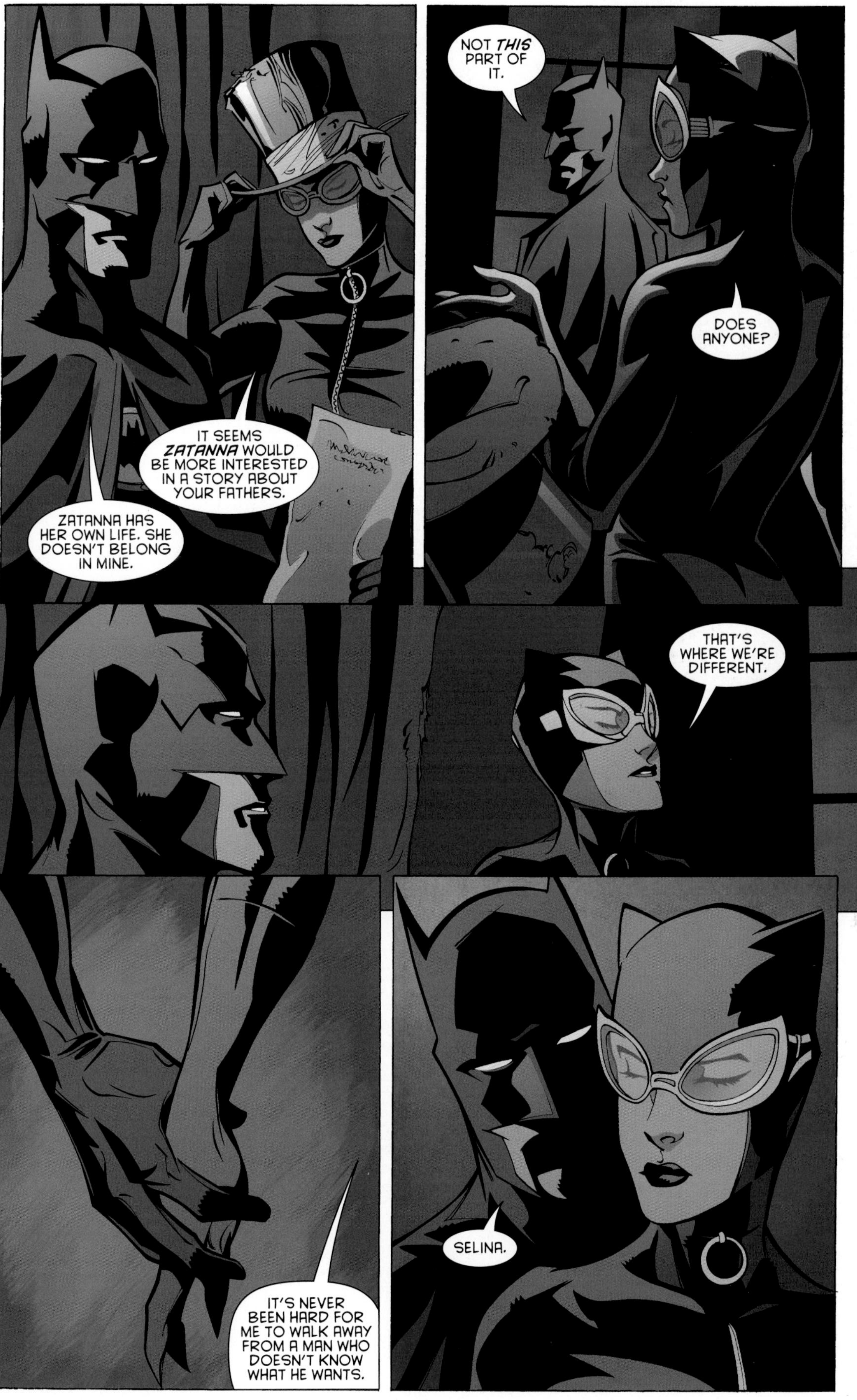

IT SEEMS ZATANNA WOULD BE MORE INTERESTED IN A STORY ABOUT YOUR FATHERS.
ZATANNA HAS HER OWN LIFE. SHE DOESN'T BELONG IN MINE.
NOT THIS PART OF IT.
DOES ANYONE?
THAT'S WHERE WE'RE DIFFERENT.
IT'S NEVER BEEN HARD FOR ME TO WALK AWAY FROM A MAN WHO DOESN'T KNOW WHAT HE WANTS.
SELINA.

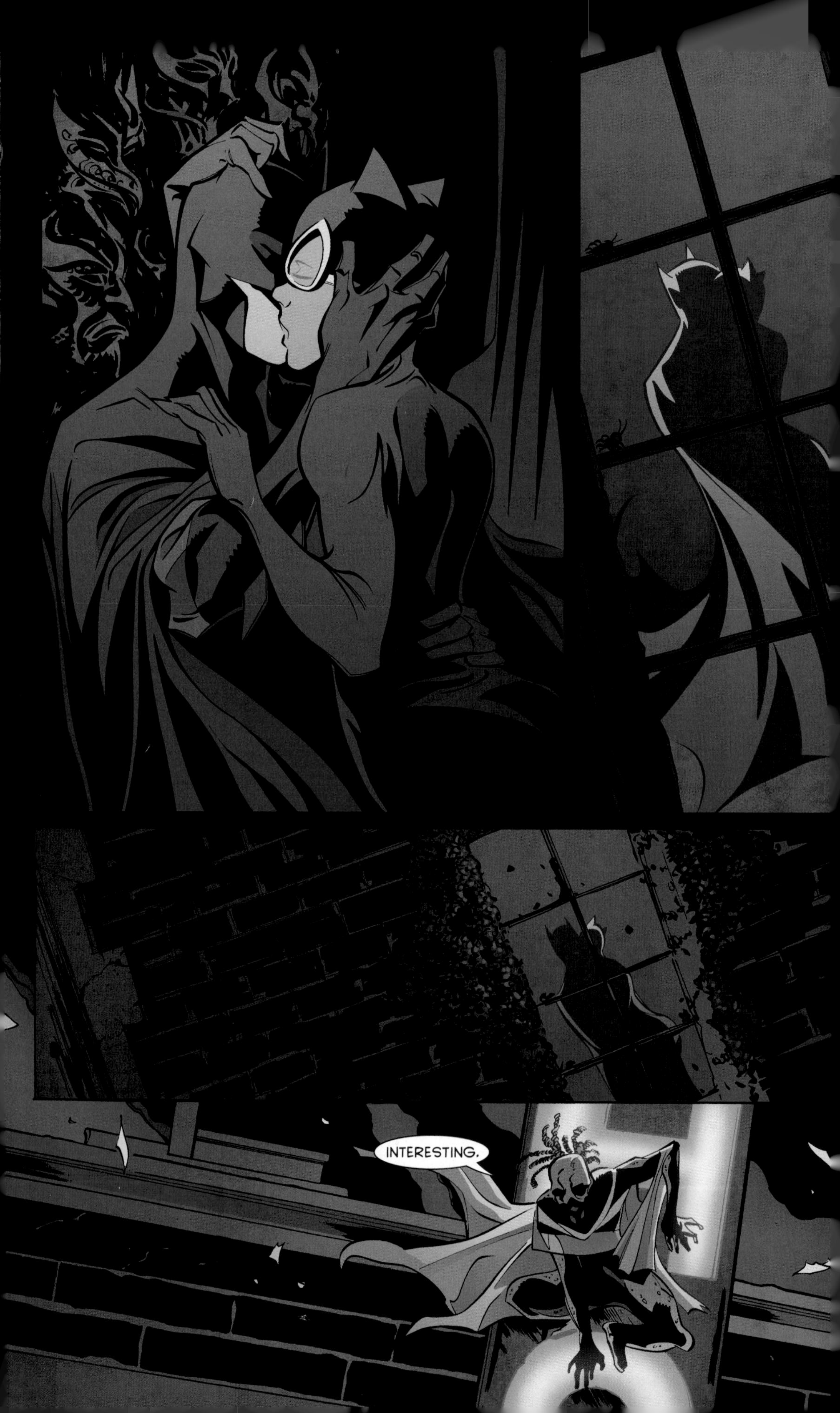
INTERESTING.

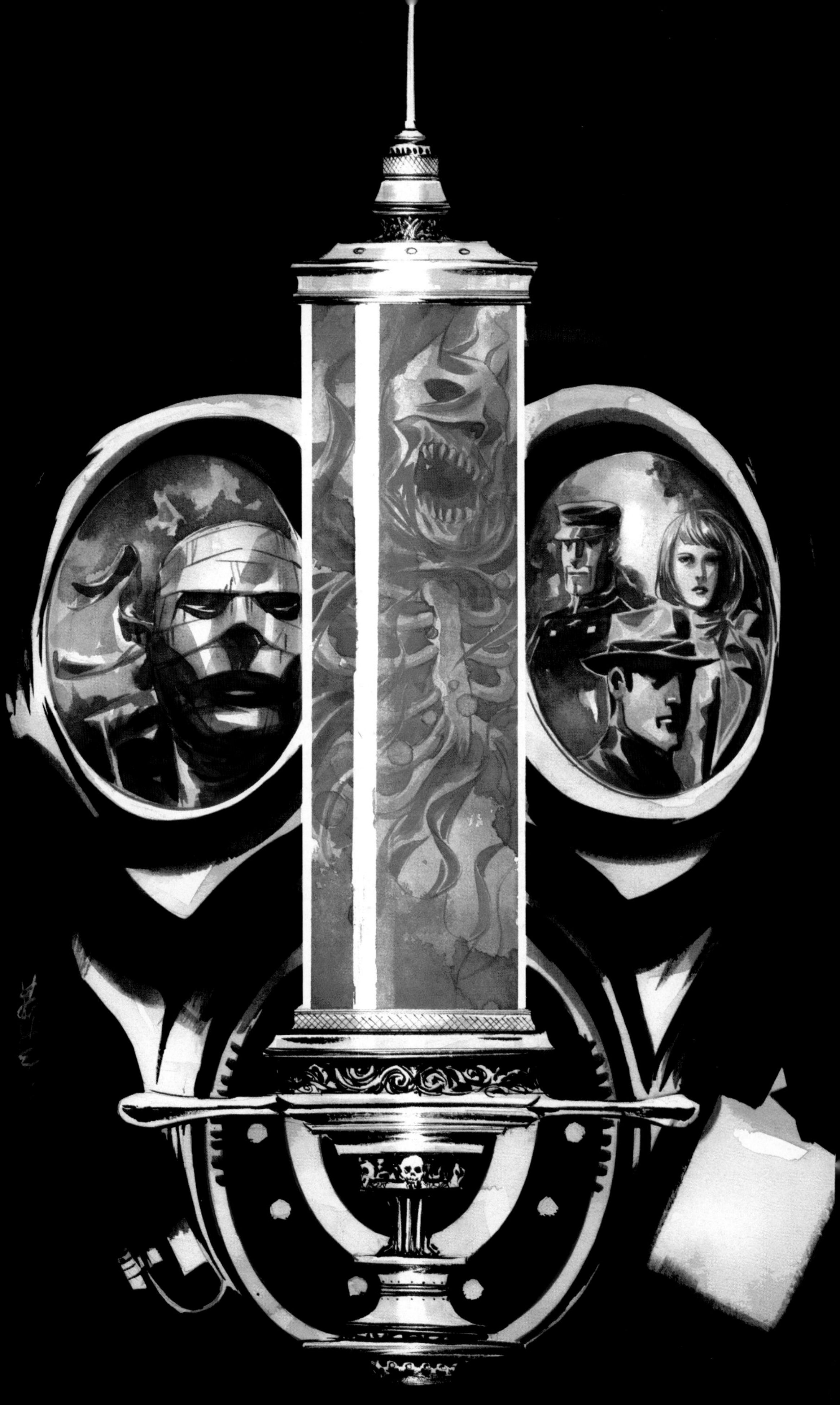

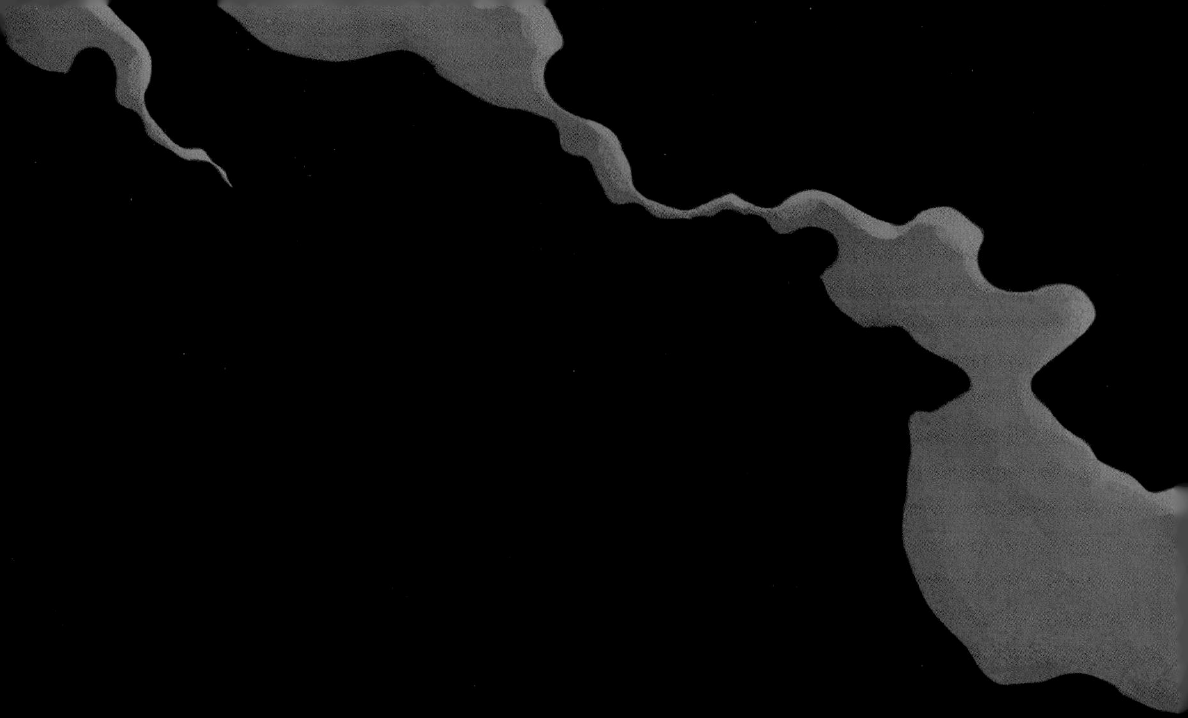

“That was the night it all changed in Gotham.”

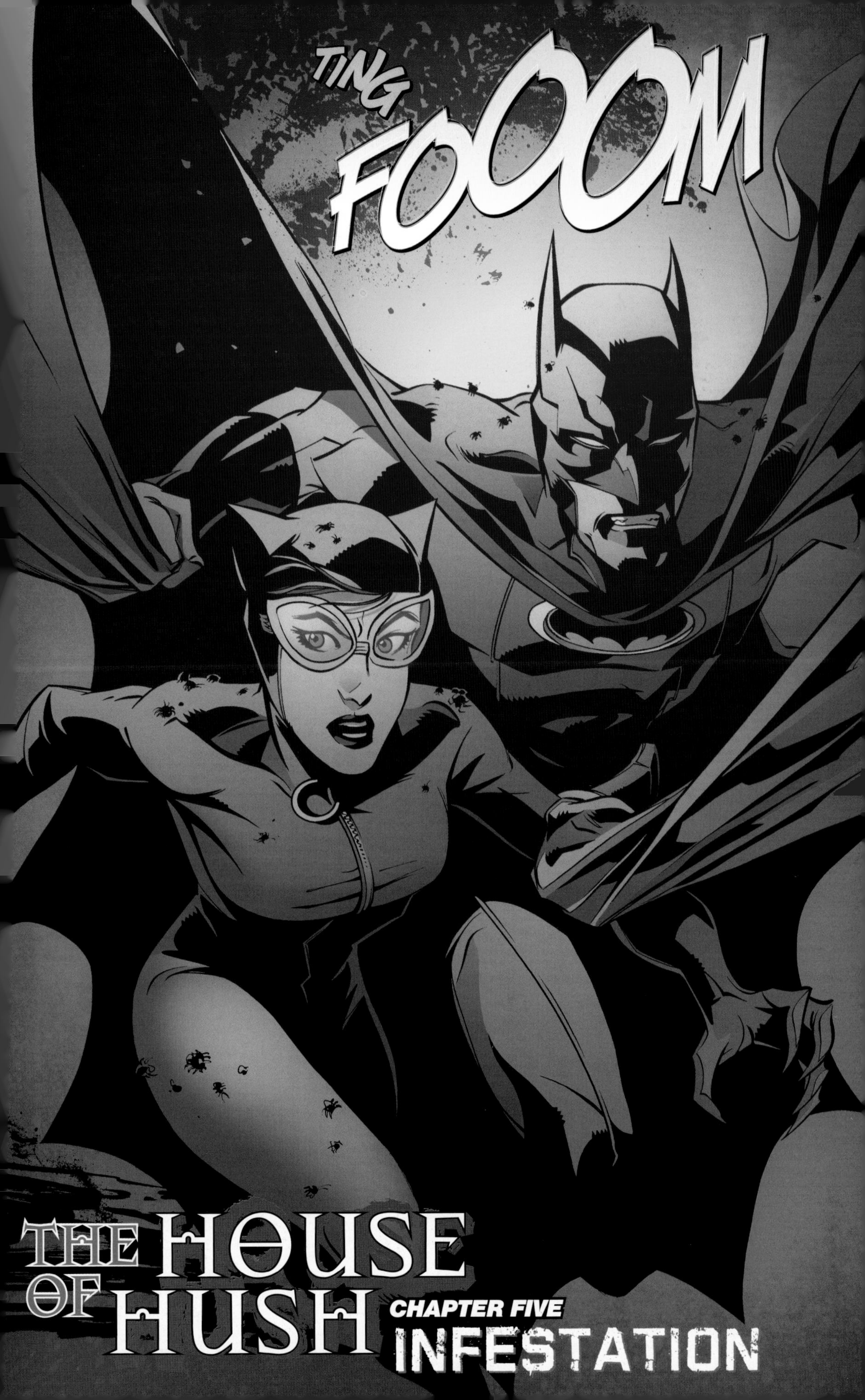
TING
FOOOM
THE HOUSE OF HUSH
CHAPTER FIVE
INFESTATION

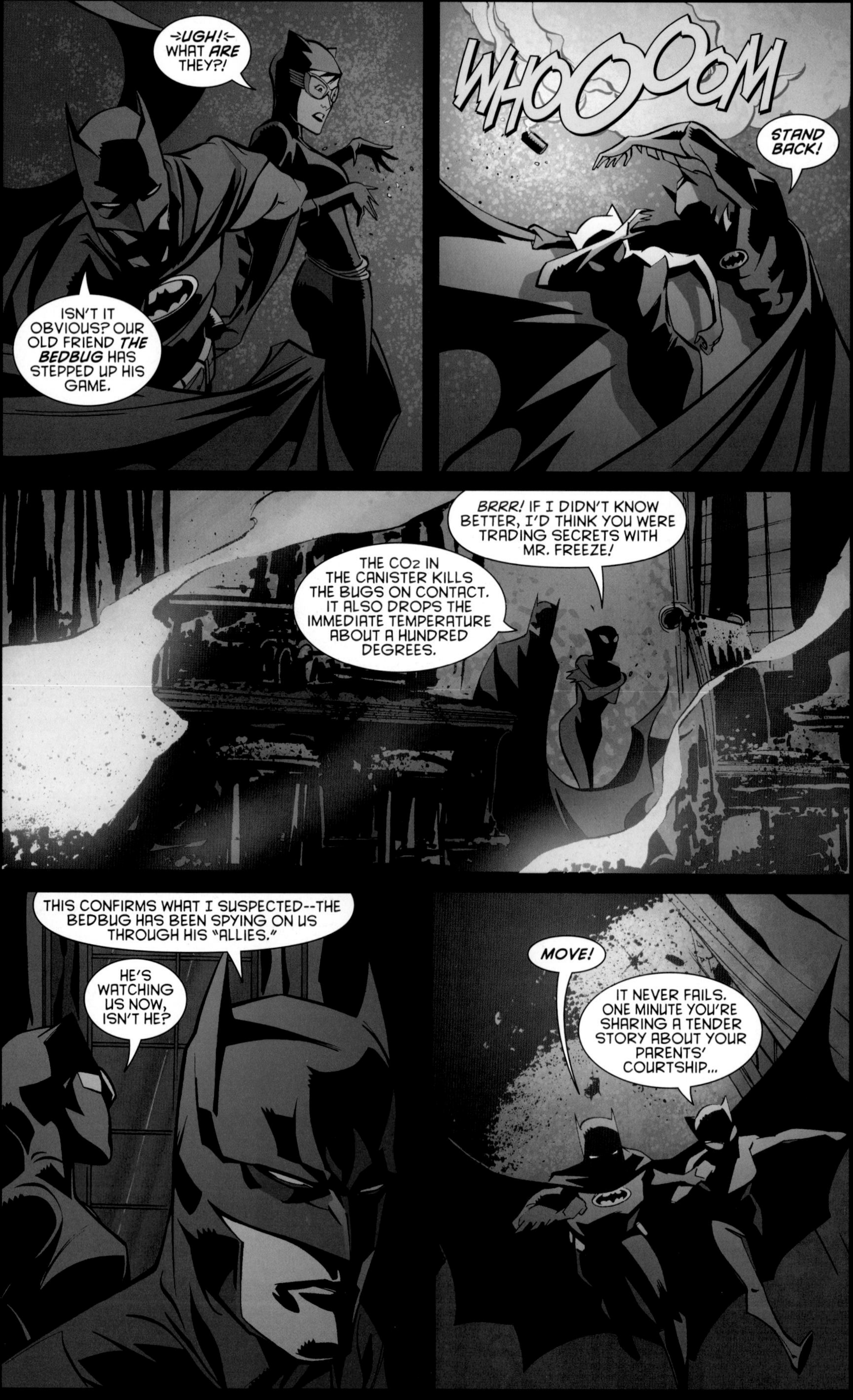

>UGH!< WHAT ARE THEY?!
ISN'T IT OBVIOUS? OUR OLD FRIEND THE BEDBUG HAS STEPPED UP HIS GAME.
WHOOOOOM
STAND BACK!
BRRR! IF I DIDN'T KNOW BETTER, I'D THINK YOU WERE TRADING SECRETS WITH MR. FREEZE!
THE CO2 IN THE CANISTER KILLS THE BUGS ON CONTACT. IT ALSO DROPS THE IMMEDIATE TEMPERATURE ABOUT A HUNDRED DEGREES.
THIS CONFIRMS WHAT I SUSPECTED--THE BEDBUG HAS BEEN SPYING ON US THROUGH HIS "ALLIES."
HE'S WATCHING US NOW, ISN'T HE?
MOVE!
IT NEVER FAILS. ONE MINUTE YOU'RE SHARING A TENDER STORY ABOUT YOUR PARENTS' COURTSHIP...

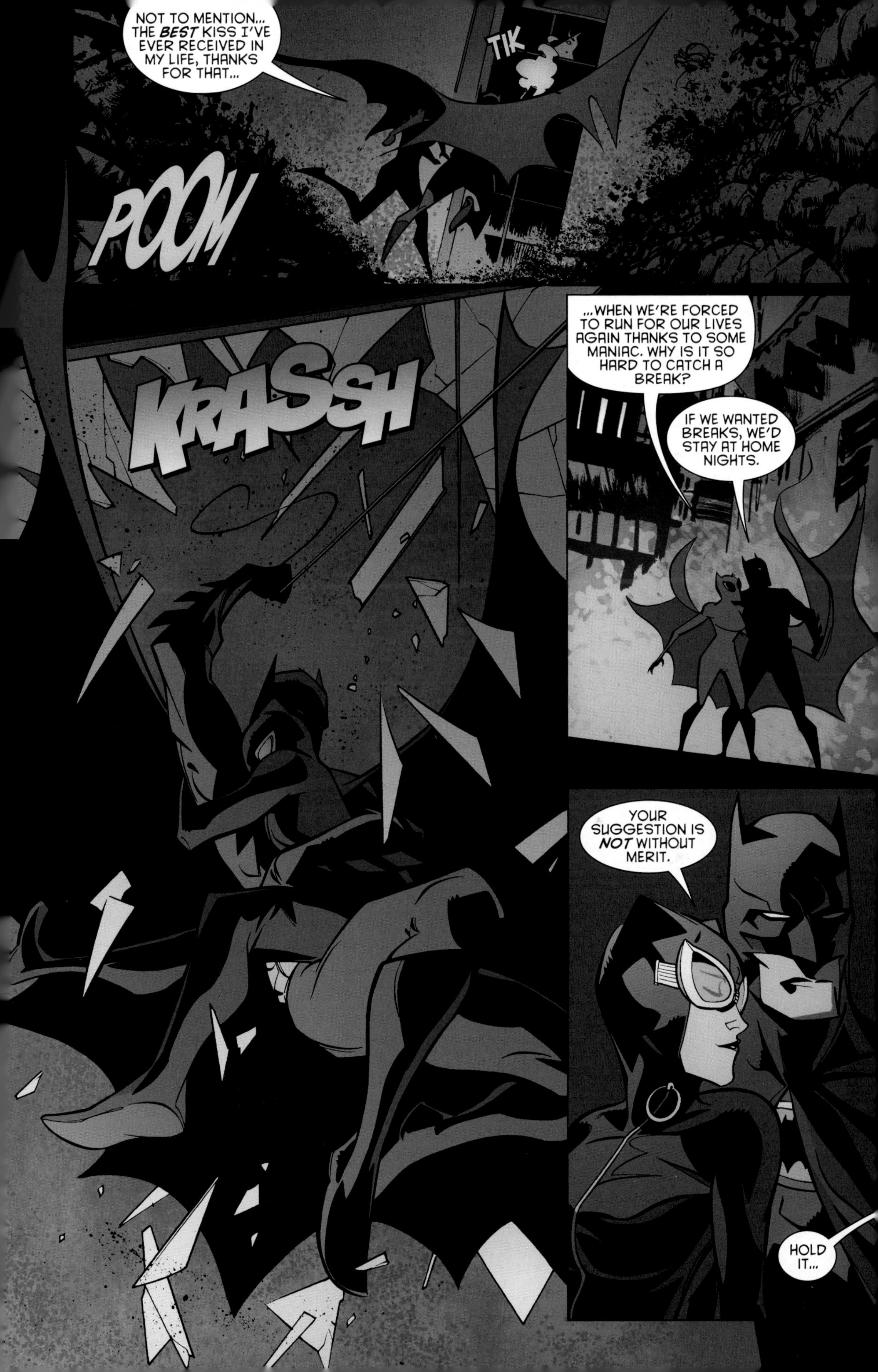
NOT TO MENTION... THE BEST KISS I'VE EVER RECEIVED IN MY LIFE, THANKS FOR THAT...
TIK
POOM
KRASSH
...WHEN WE'RE FORCED TO RUN FOR OUR LIVES AGAIN THANKS TO SOME MANIAC. WHY IS IT SO HARD TO CATCH A BREAK?
IF WE WANTED BREAKS, WE'D STAY AT HOME NIGHTS.
YOUR SUGGESTION IS NOT WITHOUT MERIT.
HOLD IT...

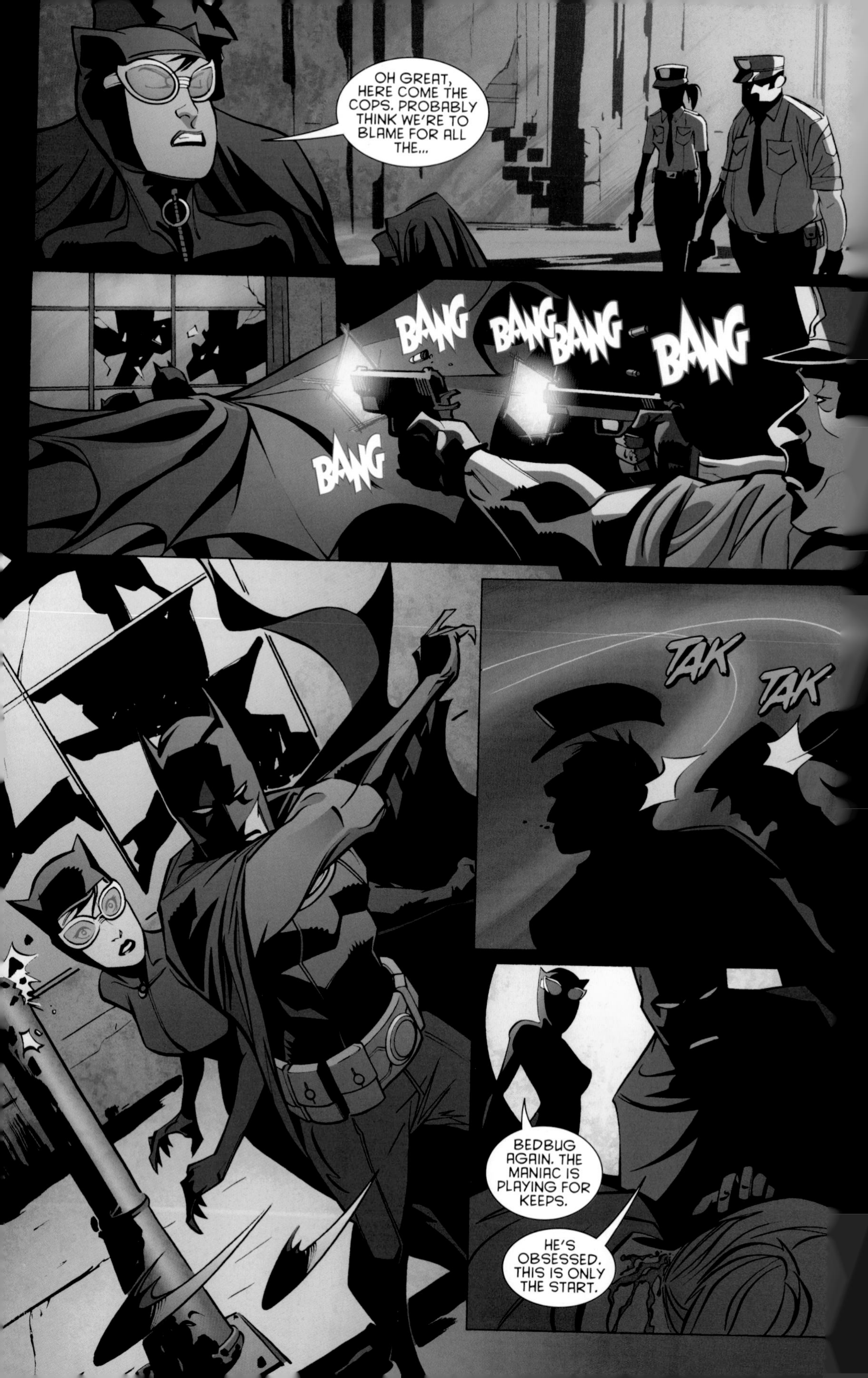
OH GREAT, HERE COME THE COPS. PROBABLY THINK WE'RE TO BLAME FOR ALL THE...
BANG
BANG
BANG
BANG
BANG
TAK
TAK
BEDBUG AGAIN. THE MANIAC IS PLAYING FOR KEEPS.
HE'S OBSESSED. THIS IS ONLY THE START.

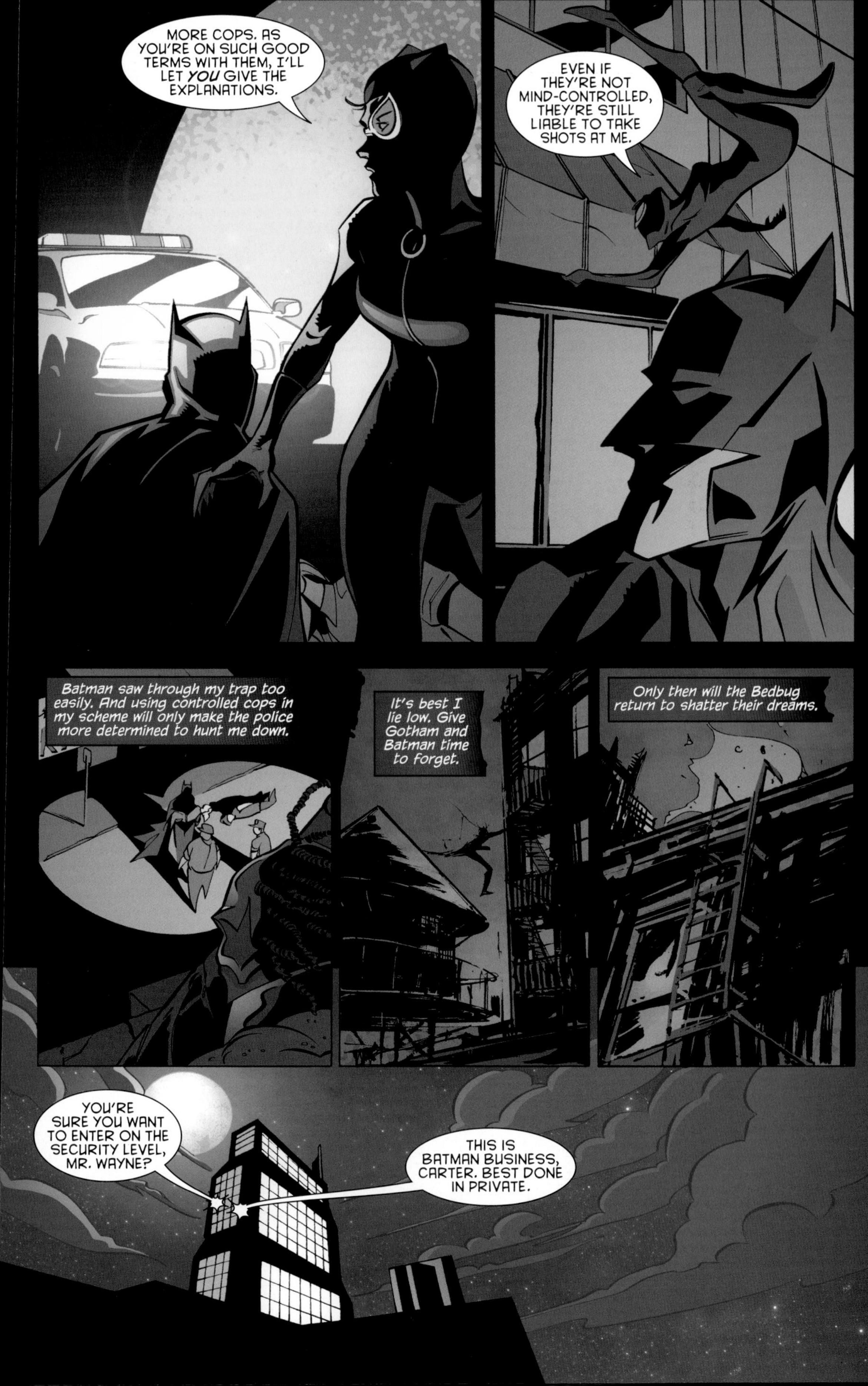

MORE COPS. AS YOU'RE ON SUCH GOOD TERMS WITH THEM, I'LL LET *YOU* GIVE THE EXPLANATIONS.
EVEN IF THEY'RE NOT MIND-CONTROLLED, THEY'RE STILL LIABLE TO TAKE SHOTS AT ME.
Batman saw through my trap too easily. And using controlled cops in my scheme will only make the police more determined to hunt me down.
It's best I lie low. Give Gotham and Batman time to forget.
Only then will the Bedbug return to shatter their dreams.
YOU'RE SURE YOU WANT TO ENTER ON THE SECURITY LEVEL, MR. WAYNE?
THIS IS BATMAN BUSINESS, CARTER. BEST DONE IN PRIVATE.

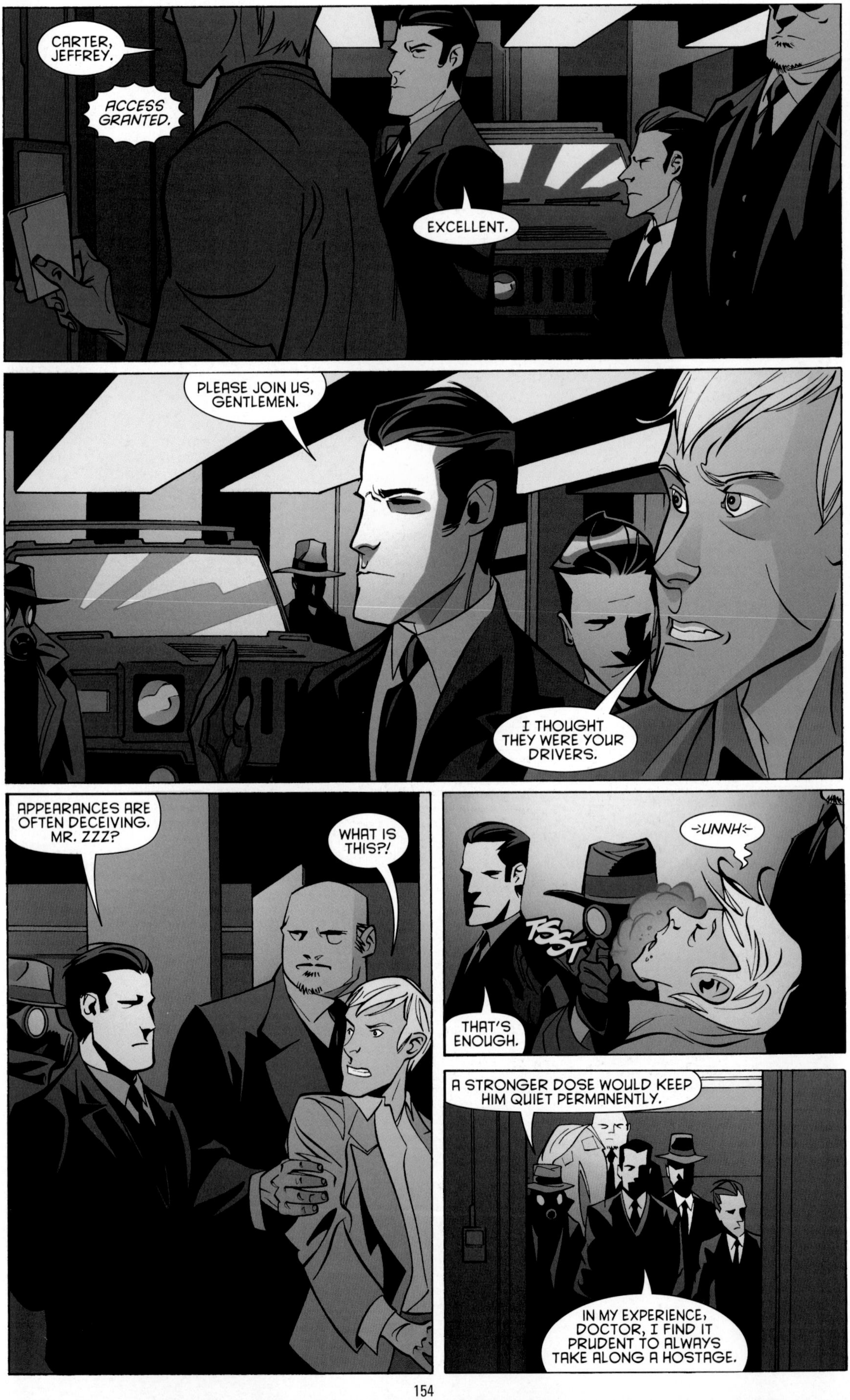
CARTER, JEFFREY.
ACCESS GRANTED.
EXCELLENT.
PLEASE JOIN US, GENTLEMEN.
I THOUGHT THEY WERE YOUR DRIVERS.
APPEARANCES ARE OFTEN DECEIVING. MR. ZZZ?
WHAT IS THIS?!
UNNH
TSST
THAT'S ENOUGH.
A STRONGER DOSE WOULD KEEP HIM QUIET PERMANENTLY.
IN MY EXPERIENCE, DOCTOR, I FIND IT PRUDENT TO ALWAYS TAKE ALONG A HOSTAGE.

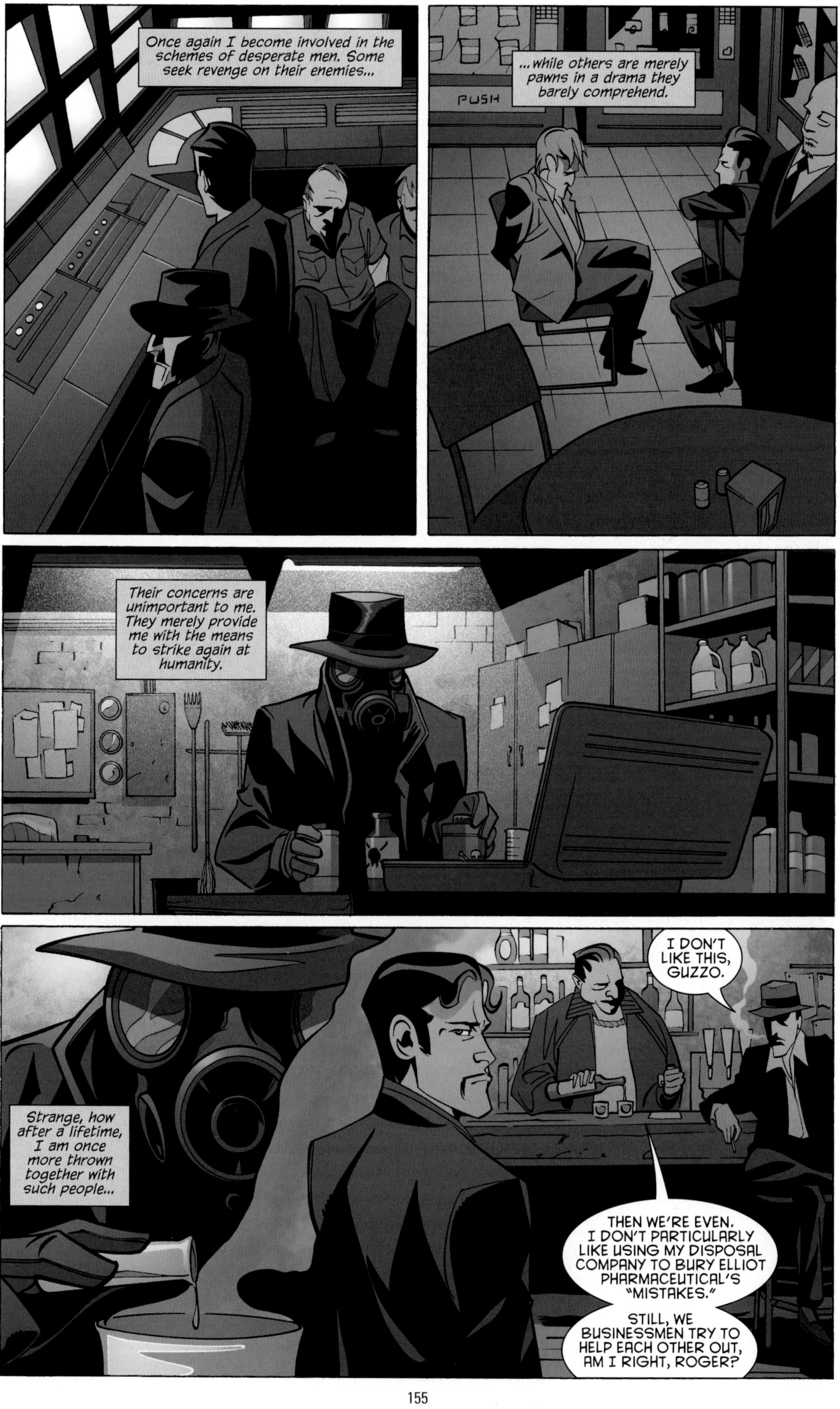

Once again I become involved in the schemes of desperate men. Some seek revenge on their enemies...
PUSH
...while others are merely pawns in a drama they barely comprehend.
Their concerns are unimportant to me. They merely provide me with the means to strike again at humanity.
I DON'T LIKE THIS, GUZZO.
Strange, how after a lifetime, I am once more thrown together with such people...
THEN WE'RE EVEN. I DON'T PARTICULARLY LIKE USING MY DISPOSAL COMPANY TO BURY ELLIOT PHARMACEUTICAL'S "MISTAKES."
STILL, WE BUSINESSMEN TRY TO HELP EACH OTHER OUT, AM I RIGHT, ROGER?

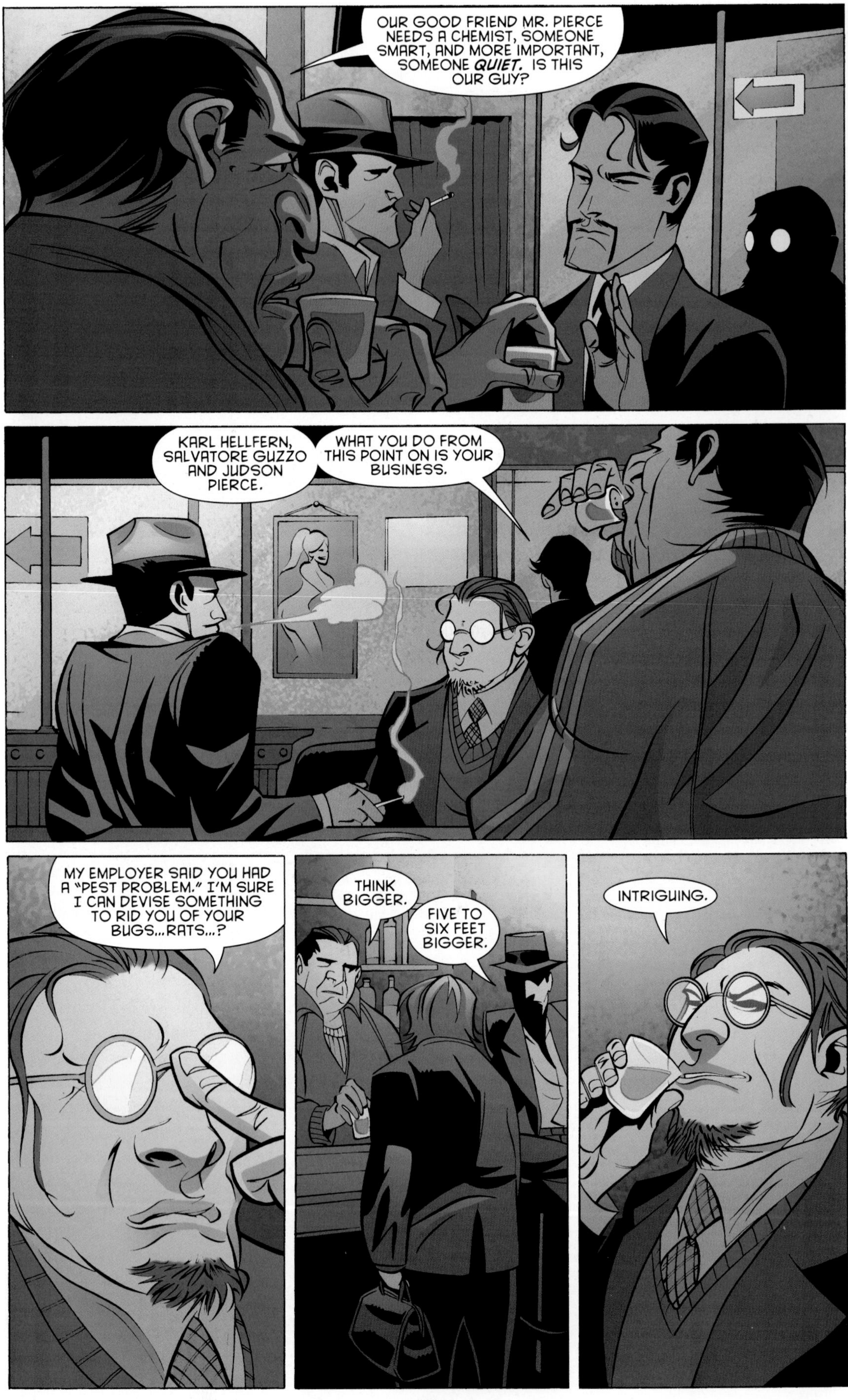
OUR GOOD FRIEND MR. PIERCE NEEDS A CHEMIST, SOMEONE SMART, AND MORE IMPORTANT, SOMEONE *QUIET.* IS THIS OUR GUY?
KARL HELLFERN, SALVATORE GUZZO AND JUDSON PIERCE.
WHAT YOU DO FROM THIS POINT ON IS YOUR BUSINESS.
MY EMPLOYER SAID YOU HAD A "PEST PROBLEM." I'M SURE I CAN DEVISE SOMETHING TO RID YOU OF YOUR BUGS...RATS...?
THINK BIGGER.
FIVE TO SIX FEET BIGGER.
INTRIGUING.

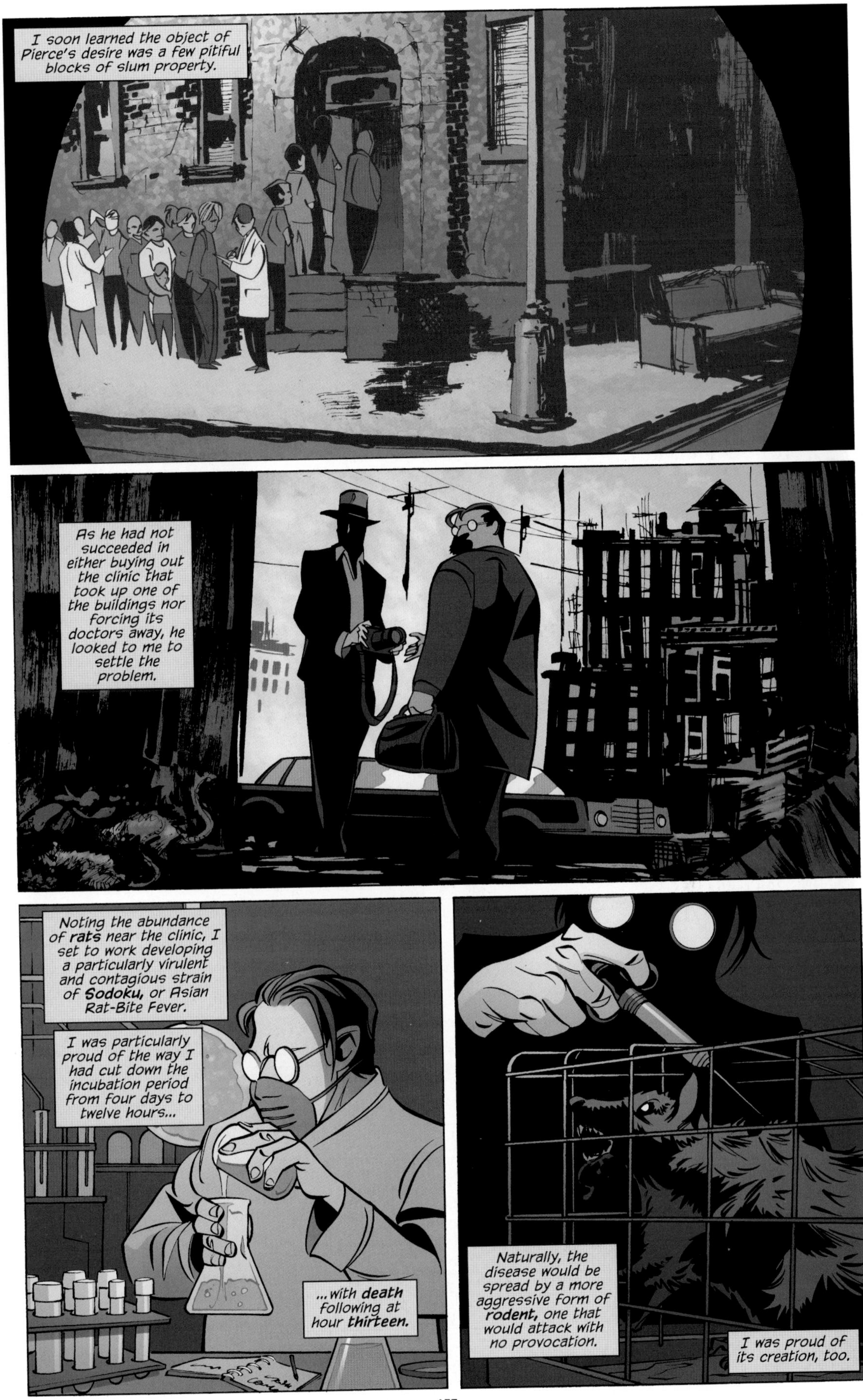
I soon learned the object of Pierce's desire was a few pitiful blocks of slum property.
As he had not succeeded in either buying out the clinic that took up one of the buildings nor forcing its doctors away, he looked to me to settle the problem.
Noting the abundance of **rats** near the clinic, I set to work developing a particularly virulent and contagious strain of **Sodoku,** or Asian Rat-Bite Fever.
I was particularly proud of the way I had cut down the incubation period from four days to twelve hours...
...with **death** following at hour **thirteen.**
Naturally, the disease would be spread by a more aggressive form of **rodent,** one that would attack with no provocation.
I was proud of its creation, too.

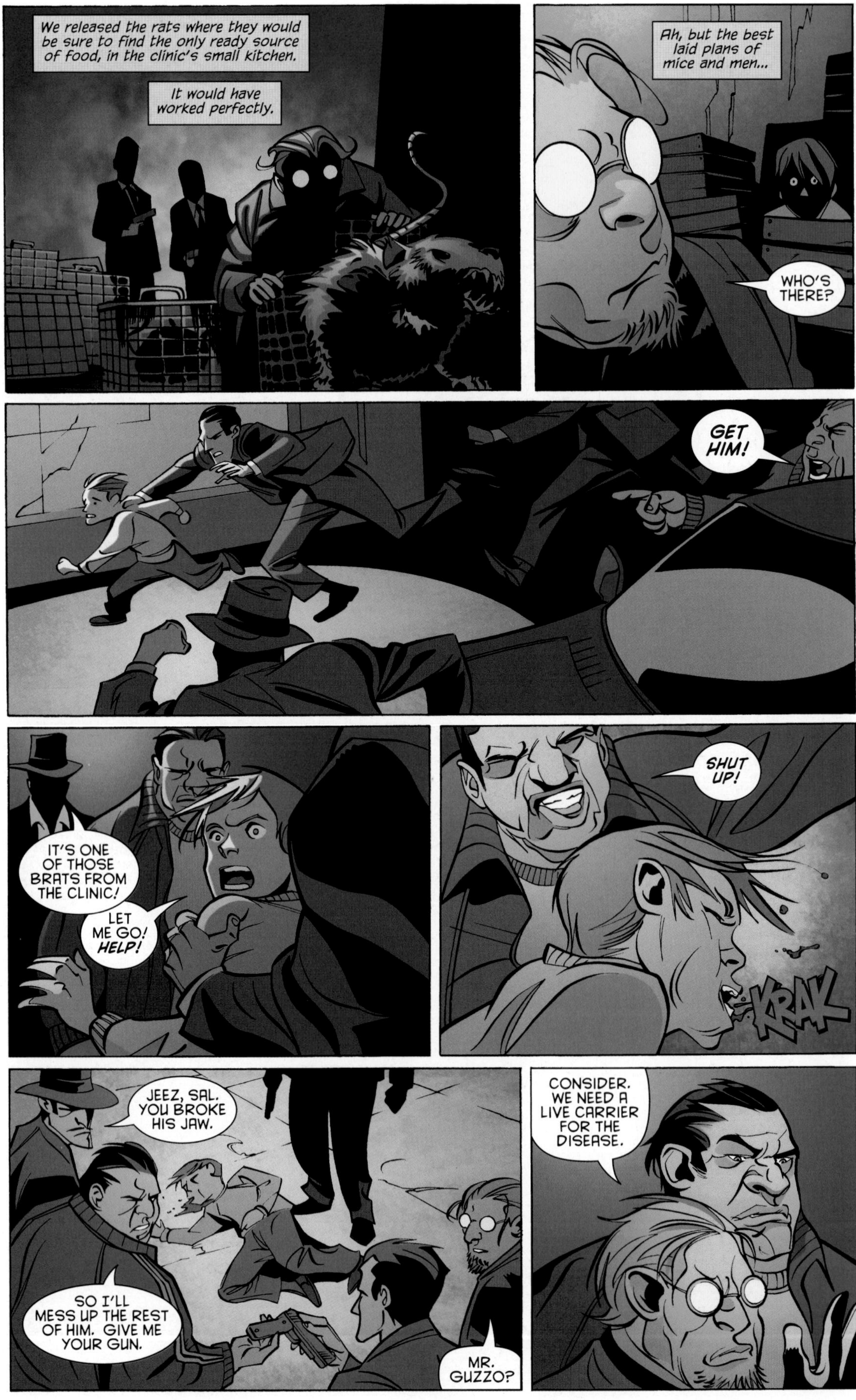

We released the rats where they would be sure to find the only ready source of food, in the clinic's small kitchen.
It would have worked perfectly.
Ah, but the best laid plans of mice and men...
WHO'S THERE?
GET HIM!
IT'S ONE OF THOSE BRATS FROM THE CLINIC!
LET ME GO! HELP!
SHUT UP!
KRAK
JEEZ, SAL. YOU BROKE HIS JAW.
SO I'LL MESS UP THE REST OF HIM. GIVE ME YOUR GUN.
MR. GUZZO?
CONSIDER. WE NEED A LIVE CARRIER FOR THE DISEASE.

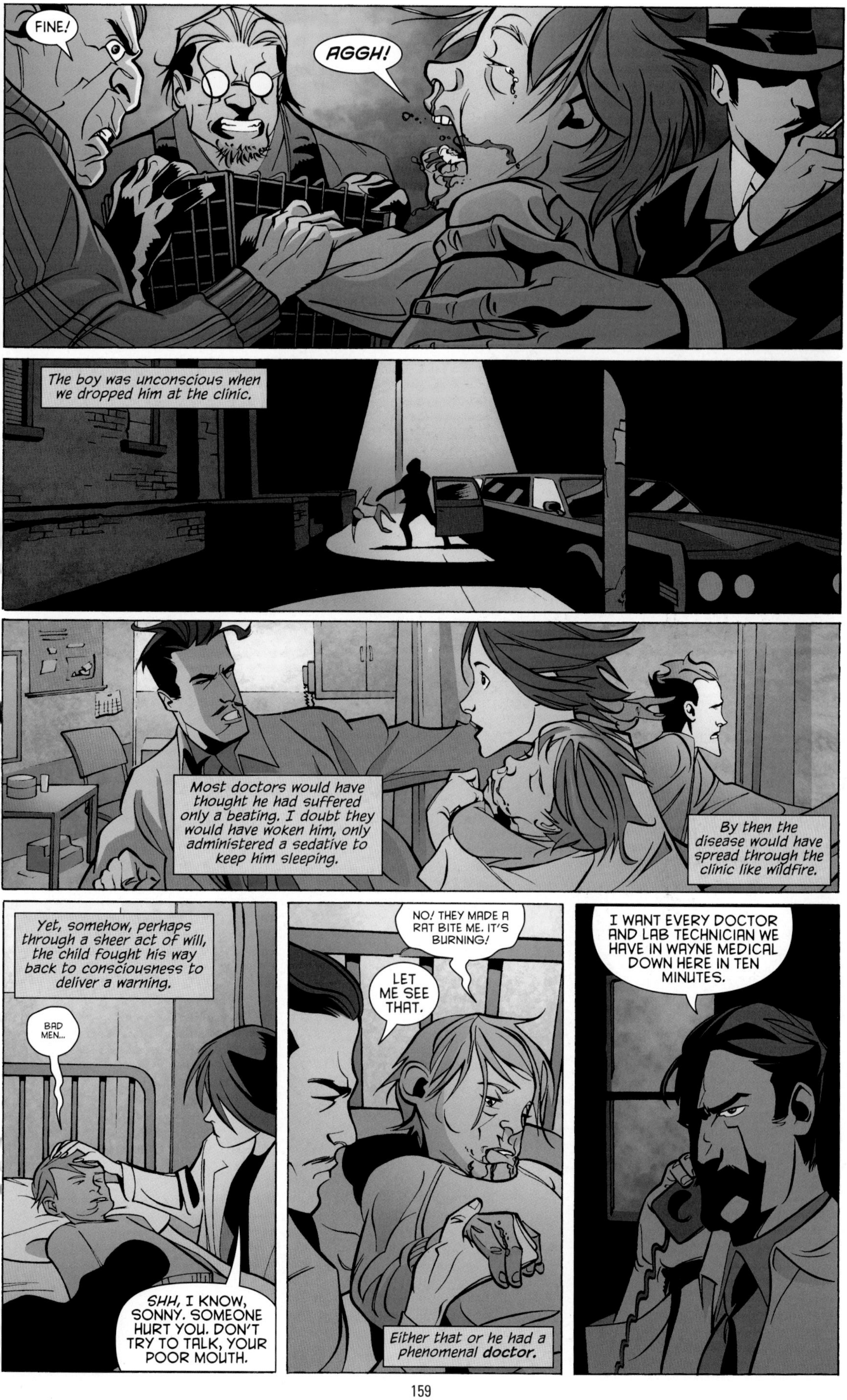
FINE!
AGGH!
The boy was unconscious when we dropped him at the clinic.
Most doctors would have thought he had suffered only a beating. I doubt they would have woken him, only administered a sedative to keep him sleeping.
By then the disease would have spread through the clinic like wildfire.
Yet, somehow, perhaps through a sheer act of will, the child fought his way back to consciousness to deliver a warning.
BAD MEN...
SHH, I KNOW, SONNY. SOMEONE HURT YOU. DON'T TRY TO TALK, YOUR POOR MOUTH.
NO! THEY MADE A RAT BITE ME. IT'S BURNING!
LET ME SEE THAT.
Either that or he had a phenomenal **doctor.**
I WANT EVERY DOCTOR AND LAB TECHNICIAN WE HAVE IN WAYNE MEDICAL DOWN HERE IN TEN MINUTES.

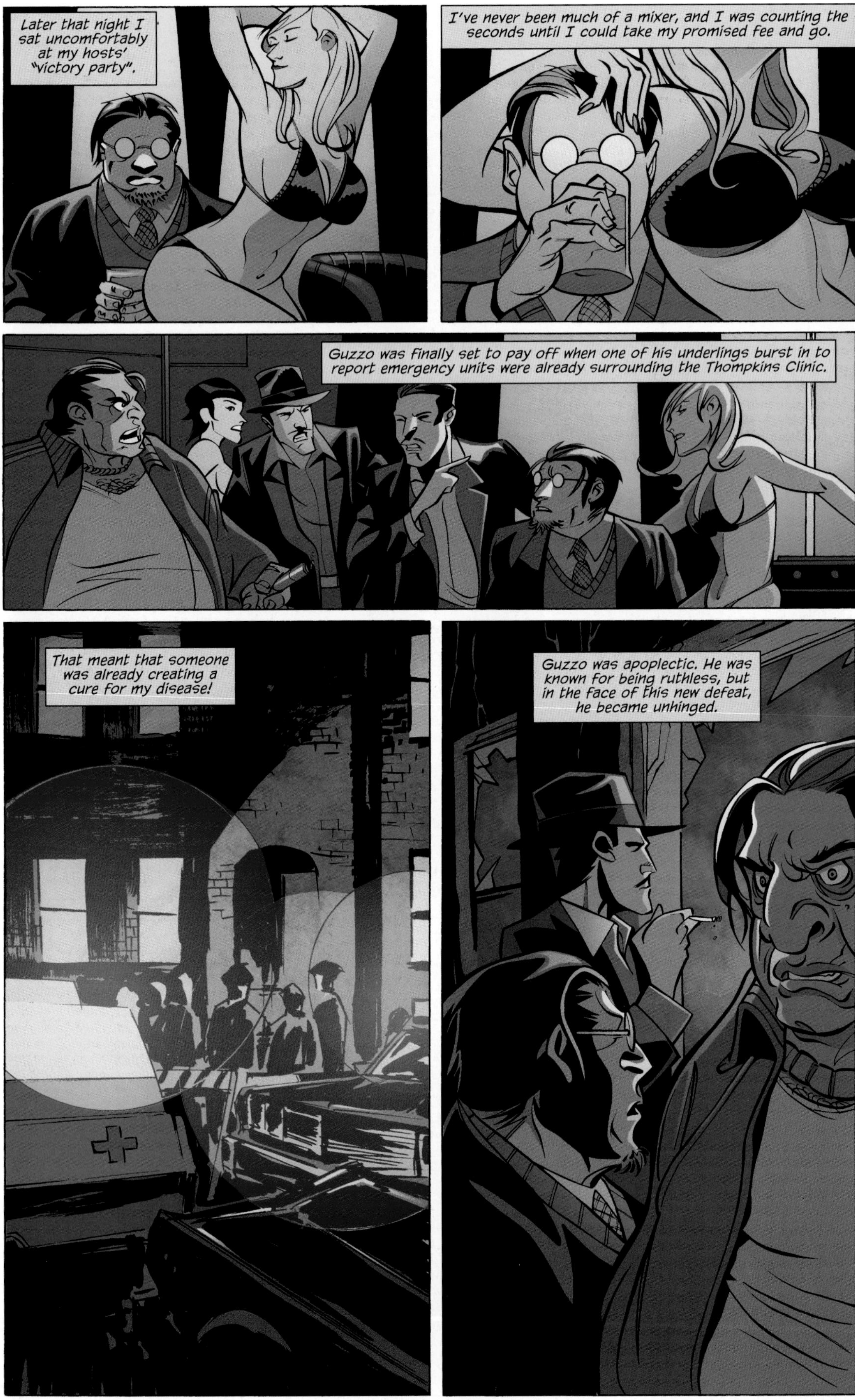
Later that night I sat uncomfortably at my hosts' "victory party".
I've never been much of a mixer, and I was counting the seconds until I could take my promised fee and go.
Guzzo was finally set to pay off when one of his underlings burst in to report emergency units were already surrounding the Thompkins Clinic.
That meant that someone was already creating a cure for my disease!
Guzzo was apoplectic. He was known for being ruthless, but in the face of this new defeat, he became unhinged.

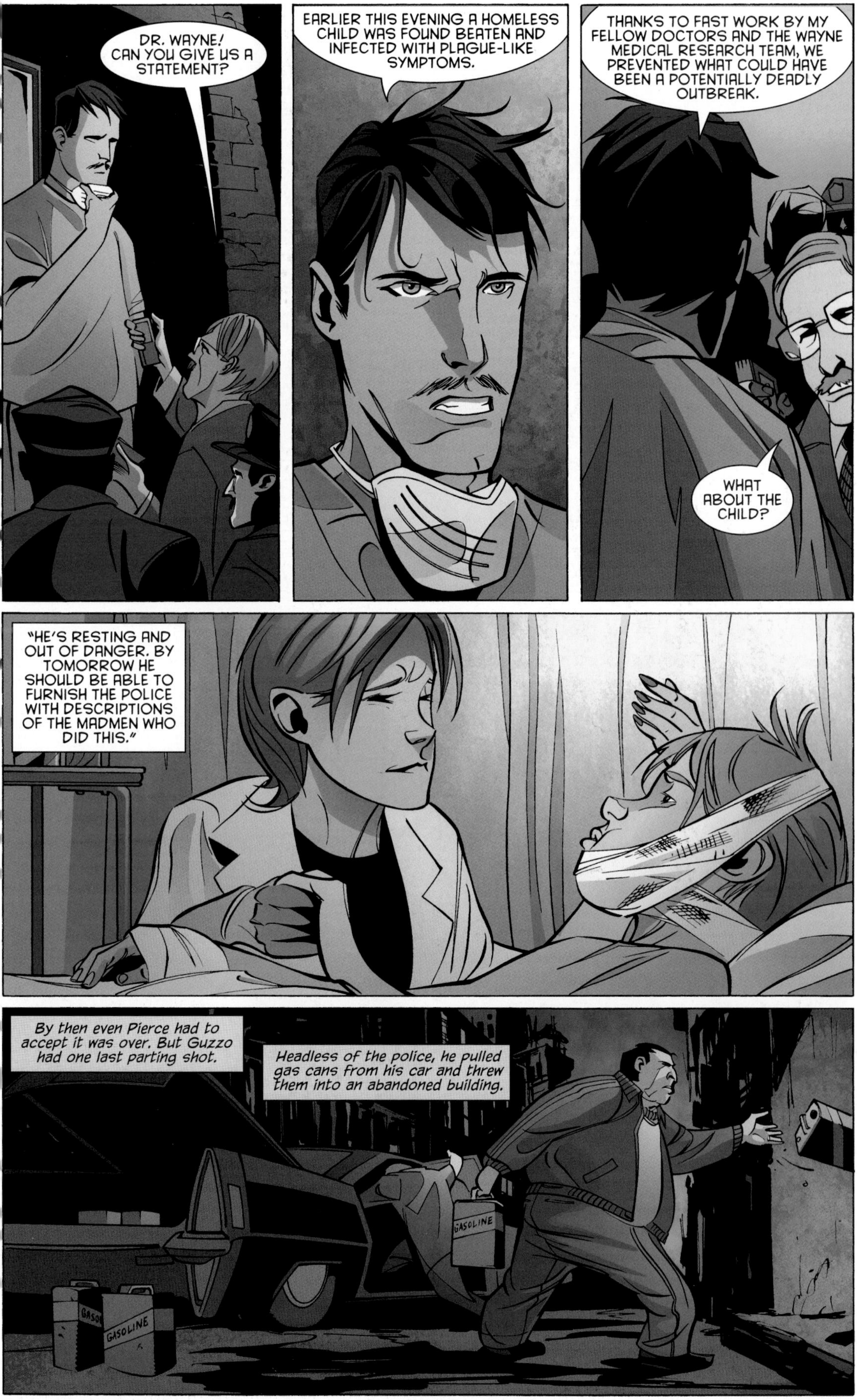
DR. WAYNE! CAN YOU GIVE US A STATEMENT?
EARLIER THIS EVENING A HOMELESS CHILD WAS FOUND BEATEN AND INFECTED WITH PLAGUE-LIKE SYMPTOMS.
THANKS TO FAST WORK BY MY FELLOW DOCTORS AND THE WAYNE MEDICAL RESEARCH TEAM, WE PREVENTED WHAT COULD HAVE BEEN A POTENTIALLY DEADLY OUTBREAK.
WHAT ABOUT THE CHILD?
"HE'S RESTING AND OUT OF DANGER. BY TOMORROW HE SHOULD BE ABLE TO FURNISH THE POLICE WITH DESCRIPTIONS OF THE MADMEN WHO DID THIS."
By then even Pierce had to accept it was over. But Guzzo had one last parting shot.
Headless of the police, he pulled gas cans from his car and threw them into an abandoned building.
GASOLINE
GASO
GASOLINE

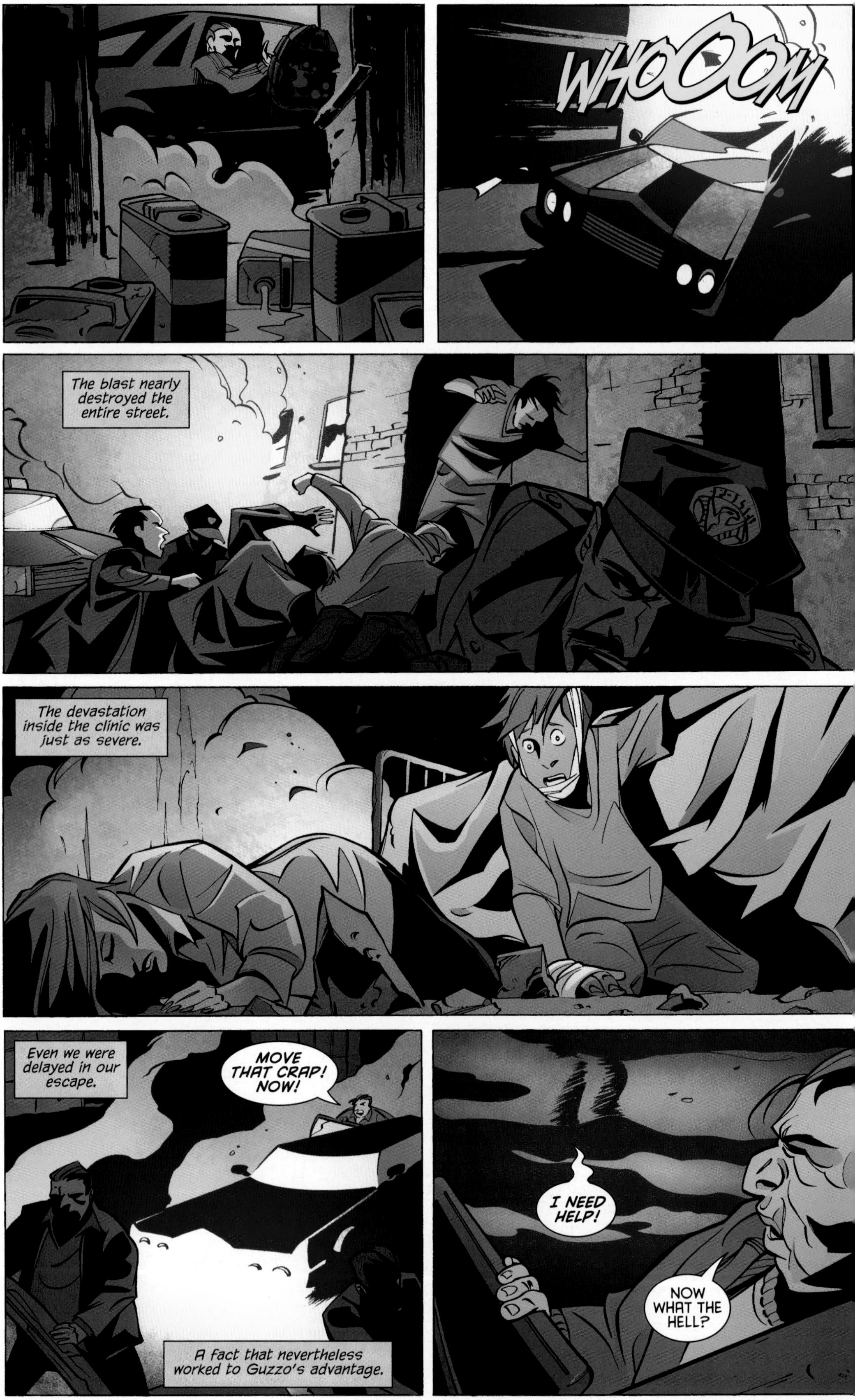
WHOOOOM
The blast nearly destroyed the entire street.
The devastation inside the clinic was just as severe.
Even we were delayed in our escape.
MOVE THAT CRAP! NOW!
A fact that nevertheless worked to Guzzo's advantage.
I NEED HELP!
NOW WHAT THE HELL?

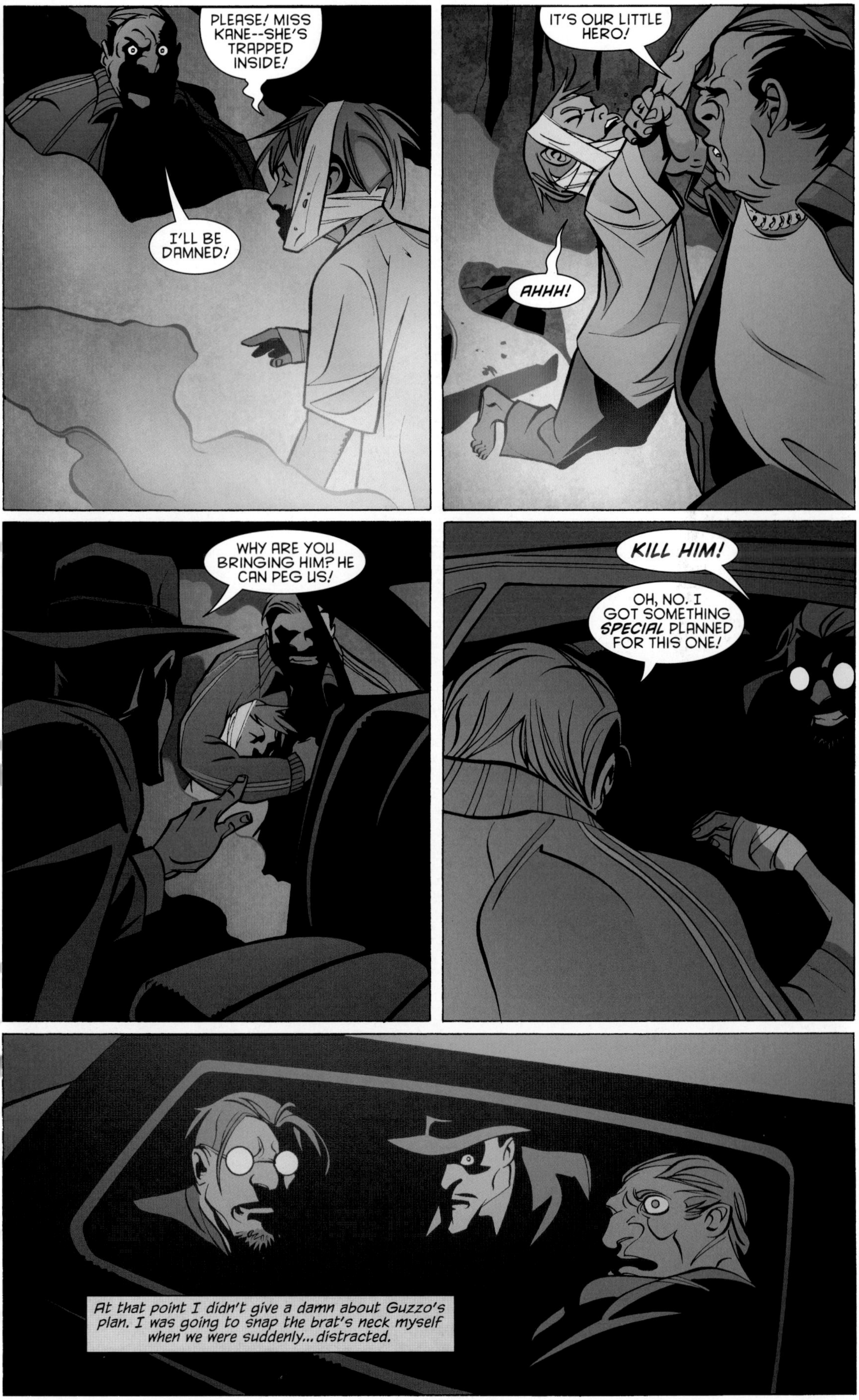
PLEASE! MISS KANE--SHE'S TRAPPED INSIDE!
I'LL BE DAMNED!
IT'S OUR LITTLE HERO!
AHHH!
WHY ARE YOU BRINGING HIM? HE CAN PEG US!
KILL HIM!
OH, NO. I GOT SOMETHING SPECIAL PLANNED FOR THIS ONE!
At that point I didn't give a damn about Guzzo's plan. I was going to snap the brat's neck myself when we were suddenly... distracted.

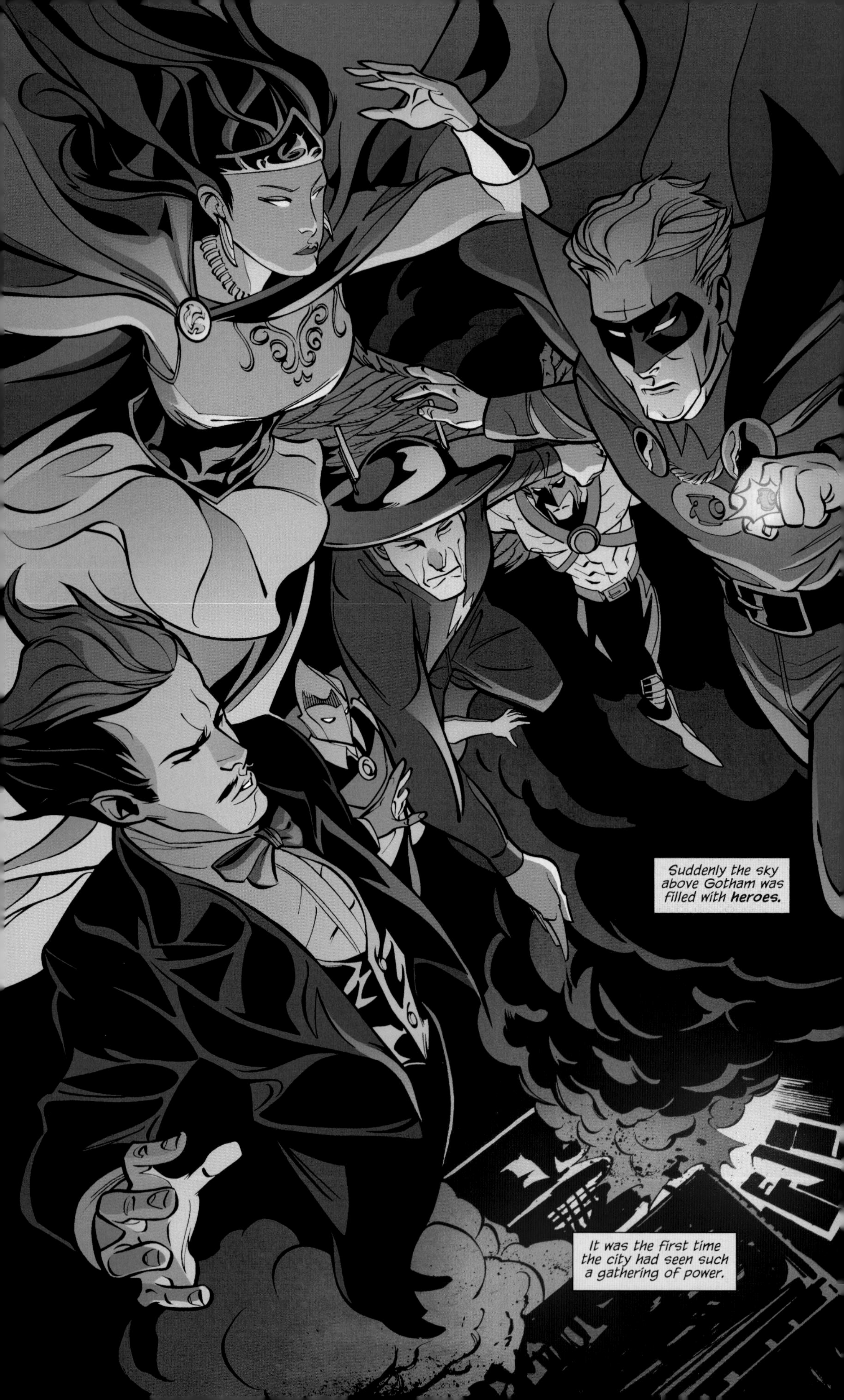
Suddenly the sky above Gotham was filled with **heroes.**
It was the first time the city had seen such a gathering of power.

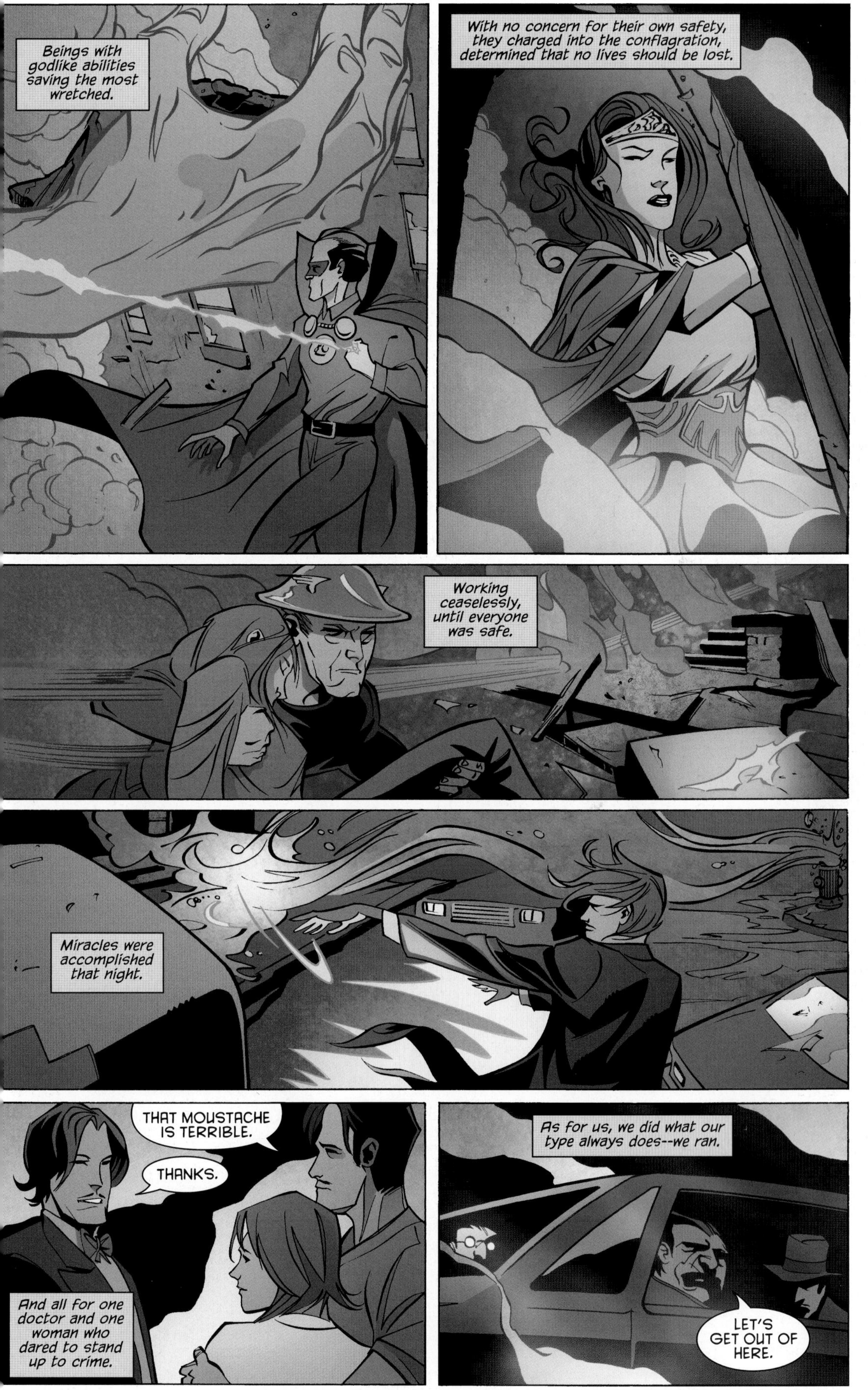

Beings with godlike abilities saving the most wretched.
With no concern for their own safety, they charged into the conflagration, determined that no lives should be lost.
Working ceaselessly, until everyone was safe.
Miracles were accomplished that night.
THAT MOUSTACHE IS TERRIBLE.
THANKS.
And all for one doctor and one woman who dared to stand up to crime.
As for us, we did what our type always does--we ran.
LET'S GET OUT OF HERE.

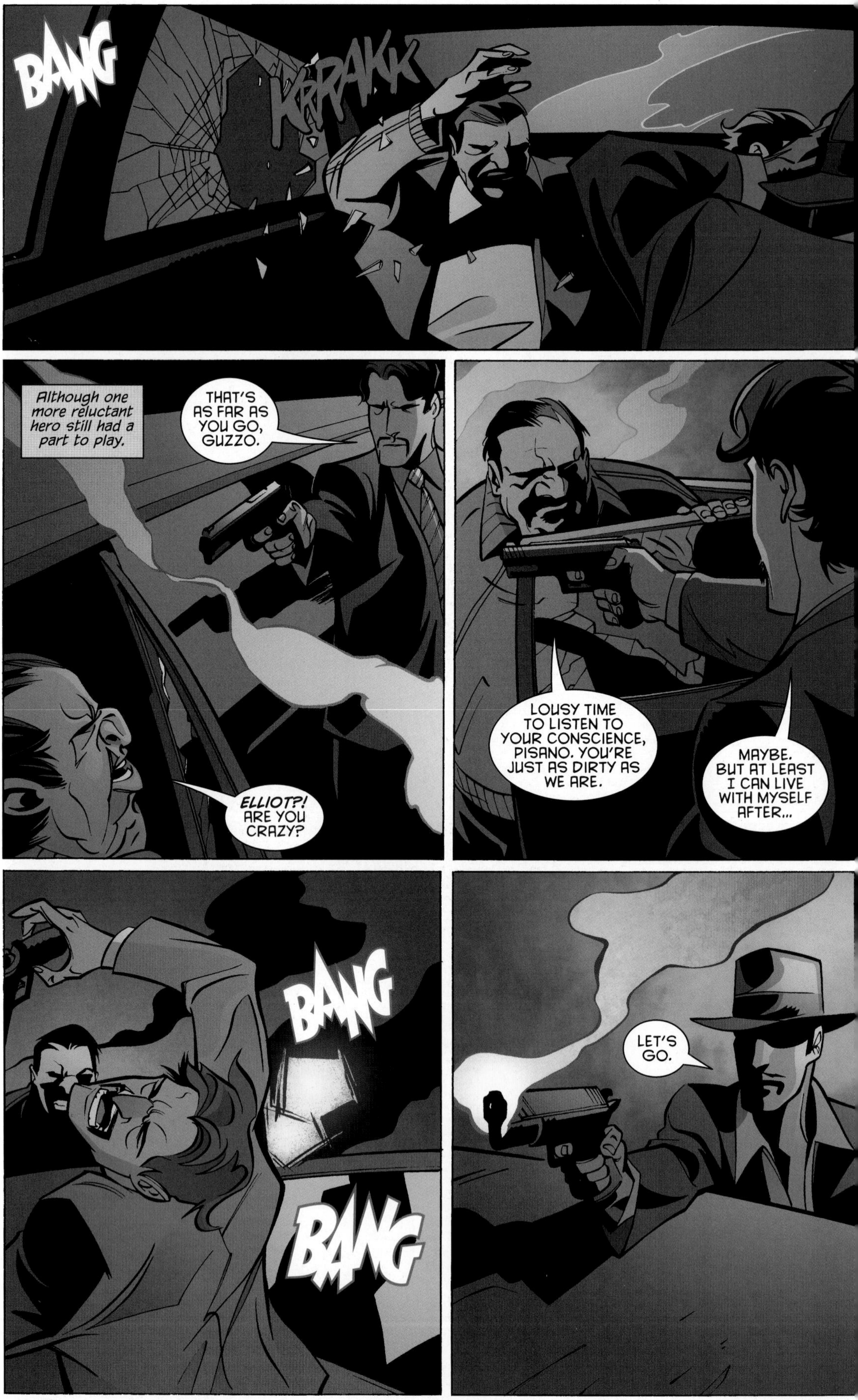
BANG
KRRAKK
Although one more reluctant hero still had a part to play.
THAT'S AS FAR AS YOU GO, GUZZO.
ELLIOT?! ARE YOU CRAZY?
LOUSY TIME TO LISTEN TO YOUR CONSCIENCE, PISANO. YOU'RE JUST AS DIRTY AS WE ARE.
MAYBE. BUT AT LEAST I CAN LIVE WITH MYSELF AFTER...
BANG
BANG
LET'S GO.

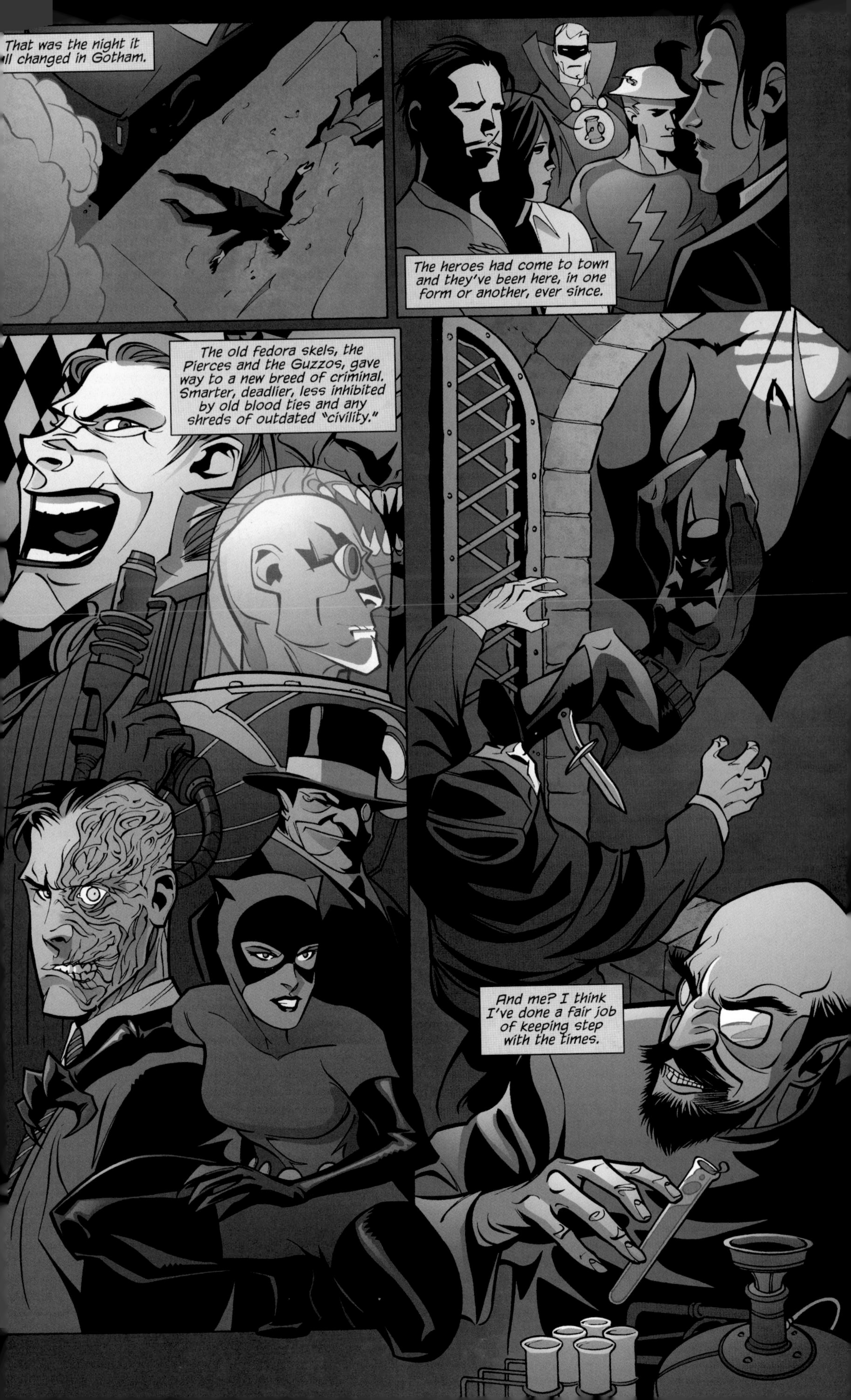
That was the night it
all changed in Gotham.
The heroes had come to town
and they've been here, in one
form or another, ever since.
The old fedora skels, the
Pierces and the Guzzos, gave
way to a new breed of criminal.
Smarter, deadlier, less inhibited
by old blood ties and any
shreds of outdated "civility."
And me? I think
I've done a fair job
of keeping step
with the times.

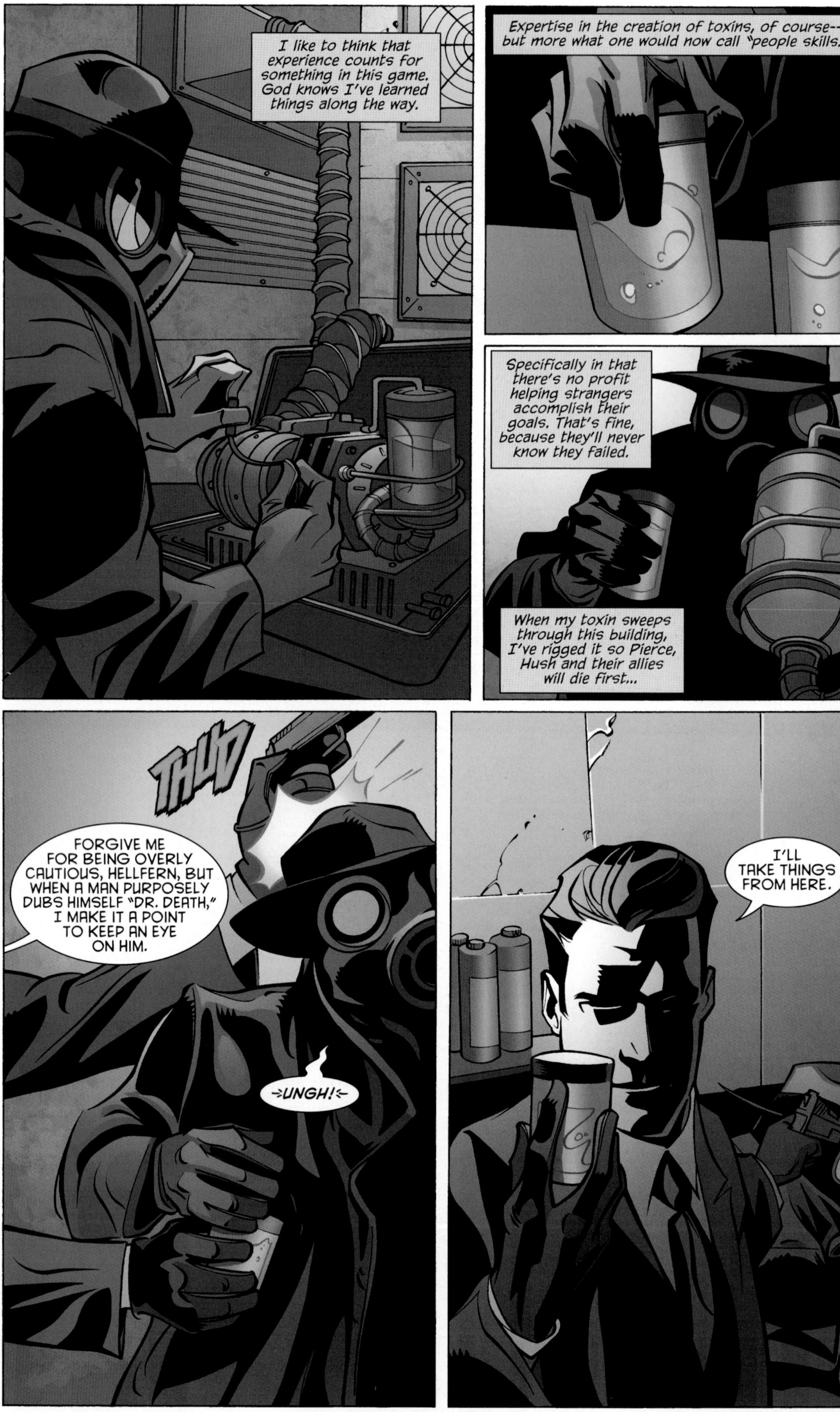

I like to think that experience counts for something in this game. God knows I've learned things along the way.
Expertise in the creation of toxins, of course-- but more what one would now call "people skills."
Specifically in that there's no profit helping strangers accomplish their goals. That's fine, because they'll never know they failed.
When my toxin sweeps through this building, I've rigged it so Pierce, Hush and their allies will die first...
THUD
FORGIVE ME FOR BEING OVERLY CAUTIOUS, HELLFERN, BUT WHEN A MAN PURPOSELY DUBS HIMSELF "DR. DEATH," I MAKE IT A POINT TO KEEP AN EYE ON HIM.
UNGH!
I'LL TAKE THINGS FROM HERE.

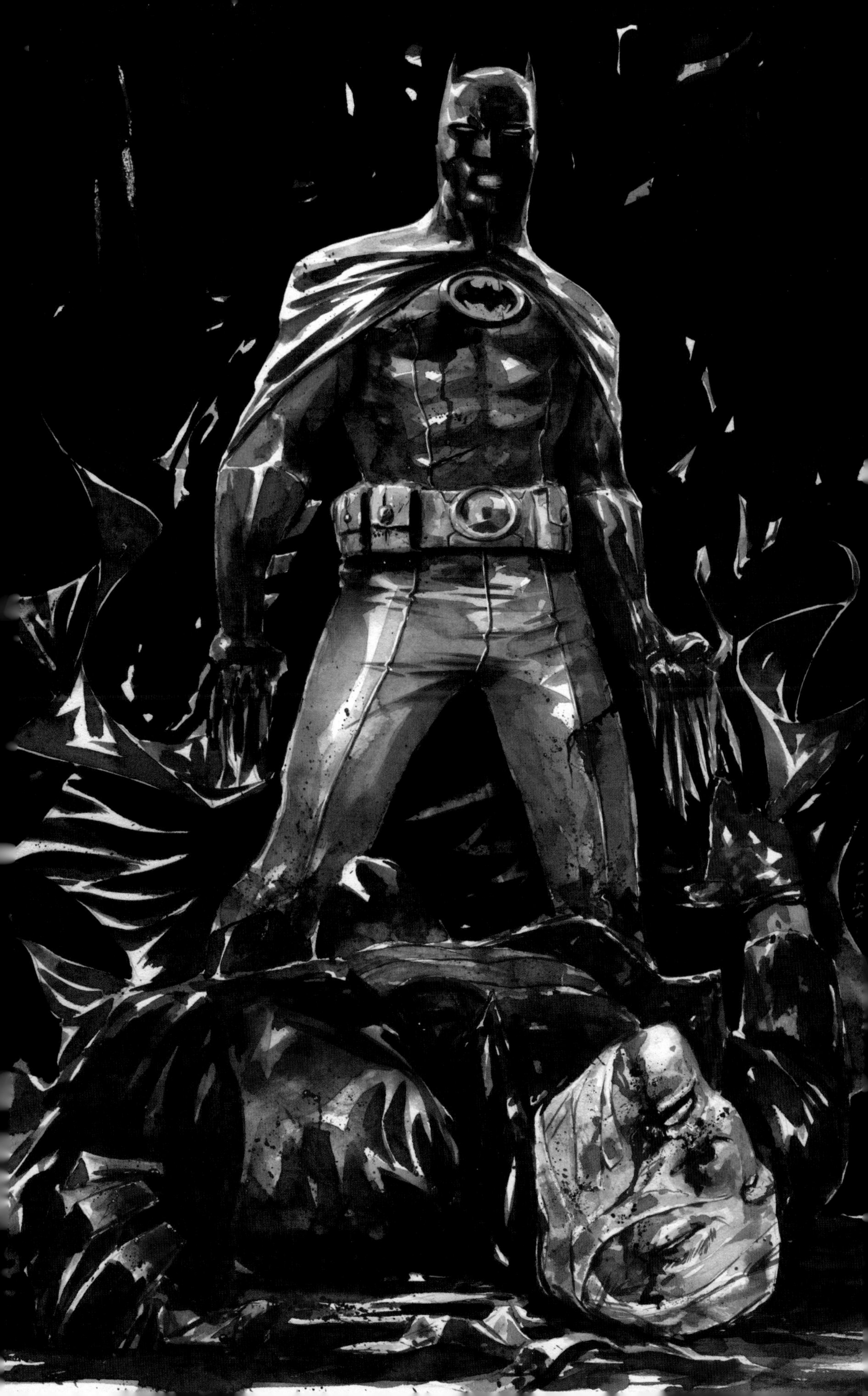

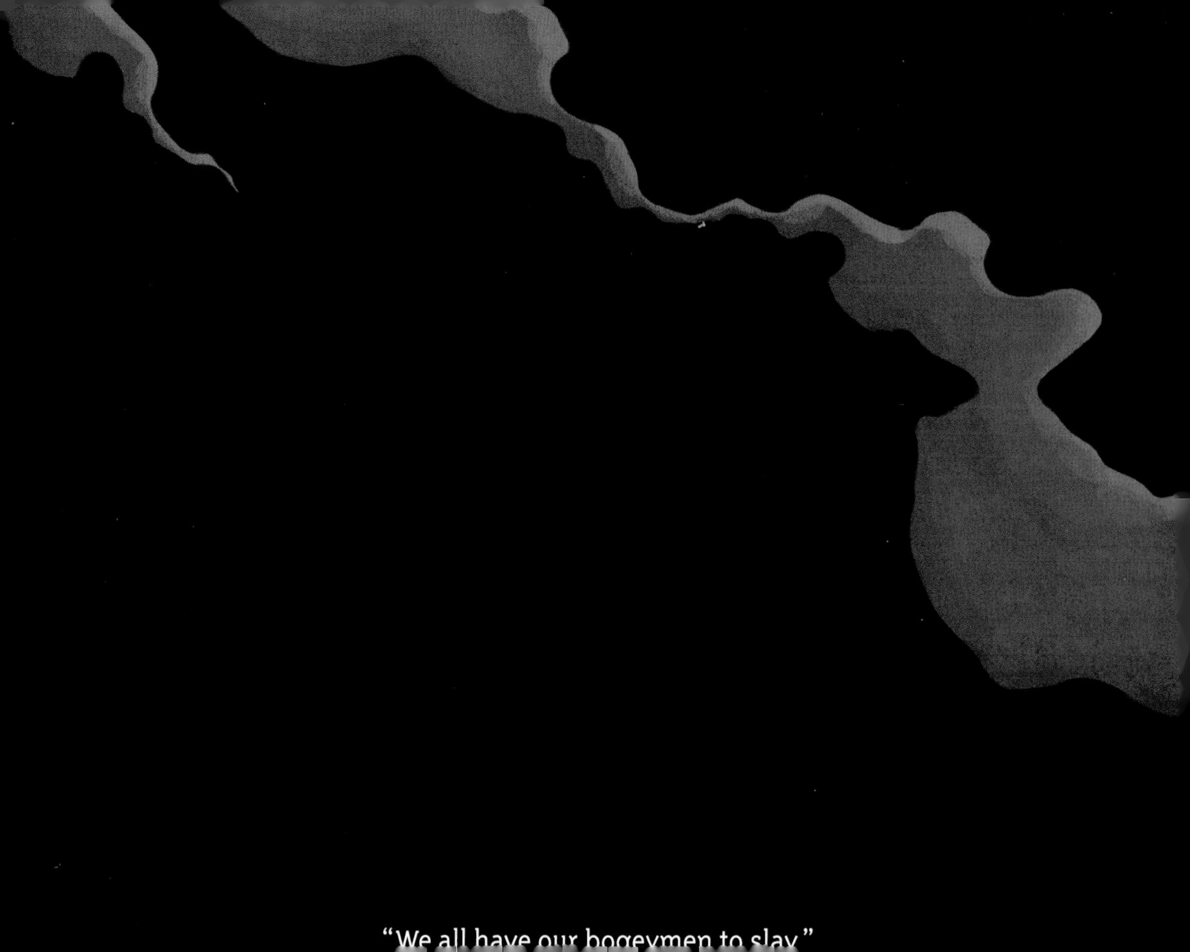
"We all have our bogeymen to slay."

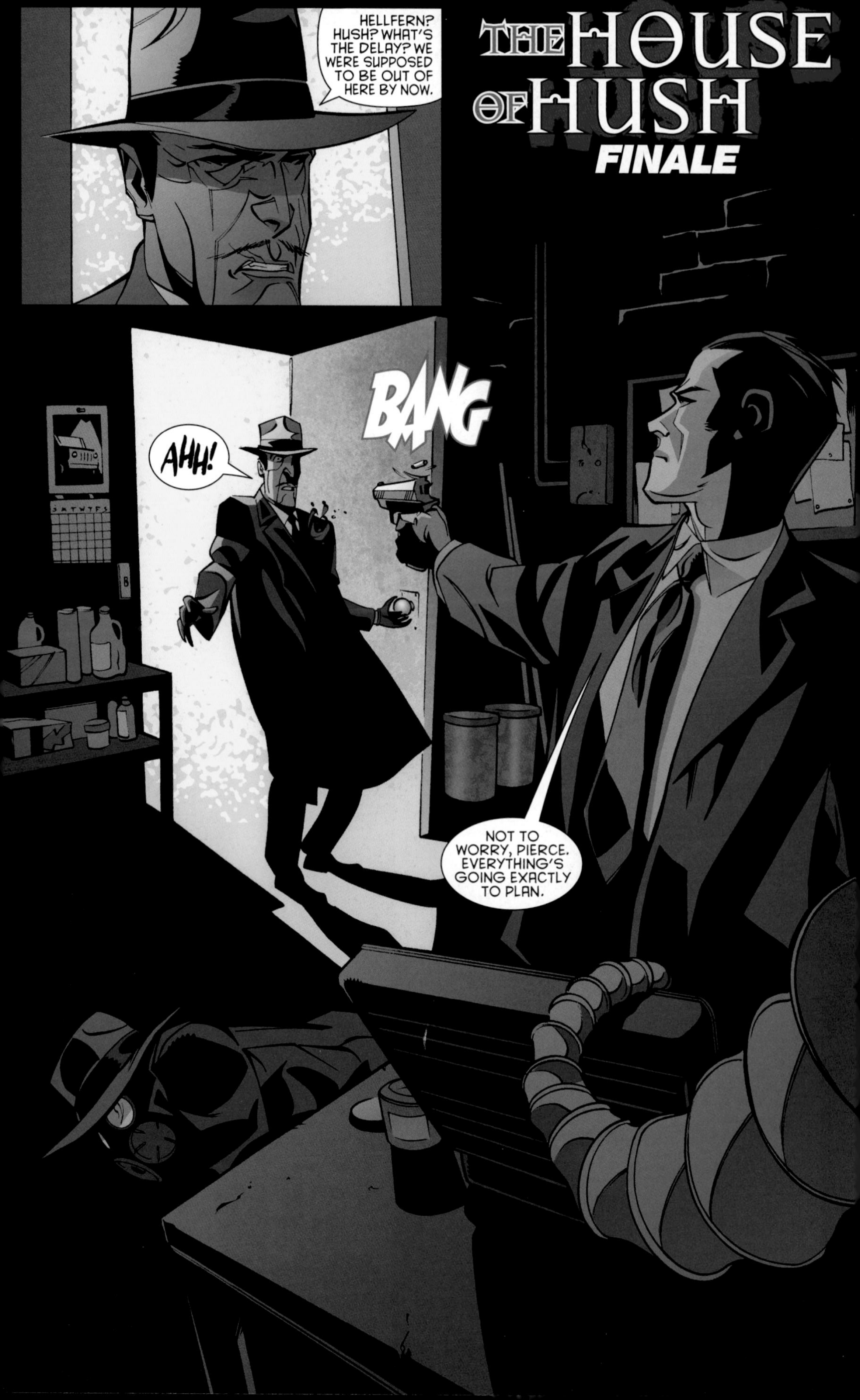
HELLFERN? HUSH? WHAT'S THE DELAY? WE WERE SUPPOSED TO BE OUT OF HERE BY NOW.
THE HOUSE OF HUSH
FINALE
BANG
AHH!
NOT TO WORRY, PIERCE. EVERYTHING'S GOING EXACTLY TO PLAN.

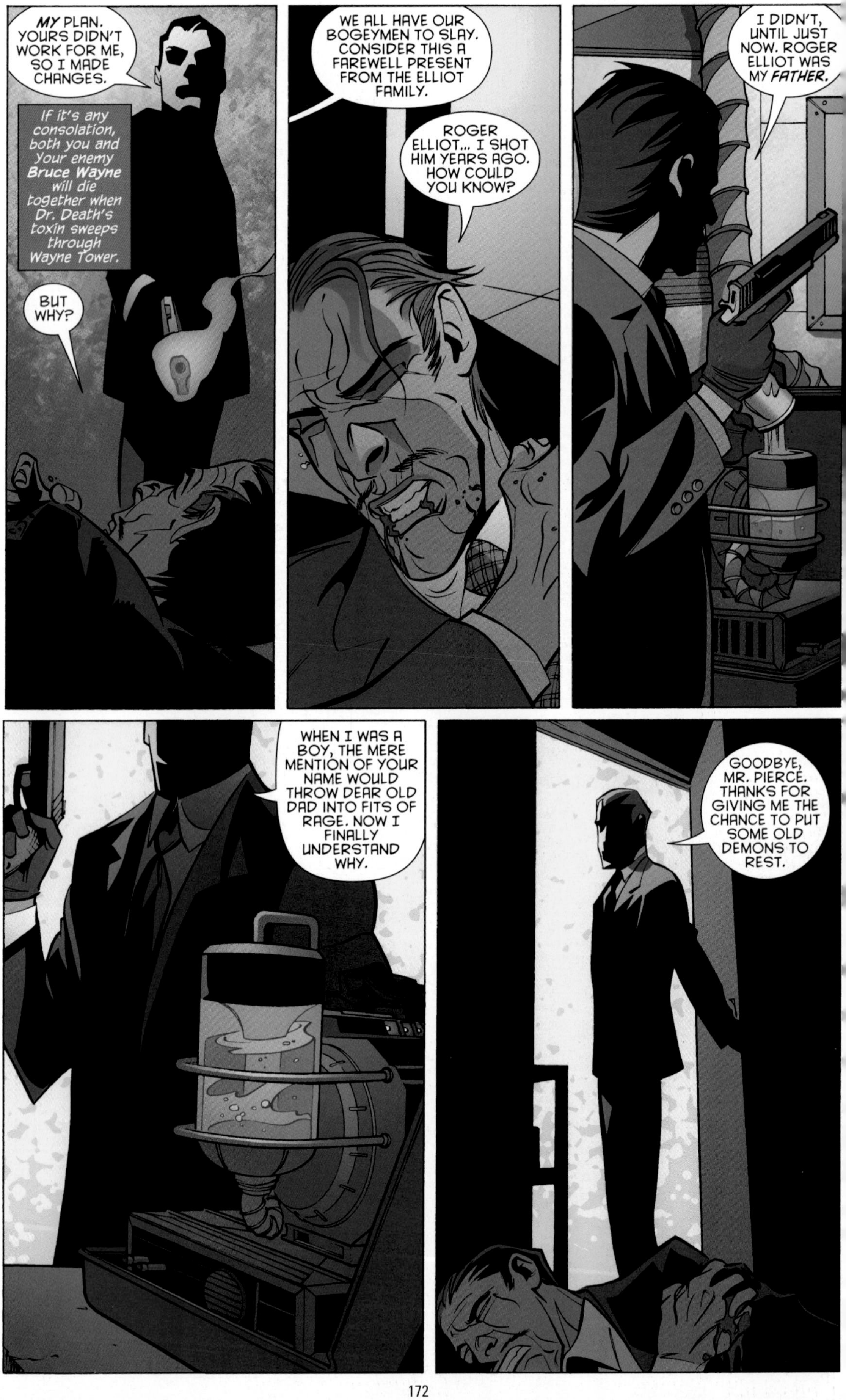

MY PLAN. YOURS DIDN'T WORK FOR ME, SO I MADE CHANGES.
*If it's any consolation, both you and your enemy **Bruce Wayne** will die together when Dr. Death's toxin sweeps through Wayne Tower.*
BUT WHY?
WE ALL HAVE OUR BOGEYMEN TO SLAY. CONSIDER THIS A FAREWELL PRESENT FROM THE ELLIOT FAMILY.
ROGER ELLIOT... I SHOT HIM YEARS AGO. HOW COULD YOU KNOW?
I DIDN'T, UNTIL JUST NOW. ROGER ELLIOT WAS MY ***FATHER.***
WHEN I WAS A BOY, THE MERE MENTION OF YOUR NAME WOULD THROW DEAR OLD DAD INTO FITS OF RAGE. NOW I FINALLY UNDERSTAND WHY.
GOODBYE, MR. PIERCE. THANKS FOR GIVING ME THE CHANCE TO PUT SOME OLD DEMONS TO REST.

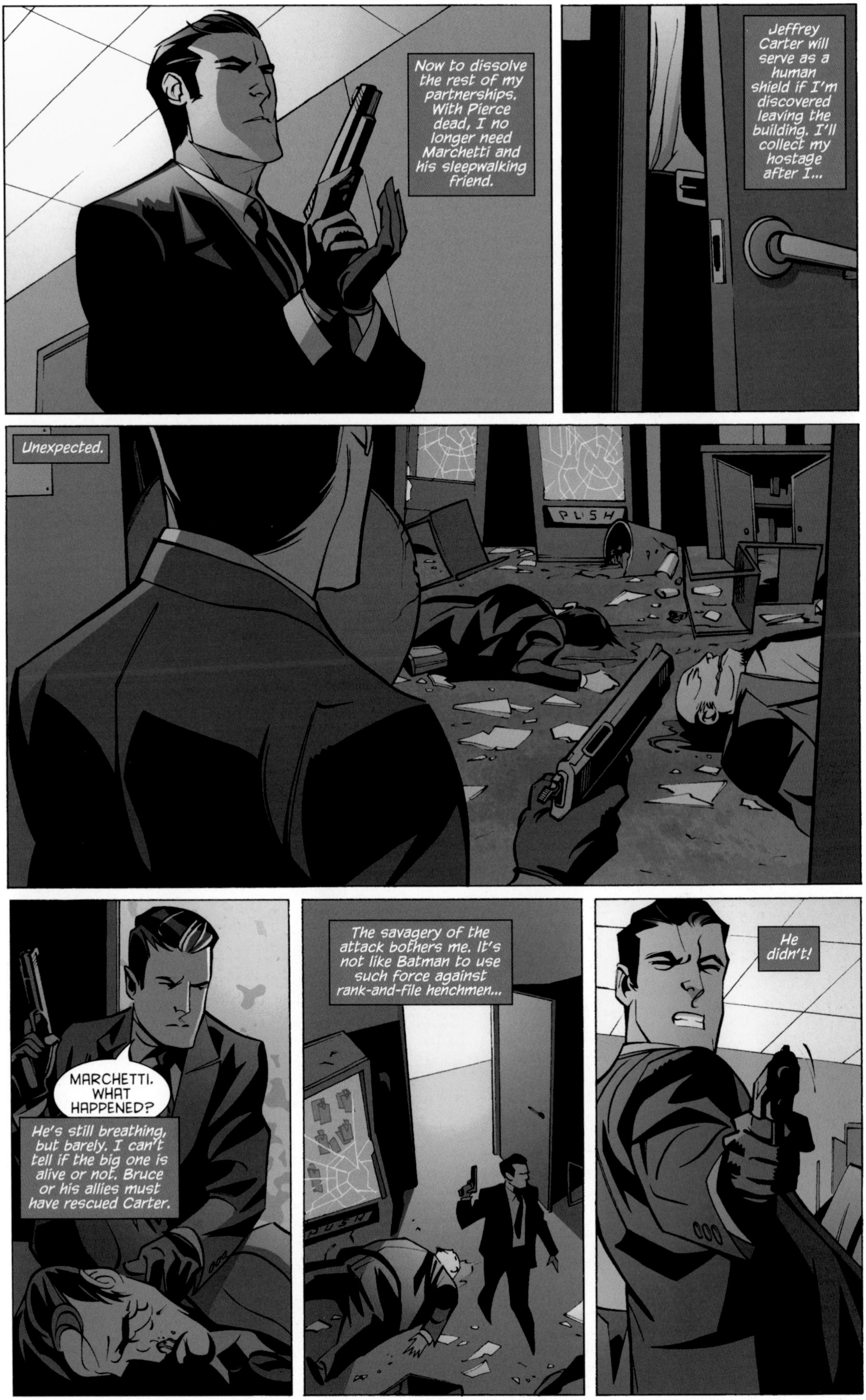

Now to dissolve the rest of my partnerships. With Pierce dead, I no longer need Marchetti and his sleepwalking friend.
Jeffrey Carter will serve as a human shield if I'm discovered leaving the building. I'll collect my hostage after I...
Unexpected.
PUSH
MARCHETTI. WHAT HAPPENED?
He's still breathing, but barely. I can't tell if the big one is alive or not. Bruce or his allies must have rescued Carter.
The savagery of the attack bothers me. It's not like Batman to use such force against rank-and-file henchmen...
He didn't!

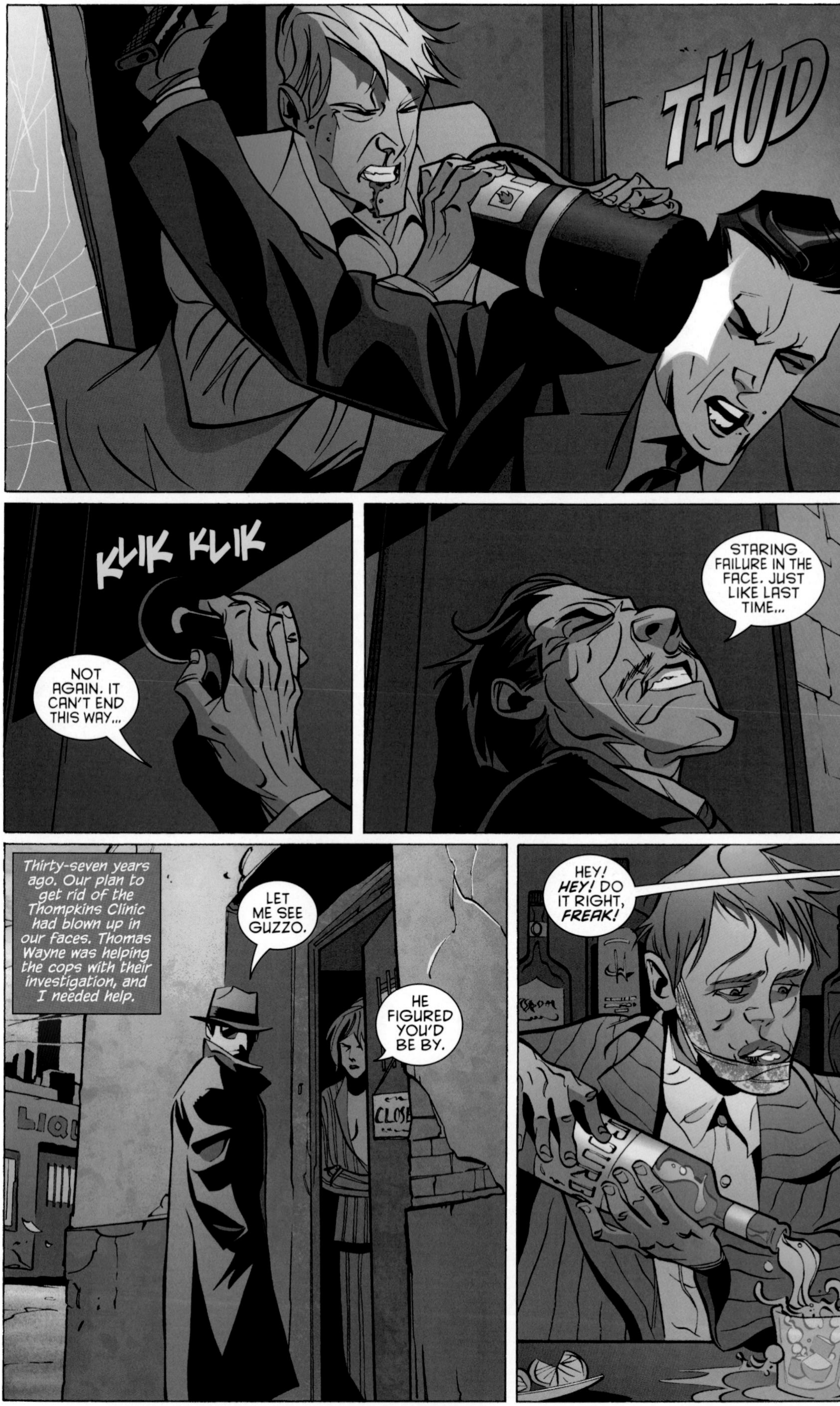
THUD
KLIK KLIK
NOT AGAIN. IT CAN'T END THIS WAY...
STARING FAILURE IN THE FACE. JUST LIKE LAST TIME...
Thirty-seven years ago. Our plan to get rid of the Thompkins Clinic had blown up in our faces. Thomas Wayne was helping the cops with their investigation, and I needed help.
LET ME SEE GUZZO.
HE FIGURED YOU'D BE BY.
HEY! *HEY!* DO IT RIGHT, *FREAK!*

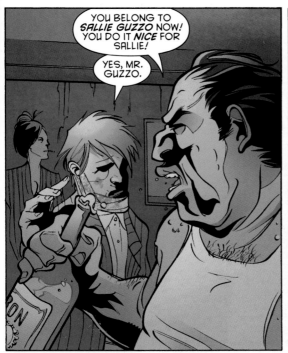

YOU BELONG TO *SALLIE GUZZO* NOW! YOU DO IT *NICE* FOR SALLIE!

YES, MR. GUZZO.

"YES, MR. GUZZO. NO, MR. GUZZO." *SHEEESH!*

I TOOK YOU HOME, GAVE YOU A NICE STORE ROOM TO SLEEP IN, AN' YOU JUST WALK AROUND WITH THAT HANGDOG *FROWN* ON YOUR *STUPID FACE!*

LIGHTEN UP, DEADPAN! EASY DOES IT! *SMILE!*

↘HUK!↙

THAT'S THE WAY I LIKE IT! NOW SMILE AND SWALLOW, LIKE YA DONE LAST NIGHT!

Y-YES, MR. GUZZO!

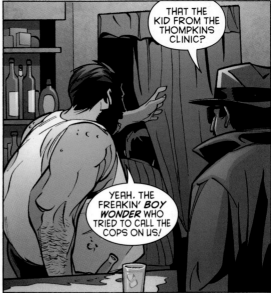

THAT THE KID FROM THE THOMPKINS CLINIC?

YEAH. THE FREAKIN' *BOY WONDER* WHO TRIED TO CALL THE COPS ON US!

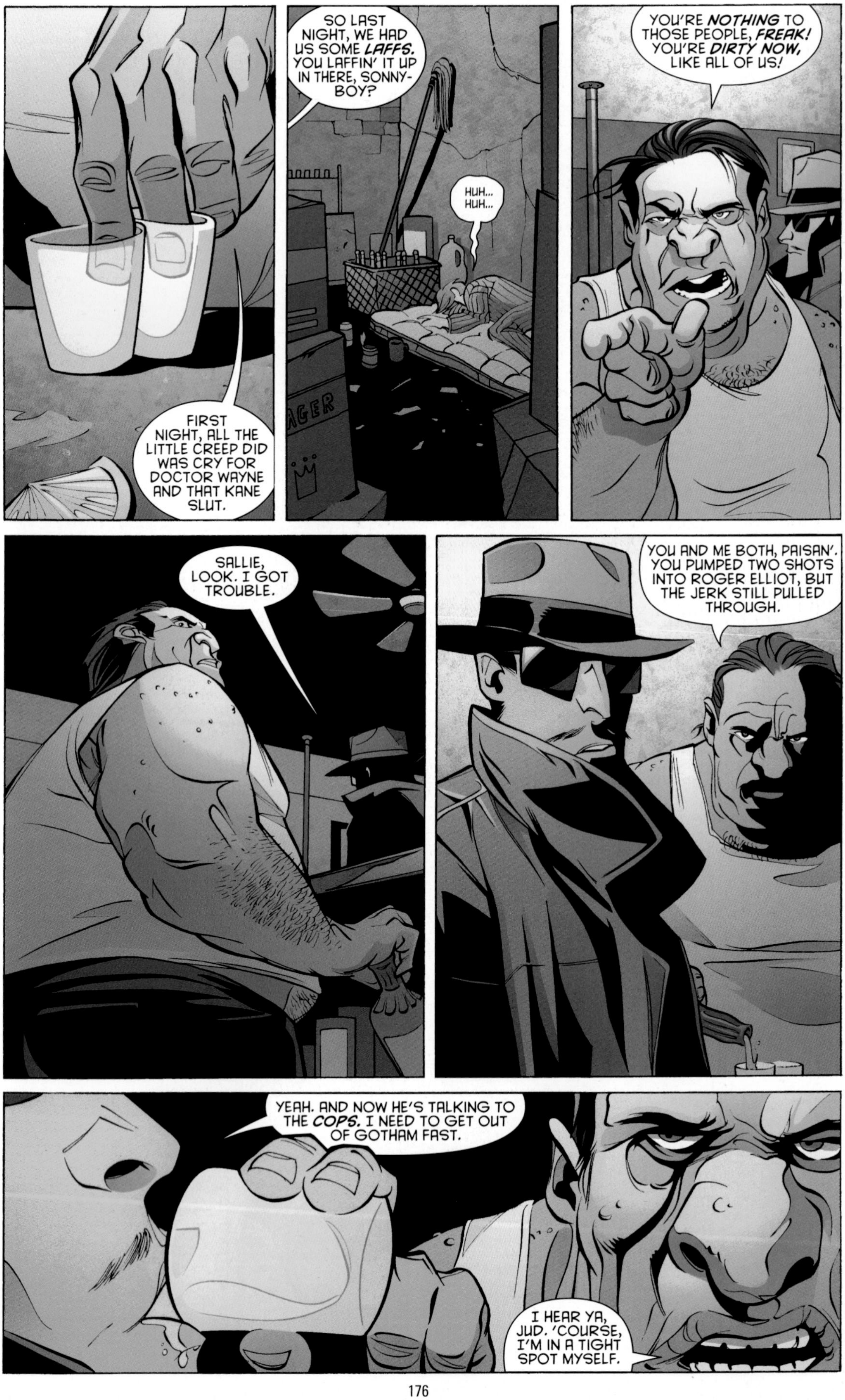
FIRST NIGHT, ALL THE LITTLE CREEP DID WAS CRY FOR DOCTOR WAYNE AND THAT KANE SLUT.
SO LAST NIGHT, WE HAD US SOME LAFFS. YOU LAFFIN' IT UP IN THERE, SONNY-BOY?
HUH... HUH...
AGER
YOU'RE NOTHING TO THOSE PEOPLE, FREAK! YOU'RE DIRTY NOW, LIKE ALL OF US!
SALLIE, LOOK. I GOT TROUBLE.
YOU AND ME BOTH, PAISAN'. YOU PUMPED TWO SHOTS INTO ROGER ELLIOT, BUT THE JERK STILL PULLED THROUGH.
YEAH. AND NOW HE'S TALKING TO THE COPS. I NEED TO GET OUT OF GOTHAM FAST.
I HEAR YA, JUD. 'COURSE, I'M IN A TIGHT SPOT MYSELF.

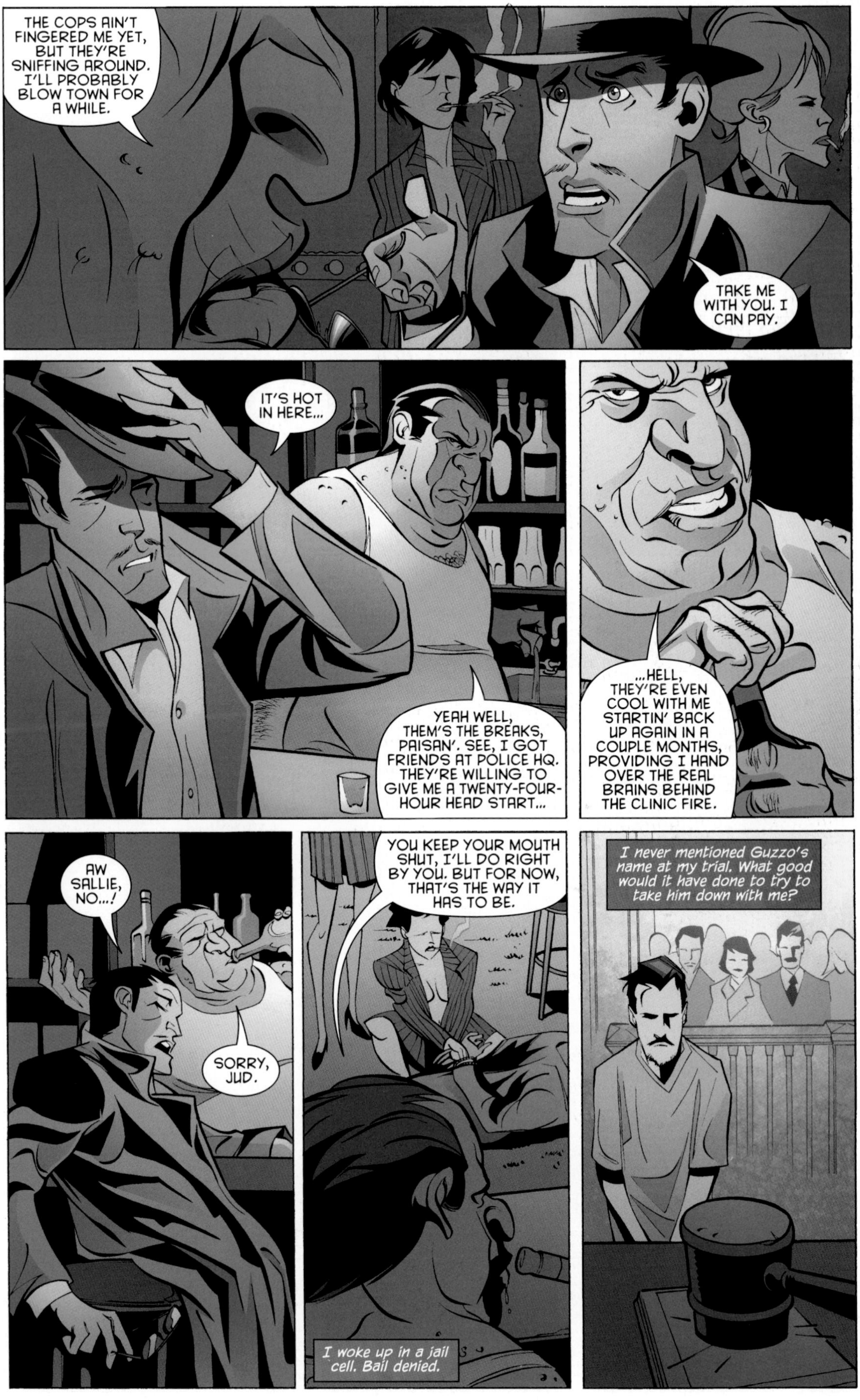
THE COPS AIN'T FINGERED ME YET, BUT THEY'RE SNIFFING AROUND. I'LL PROBABLY BLOW TOWN FOR A WHILE.
TAKE ME WITH YOU. I CAN PAY.
IT'S HOT IN HERE...
YEAH WELL, THEM'S THE BREAKS, PAISAN'. SEE, I GOT FRIENDS AT POLICE HQ. THEY'RE WILLING TO GIVE ME A TWENTY-FOUR-HOUR HEAD START...
...HELL, THEY'RE EVEN COOL WITH ME STARTIN' BACK UP AGAIN IN A COUPLE MONTHS, PROVIDING I HAND OVER THE REAL BRAINS BEHIND THE CLINIC FIRE.
AW SALLIE, NO...!
SORRY, JUD.
YOU KEEP YOUR MOUTH SHUT, I'LL DO RIGHT BY YOU. BUT FOR NOW, THAT'S THE WAY IT HAS TO BE.
I woke up in a jail cell. Bail denied.
I never mentioned Guzzo's name at my trial. What good would it have done to try to take him down with me?

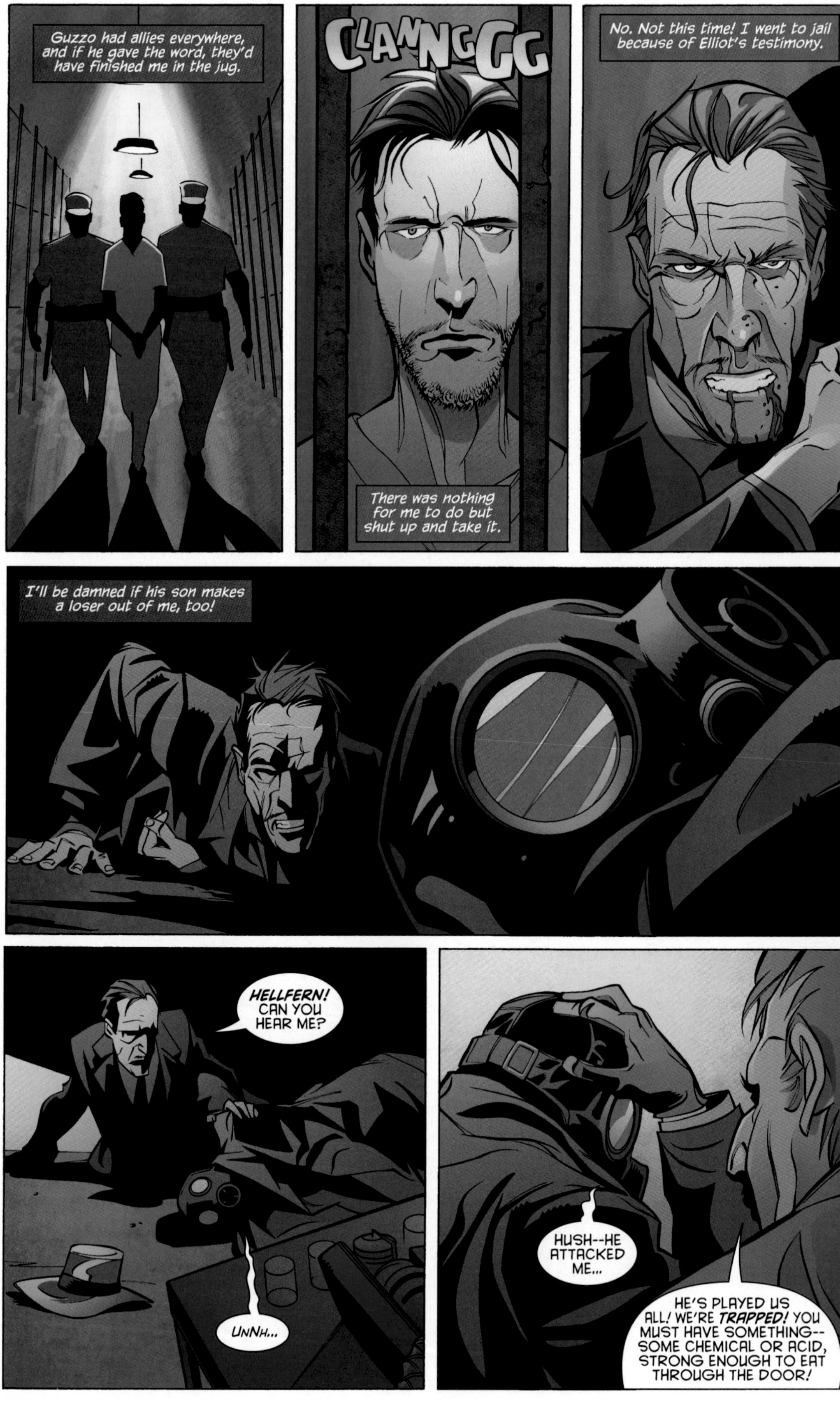
Guzzo had allies everywhere, and if he gave the word, they'd have finished me in the jug.
CLANNGGG
There was nothing for me to do but shut up and take it.
No. Not this time! I went to jail because of Elliot's testimony.
I'll be damned if his son makes a loser out of me, too!
HELLFERN! CAN YOU HEAR ME?
UNNH...
HUSH--HE ATTACKED ME...
HE'S PLAYED US ALL! WE'RE TRAPPED! YOU MUST HAVE SOMETHING-- SOME CHEMICAL OR ACID, STRONG ENOUGH TO EAT THROUGH THE DOOR!

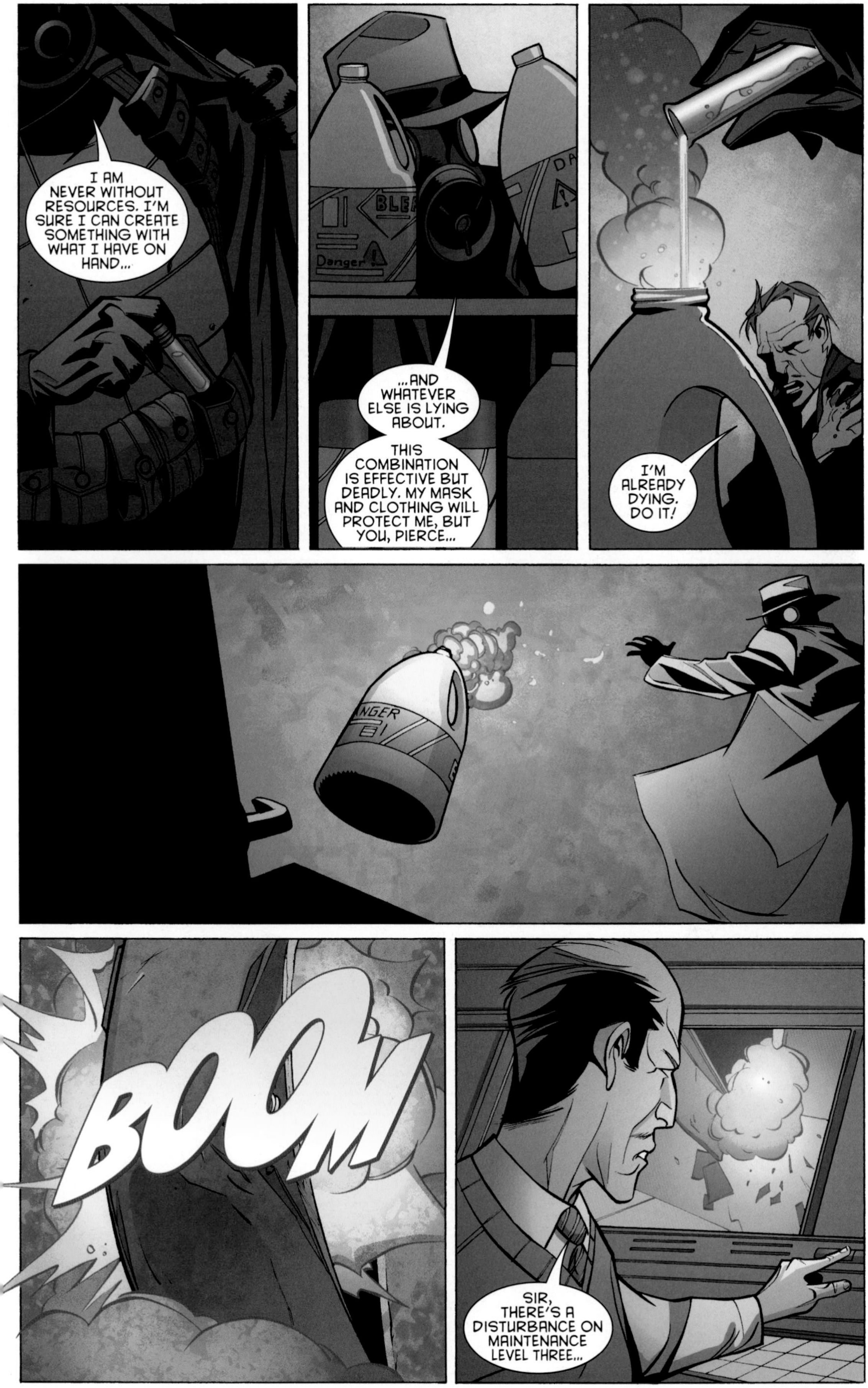
I AM NEVER WITHOUT RESOURCES. I'M SURE I CAN CREATE SOMETHING WITH WHAT I HAVE ON HAND...
BLEA
Danger
...AND WHATEVER ELSE IS LYING ABOUT.
THIS COMBINATION IS EFFECTIVE BUT DEADLY. MY MASK AND CLOTHING WILL PROTECT ME, BUT YOU, PIERCE...
I'M ALREADY DYING. DO IT!
NGER
BOOM
SIR, THERE'S A DISTURBANCE ON MAINTENANCE LEVEL THREE...

WE'RE FREE. STILL WITH ME, PIERCE?

HRM. JUST AS WELL.

HELLFERN... WAIT...

I'M BURNING! MY SKIN...!

"MY FACE...EVERY NERVE IS ON FIRE!"

What happened? Carter, he...

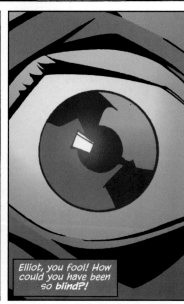

Elliot, you fool! How could you have been so blind?!

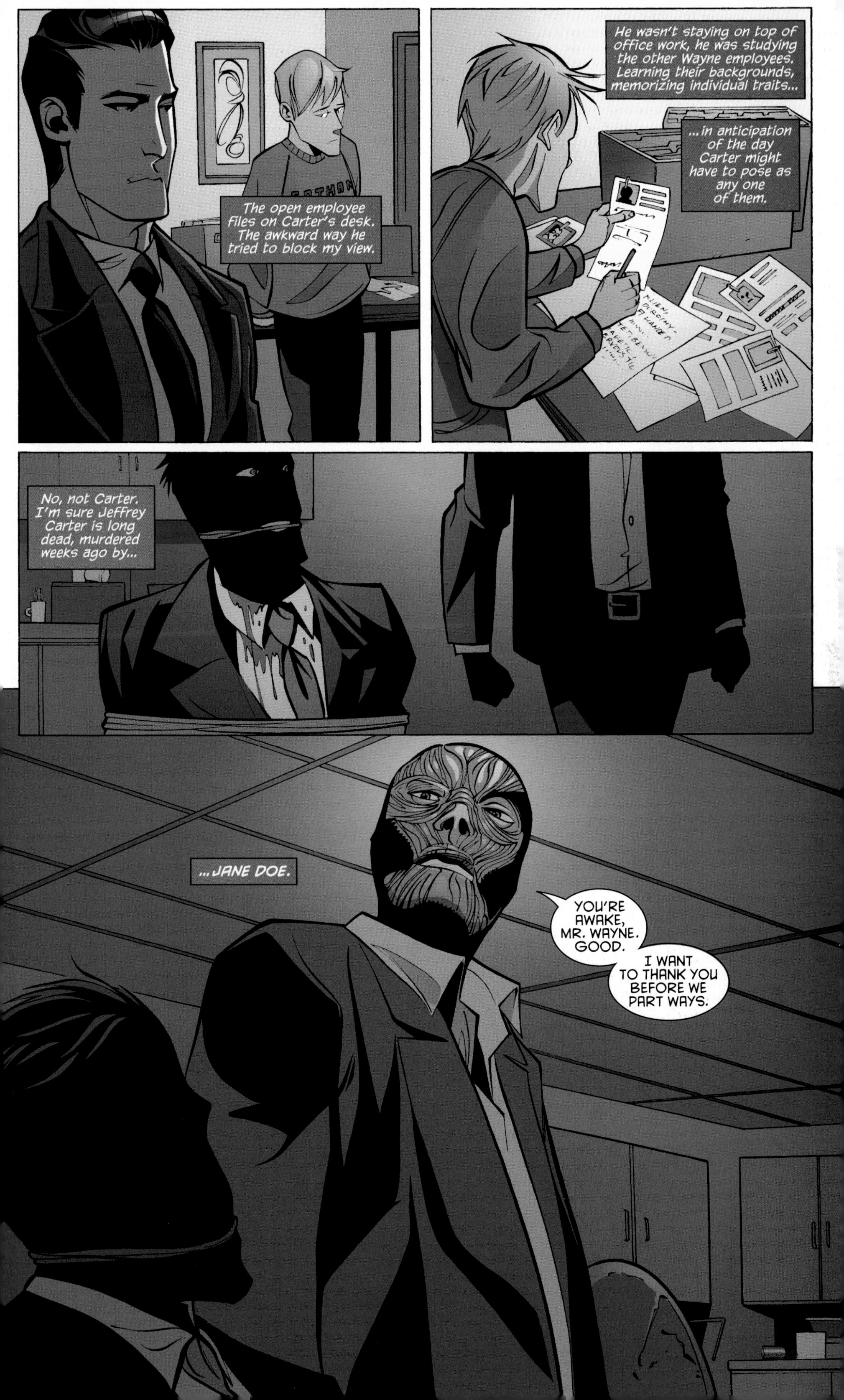
The open employee files on Carter's desk. The awkward way he tried to block my view.
He wasn't staying on top of office work, he was studying the other Wayne employees. Learning their backgrounds, memorizing individual traits...
...in anticipation of the day Carter might have to pose as any one of them.
No, not Carter. I'm sure Jeffrey Carter is long dead, murdered weeks ago by...
...JANE DOE.
YOU'RE AWAKE, MR. WAYNE. GOOD.
I WANT TO THANK YOU BEFORE WE PART WAYS.

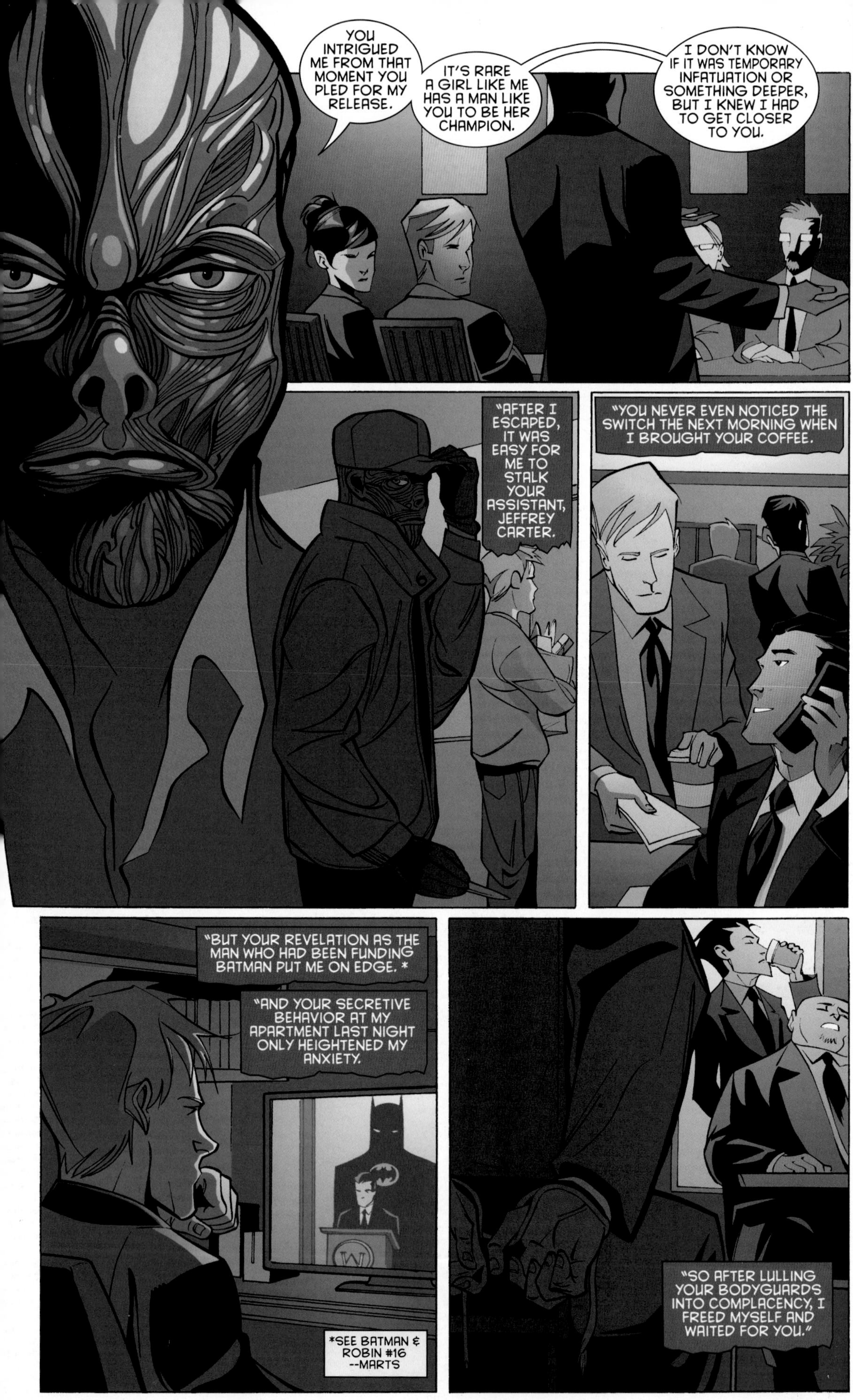
YOU INTRIGUED ME FROM THAT MOMENT YOU PLED FOR MY RELEASE.
IT'S RARE A GIRL LIKE ME HAS A MAN LIKE YOU TO BE HER CHAMPION.
I DON'T KNOW IF IT WAS TEMPORARY INFATUATION OR SOMETHING DEEPER, BUT I KNEW I HAD TO GET CLOSER TO YOU.
"AFTER I ESCAPED, IT WAS EASY FOR ME TO STALK YOUR ASSISTANT, JEFFREY CARTER.
"YOU NEVER EVEN NOTICED THE SWITCH THE NEXT MORNING WHEN I BROUGHT YOUR COFFEE.
"BUT YOUR REVELATION AS THE MAN WHO HAD BEEN FUNDING BATMAN PUT ME ON EDGE. *
"AND YOUR SECRETIVE BEHAVIOR AT MY APARTMENT LAST NIGHT ONLY HEIGHTENED MY ANXIETY.
*SEE BATMAN & ROBIN #16 --MARTS
"SO AFTER LULLING YOUR BODYGUARDS INTO COMPLACENCY, I FREED MYSELF AND WAITED FOR YOU."

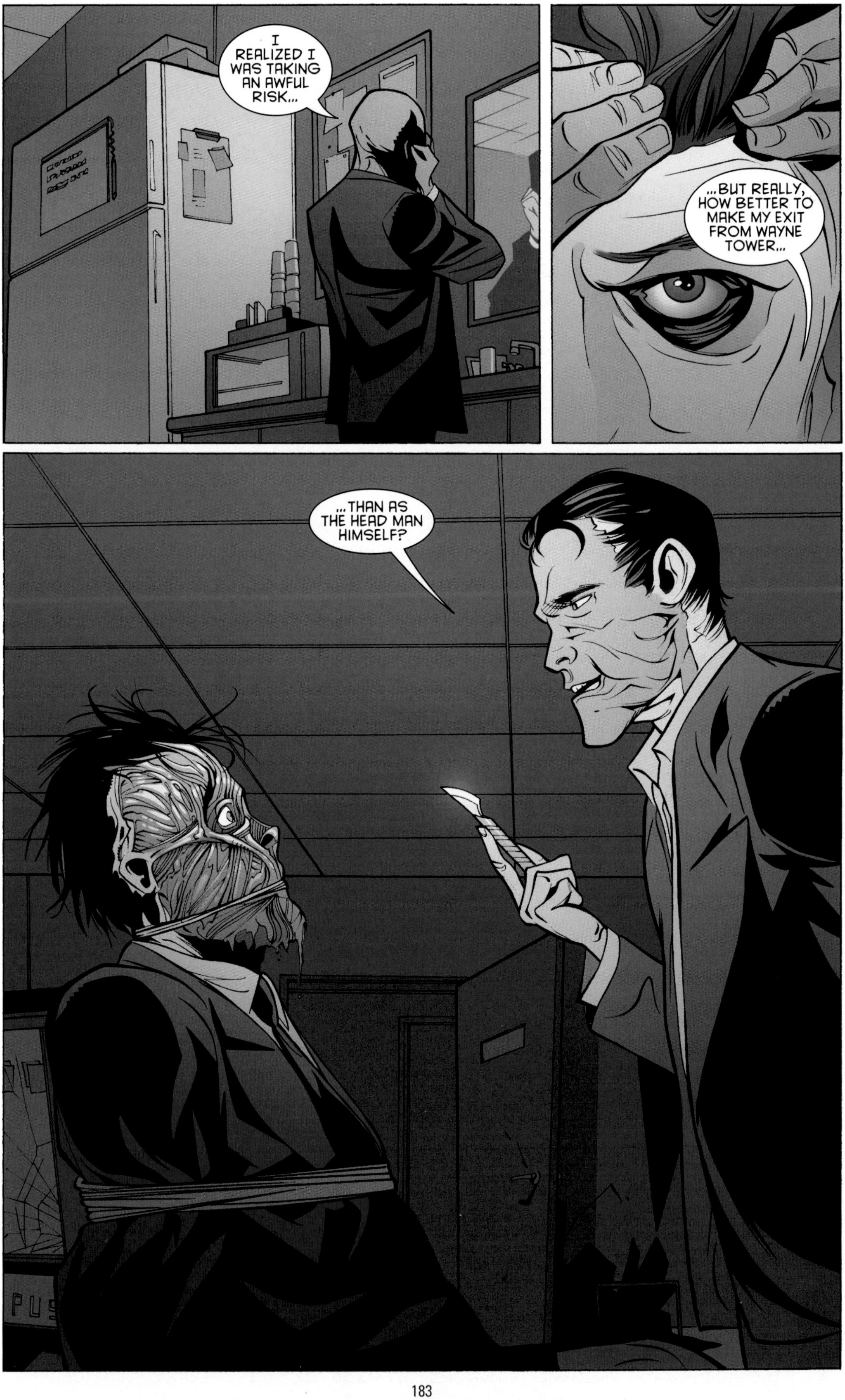
I REALIZED I WAS TAKING AN AWFUL RISK...
...BUT REALLY, HOW BETTER TO MAKE MY EXIT FROM WAYNE TOWER...
...THAN AS THE HEAD MAN HIMSELF?
PUS

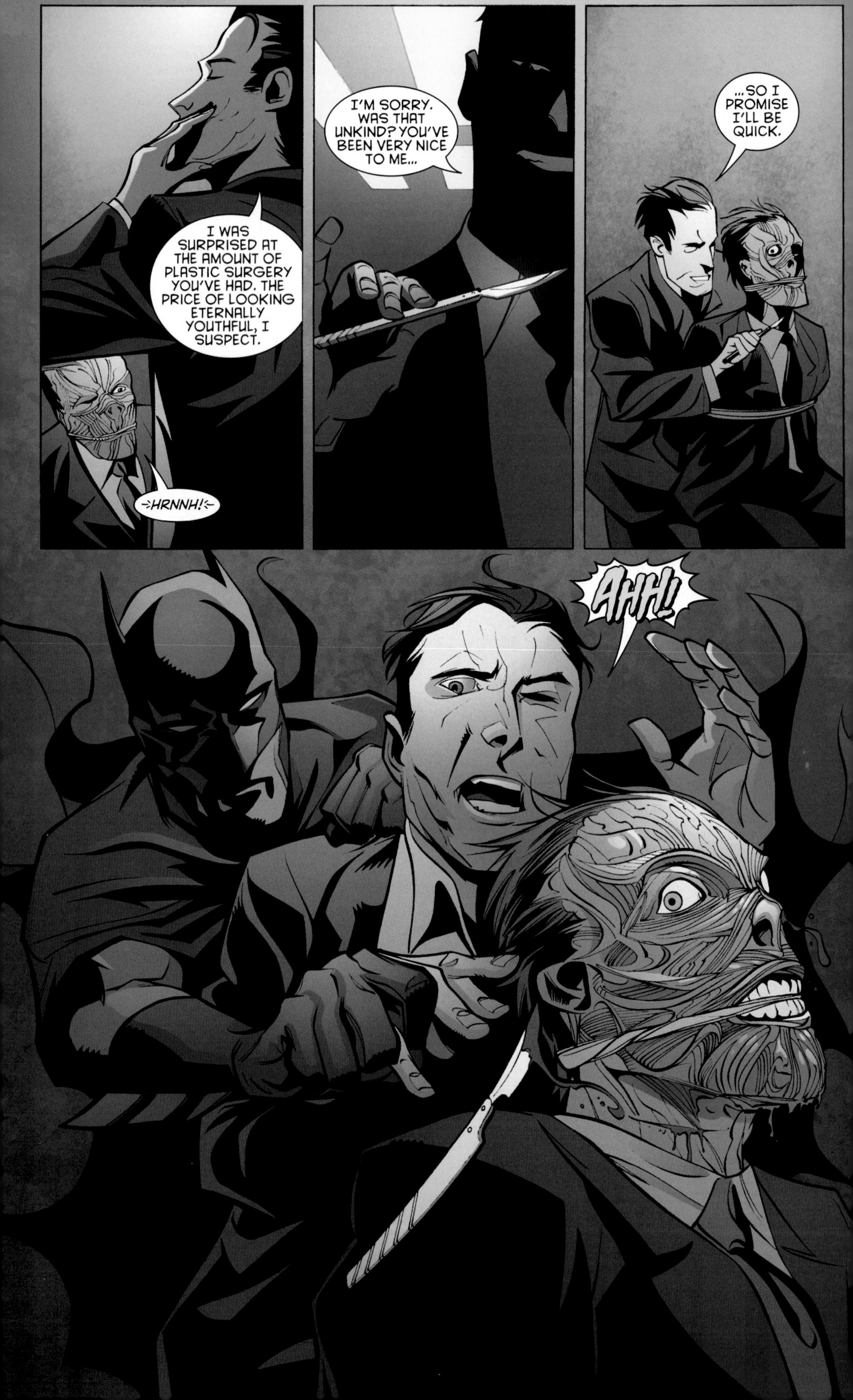
I WAS SURPRISED AT THE AMOUNT OF PLASTIC SURGERY YOU'VE HAD. THE PRICE OF LOOKING ETERNALLY YOUTHFUL, I SUSPECT.
HRNNH!
I'M SORRY. WAS THAT UNKIND? YOU'VE BEEN VERY NICE TO ME...
...SO I PROMISE I'LL BE QUICK.
AHH!!

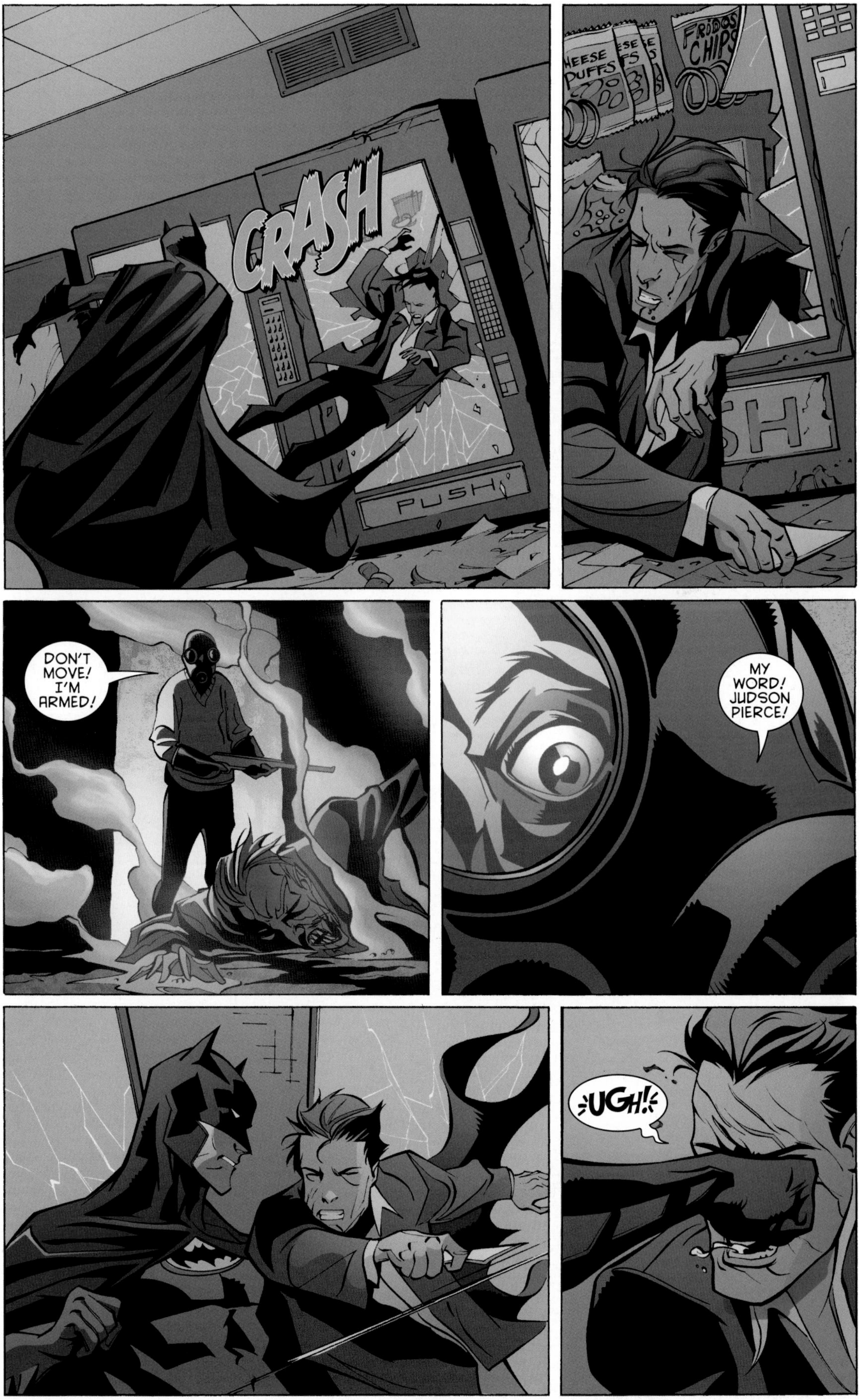
CRASH
PUSH
FRIDOS CHIPS
DON'T MOVE! I'M ARMED!
MY WORD! JUDSON PIERCE!
UGH!

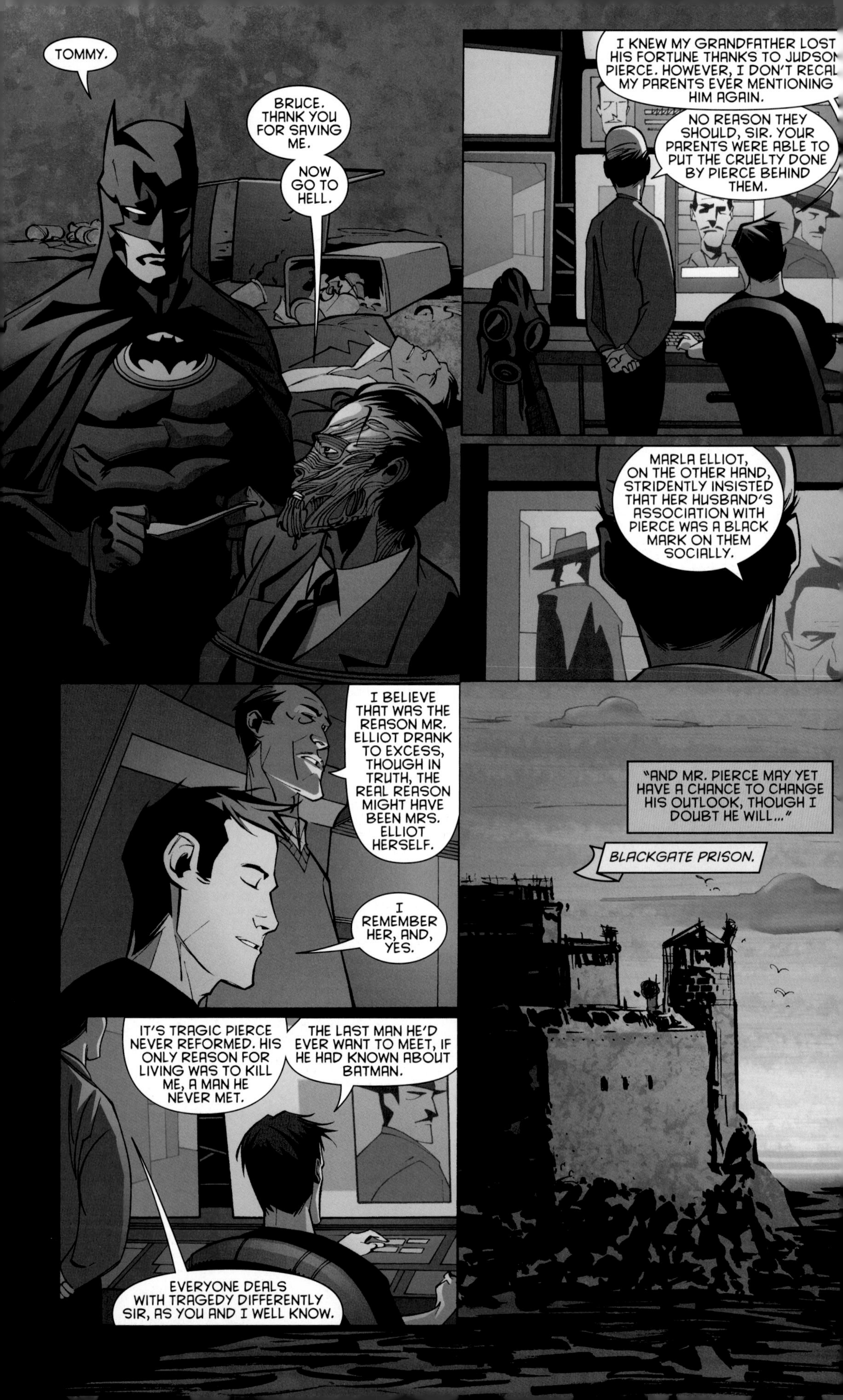
TOMMY.
BRUCE. THANK YOU FOR SAVING ME.
NOW GO TO HELL.
I KNEW MY GRANDFATHER LOST HIS FORTUNE THANKS TO JUDSON PIERCE. HOWEVER, I DON'T RECAL MY PARENTS EVER MENTIONING HIM AGAIN.
NO REASON THEY SHOULD, SIR. YOUR PARENTS WERE ABLE TO PUT THE CRUELTY DONE BY PIERCE BEHIND THEM.
MARLA ELLIOT, ON THE OTHER HAND, STRIDENTLY INSISTED THAT HER HUSBAND'S ASSOCIATION WITH PIERCE WAS A BLACK MARK ON THEM SOCIALLY.
I BELIEVE THAT WAS THE REASON MR. ELLIOT DRANK TO EXCESS, THOUGH IN TRUTH, THE REAL REASON MIGHT HAVE BEEN MRS. ELLIOT HERSELF.
I REMEMBER HER, AND, YES.
IT'S TRAGIC PIERCE NEVER REFORMED. HIS ONLY REASON FOR LIVING WAS TO KILL ME, A MAN HE NEVER MET.
THE LAST MAN HE'D EVER WANT TO MEET, IF HE HAD KNOWN ABOUT BATMAN.
EVERYONE DEALS WITH TRAGEDY DIFFERENTLY SIR, AS YOU AND I WELL KNOW.
"AND MR. PIERCE MAY YET HAVE A CHANCE TO CHANGE HIS OUTLOOK, THOUGH I DOUBT HE WILL..."
BLACKGATE PRISON.

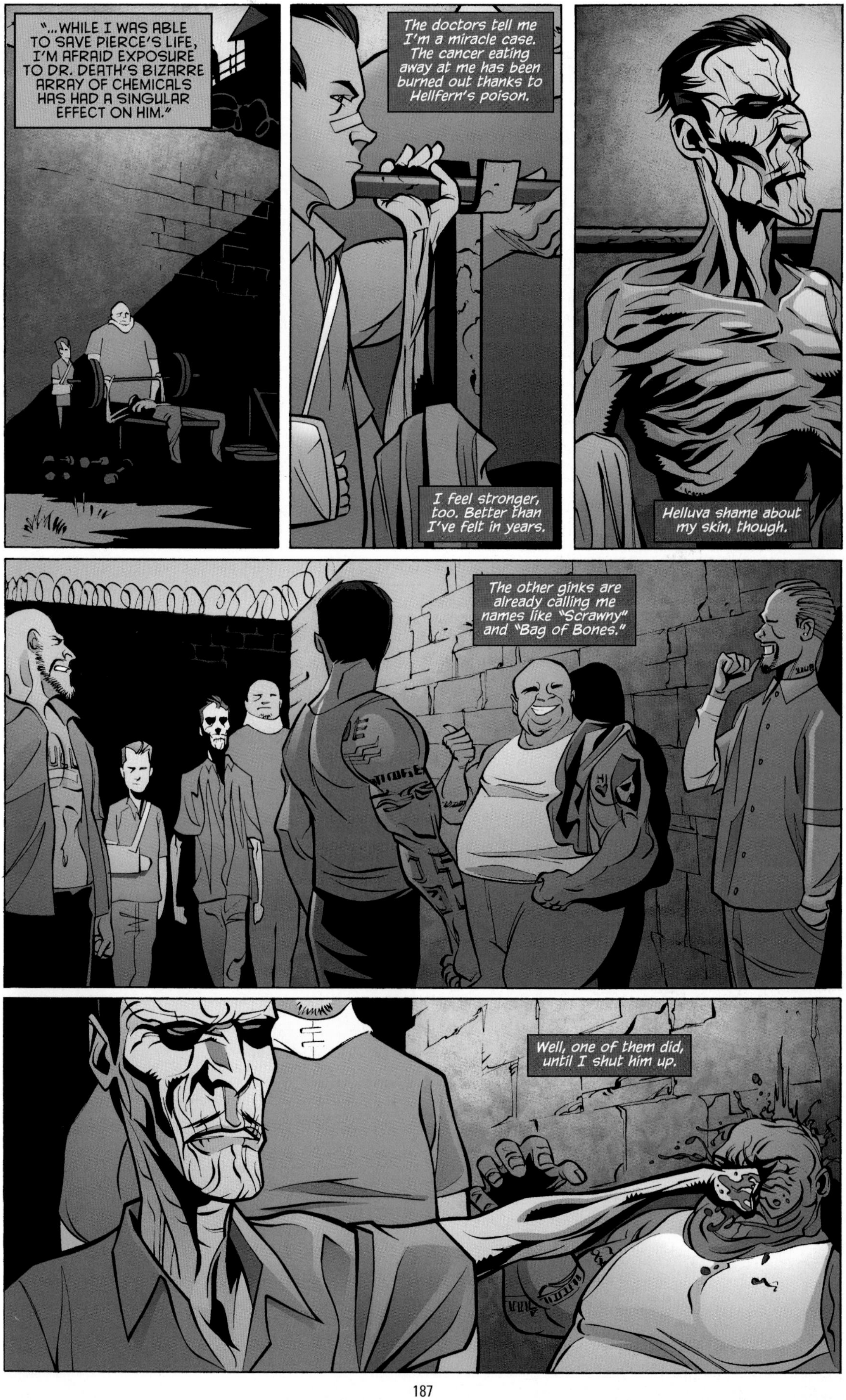
"...WHILE I WAS ABLE TO SAVE PIERCE'S LIFE, I'M AFRAID EXPOSURE TO DR. DEATH'S BIZARRE ARRAY OF CHEMICALS HAS HAD A SINGULAR EFFECT ON HIM."
The doctors tell me I'm a miracle case. The cancer eating away at me has been burned out thanks to Hellfern's poison.
I feel stronger, too. Better than I've felt in years.
Helluva shame about my skin, though.
The other ginks are already calling me names like "Scrawny" and "Bag of Bones."
Well, one of them did, until I shut him up.

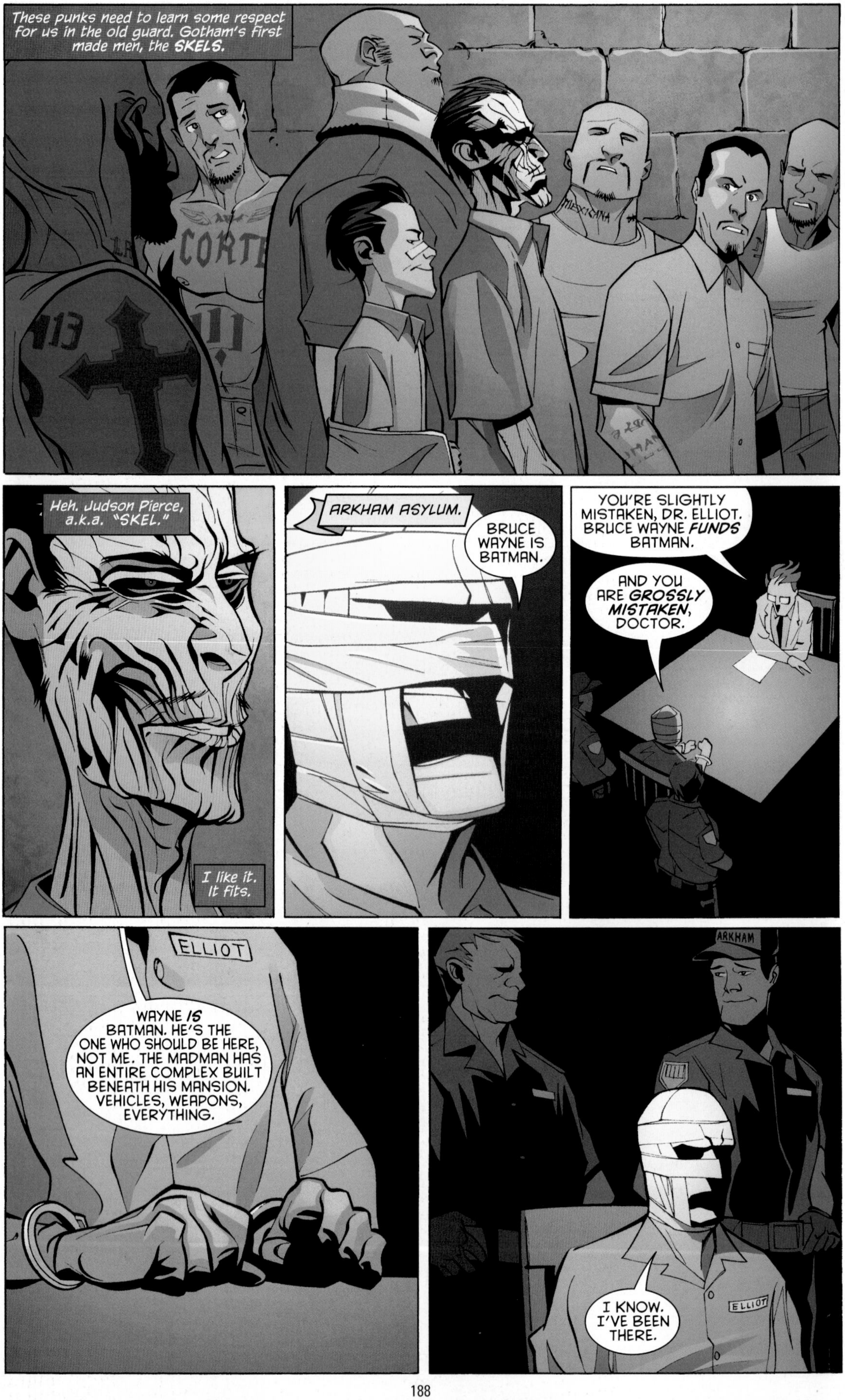
These punks need to learn some respect for us in the old guard. Gotham's first made men, the **SKELS.**
CORTE
MEXICANA
Heh. Judson Pierce, a.k.a. "SKEL."
I like it. It fits.
ARKHAM ASYLUM.
BRUCE WAYNE IS BATMAN.
YOU'RE SLIGHTLY MISTAKEN, DR. ELLIOT. BRUCE WAYNE ***FUNDS*** BATMAN.
AND YOU ARE ***GROSSLY MISTAKEN,*** DOCTOR.
ELLIOT
WAYNE ***IS*** BATMAN. HE'S THE ONE WHO SHOULD BE HERE, NOT ME. THE MADMAN HAS AN ENTIRE COMPLEX BUILT BENEATH HIS MANSION. VEHICLES, WEAPONS, EVERYTHING.
ARKHAM
ELLIOT
I KNOW. I'VE BEEN THERE.

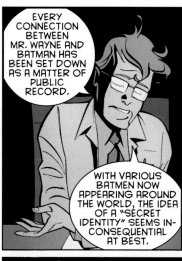

EVERY CONNECTION BETWEEN MR. WAYNE AND BATMAN HAS BEEN SET DOWN AS A MATTER OF PUBLIC RECORD.

WITH VARIOUS BATMEN NOW APPEARING AROUND THE WORLD, THE IDEA OF A "SECRET IDENTITY" SEEMS IN-CONSEQUENTIAL AT BEST.

IT WAS A MASTER STROKE, REALLY. BY GOING PUBLIC, HE REMOVED THE ONE THING I COULD STILL USE AGAINST HIM. CHECK AND MATE, BRUCE.

DR. ELLIOT...

...YOU NEED TO STOP OBSESSING OVER THESE THINGS IF WE'RE GOING TO MAKE PROGRESS IN YOUR RECOVERY.

I'M MUCH MORE INTERESTED IN DISCOVERING: "WHO IS TOMMY ELLIOT?"

WON'T YOU LET ME MEET TOMMY ELLIOT?

CERTAINLY.

Who is Tommy Elliot?

There are many ways to answer that, Doctor. Tommy Elliot is a cipher. A ruined shell, a lost child, a distorted shadow of another man...

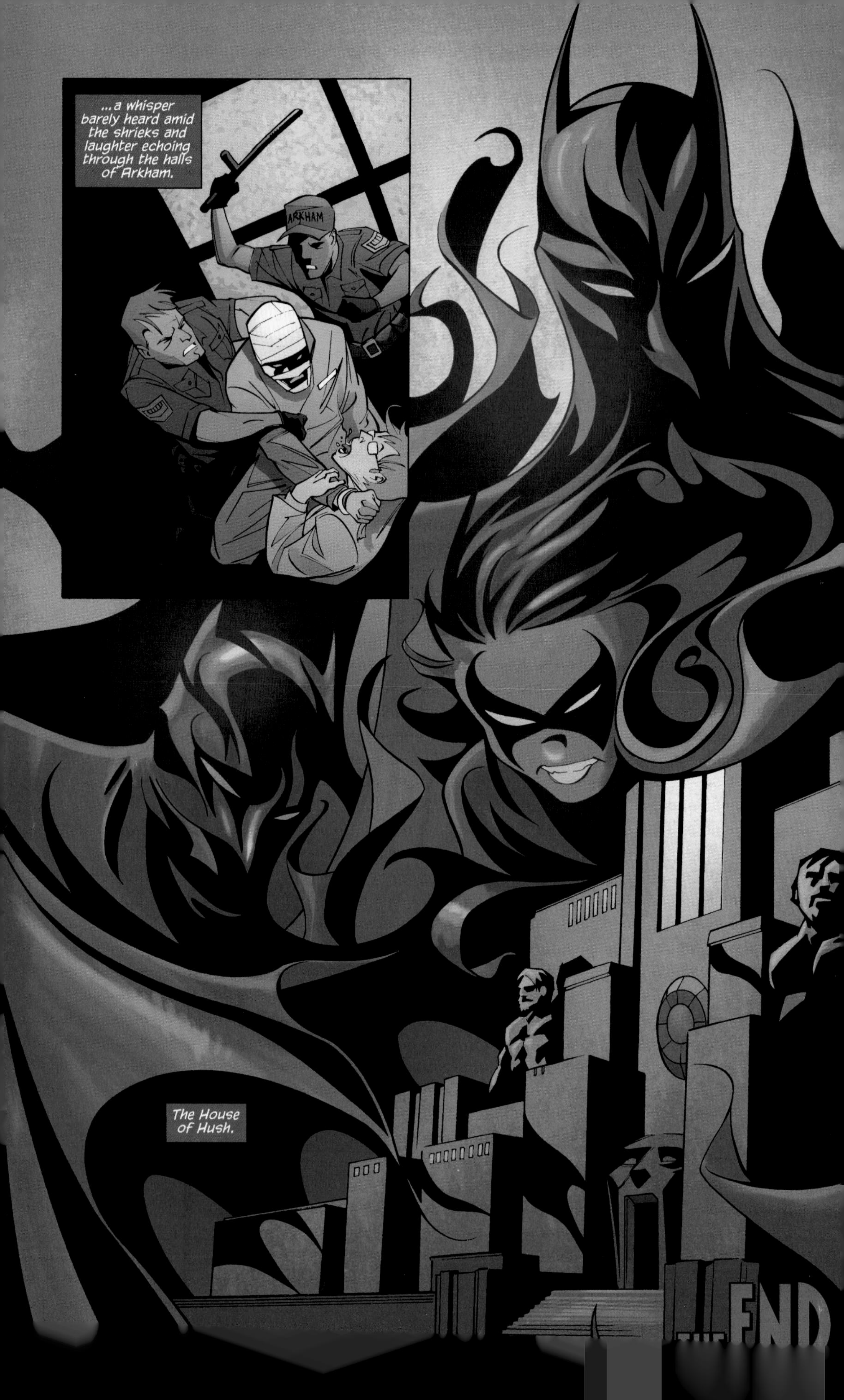

...a whisper barely heard amid the shrieks and laughter echoing through the halls of Arkham.
ARKHAM
The House of Hush.
THE END

MORE CLASSIC TALES OF THE DARK KNIGHT

BATMAN: HUSH

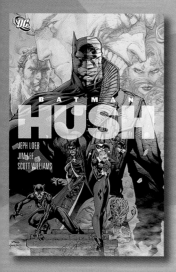

JEPH LOEB
JIM LEE

BATMAN: UNDER THE HOOD
VOLS. 1 & 2

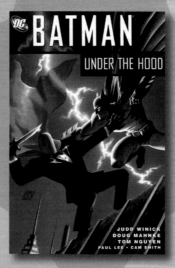

JUDD WINICK
DOUG MAHNKE

BATMAN:
THE LONG HALLOWEEN

JEPH LOEB
TIM SALE

BATMAN:
DARK VICTORY

JEPH LOEB
TIM SALE

BATMAN:
HAUNTED KNIGHT

JEPH LOEB
TIM SALE

BATMAN:
YEAR 100

PAUL POPE

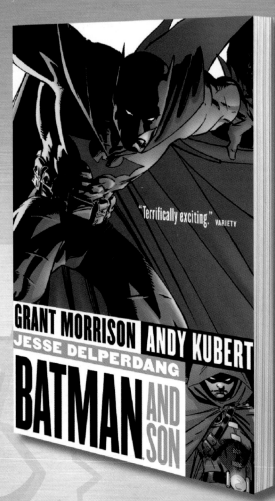 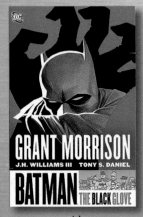